THE SIEGE OF LOYALTY HOUSE

ALSO BY JESSIE CHILDS

Henry VIII's Last Victim:
The Life and Times of Henry Howard, Earl of Surrey

God's Traitors:
Terror and Faith in Elizabethan England

The SIEGE of LOYALTY HOUSE

A STORY OF THE ENGLISH CIVIL WAR

JESSIE CHILDS

PEGASUS BOOKS

NEW YORK LONDON

THE SIEGE OF LOYALTY HOUSE

Pegasus Books, Ltd.
148 West 37th Street, 13th Floor
New York, NY 10018

ISBN: 978-1-63936-310-0

10 9 8 7 6 5 4 3 2 1

Printed in the United States of America
Distributed by Simon & Schuster
www.pegasusbooks.com

For Fletch

We look on past ages with condescension, as a mere preparation
for *us* . . . but what if we're only an after-glow of *them*?

J. G. Farrell, *The Siege of Krishnapur* (1973)

Contents

PART FOUR
The Storm

Author's Note

During an argument at a London apothecary in 1639, Sarah Wheeler called Sampson Sheffield 'fatt gutts' (he had called her a whore, and her husband 'a rogue, a rascal, base fellow, a peasant, an apothecary slave and one that lived by the turds and farts of gentlemen').[1] It would be a shame, I think, to lose the visual thickening of those double 't's. Therefore, when the original spelling of a word adds charm, effect or, indeed, girth, I have retained it. For the most part, however, I have modernised spelling and punctuation.

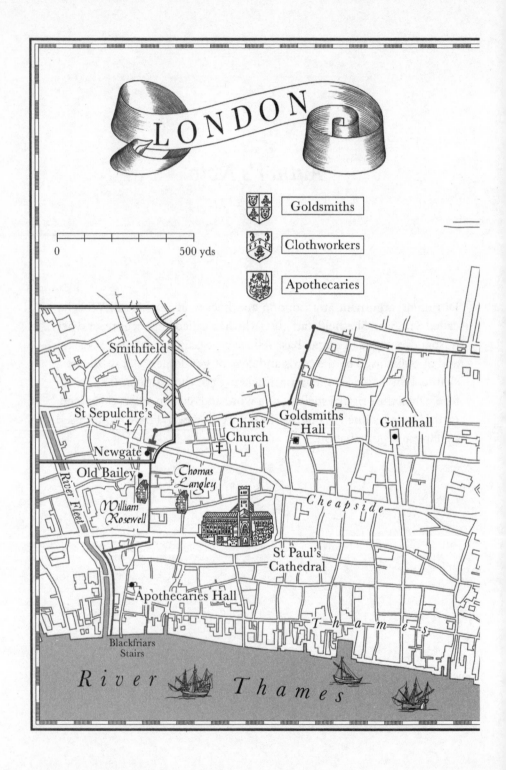

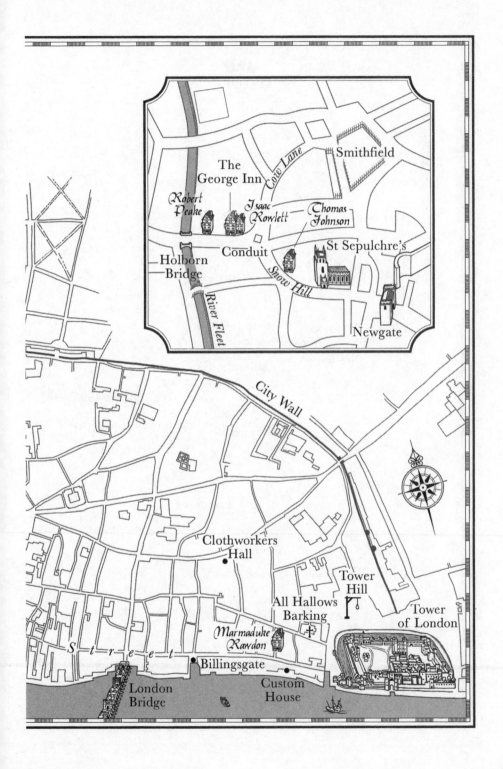

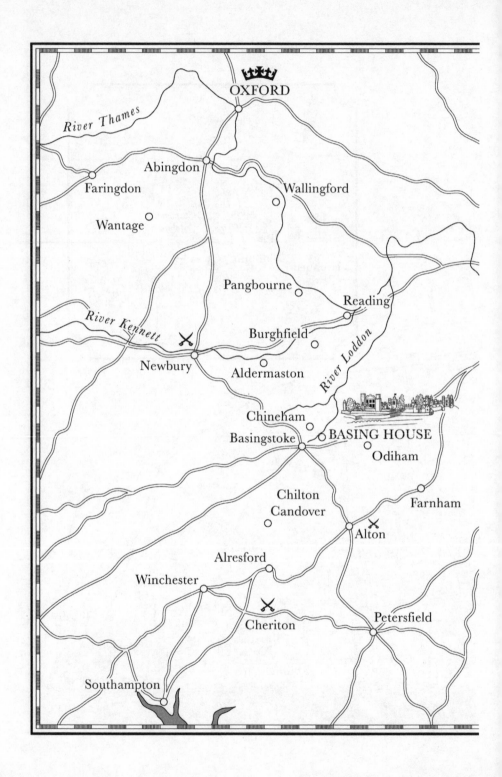

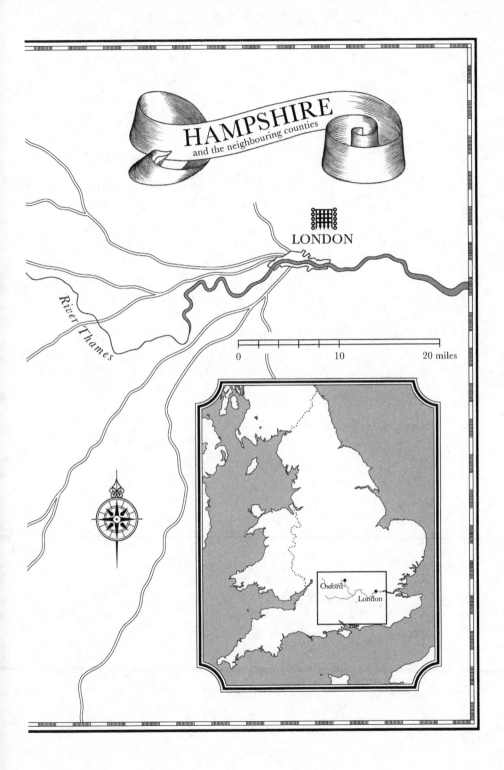

HAMPSHIRE
and the neighbouring counties

LONDON

River Thames

0   10   20 miles

Oxford
London

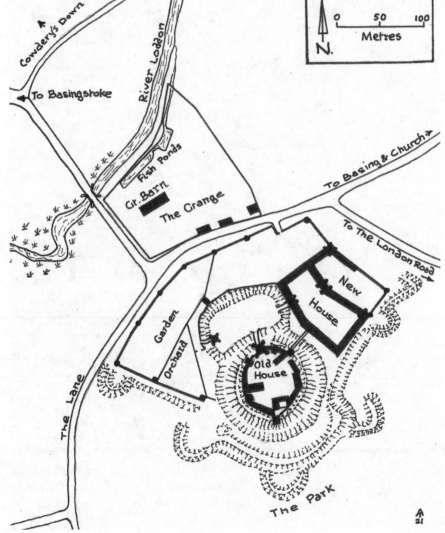

BASING HOUSE

Introduction

In 1786, two Americans walked a battlefield. They were in the heart-lands of England, not far from Shakespeare country. As they circuited the site of the battle of Worcester, where in 1651 Charles I's son was put to flight, John Adams and Thomas Jefferson, the future second and third presidents of the United States, had questions for the locals. None seemed capable of or even interested in answering them. Adams couldn't believe it. 'Do Englishmen so soon forget the ground where Liberty was fought for?' he asked. 'Tell your neighbours and your children that this is holy ground, much holier than that on which your churches stand.'[1]

More than two centuries on and there is still some bafflement, and occasional outrage, at the Englishman's unfamiliarity with his nation's brightest, and darkest, hours. This despite the civil wars creating fault lines that are still evident in the way we divide and vote. This despite the seventeenth century being one of the most formative periods in British and Irish history. Everything seemed to expand in this moment, from the population and marketplace to the natural world and the very heavens. With telescopes and microscopes, people could see further and closer than ever before. There were exciting discoveries and terrible new prospects. Merchants grabbed lands and forced enslaved Africans to work them. England's position in the world, in Europe and in its own archipelago was transformed. The public became more literate, litigious and opinionated. There were culture wars and the first newspapers. Preachers and politicians fashioned themselves accordingly. Plague stalked the earth. There was a growing feeling that the end days were coming and that an apocalyptic showdown between the forces of darkness and light was imminent. It was a terrifying, electrifying time.

People called it the 'Iron Century'. We now know that they were living through the most intense phase of the Little Ice Age, a period of climatic cooling that saw some of the coldest weather on record. This meant long winters and wet summers, failed crops and food shortage. There was political turbulence across the globe – the Thirty Years War in Europe, rebellion in Russia, sultanicide in the Ottoman empire, civil war in the Mughal empire and violent regime change in China. 'Monstrous things have happened,' wrote the Welshman James Howell, 'it seems the whole world is off the hinges.'[2]

It was hoped, at first, that Britain might escape the convulsions. 'God be thanked,' preached Matthew Griffith at St Paul's Cathedral on 2 October 1642, 'we have lived in peace and plenty. God be thanked, we never yet knew what it is to hear the murdering pieces about our ears.' He implored his listeners to look at the rest of the world in turmoil, 'whilst this our Britain (like the centre) stood unmoved'.[3]

But Britain was not, it turned out, exceptional, and by the end of the month, the preacher was in prison and the battle of Edgehill had reaped the first ghastly harvest of a civil war that would claim a greater proportion of British lives than the First World War.[4] The most notorious casualty was King Charles I, executed at the Banqueting House in Whitehall on 30 January 1649. The monarchy and the House of Lords were abolished and so was the Church of England in structure and liturgy. In came a republic, a Directory for Public Worship, two written constitutions and Oliver Cromwell.

In 1660, the son of the dead king returned from exile as Charles II. He restored the lords and the bishops (if not the status quo ante bellum). An Act of Oblivion offered a general pardon for offences committed during the 'distractions', and people were required to lacquer their pain in a coat of amnesia. Words in 'any way tending to revive the memory of the late differences' were banned.[5]

Yet words – and memories – could not be effaced. They remain in the archives, unvarnished and raw. In the Essex Record Office, the petition of Jeremiah Maye, a disabled parliamentarian soldier, explains that he and his family need rescuing from 'the hungry jaws of want'. In a petition in the Berkshire Record Office, a royalist widow describes seeing her house 'violently torn' and torched 'by the cruel soldiers'. Amongst the papers of the Committee for Advance of Money is an account of the torture of a parliamentarian prisoner who was 'burnt with lighted matches' in Aberystwyth Castle.[6]

Other documents are less explicit, but equally poignant. A little love poem flits between the pages of an army account book from royalist Oxford – 'What thing / is love is love / . . . It is a pretty thing'. It has been crossed out. In the Hampshire Archives, a royalist protection order is striped with damp, presumably because its frightened recipient hid it under his floorboards (see plates). In the Leeds branch of the West Yorkshire Archives, a tatty notebook catalogues the contents of a garden. Old words tumble out of it: Kentish Codlings, Granado Gilliflower, Melancholy Monkshood. One page is devoted to 'my best tulips'. When war came, the gardener flipped his book over and began new lists. One is headed 'The Postures of the Musket'.[7] Out went seeds, bulbs and stakes. In came powder, shot and scouring stick. A world was turned upside down.

This book is an attempt to recover the shock of that experience and to look upon the face of the war through the story of one particularly dramatic episode. The siege of Basing House in Hampshire belongs to the first civil war, 1642–6, which ended with Charles I in custody. The house was said to be the largest private mansion in England. It rose above the banks of the River Loddon and seemed perpetually enveloped in mist. It was known as 'Loyalty House', after the motto 'Aimez Loyauté' ('Love Loyalty') of its owner, the Marquess of Winchester, and it had strategic importance because it commanded the main road between London and the west.

It mattered even more symbolically. To its enemies, Basing House was a microcosm of Stuart degeneracy, personified by its Catholic owner, his half-Irish marchioness and their most famous guest, Inigo Jones, the architect who had done so much to exalt the dynasty. It hardly mattered that Jones and many others in the house did not share the Winchesters' faith. In the press and pulpits, Basing House was a bastion of 'popery', 'a limb of Babylon', 'a nest of the vilest vermin in all the kingdom'. It was here, announced a parliamentarian preacher, that 'religion and laws and liberties and the very being of our English nation lie at stake'.[8]

For over two years, Parliament's forces tried to shoot, shell, starve and smoke the royalist soldiers and civilians out of their stronghold. Things happened, we are told, 'which the nature of man doth tremble at', things that anticipated not only Oliver Cromwell's sectarian fury in

Ireland, but also, in the rudimentary use of chemical warfare, the fumes in Flanders fields. 'You must remember *what* they were,' reported a parliamentarian newsbook, 'they were most of them papists; therefore our muskets and our swords did show but little compassion.'[9] The royalists grew equally ruthless. In their struggle to survive, they turned on their neighbours and they turned on themselves.

If Basing House offers a lesson in the descent of man into savagery, it can also point to his ascent. For this was a place of beauty and wonder too. It saw heroic deeds, miraculous escapes and even a wedding. It was witness to the power of love – from the sacrifice of a daughter for her father to the love of life that provides hope when all else is lost. Basing House acquired an aura. People began to wonder if it would ever fall; if, indeed, God might not want it to fall.

Because the ruins are so evocative, and the archaeology so rich (with the added allure of hidden treasure), and because the mists still come to haze time and space, Basing House is, for me, a numinous place. It captures the push and pull of the past and the transience of human life, 'the poetry of history', as G. M. Trevelyan called it: 'the quasi-miraculous fact that once, on this earth, once, on this familiar spot of ground, walked other men and women, as actual as we are today, thinking their own thoughts, swayed by their own passions, but now all gone, one generation vanishing after another, gone as utterly as we ourselves shall shortly be gone, like ghost at cock-crow'.[10]

A stirred imagination is an impetus that need not adulterate the facts, nor denote partisanship. This story is told mainly from inside the house looking out, but I have also tried to breach the minds of the besiegers and the neighbours who were caught in the crossfire. By dint of the trades and skills of those who came to Basing House, a sort of garrison of all the talents, we can also look out beyond the lines onto other vistas – artistic, scientific, commercial – to see why this was such a dynamic age.

I hope that readers who came for the fighting will stay for the long build-up and the lulls (an authentic siege experience, after all), just as I hope that those who have little interest in military history will better appreciate its value. There is something about war, particularly civil war, and most especially the conditions of a siege, that brings out the best and worst of humanity. By looking at it in detail, it may even be possible to see a world in a grain of sand.

Above all, and quite simply, I hope that the story that follows might make the civil war seem more vital: that it might enable us to follow the drama on the ground, so to speak, as chaotic and bewildering as the experience often was, and that it might restore life to some of the players. The defenders of Basing House were not a monochrome Cavalier elite. They included an apothecary, a print-seller and a scrivener, a merchant, an engraver and a vintner, an actor and a clergyman and his brave young daughters, who were all thrust upon the stage in one theatre in an especially brutish century.

'All England should come in pilgrimage to this hill once a year,' John Adams declared at Worcester. Other hills provide different views of Liberty. Our story begins on a city hill, fifty miles north-east of Basing House, where the bells of Old Bailey are calling.

PART ONE

THE SHOP OF WAR

I

Snow Hill

> When will you pay me?
> Say the bells at Old Bailey.

The bells at Old Bailey were, in fact, the bells of the church of St Sepulchre, at the top of Snow Hill in the ward of Farringdon Without Newgate. Just as no seventeenth-century Londoner could picture the River Thames without its boats and swans, so none could cross the City and not feel the clangour of its bells. St Sepulchre's, which lay just outside the city wall, had six main bells in the tower, with new clappers and ropes a regular outlay in the parish accounts. They marked the hours and called people to prayer, fixing them to time and place and connecting them – especially at moments of celebration, commemoration or crisis – to the four hundred thousand inhabitants that made up the City and Liberties of London.

Of different tone and timbre was a small handbell, today on display in a glass case in the nave, that was taken across the road to Newgate Prison and tinkled outside the cell of condemned felons on their last night of life. Then, at six o'clock the following morning, the church's tenor bell tolled for the prisoner. It continued as he was carted past the church, down the hill, over Holborn Bridge and along the Oxford road to Tyburn. At ten, 'or at such time as knowledge may be truly had of the prisoner's execution', it rang out for fifteen minutes, then ceased. The intention was to move all hearers to pray for the prisoner's salvation, and for their own. As John Donne, the vicar down the road at St Dunstan-in-the-West, had put it, 'every man is a piece of the continent, a part of the main'. This was a noble sentiment, but London was never so united. A single death might diminish mankind, but for the youths

jeering on the churchyard wall and the punters of the taverns that dotted the route to Tyburn, it was terrific sport.[1]

Near the foot of Snow Hill, an apothecary opened his shop to
the more quotidian harmonies of the sweepers and scavengers and the
water-carriers and coalmen with their buckets and barrows. His neighbours were leathersellers, a widow, a vintner and the grocer who sold
'Luke olives' and oil from his ground-floor shop. On the afternoon of
16 July 1639, a fight that had broken out in the Holy Lamb tavern was
resolved in the vintner's house, where the offender made a bare-headed
apology in front of the grocer and six other citizens.[2] A few years later,
when the widow drew up her will, she put three pounds aside for select
neighbours to have a funeral supper together.[3] Thus, beyond London's
Common Council and wardmote, the livery hall and the vestry, a little
community was settled and the frayed edges just about contained
within the warp and weft of Snow Hill.

'The name is such a good one,' Charles Dickens would write two
centuries later. This was before Holborn Viaduct arose from the clay
and changed its contours and character; when the hill was still so steep
that horses ascending from the Fleet valley 'seriously think of falling
down on purpose'.[4] When it rained, the detritus of the street would
plunge down to meet the muck of Smithfield Market:

> And in huge confluent join at Snow Hill ridge,
> Fall from the Conduit prone to Holborn Bridge.
> Sweepings from butchers' stalls, dung, guts, and blood,
> Drown'd puppies, stinking sprats, all drench'd in mud,
> Dead cats and turnip-tops come tumbling down the flood.[5]

At the end of August every year, the slaughter stopped and the
smooth field of Smithfield was transformed into Bartholomew Fair.
Conjurors and jugglers came to town, men on stilts and pigs on spits,
wrestlers, ballad-sellers, prostitutes, puppeteers and shoals of pick-
pockets. In his 1614 play *Bartholomew Fair*, the dramatist Ben Jonson
introduced audiences to Zeal-of-the-land Busy, a Puritan fundamental-
ist 'of a most lunatic conscience', who wants to ban it all. 'Thou art the
seat of the Beast, O Smithfield,' he spits. Busy sees sin in all things: long
hair ('an ensign of pride'), tobacco ('mist and error'), a hobby-horse ('a
very idol') and the 'fleshly' woman. 'He is a fellow of a most arrogant

and invincible dullness,' sighs Quarlous the gamester, but the real Puritans were not so easy to dismiss, especially by 1631, when Jonson's play was printed and opposition was growing to a king who had decided to rule without Parliament.[6] It was downright dangerous to ridicule them a decade later, when a reworking of *Bartholomew Fair* appeared in an anonymous pamphlet with a Puritan protagonist more menacing than Jonson's canting cartoon.

In this version, the Puritan enters a gallery in Christ Church cloisters, a stone's throw from Snow Hill, where he spies a picture of Jesus with the twelve apostles, the Virgin Mary and the saints. He falls into a frenzy, jabbing at the canvas and railing at the Whore of Babylon.*[7] That he brandishes a child's wooden sword and is soon put in the stocks does not quite render him ludicrous – not in 1641, and not at Christ Church, where, in December, the minister was stripped of his surplice to cheers from the congregation 'as if they had got a greater victory than even Alexander the Great could attain'. One of the defrockers was a blind old woman, transformed in her zeal into a 'young Amazonian'.[8]

It was the same story elsewhere that year. At St Mary's, Chelmsford, in Essex, a group of parishioners had tried to tear 'the rags of Rome' off their vicar. Two weeks earlier, on 5 November, the church's east window, a stained-glass depiction of the life of Christ, had been stoned. Twenty-five miles away in Earls Colne, the 'popish' Book of Common Prayer had been subjected to 'swimming' and burning, as if it were both witch and heretic. At Hillingdon the following summer, surplices were ripped up and recycled as menstrual cloths.[9]

This was no sacrilege, Puritans argued, since there had never been anything sacred in these objects, only the filth of the Antichrist. 'Thou shalt not make unto thee any graven image, or any likeness of any thing,' God had commanded. The Catholics and some of the early Protestant reformers had folded this prohibition into God's First Commandment, which admonishes the faithful that there is only one God.

---

* 'Babylon': the ancient Mesopotamian city, a symbol of glamour, worldly corruption and doom, often personified by the Whore of Babylon riding the seven-headed beast of the Apocalypse. According to the Book of Revelation, Babylon would fall at the Second Coming, in the final cosmic battle, ushering in the kingdom of Christ on earth. To many English Protestants, Babylon was synonymous with the 'popish tyranny' of Rome.

But later Protestants upgraded it to a stand-alone Second Commandment and made it a central tenet of their faith.[10] For the Puritans, anything that adulterated the pristine Word of God – in image, ritual or clerical fancy dress – was an obstacle on the pathway to heaven. And all those who failed to destroy such obstacles would, like the worshippers of the golden calf, incur God's horrible wrath. At a time of decayed trade, harvest failure, epidemics and wild weather, this was a pregnant threat. 'The Lord hath showed us, of late years, that He is displeased with us by His sending unseasonable weather the last harvest, and then in the seed time, and now this spring season,' the parishioners of St Sepulchre's were warned.[11]

No one wanted to be called a Puritan. It was an insulting term. They did not much like 'the hotter sort of Protestants' either, though it gave a good sense of their ardour.[12] They preferred 'the godly', or 'the Saints' or, indeed, 'the Elect', since most believed in the Calvinist doctrine of predestination – that God had already decided which lucky few would receive the unmerited gift of salvation – and naturally they cleaved to the view that they were the special ones. This might lead to complacency, but most Puritans were twitchy about their status and constantly on the lookout for signs of assurance. 'Keep your day book,' urged Hugh Peter, a popular preacher at St Sepulchre's, 'write down your sins on one side, and on the other side God's little mercies.'[13] Thousands of columns were filled this way. A London woodturner chastised himself for eating a pear without lifting his heart to God. An Essex cleric blamed the death of his baby boy on 'unseasonable playing at chess'. The parliamentary journalist Sir Simonds D'Ewes, who survived a childhood fall in a dung pit, would forever ponder its meaning. While Puritans invited derision, the integrity of their thoughts goes some way to explaining the violence of their deeds and, indeed, their busyness. The Lord, wrote Jean Calvin, 'would by no means have those persons inactive, whom He Himself has placed on the watch'.[14]

Puritans did not think the Reformation in England had gone far enough in cleansing the Church of ignorance and idolatry. They had been frustrated by the moderation of Elizabeth I and appalled by her successor James I's appeasement of the House of Habsburg during the Thirty Years War in Europe. This was a political and religious conflict centred on the Holy Roman Empire but drawing in all the major European states. It had special significance for English Protestants since it had stemmed from the acceptance of the crown of Bohemia by James's daughter Elizabeth and her husband, Frederick V, Elector Palatine, after a Protestant revolt against Habsburg rule in 1618. The deposed king-elect, Ferdinand, who was subsequently crowned Holy Roman Emperor, sent troops to retake his throne, re-Catholicise Bohemia and seize Frederick's ancestral lands in the Lower Palatinate. Frederick and Elizabeth were defeated, exiled and ever after mocked as the 'Winter King and Queen'. They appealed to James for help, but he refused them asylum in England and insisted, fruitlessly, on a diplomatic solution.

The Puritans saw the ensuing war in Europe as an apocalyptic showdown between Christ's Protestant soldiers and the Catholic forces of the resurgent Antichrist. They believed that England was the new Israel, God's chosen nation, and that Englishmen should therefore be on the front line alongside their struggling brethren. They linked Protestant setbacks in Europe to the advance of 'popery' at home and they were horrified to see both James and his son, Charles, promote bishops who seemed addicted, as one Puritan put it, to 'ikon slavery'.[15]

Charles, who succeeded his father in the great plague year of 1625, was Protestant, but his French wife Henrietta Maria was devoutly Catholic and there were several high-profile conversions at court. As a young man, Charles had been beguiled by the majesty of Madrid, the seat of the Iberian Habsburgs, and he also believed in the 'beauty of holiness'. This was a phrase that his Archbishop of Canterbury, William Laud, and his bishops took from Psalm 96 to signify a sublimity of worship in the service and house of God. They believed that true Christian communion was facilitated by decorum in church and the enrichment of its fabric. While many buildings, including St Sepulchre's, had been 'repaired and trimmed' in the previous reign, Charles, Laud and their allies believed that there was still work to be done in cleaning up God's house. Ecclesiastical court records for the Archdeaconry of Essex, for example, mention one ruined church with grave-grubbing hogs in the yard, a man who 'did piss in the church into the hat of one that sat by him' and Susanna Cooke of Baddow Parva, who dried her laundry in the church, for she 'might hang her rags there as well as the surplice'.[16]

Worse for those bishops who vaunted the Eucharist as the most intense interaction with Christ was the profanation of the communion table, which they claimed was treated more like a place 'to eat oysters on than the holy table fit for God's sanctuary'.[17] Stories abounded of hats and bags being dumped on communion tables and of naps being taken beneath them. Reverence was restored in many churches in the 1630s, when the tables were returned to their pre-Reformation position at the east end of the church, raised onto a platform and railed off from the hoi polloi. To many Protestants (and not just Puritans) this looked very much like the return of the sacrificial altar of the Catholic Mass and the adoration of a 'breaden God'. Back too were performative devotions like bowing at the name of Jesus and kneeling to receive communion, as well as organ music, clerical vestments, candlesticks, crucifixes and religious imagery in the windows. This vision of church and soul aglow with the beauty of holiness had integrity and scriptural rationale to its adherents, but to many others, including the poet John Milton, it was a profane tarting-up of the gospel with 'all the gaudy allurements of a whore'.[18]

Imperative to the ideal of immaculate order was a royal insistence on conformity, an uglier and more jagged process achieved through prerogative court and pillory as the Puritan lawyer William Prynne could attest. Towards the end of 1632, he had released a book against stage plays in which he applauded the Roman assassins of theatre-loving emperors and likened actresses to 'notorious whores'. Henrietta Maria, who was in rehearsals for a masque at the time, was neither named nor exempted. Prynne was tried before the Court of Star Chamber and sentenced to life imprisonment and the loss of his ears. While in the pillory, he was also forced to watch a bonfire of his books – the first time a book was publicly burned by the common hangman in England. Four years later, having smuggled out more offensive tracts, Prynne was again convicted of sedition. His ears, having been cropped before, were now completely sheared off. His nose was also slit and his cheeks were branded with 'S. L.' for 'Seditious Libeller' (or 'Stigma of Laud', as Prynne had it).[19]

Thousands of Puritans fled across the Atlantic to search for God in a New England. One was Hugh Peter, the preacher who had attracted thousands to his whippy sermons at St Sepulchre's and who had been imprisoned for praying that the queen forsake idolatry. (Vile rumour had it that he was also running from a Smithfield butcher whose wife he had enjoyed.) Peter became pastor of the congregational church at Salem, Massachusetts, and a founder of Harvard College. He would return when the time was right.[20]

Charles, a life-long stammerer, held firm to his belief that Caesar and God spoke with one voice. His father had taught him that he ruled by divine right: he was God's viceroy on earth and subject to no earthly authority. When a new east window was put into the chapel of Lincoln College, Oxford, the images of Christ bore the beard and moustache of Charles.[21]

With the king's weight behind them, the church courts increasingly intruded into ordinary lives and pockets. Charles backed the bishops in improving their revenue streams and the cathedral canons in local disputes with civic corporations. In London, his intended showpiece, the classical makeover of St Paul's Cathedral, with statues of himself and his father upon a new west portico, was steamrollered through by his surveyor, Inigo Jones, with scant regard for St Gregory's church next door. Jones allegedly threatened the parishioners that they would be 'laid by the heels' – imprisoned in shackles – if they objected to its destruction.[22]

The authoritarianism of a leeching church and state fed wider fears of 'popish' infection. Charles's heavy hand, which also waved in arbitrary taxation, imprisonment without charge and, since 1629, governance without Parliament, was considered a smooth fit in the glove of continental absolutism. This strain of the popish disease might not have been as aggressive as the Elizabethan version, with its invading Spaniards and Jesuit plots, but it was deemed no less virulent. Here was a popery that hid in plain sight, wafting into court behind the Catholic queen and through the vestries of those grace-disgracing bishops. Puritans trotted out the old anti-Catholic tropes and recalled popery's worst excesses: 'Bloody' Mary's burning of Protestants at Smithfield in the 1550s, the Spanish Armada in Elizabeth's day, the Gunpowder Plot in James's reign and, most recently, Habsburg atrocities in the Thirty Years War. So when the bells pealed every fifth of November to celebrate the foiling of the powder treason, they also chimed a warning; bolder Puritans fulminated against a new popish plot, sponsored by crown and mitre, that was undermining God's house more effectively than thirty-six barrels of gunpowder ever could have done.

The innovations in church and state drove many mainstream Protestants towards the Puritan clamour for lost liberties, but it was Charles
I's 'Britannic vision' that ultimately triggered the series of events
that edged his three kingdoms towards civil war. For another of
his ambitions – inherited from his father, but pursued with none of his
finesse – was to bring Scotland and Ireland into closer alignment with
England. North of the border, this culminated in a ceremonial prayer
book foisted onto a kirk that had long preferred a pared-down form of
worship. The Scots called it 'a Popish-English-Scottish-Mass-Service-
Book' and threw stools at the Dean of St Giles' Cathedral in Edinburgh
when he tried to read from it in July 1637. As with much of the iconoclasm in England, 'rascally' women were blamed.[23] Riot led to rebellion,
to two 'Bishops' Wars', both lost by Charles, and eventually, on
3 November 1640, to the opening of what would become known as the
Long Parliament: the Parliament that would go to war with the king.
Charles was desperate to end the Scottish crisis, but only Parliament
could grant him the funds required to deal with it. 'The game was well
begun,' reported Hugh Peter's patron, Robert Rich, 2nd Earl of Warwick, one of a small group of Puritan peers who had encouraged the
Scots to invade and occupy the north of England in August in order to
force the king's hand.[24]

In the days before the opening of the Long Parliament, the altar of
St Paul's Cathedral was attacked and the offices of the hated Court
of High Commission were vandalised. In Parliament's third week, an
official tasked with compiling a list of Westminster recusants – those
refusing to attend Anglican church services – was stabbed by 'a Roman-
ist with a long dagger'. The next day, Sunday 22 November, Catholic
worshippers leaving the Inigo Jones-designed Queen's Chapel on the
Strand were pelted with stones. Two anti-Catholic petitions were presented to Parliament the following day. One complained of their
presence at court. The other wondered if it might not be a good idea
for the 'thousands upon thousands' of papists in London to be 'distinguished from Protestants by their apparel'.[25]

The fearless, earless William Prynne, meanwhile, was released from
prison by order of Parliament and returned to bells, cheers and flowers
at his feet. On 11 December 1640, a huge petition signed by 15,000 Londoners called for the destruction of the episcopal hierarchy, with its

archbishops and bishops, and the root-and-branch reform of the Church. A week later, Archbishop Laud was impeached for high treason. He was branded a handmaiden of tyranny, a debaser of true religion and – by one Harbottle Grimston, M P – 'the corrupt fountain that hath infected all the streams'.[26] The Puritans took over the pulpits and censorship collapsed. On it went 'as hot as a toast', reported one nervous observer.[27]

There was so much hope amongst the Puritans these days, so much confidence in divine momentum, so much Revelation in the pulpits: 'Babylon is fallen, is fallen.'[28] Charles's most hated churchman was in custody and his most hated adviser, Thomas Wentworth, Earl of Strafford, Lord Deputy of Ireland, was impeached. On 12 May 1641, Strafford was executed for treason before the avid eyes of 100,000 spectators. A Triennial Act, guaranteeing parliaments at least every three years, was passed and the apparatus of the king's Personal Rule dismantled. There was not a lot that Charles could do about it, because only Parliament could pay off the Scots, who continued to occupy northern England throughout a very uneasy and costly truce. Another act ensured that Parliament could not be dissolved without its own consent. Any show of royal force, such as the refortification of the Tower of London, or Charles's attempts to rescue Strafford, only raised the political temperature. 'Justice! Justice!' a 12,000-strong crowd chanted outside the Banqueting House as Charles agonised over giving his assent to Strafford's attainder.[29] This moment has been called 'the English spring'.[30] Certainly, to Puritan preachers, 1641 was an 'annus mirabilis', 'the year of mercies', 'this wonderful year': 'The winter is past, the rain is over and gone, the flowers appear on the earth, the time of the singing of birds is come.'[31]

The summer of 1641 was the third coldest on record for the northern hemisphere over the past six centuries.[32] In August, Charles travelled to Edinburgh to ratify a treaty with the Scots. He conceded to their demands, including the abolition of bishops and a veto on government appointees. (A botched plot, known as 'the Incident', to arrest his chief Scottish opponents on 11 October revealed how he felt about the capitulation.) In Westminster, an order was published reversing Archbishop Laud's innovations in the Church.[33] This quickened the hearts of Puritans and fired an iconoclastic surge in the parishes. Altar rails were wrenched away, 'scandalous pictures' were destroyed and ministers who dared still to wear their surplices were assaulted and abused. Zeal-of-the-land Busy wasn't a laughing stock any more.

The English and Scots spoke bravely of getting involved in the war on the Continent and recovering lost Protestant lands. The Earl of Warwick and his allies in the Lords and Commons – 'the Junto' – strategised over how to strip Charles of his last major powers: the control of ministerial and military appointments. They faced substantial resistance from an emergent 'king's party' that was alarmed by the radical turn and did not wish to see an English monarch reduced to a doge of Venice.[34] Few, though, were paying proper attention to Ireland, the overwhelmingly Catholic land that had been rigorously planted by James I, ruthlessly taxed by Charles I and was now suffering from a terrible harvest. But the Irish had been looking across the sea. 'Yea,' said one, 'the Scots have taught us our A.B.C.'[35]

On 23 October 1641, Irish Catholics rose up against the Protestant settlers and what they increasingly viewed as an existential threat from Westminster. 'This rebellion came as suddenly upon us as lightning,' wrote the Earl of Cork. 'No man foresaw it, nor suspected it, nor had munition, nor anything provided.' The settlers were 'planet-strucken' with fear.[36] Thousands were cast out of their homes, 'stark naked', into the snow. A farmhand recalled seeing about 140 bodies in a pit. They were laid 'thick and close together', he said, like 'the packing up of herrings'.[37]

Reports of Catholic atrocities were read in Parliament and embellished in the pulpits. Lurid pictures of dismembered bodies, and of babies on pitchforks, perked up the pamphlets that now glutted the market. They were similar to the images arriving from war-torn Europe. To her enemies, the Whore of Babylon was the same whether she was scything citizens in Magdeburg or roasting infants on an Ulster spit. Babylon was not fallen; Babylon was rising. The half-clothed, half-crazed refugees who made it across the Irish Sea and threw themselves upon the mercy of parishes throughout England and Wales bore witness to her savagery. 'O what fears and tears, cries and prayers, night and day,' Joseph Lister remembered, 'in my dear mother's house' in Bradford. There was a rumour, neither proven nor implausible, that the king and queen had encouraged the revolt to raise an army. There was also a proverb: 'He that will England win must first with Ireland begin.'[38]

The bonfires and bells of the fifth of November were especially lively that autumn. After the 'Incident' in Scotland and the 'massacre' in Ireland, it seemed only a matter of time before a new popish plot would hiss and jolt into action. These were frosty days, 'dry and hard, with a great mist for the thieves'.[39] Stories circulated about sleeper cells and underground armies. Witness statements read out in the Commons carried the whiff of sulphur: 'the Protestants' heels would go up apace'; 'the Protestants should shortly have a blow'.[40] Catholic recusants were disarmed. Earlier that summer, an informant had told the House of Commons of a stockpile of weapons large enough to equip 1,500 men at Basing House in Hampshire, the seat of the Catholic Marquess of Winchester. Now he was ordered to sell them all off, but only to Protestants, and with the receipts submitted to the Commons.[41]

On 25 October, John Pym, the king's key opponent in the Commons, was handed a letter in the chamber. The porter said that he had received it that morning on Fish Street Hill from a man on a horse with a red ribbon around his arm. The rider's face was covered by a montero (a flapped hunting cap), but the porter had noticed a wart on his nose, and the twelvepence reward. He passed the letter to Pym. It contained a bandage saturated in plague pus and a note stating that if the infection did not kill him, a dagger would follow.[42]

The following month saw Pym – 'Mr Pimp' or 'King Pym' to his critics – present an extraordinary document to Parliament.[43] Known to posterity as the Grand Remonstrance, it catalogued every error and policy failure of Charles I's reign, from taxes and monopolies to the obstructiveness of the bishops and 'popish' peers in the House of Lords. It was a forensic dissection of a corrupted body politic with every 'malignant' humour exposed. A king who relied upon 'evil counsel', Pym argued, was not a king who could be trusted with appointments to high office.[44]

A furious fourteen-hour debate ensued between Pym's allies and the more moderate MPs, who felt that Charles had conceded quite enough this Parliament. Tempers were lost and swords were grasped, but in the small hours of Tuesday 23 November 1641, the Grand Remonstrance was passed by 159 votes to 148 (or 52 to 48 per cent). The MP for Cambridge reportedly stated that if it had been rejected, he would have packed up the next morning 'and never seen England more'. His name was Oliver Cromwell.[45]

On a mid-December afternoon three weeks later, after many MPs had gone home for the day, a previously defeated motion to have the Grand Remonstrance printed was slipped into the agenda and carried. Hitherto 'that great Buggbeare to affright the people', as one critic called it, had only circulated in manuscript. Now many more people could read all about it. This was something new in parliamentary politics – a direct appeal, over the heads of the elite, to public opinion. 'I did not dream that we should remonstrate downward,' Sir Edward Dering protested, or 'tell tales to the people'.

'It's time to speak plain English,' said Pym.[46]

These December days were the most frightening, and thrilling, in living memory and they shattered the rhythms of Snow Hill and other communities throughout the city and the realm. Near the top of the hill, at Newgate Prison, there was a riot. About twenty inmates who were condemned to hang on 13 December heard that the seven Catholic priests due to be executed alongside them had been reprieved by the king. The prisoners managed to get hold of some weapons and overcome the guards. The trained bands, London's citizen militia, were called, but order was only restored after nightfall. The following morning, at the tolling of St Sepulchre's bell, the prisoners were carted off to Tyburn. It was a tense procession, accompanied by the 'great murmuring of the common people'.[47]

There was 'a great disturbance' in church the following Sunday when a religious radical attempted to give an impromptu sermon from the gallery. Speaking on the Book of Revelation, he urged repentance and threatened war, before being shouted down and bustled out. The same day, in the neighbouring parish of Christ Church, the minister was handed a note asking him to pray for the apprentices in their efforts 'to extirpate all innovations of the bishops'.[48]

There were stirs throughout the City now. The king's party and the Warwick–Pym Junto clashed over who should control the army needed to put down the Irish rebels, who should defend the Tower of London, who should guard Parliament and who, ultimately, was in charge of the streets. On 12 December, Charles ordered 210 absentee MPs and peers to return to Westminster within a month. This put pressure on the opposition, who faced the prospect not only of losing their majority in the Commons but also of Charles's threatened vengeance. In order to pass an impressment bill, which would give them control of an army for Ireland (and strip the king of his prerogative power to conscript men in an emergency), they needed to overturn his majority of peers and bishops in the Lords before losing their own in the Commons.[49]

'All things grow daily into a more dangerous expectation,' noted Captain Guy Molesworth on 16 December; 'continual petitions from all counties for and against bishops.' As the clock ticked on, and the newly printed Grand Remonstrance passed from hand to hand, 'factious' crowds gathered at Westminster to protest: 'No bishops! No popish lords!' they cried.[50]

The following week, crucial elections for London's legislative body, the Common Council, were held and there was a strong swing towards Junto-leaning 'new men'. This would enable them to wrest control of City governance – and the trained bands – from the Lord Mayor and Aldermen, who were mainly loyal to the king. In theory, the new councillors were not to be installed until the Monday after Twelfth Night, 10 January, but according to one hostile account, this interim period was 'a very active time and that which laid the groundwork of that revolt of this city, from their loyalty to rebellion'.[51]

There was another changing of the guard at the Tower of London, where Charles appointed a new lieutenant: Colonel Thomas Lunsford, a flame-haired young officer who had fought the Scots in the north. The great city fortress, which was studded with cannon and housed the main arsenal and mint, was now in the hands of an erstwhile outlaw and soldier of fortune who had once served under the banner of the King of France. Subsequent rumours that Lunsford was a child-eater were spread more in mirth than credulity, but his appointment was deeply unpopular and framed by Charles's enemies as a Franco–popish plot. There were official protests in the Commons and demonstrations on the streets.[52]

Charles soon realised his mistake and removed Lunsford from the post, but the swaggering colonel did not go away. On Monday 27 December, he and a party of demobbed officers clashed with demonstrating citizens, apprentices and sailors inside Westminster Hall. According to one account, Lunsford and his men charged at them, scattering them into the upstairs courts. The demonstrators, including John Lilburne, the future leader of the Levellers, retaliated with

Lunsford's charge. In plumed hat and fancy (if soon-sodden) breeches, the colonel
raises his sword and leads his 'ruffinly Cavaleires' towards a herd of anonymous
and – in this etching at least – unarmed protesters.

swords, clubs, and bricks prised from the floor. Facing a swelling crowd,
Lunsford and his men beat a swift retreat. He only just escaped, by
wading into the Thames until the water seeped over the tops of his
boots.[53]

Here, then, is the cartoon Cavalier: hotspurred and ruthless and
also – since the word was imported from the Spanish *caballero*, the Italian *cavaliere* and the French *chevalier* (for 'horseman') – a little bit
papist. The word had been used before this point both positively (to
denote chivalry) and pejoratively (for roistering rakehells), but now it
gained currency as a political label in the menacing Lunsfordian mould.
New, too, to the lexicon was the word Roundhead, deployed that day
at Westminster by an officer threatening to cut the throats of the
'round-headed dogs that bawled against bishops'.[54] He was referring to
the short hairstyles of the apprentices: young men in their late teens
and early twenties who were bound for the best part of a decade to
their masters in the City guilds. They were used to hard work, strict
regulation and, in recent years, depressed conditions. Not all

apprentices were against the bishops, but a great many were in the crowd at Westminster on Monday in their first violent clash with the Cavaliers.

That evening, the gates to the City of London were shut and a treble watch was imposed. Lord Mayor Gurney and his sheriffs patrolled the streets in person. The next day, a proclamation was issued against 'riotous assemblies'. It was too little too late for the bishops, who were thoroughly spooked. They had been jostled upon arrival at the House of Lords and heckled in their coaches as they left. According to one witness, 'a lane was made in both the palace yards and no man could pass but whom the rabble gave leave to, crying: "A good Lord" or "A good man – let him pass!" '55 The Archbishop of York scuffled with a group of protesters and his gown was torn. His residence next to Westminster Abbey was also attacked and his men were forced to defend the church, throwing stones from the roof at would-be iconoclasts. Bishops arriving by water were prevented from landing by a barrier of apprentices on the wharf. Twelve bishops made it to the Lords on Monday, two on Tuesday, none on Wednesday. Two seasonal elements spiced the cocktail. It was the bitterest of winters, with frosty wind, snow and thunderstorms, and it was Christmastide, the season of good will but also misrule.

On Wednesday 29 December, earth stood hard as iron. Whitehall Palace, the residence of Charles and his family, was railed in and defended by a Court of Guard. Between three and four in the afternoon, as the light dimmed, two hundred demonstrators drifted back from Westminster to the City. When they passed Whitehall Gate, they exchanged taunts with the soldiers on duty. Then they threw icy snowballs at them. The guards drew their swords, vaulted the rails and slashed at the crowd. No protester was killed outright, but several suffered wounds to their faces and arms, and a handful may have died afterwards of their injuries.56

Later that night, two thousand apprentices converged on Cheapside, London's main marketplace. According to one source, they were armed with clubs, swords and halberds (a sort of poleaxe). Some had been blooded in the Whitehall skirmish and wanted to storm the prisons where their friends were being held. John Venn, an MP and militia captain, who seems to have colluded with various apprentice groups during the demonstrations, tried to settle them. He assured the young men that he was on their side, and promised to secure the release of every apprentice arrested that day. 'Home, home, home,' most now cried, but some hived off into the streets, attacking prisons and property. One pamphlet absolved the apprentices of blame, pointing the finger instead at 'papists and atheists, who swarm like the frogs of Egypt over the whole land'. Peace would not return, the writer insisted, until God swept them into 'the Red Sea of their own blood'.[57]

Reflecting on the past few days, the navy captain Robert Slingsby was not hopeful: 'I cannot say we have had a merry Christmas, but the maddest one that ever I saw.' The court was under guard. Westminster Abbey was full of soldiers. Twelve bishops, having protested that Parliament was no longer free, were in custody. 'The citizens for the most part shut up their shops,' Slingsby continued, 'and all gentlemen provide themselves with arms as in time of open hostility. Both factions talk very big and it is a wonder there is no more blood yet spilt, seeing how earnest both sides are. There is no doubt but if the king do not comply with the Commons in all things they desire, a sudden civil war must ensue, which every day we see approaches nearer.'[58]

As Charles pondered his next move, rain flayed the streets and charged down Snow Hill. Some citizens hid behind their shutters. Others tooled up and stood guard. There were more soldiers now mustering at the alarm points at Newgate at the top of the hill, and at Holborn Conduit, at the ridge where the floodwater pooled with the detritus of Smithfield. There were more horses struggling to stay upright. And there were more bells, discordant now, sending their warning to the print-seller and his apprentices at the conduit, and the scrivener who lived with his sister next to the sign of The George, and to Thomas Johnson, the apothecary of Snow Hill.

2

The Apothecary

My subject is nature, that is, life.

Pliny, *Natural History* (AD 77)

They did not want a civil war. They had bills to pay and mouths to feed. Robert Peake had prints to display. Isaac Rowlett had wills to transcribe. Robert Amery had wine to sell. Marmaduke Rawdon had ships to buy and colonies to plant. The four of them enjoyed dressing up in military garb and parading at the Artillery Garden near Bishopsgate, but this was not war. William Faithorne had an apprenticeship to finish and copper plates to engrave. Thomas Fuller and Matthew Griffith had children and parishioners to look after. William Robbins was playing the fool at the Cockpit Theatre in Drury Lane. And the great old maestro Inigo Jones was busier than ever, reshaping the architectural and theatrical landscapes of the land.

Thomas Johnson had a shop to run and patients to treat, books to write, plants to find. There is nothing in his words or deeds to suggest that he was living under a tyranny or anticipating a revolution in any world other than the medical one. His flintiest remarks went to the snobs at the College of Physicians and the 'careless druggists' who allowed themselves to be gulled by the old women in the herb market.[1] He was intensely observant and boundlessly active, but he does not appear to have been spurred by politics. When he went to Westminster, it was to admire the gillyflowers in his friend Ralph Tuggy's garden.[2] He kept copious notebooks, but they were filled with the English and Latin names of plants, not the debits and credits of God's favour. There is no evidence to suggest that he was exercised by the raising, or razing, of altar rails, but he would dive into a bog for a butterwort.[3]

He weathered Virgilian storms and vertiginous mountains to take cuttings of interesting plants. He wrote about cudweed and catsfoot, marsh-mallow and chalice moss, great burdock, hedgehog parsley and the very small red wild campion. He wrote about giant throatwort and petty spurge, Coventry bells and ivy bells, lady's slipper, freshwater soldier, and a sea urchin 'so delicate and fragile that it could scarcely be handled'. He wrote about sea thistle and musk thistle, spear thistle and milk thistle, woolly-headed thistle and thistle-upon-thistle. He found 'knotberry and cloudberry on the tops of the high mountains both in the North and in Wales', and 'red wortle or hurtle berries in the wild moors of Northumberland'. He wrote about the prick mushroom (*Fungus virilis penis arecti forma*) and the great jujube tree, which 'grows to the height of an indifferent pear tree'. And he described the grass 'with which we in London do usually adorn our chimneys in summer time; we commonly call the bundle of it handsomely made up for our use by the name of bents'.[4]

Thomas Johnson was an apothecary. Every morning he would wake up in his house on Snow Hill, go downstairs and open his shop. He would check the prescriptions and compound his ingredients. Like most Londoners, he had not been born in the city. He was sired in Selby in Yorkshire around the turn of the century (his name is not the researcher's friend). On 28 November 1620, he was apprenticed to the London apothecary William Bell. Eight years later, having completed his training and passed the exam, he became a freeman of the Worshipful Society of Apothecaries and ceremonially 'gave a spoon' to signify his new status as a dispenser of medicine.[5]

The society was an offshoot of the Worshipful Company of Grocers, one of the Great Twelve livery companies, whose members dealt wholesale (*en gros*). The apothecaries (from the Greek *apotheke*: storehouse) started off as merchants too, selling everything from paper to pepper. In 1617, a royal charter gave them an exclusive licence to sell medicine, but only those medicines prescribed by the College of Physicians – an older, better-educated and altogether more august institution, or so said its members.[6]

Like pharmacists today, apothecaries might dispense advice with their syrups and pills. They prepared the treatments themselves from single plants and herbs ('simples') and tried to attract customers with curiosities: dead and dried things mainly, and something exotic to showcase global reach. On his grim road to suicide, Shakespeare's Romeo encounters an apothecary in whose:

> . . . needy shop a tortoise hung,
> An alligator stuffed, and other skins
> Of ill-shaped fishes; and about his shelves
> A beggarly account of empty boxes,
> Green earthen pots, bladders, and musty seeds,
> Remnants of packthread, and old cakes of roses
> Were thinly scattered, to make up a show.[7]

On 10 April 1633, five months before William Laud was confirmed as Archbishop of Canterbury and a decade before the country waged war on itself, Johnson made up his own show on Snow Hill with a strange fruit from Bermuda. 'I drew [it] as soon as I received it,' he wrote, and he described it as precisely as he could:

The fruit which I received was not ripe, but green, each of them was about the bigness of a large bean; the length of them some five inches, and the breadth some inch and half: they all hang their heads downwards, have rough or uneven ends, and are five cornered, and if you turn the upper side downward, they somewhat resemble a boat . . .

The pulp is white and soft, the stalk whereby it is fastened to the knot is very short and almost as thick as one's little finger . . .

The pulp or meat was very soft and tender and it did eat somewhat like a musk-melon.[8]

Melon, in the early-modern period, was the food of the gods. Montaigne considered it one of life's greatest pleasures – alongside fresh air, wine and the wife – while another Frenchman wrote a poem, *Le Melon*, in praise of its soul-tickling charms.[9] Johnson's bananas did not impress, however, or at least no one bought them. They stayed on their hook, turning from green to yellow to black throughout April, May and into June. One can only hope that he did not discard the skins onto that very steep street of his.

Bananas drawn by Thomas Johnson, 10 April 1633. This bunch came from Bermuda, but the fruit originated in Asia. 'Some', wrote Johnson, 'have judged it for the forbidden fruit.'

Strictly speaking, only formally licensed physicians were allowed to diagnose disease and prescribe medicine, and only the barber-surgeons could cut into flesh. (Red-and-white poles, denoting blood and bandages, still swirl outside traditional barber shops.) But in a city of 400,000 people, the market was necessarily porous. Apothecaries outnumbered the university-educated physicians, and there was cheaper competition from 'cunning' men and women, midwives, healers, 'piss-prophets' and refugees from Europe, where medical knowledge was more advanced. The quack doctor, like the precise Puritan, became a stock figure in seventeenth-century literature, one of Ben Jonson's 'turdy-facey-nasty-patey-lousy-fartical rogues'.[10]

The College of Physicians tried to police unlicensed practice. Johnson's friend, the 'very insolent' John Buggs, who was an actor as well as an apothecary, was fined and imprisoned after the death of a patient, but the College had no real hope of defending its monopoly.[11] In medicine, no less than politics and commerce, the seventeenth century was an age of expansion and of questioning old traditions. The Galenic system based on balancing the body's four humours (black bile, yellow bile, phlegm and blood) was being challenged, if not yet replaced, by new chemical and empirical methods. There was no technology upon which to rely, no painless way of looking into an ailing body, no antibiotics or germ theory. Results mattered more than a university degree. Then came reputation and, with luck, patronage.

In the summertime, before Bartholomew Fair spilled into his street, when the city became salty and the bundles of bents started to line people's hearths, Thomas Johnson and his apothecary friends went 'herborising'. Their first major trip was to Kent, in July 1629, where they spent five days striding through bright yellow rape fields and along the water's edge. 'On the way, we found the plants whose names follow,' wrote Johnson, in Latin, before launching into the first of many lists.[12] He plucked lichen from the side of a Rochester inn, fern from a church wall in Gillingham and cannabis from the roadside between Stoke and Cliffe.

His pen was as sharp as his eye. The mayor of Queenborough, who had summoned the eccentric little party to his presence, is neatly skewered. 'The ancient kings of this realm decided to grant great and far-reaching privileges to this borough,' the official intoned, '. . . so for me, who am at this time entrusted with the public protection of this place, it is a duty to discover the cause of your journey to this island of ours.' The travellers were supremely unctuous. 'I will expound to you, Sir, the reason for our journey, though it is scarcely worthy of your attention,' oiled John Buggs, the actor-apothecary. 'We are devoted [addicti] to the study of the discipline and nature of medicine. That is why we have come to this place to discover the rare plants that grow in your island.'

'Another reason,' interjected Jonas Styles, is 'to have the opportunity of seeing a man of such merit as yourself, especially as I know that you are so well versed in seamanship. It is especially gratifying to me to become acquainted with so eminent a man.'

The mayor was thoroughly mollified and offered his new acolytes 'excellent beer' and free rein in his domain. At Queenborough Castle, Johnson transcribed verses to 'the never sufficiently belauded Queen Elizabeth' and then plucked a fern from the parapet. 'We then hurried to the seashore and our usual task.' The verbs Johnson uses most in this account are *festinare* (hurry) and *propero* (hasten). He even wrote 'with a hurrying pen'. After one particularly exhausting trek, his fellows took a brewer's dray to Rochester, but Johnson and Styles left them 'lolling amongst the barrels in the wagon' and rushed off to meet more plants. By the end of the expedition, they had catalogued around 270 specimens, several of which were the first records for Britain. It was a successful trip and a fun one, inflected by Johnson's fizzing zeal. His eye clocked everything, from the 1,200-ton *Prince Royal* docked in Chatham to the sugar cane and 'big Indian nut' on a merchant ship returning from the East Indies.

In a house in Gillingham, Johnson had admired a portrait of an Elizabethan constable of Queenborough Castle. At 'great expense and toil',
the constable had collected the portraits and escutcheons of all his pre-
decessors. Johnson noted the painting's inscription: 'Things scattered
and neglected I assembled'. The phrase seems to have tickled him, for
he was trying to do something similar in his own work. He believed
that 'God, of his infinite goodness and bounty, hath, by the medium of
plants, bestowed almost all food, clothing and medicine upon man.'[13]
These divine prescriptions had been lost over time, but could be recovered, reordered and relearned. Paradise lost might be regained. 'These
rambles of ours,' Johnson concluded, were 'not for show but for use'
and 'merely a prelude to others to be tackled in the years that follow'.

Not all the fellows of the Worshipful Society of Apothecaries
approved. Some labelled the trip 'vain and superfluous'. Johnson was
stung by the criticism. Apothecaries, he argued, were no better than
quacks if they didn't know what went into their medicines: 'Almost
every day in the herb market one or other of them, to the great peril
of their patients, lays himself open to the mockery of the women who
deal in roots. These women know only too well the unskilled, and thrust
upon them brazenly what they please for what you will.' If an apothecary
looking for peony roots, for example, bought instead those of hemlock
water dropwort, an accessible but highly toxic Thames-side plant, the
results could be fatal.[14] Johnson's mission was to locate and label every
indigenous plant in England and Wales and log his findings into a comprehensive flora that would bring the apothecaries up to scratch.

Indeed, he went further. In three lectures delivered at Apothecaries
Hall in 1634, he also rapped physicians for not being botanically
learned.[15] Hippocrates, Galen and the ancients had all known about
plants and made their own medicines, he said. As apothecary-physicians,
they had understood that their discipline could only be mastered with
a proper grasp of its practical, 'operative' parts, which included pharmacy. Over time, however, the apothecary had been misrepresented
and downgraded in relation to the physician. He had been branded
a mountebank and a 'mere mortar-man'. He had been called 'unguen-
tary' and effeminate: 'You see what it is to be younger brothers or
at least to lose our birthright,' Johnson groused. He marshalled an
impressive array of ancient and humanist sources to return the apothecary to his legitimate place in the medical lineage. 'We fetch our

pedigree from the same ancestors,' he said. 'It is curing not talking, nor writing, that is the chief act of physic.' The natural corollary to this argument was that those 'self-opinionate[d]' fellows of the College of Physicians who did not care for pharmacy might not be the true, or at least not the prime, heirs of the universal doctor of antiquity. It was a combative argument delivered at a time when tensions between the apothecaries and physicians were at their height. Thomas Johnson was a brave man.

Johnson went on two herborising trips to Hampstead Heath and another to Kent, where he recorded a stuffed snake in an apothecary shop in Sandwich ('fifteen feet long and thicker than an arm', apparently).[16] He went to Bath, Bristol and Hampshire in 1634, and Wales in the summer of 1639, where he decided to climb Mount Snowdon. The whole mountain was shrouded in cloud, but his effort was rewarded with French sorrel, heath cypress, violets, sedums and hairy kidney-wort. He was enchanted by Wales. 'The refinement of its inhabitants,' he wrote, 'and the variety of the scenery have so delighted me that there would be nothing more delectable, or more joyful, than again to visit when the aspect of the sky is kinder and when I have greater leisure.'[17]

He also undertook two major publishing projects that would prove immeasurably useful in the coming decade. One was a translation of the works of the sixteenth-century battlefield surgeon Ambrose Paré. The other was a revised edition of the 1597 *Herball* of the Elizabethan barber-surgeon John Gerard. This was an enormous catalogue of plants, listing their characteristics and medicinal properties. Gerard's original had been a crude, error-strewn mash-up of two Flemish texts. 'I know not what our author meant by this description,' Johnson despairs as he edits a section on coral moss. He only had a year to enlarge and amend Gerard's text, but with extensive (and acknow-ledged) help from his great friend the Hampshire botanist John Goodyer, he fulfilled his brief. Johnson's edition was published in 1633 with around 800 new entries and over 2,500 woodcuts. It was, as he freely admitted, horribly rushed, but it was a vast improvement on the original and it made his name.[18]

A second edition followed in 1636, a copy of which, stamped with the arms of Charles I, is now in the Royal Collection. On 2 July 1637, the provost of Eton College, Sir Henry Wotton – an eminent statesman now best known for the apophthegm that 'an ambassador is an honest man sent to lie abroad for the good of his country' – wrote to Johnson with 'two or three requests': where could he find a well-bound copy of 'one of your Gerards'? Where could he get coloured pinks or other scented flowers for his garden? Thirdly, did Johnson know anyone suffering from *melancholia hypochondriaca*, 'wherewith I have been troubled of late in some measure'? Wotton didn't want to know what was written in the books. He wanted Johnson's opinion on the best new treatments.* He addressed the letter 'To my very loving and learned friend Mr Johnson Apothecary, at his house on Snow Hill, London.'[19]

The boy from Selby had arrived. He had prestigious clients and influential friends, including John Argent, the rotund president of the College of Physicians, who had sent him those bananas in 1633 – proof that physicians and apothecaries could, in practice, get along.[20] By the end of the decade, he had herborised through twenty-five counties and was well on his way to realising his dream of a comprehensive flora of England and Wales. According to the physician Christopher Merrett, a future founder member of the Royal Society – and, incidentally, the man who, thirty years before Dom Pérignon, first recorded how to put bubbles into wine – Johnson was 'an exceptionally industrious man'.[21] He seemed unstoppable.

On 3 August 1640, exactly three months before the opening of the Long Parliament, Johnson was appointed to the governing body of the Society of Apothecaries. According to a poll tax assessment the following year, he had two male apprentices, two female servants and one of the bigger houses on Snow Hill. He also had a garden where he cultivated various plants.[22] Roger Reeve, the 'oyleman' who lived three doors down from him and was assessed at the same high tax rate, boasted twelve leather chairs in his parlour, three spits in his kitchen, a still in the cellar, a summer house, well-yard, wash-house and stable.[23] St Sepulchre's has often been portrayed as a seedy suburb, 'infamous for filth, crime and plague', and it is true that some parts, especially around

---

* Johnson's reply has sadly not survived, but his friend, the king's physician Theodore de Mayerne, might have told him about one of his patients, a 'Monsieur Cromwell', who had been 'very melancholy' in 1628. (Ronald Hutton, *The Making of Oliver Cromwell* (2021), 26.)

Smithfield, struggled hard, but Johnson's street in the Holborn Cross precinct was substantial and salubrious.[24]

The tax assessment lists two little words after Johnson's name: '*et uxor*' – 'and wife'. The parish registers of St Sepulchre were destroyed in the Great Fire, but the marriage of an apothecary called Thomas Johnson was announced at nearby St Martin-in-the-Fields on 22 July 1629. There was more than one apothecary called Thomas Johnson knocking about London at the time, but the dates fit and the groom's signature is a close match for Johnson's later hand. By this record, he was twenty-seven, recently out of his apprenticeship and just back from his Kent trip (perhaps another reason for the hurry). His bride was Jane Darling, aged twenty, the daughter of a vintner of the parish. They would have at least two daughters and a son.[25] We do not know if he was a good husband or if she was a good wife. We do not know if she helped him in the shop or followed him to the wars. We must leave her, therefore, in a back room, or a shadow in the garden.

On 13 March 1643, Johnson's next-door neighbour, the widow Dorcas Ball, made her will. She left him a 'chest with drawers', a good thing to give an apothecary, and appointed him overseer along with three others. Johnson was the only one of the four not to witness the signing and sealing of the will. Sometime afterwards, finding her estate 'declining', Ball added a codicil. She reduced some legacies and struck out others. 'Mr Thomas Johnson is no overseer,' the document now states. The codicil is endorsed by just one person: Johnson's kinsman and former apprentice George Johnson.[26] Perhaps, then, he was the one who told Dorcas that Thomas had gone on a different kind of field trip and would not be back soon – that he was, in fact, in Oxford with the king.

3

Waves of the Sea

On 4 January 1642, in an attempt to break the deadlock after the December tumults, Charles I tried to arrest John Pym and four other Members of Parliament for treason. The king left Whitehall with four hundred troops. The five members received a tip-off just in time and escaped downriver to the City. Finding his birds flown, Charles left the chamber to cries of 'Privilege! Privilege!'

The following morning, he tried again, taking his gilded coach into the heart of the City to request that the Common Council hand the fugitives over. Again he was denied and again the chorus rang in his ears: 'Privileges of Parliament!' When Charles afterwards dined at Sheriff Garrett's house near St Paul's, thousands thronged 'from all parts of the City, and the clamour still was Privileges of Parliament'. When he returned to his coach, the crowd pressed against it, leering in and holding on 'in a most undutiful manner'. A red-bearded preacher called Henry Walker, once an ironmonger's apprentice in Newgate, threw a pamphlet at the coach. It bore the revolutionary rallying cry: *To your tents, O Israel.*[*]

On his return from escorting Charles out of the City, the Lord Mayor of London, sixty-three-year-old Richard Gurney, was roughed up by a gang of 'uncivil women' near Ludgate. They pulled him from his horse, ripped his gown and tore the chain of office from his neck. Unable to guarantee its members' safety, Parliament adjourned and reconvened by committee at London's Guildhall. Word on the street was of military manoeuvres at Whitehall in the west and the Tower in

---

[*] 'So when all Israel saw that the king hearkened not unto them, the people answered the king, saying, What portion have we in David? Neither have we inheritance in the son of Jesse: *To your tents, O Israel*: now see to thine own house, David. So Israel departed unto their tents.' (1 Kings 12:16)

the east. People were terrified that London would be sacked and burned. They thought of the Protestant city of Magdeburg, scorched by Habsburg troops a decade earlier. They pictured babies on pitchforks in Ireland. They closed their shops and stood guard, 'possessed with strange fears and imaginations'.

The next day produced a fitting finale to the 'maddest' Christmas that had ever been. Around midnight, the City and suburbs awoke to screams that the Cavaliers were coming. 'There was a great bouncing at every man's door,' one eyewitness recalled. In little more than an hour, and without the necessary mayoral authority, the trained bands were up in arms. Around 100,000 more Londoners presented themselves with swords, clubs and whatever else they could find. 'Women and children did then arise and fear and trembling entered on all.' The city gates were shut, portcullises were dropped and chains were dragged across the streets to obstruct horses. Women boiled water to throw onto the Cavaliers and fashioned barricades out of stools, benches and tubs. Then they waited. They waited for the sound of horses' hooves until the water went cold in their pots and pans. Some reportedly lost the babies in their bellies, but the enemy, it turned out, was not at the gate. It was a false alarm, raised – according to one royalist satirist, writing under the pseudonym Mercurius Civicus – to gauge the extent of City support for Parliament.

'Had you been at the Lord Mayor's that night, as I was,' he wrote a year and a half later, 'you might, upon the aldermen's coming to him to consult against the common danger, easily perceive which of the aldermen were privy to this design.' They were the spruce ones in perfect ruffs, 'as if they had spent the whole day to be trim at midnight, their beards put into a feasting posture, not a hair awry, a clear demonstration that they had not consulted their pillows that night'. Others had plainly been kept in the dark. One arrived in his nightcap and forgot his hat. Another remembered his hat, but forgot his ruff. 'One trots along in his slippers', while another, having neglected his garter, shuffled over with his stockings at his feet.[2]

Whether contrived or not – others attributed the panic to accidental gunfire at Whitehall and drunken duellers in Covent Garden – Parliament's allies in the City were emboldened by the rapid response of its residents. On 8 January, Mayor Gurney was again blindsided when Common Council, liaising with the parliamentary committees in London, resolved that the City trained bands would protect the five members on their return to Westminster. Charles, realising that he had lost his capital, and fearful for the safety of Henrietta Maria and the children, slipped away with them on 10 January. 'So fleeting and so friendless', and with Hampton Court barely ready to receive them, they kept each other warm that night in one bed.[3] The following day, the five MPs and one impeached peer returned to Westminster in noisy triumph. They were accompanied by trumpets, drums and salvoes from a flotilla on the river. The king was gone. Parliament was back.

Marmaduke Rawdon looked on in dismay. Little more than a month earlier, it had been the king, returning from the negotiations in Edinburgh, who had received the welcoming party. The message then, in late November 1641, had been that while Charles had effectively lost Scotland and was struggling with Ireland, he could still count on the love and loyalty of England and her capital. John Venn, MP for London, had protested that the pageant was 'displeasing to the Parliament', but he had been overruled. Five hundred liverymen had ridden out in their velvet and plush, with gold chains around their necks and swords at their sides. Rawdon, who was fifty-eight, had been there with the Clothworkers' Company. It had been quite a show: cannon roared, claret flowed and a torchlit procession had carried the royal couple along the Strand to Whitehall.[4] But it was a mirage, and Rawdon, who had felt the heat for some time, knew it.

Time was when he and John Venn had walked down the same path. Both were children of Gloriana: Rawdon had been five when the Spanish Armada had loomed in 1588; Venn two. Both were migrants to the City and merchants by training: Rawdon specialised in wine; Venn, silk. Both were apprentices in the first decade of the new century and quickly moved up the ranks of their respective companies, Rawdon at the Clothworkers and Venn with the Merchant Taylors. Both were officers in London's trained bands and early members of the Honourable Artillery Company. Rawdon enrolled in 1612 and Venn two years later.[5] In 1631, they both vied for the job of captain-leader and their paths diverged.

The Honourable Artillery Company had been established in 1611, with its roots in two Tudor citizen militias: the 1537 Fraternity of St

George and the Elizabethan Captains of the Artillery Garden, who were appointed to command and drill the militia raised in response to the Catholic threat from Europe. They modelled themselves on the Protestant merchants of Antwerp, who had fought valiantly, if vainly, against Spain's besieging forces in 1584–5. Most of the captains had been at Tilbury Fort when Elizabeth I had given her rousing Armada speech. This spirit of militant Protestant patriotism infused the later Jacobean academy that Rawdon and Venn joined.[6] It was a voluntary body of infantry ('artillery' only in the old sense of the word, denoting missile weapons) and almost five hundred strong when Rawdon took a muster in 1631. Every week, members would go up to the fields north of the city wall to drill with musket and pike. They also studied the latest tactics from Europe and the conventional laws of war. Occasionally they put on a show, like the mock battle between the crescent and the cross at Merchant Taylors' Hall in 1638, when a company of scimitar-wielding 'Saracens', dressed in 'the Persian and Turconian manner', were vanquished – and at the last converted – by John Venn's 'modern' musketeers. 'Behold,' announced one militiaman to his audience, 'the soldier and the citizen / make but one man.'[7]

Bigger and more public was the company's annual feast day, when members would buff their boots and parade before big crowds. This was followed by a blood-and-thunder sermon in one of London's churches, and then onward the Christian soldiers would march to a banquet, where toasts were raised to Mars and Bacchus. Like Thomas Johnson and his herborisers, Artillery men had a perhaps-deserved reputation for enjoying themselves a little too much, but they believed, as did the apothecaries, that they were the key workers of the commonwealth.*[8] When the Whore of Babylon came for Christ's citadel, the citizen-soldiers of the Honourable Artillery Company would man the defences. In the meantime, they went about their business and strived to uphold their motto: 'Arma pacis fulcra' – 'Armed strength for peace'.

Fraternity was important to Marmaduke Rawdon, the middle of five brothers who had grown up in Stearsby, beneath the North York

---

* In the company's history, only two members have been struck off the Ancient Vellum Book: Francis Colman for 'unmanly carriage' towards his captain in 1670, and John Currey, also in 1670, 'for his unmanly action in biting off his wife's nose'. (AVB, xii–xiii.)

Moors. His father Ralph was a big bear of a man and 'a great friend of inoffensive mirth'. He taught his son the importance of credit. When Marmaduke had ventured to London at the age of sixteen, he had thrived as a wine merchant's apprentice and then as his factor in Bordeaux. Returning in 1610, he bought a house by the Thames on Water Lane, in the shadow of the Tower of London. The following year, he married a nineteen-year-old heiress called Elizabeth Thorowgood. She gave him an estate in Hertfordshire, ten sons, six daughters and a quite fabulous stepmother-in-law called Martha Moulsworth, who wrote an autobiographical poem extolling past marriages ('Three husbands me, and I have them enjoyed / Nor I by them, nor they by me annoyed . . .') and female education:

> And why not so? The muses female are
> And therefore of us females take some care
> Two universities we have of men
> Oh that we had but one of women then
> Oh then that would in wit, and tongues surpass
> All art of men that is, or ever was.[9]

With funds had come freedom. This was the first truly global age, and Rawdon made the most of it, investing in ships (including the eponymous *Marmaduke*) and trading in the Mediterranean, Levant, West Indies and the wine-producing Canary Islands off the Moroccan coast.[10] He survived 'several dangerous voyages' and financed others, including an early expedition to New England in 1614 (piloted by John Smith of Pocahontas legend) and an attempt to discover a north-west passage to Asia, which returned only 'an unicorn's horn of small value'.[11] More profitable, if not in his lifetime and not in the tobacco crop that he envisaged, was Barbados, where Rawdon's syndicate obtained 10,000 acres of land in 1628 and – with the help of a royal charter – ruthlessly wrenched control of the island from its first settlers.*[12]

---

* Initially known as the 'tobacco island', Barbados could not compete with Virginia, whose smooth, superior weed dominated the market. The shift to sugar – and slavery – came in 1641. There had been enslaved people on the island before, but the majority of labourers were indentured servants. Between 1642 and 1660, however, an average of 2,000 West Africans a year were transported to Barbados. (Gragg,

That year, Rawdon became a Member of Parliament. He represented Aldeburgh on the Suffolk coast and earned his constituents' enduring thanks in the form of 'a small present of excellent fish' every Lent. Ships, Rawdon told the House, were 'the jewels that adorn the kingdom and the walls of the land'. He was not afraid to criticise the government – some years, he said, he had spent more on tax than on stock – and he doggedly secured the release of merchants imprisoned for resisting a new wine duty. More often than not, though, he sought accommodation with the Crown and backed its request for subsidies.[13]

His nephew, writing in 1667, called him a 'royal merchant' and boasted that he had been consulted privately, and often, by both James I and Charles I.[14] He was also esteemed by the glamorous royal favourite, the Duke of Buckingham, 'who would keep him sometimes two or three hours together asking his opinion about concerns of state'. It was as well that forty years had passed when Rawdon's nephew wrote this, since George Villiers, Duke of Buckingham, who was stabbed to death in the summer of 1628, was widely blamed for the most egregious Stuart policies, particularly Charles's disastrous attempts to fight Spain and France. When the English fleet had straggled home in 1625 after an abysmal (and inebriated) attempt to recapture Elizabethan glories in Cadiz, the joke in Europe had been that 'there were now no more Drakes in England, all were hens'.[15]

When it came to 'Ship Money', probably the most controversial single issue of the 1630s, Rawdon had not opposed the Crown. This was a tax raised to strengthen the navy. It had traditionally been levied on coastal towns in times of emergency, but Charles had demanded it of everyone, even inland, even in peacetime. Several people had dragged their feet and raised only a small percentage. Others, notably John Hampden of Buckingham in 1637, refused outright to pay. The case went to court and the judges ruled for the king. At stake was not just the legality of the tax, or a subject's right to property, but the extent to which Charles could rule at will, since a king who could grant himself unlimited funds, unchecked by the law, was not one in need of a parliament. Who, then, would call him to account for other impositions, or

---

Englishmen Transplanted, 88–91, 119.) One of the island's first – and most ruthless – sugar planters was Rawdon's factor and former apprentice, James Holdip. For more, see the Epilogue.

monopolies, or the billeting of troops on people's homes, or the arrest
of subjects without charge, or the 'popish' innovations of his bishops?
The list was long.

'In all my life,' wrote the Puritan MP Simonds D'Ewes, 'I never saw
so many sad faces in England as this new taxation called Ship Money
occasioned.' He regarded it as 'the most deadly and fatal blow' to
English liberty in five centuries and foresaw 'an Iliad of miseries' if it
was not dropped.[16] For Rawdon, though, it was a tax to build boats and
fight pirates, specifically, in 1637, the Moroccan corsairs who were
threatening his shipping and creeping up the Channel, enslaving
English fishermen. That he was himself a pirate when it suited – or at
least a 'privateer' licensed by royal letters of marque – was neither here
nor there.[17] As the Honourable Artillery Company's mock battle of the
crescent and cross at Merchant Taylors' Hall in 1638 showed, piety and
profit had a habit of reinforcing one another.

Rawdon had two mottoes in life. The official one – *Magna est veritas
et praevalet* ('Truth is great and prevails') – was scrolled on his coat of
arms and carved into the oak of the chapel in Hoddesdon, Hertfordshire where he built his grand manor. His second saying was more
reflective of the mercantile, often mercenary, world of cut-throat
glamour that he inhabited: 'Win gold and wear gold'.[18]

He was a big man, taller than average, with a long, weathered face
and a prominent nose, 'something rising'. He had a great shag of black-
brown hair, thick eyebrows and a full moustache. 'His bones were
strong.' He was a 'modish' dresser and expected his family and servants
to be 'well clad and fashionable'. He ran a tight ship, with 'much order
and little noise', and he was a peacemaker, 'a great compounder of differences'. He would 'as freely talk with the poor as the rich and would,
with much patience, hear what they had to say and relieve them if it lay
in his power'. His weakness was horses. He was fond of saying that
whoever sold him a fine one, whatever the cost, was a friend for life.
This description comes from his nephew, also called Marmaduke
('Duke'), whose father had died when he was sixteen. Rawdon had
taken the lad in and put him to work in the firm. Rawdon's other, older
brother, Robert, a fishmonger on Thames Street, was similarly open-
armed. He had been quick with his fists in his youth, but was 'a great
lover of his own countrymen . . . and if he met any Yorkshireman of his

acquaintance that were poor, he would carry them to his house and furnish them both with money and clothes'.

We can imagine these two brothers striding towards Marmaduke's tavern in Billingsgate, the tang of the Thames in their nostrils. Robert 'a burly fat man', 'jocular and facetious' with a wide swagger. Marmaduke stiff, alert, 'his eyes grey, his body straight', a more measured gait. He was tough in business, but 'pleasant and cheerful' amongst friends.[19] This, at least, is how Duke chose to remember his uncle twenty-one years after his death. And if others accused him of piracy or running a wine cartel or bullish behaviour in Barbados, you had to win gold to wear gold.

He did also share the gold, conspicuously. He made significant donations to the chapel and market house at Hoddesdon, and installed a conduit in the centre of town so that everyone could have spring water piped from Rawdon House. The fountainhead was a limestone Samaritan woman, who inspired verses to the 'blest man' from rival clergymen. She now stands in the grounds of the Lowewood Museum on Hoddesdon high street.[20]

Rawdon's legacy in London is less visible. War and fire have scratched him from the palimpsest. Yet in his lifetime, his mark was everywhere: on the colours of the trained band company that marched under his command; in the bricks of Clothworkers' Hall, rebuilt under his mastership; in the regulations of the hospital he oversaw and the windows of the churches where he prayed. His ships were on the river and his wine was in the vaults.[21] His name was in the minutes of the Levant Company, the French Company, the New River Company and the hugely influential City Lands Committee. This dealt with the management of leases. Its grant book is unspectacular, but completely thrilling, not because of the minutiae it contains, but because of the power it represents. At Rawdon's first committee meeting, held on 28 January 1639, a lease for his brother Robert was renewed. At his last, on 23 June 1640, he was asked to resolve a rent dispute. His name did not reappear after the summer. At the next committee meeting, which was held a fortnight after the opening of the Long Parliament, one of the new members was the Puritan silk merchant John Venn.[22] His rise reflects other subtle shifts going on elsewhere in the City. Cumulatively they represent a draining of influence away from the old chartered

company men, who enjoyed royal favour, towards the 'new merchants', who were more likely to be freewheeling in business and
reformist in religion.[23]

As a maverick transatlantic trader, Marmaduke Rawdon did not
quite fit the Establishment bill. One of his proudest achievements as a
young Common Councilman had been to end the tradition of citizens
having to remove their hats in the presence of the Lord Mayor and
Aldermen. But he had a full book of elite contacts – at court, in the
Custom House and on the aldermanic bench – and he was a prominent
supporter of Archbishop Laud's vision for the beautification of the
Church. Tellingly, he did not subscribe to the Irish Adventure scheme
to colonise Ireland, nor to the more 'godly' colonies like Providence
Island and Massachusetts Bay, which attracted Puritans like the Earl of
Warwick in the Lords, John Pym in the Commons, the preacher of St
Sepulchre's (and Salem) Hugh Peter, and John Venn – the merchant
who had always been in Rawdon's slipstream, but was now edging
ahead.

'When we would have any great things to be accomplished,' one
Puritan minister said, 'the best policy is to work by an engine which
the world sees nothing of.'[24] The godly boardrooms, the radical parishes, the houses of reforming magnates, and the Honourable Artillery
Company provided engine rooms for change during the tyranny, as
they saw it, of Charles I's eleven years of Personal Rule. This was a
tyranny that was offensively popish to them, an 'ikon slavery' that
encouraged thousands to emigrate, but also – perhaps more so for
those with stakes in the ground – it was about monopolies, colonies,
money and power.

Rawdon and Venn had first clashed in 1631, over the leadership of the
Honourable Artillery Company. Venn had been elected captain-leader
by the members, but the Lord Mayor and Aldermen, who preferred
Rawdon, had faulted the procedure and insisted upon a second vote.
Three candidates were put forward: Venn, Rawdon and Rawdon's son-
in-law, Edmund Forster. Rawdon was elected. Venn and his supporters
objected 'in a factious manner' and there had been an almighty row
that had dragged in the king. The company came close to dissolution
and a 'royal regiment' was mooted, but in the end Charles appointed a
compromise candidate and Rawdon and Venn accepted lesser posts.[25]

The company stagnated for a while, with few new recruits (18 in 1633, 16 in 1634) and poor attendance at training. In 1635, though, there was a surge of 330 recruits. Four years later, with the ranks still swelling, Venn had risen to vice president of the company and the new captain-leader was Philip Skippon, a veteran of the wars on the Continent with Puritan sympathies. Skippon was something of a hero, having been shot in the neck two years earlier while holding off two hundred Spaniards with thirty pikemen. It was not a record that Rawdon could hope to match. He still had allies in the company, including Forster and the Guinea trader Nicholas Crisp, but it was not the same outfit that he had joined almost thirty years earlier.[26]

'We were wont, you know,' wrote a royalist in 1643, 'to make very merry at their training; some of them in two years' practice could not be brought to discharge a musket without winking. We did little imagine then that they were ever likely to grow formidable to the state, or advance to that strength as to be able to give the king battle, but after a while they began to affect, yea, and compass the chief offices of command.'[27]

This writer, the satirical Mercurius Civicus, accused the Puritans of deliberately packing the company once 'it was instilled into them that the blessed Reformation intended could not be effected but by the sword'. In 1648, another royalist pamphlet, Persecutio Undecima, would assert much the same thing, adding that Skippon had been brought over from Europe as 'a confiding brother to the cause'.[28] Of course it suited royalists, retrospectively, to characterise the civil war as the Puritan endgame, whereas few of the new recruits in the 1630s would have been seriously thinking of turning their swords on their compatriots. What the Honourable Artillery Company did provide – increasingly, if never exclusively – was a discreet space for disaffected reformers to gather and exercise arms, opinions and tactics. By the end of the decade it exerted a far stronger pull on those who felt, like Venn, that the Church was in need of purification than on members like Rawdon who championed its ornamentation. It was, therefore, the perfect arena for Calybute Downing's feast-day sermon of 1 September 1640.

This was four days after the invading Scots had routed the English at Newburn. New artillery platforms were going up at Whitehall and the Tower of London. Rawdon would have heard the hammering as he left his house in Water Lane. The preacher, Downing, was the vicar of

Hackney and almost certainly Philip Skippon's cousin. In his sermon, he denounced popery as the enemy of mankind and went so far as to justify resistance against an unlawful king. For the safety of the people, he argued, 'extraordinary times' allowed for 'extraordinary undertakings'.[29] Something unthinkable – treasonous – was being expounded in a pulpit to the officers of the trained bands of London. They would have discussed it afterwards at their feast, and later on in shops, taverns and on the street. Downing slipped out of London soon afterwards and found refuge at Leez, the Earl of Warwick's house in Essex.

Later that month, John Venn went from ward to ward securing signatures to a 10,000-strong petition demanding the recall of Parliament. There was some talk of coercion, but the vast majority of citizens, including many future royalists, welcomed the opportunity to air their grievances. The Long Parliament opened on 3 November 1640 and, as we have seen, burned 'as hot as a toast' through the king's chief advisers, his courts, bishops and, ultimately, his prerogative.

There had also been petitions, hundreds of them, flying in from all over the country, expressing fears of an imminent popish plot and venting eleven years of compressed complaint. The first county petition, read on 7 November, came from Hertfordshire, Rawdon's adoptive county, and the first from a London parish targeted his vicar, Edward Layfield, of All Hallows, Barking. Dr Layfield was accused of corruption, of calling his critics 'black toads, spotted toads, and venomous toads like Jack Straw and Wat Tyler', and of imposing perilous innovations on the church. The carved wooden angels that had adorned the All Hallows altar rail were presented to the Commons as proof of his malignancy.

Rawdon and his allies, most of whom had sponsored the church's refurbishment, launched a counter-petition, repudiating the 'false and scandalous' charges against Layfield and pointing out that the angels pre-dated his incumbency. He was, they insisted, a man of 'reverence, religion, gravity and devotion'.[30] He was also the nephew and chaplain of Archbishop Laud and Rawdon could not save him. Nor did his hand on a petition of 26 July 1641 in support of 'the ancient laws and customs' of the City have any discernible effect. As a Thames waterman rejoiced, 'it was Parliament time now, and the Lord Mayor was but their slave'.[31]

John Venn, on the other hand, had a marvellous Parliament, linking

up with the Scottish commissioners, agitating for root-and-branch religious reform and campaigning for the trial and execution of the king's
'evil counsellor', the Earl of Strafford. A clerk's note on the back of a
House of Lords order reveals that in the protests against the king's
hated minister in May 1641, 'Cap. Venn spake for the rest'. The following month, upon the death of a City MP, Venn became a Member of
Parliament himself. He was a forceful backer of Pym's Grand Remonstrance in November 1641 and he was accused several times of
coordinating the demonstrations around Westminster. The protesters
were politically engaged and needed no great nudge, but Venn was
certainly in the thick of it, as was his wife, Margaret, who was also
accused of rallying support. If Venn had any kind of handle on the
popular pressure during the mad December days of 1641, though, he
had not always been able to contain it. As we have seen, at Cheapside
Market on 29 December, following the snowballs and skirmishes outside Whitehall, some apprentices had listened to him and gone home,
but others had hived off to attack prisons and property. Mercurius Civicus was certainly partisan, and no doubt exaggerating when he wrote
of dark forces in the City, but he was not wrong to finger Venn as a key
player in the radical takeover of London.[32]

'Moderate men are suspected,' read Edward Pitt in Hampshire in a letter from Westminster at the end of January 1642, 'violent men are
thought saints with whom too great a stream runs. Fears and jealousies daily increase . . . His Majesty's servants, and such as have relation
to his service (if times timely mend not), suffer most.'[33]

On Thursday 13 January 1642, three days after Charles had fled London, Lord Mayor Gurney was informed by Parliament that henceforth
he must summon meetings of the Common Council 'as often, and at
such times, as shall be desired' by the Committee of Safety. This was
the first of the final series of manoeuvres that completed the parliamentary takeover of the trained bands and the emasculation of old
Mayor Gurney. John Venn was the link man between the Commons
and the City. Philip Skippon, now sergeant major general of the trained
bands, and – thanks to Venn – a member of the newly named Militia
Committee, secured the Tower of London.[34]

On 24 February, Gurney's allies fought back with a petition that
defended the ancient right of the City to order its arms. It had gained

351 signatories, including both Rawdon's brother and his business partner, before it was intercepted and denounced as 'a dangerous design'. Its author, George Benyon, was fined £3,000 and sent to the Tower. Another promoter, the City Recorder Sir Thomas Gardiner, was impeached. Over half the subscribers subsequently withdrew their support.[35]

The following month, the Militia Ordinance was passed, giving Parliament control of the county trained bands. It was an ordinance, not an act, because an act required royal assent and Charles I did not assent to this. Parliament claimed the force of law and appointed new lord lieutenants in the counties. Back in the capital, the trained bands were expanded from 6,000 to 8,000 men and reorganised into forty companies within six regiments. They were named after the colour of their ensigns. Marmaduke Rawdon was appointed lieutenant colonel of the Red Regiment, the senior unit covering the eastern wards around the Tower.

On 10 May, the re-formed regiments mustered in Finsbury Fields in express defiance of the king, who was in York, finally gaining support after failing to take the armories at Portsmouth and Hull. The queen was in Holland, trading crown jewels for arms. Some moderates in Westminster, alarmed by the recent constitutional violations, were peeling off from Parliament and heading north. A paper war was being waged, each side claiming the high ground of the ancient constitution and the true Protestant religion. Armed conflict seemed increasingly likely, but no one wanted to draw first blood.

The London muster was the first test of the Militia Ordinance and was attended by a huge crowd. Parliamentary grandees watched from a special marquee. It was a fine display of force, unity and discipline, though Rawdon's commanding officer, Colonel Atkins, rather let the side down when, upon the sudden discharge of a musket, he shat himself. It might be put more delicately, but it wasn't at the time:

> I sing the strange adventures and sad fate
> Which did befall a colonel of late,
> A portly squire, a warlike hardy wight,
> And pity 'tis you cannot call him knight,
> Stout man at custard, and a son of Mars,
> But oh the foul disaster of his arse

Before the worthies and the rest beside,
Who saw how he his courser did bestride,
Wielding his truncheon like a weaver's beam,
And yet beshit his hose in every seam.*[36]

There was little else to laugh about. Four days before the muster, Rawdon had bailed the Bishop of Hereford out of the Tower of London. He was one of the twelve 'protesting bishops' who had complained about crowd intimidation at the end of December. They had said that Parliament was no longer free. They had all been impeached. Before he became a bishop, George Coke had been a country parson in Bygrave, Hertfordshire. His wife was the aunt of Marmaduke Rawdon's wife, which is why the Rawdons called him 'uncle' and sent one of their sons to be educated in his household. He was seventy-one years old, 'a meek, grave and quiet man' with failing eyes, when Rawdon secured his release in May.[37]

The following month, the king issued his version of the Militia Ordinance: Commissions of Array, which instructed local magnates to raise and equip men in his name. Mayor Gurney had the commission proclaimed in London and was sent to the Tower. It was noted that Marmaduke Rawdon visited him there on Tuesday 12 July.[38] A week later, Rawdon was elected Master of the Clothworkers' Company.[39]

Preparations for war continued throughout the summer of 1642. 'Well-affected' Londoners were encouraged to give money, plate and horses. John Venn was an active proponent of the fund-raising campaign, and there was a big push from the pulpits. Women were most responsive, hugging their husbands into rebellion, according to sneering royalists, and donating their wedding rings, thimbles and bodkins,† 'insomuch that it was a common jeer of men disaffected to the cause, to call it the thimble-and-bodkin-army'. The response was impressive, but not enough, and in August a voluntary donation became an

---

* The Victorian cataloguer of the State Papers only printed the first four lines of these 'facetious verses'. Scat-happy seventeenth-century balladeers had no such qualms, and poor Atkins was never allowed to forget the incident.

† Bodkins were thick, blunt needles, sometimes silver, used for sewing, or as hairpins. They could be very ornate. The will of Rawdon's associate Sir John Jacob, for example, mentions 'one bodkin of small diamonds with an emerald in the middle thereof'. (TNA PROB 11/320/104.)

obligatory duty. The names of non-contributors were noted, 'so it may be more clearly discerned who stand well-affected and who not'.[40]

The livery companies were also required to contribute. On 2 August, Rawdon, as the new master of the Clothworkers, was summoned to explain why they had not paid their share. 'He had been but ten or twelve days Master,' he protested. 'It was his only business and care . . . some of it was carried in . . . daily they did endeavor the bringing in of it.' He took the opportunity to remind the House of an outstanding petition that the Clothworkers had submitted to the Commons. The company remained in arrears for the rest of the year.[41]

Rawdon's personal sympathies seemed to be all for the king, or perhaps more accurately, the king's men – Lord Mayor Gurney in the Tower, 'Uncle' Coke the protesting bishop, Edward Layfield his ejected vicar (soon to be dragged from the pulpit and forced to ride to prison with the Book of Common Prayer dangling from his neck), and even, it seems, Layfield's uncle, the impeached Archbishop of Canterbury. But Rawdon was still a senior officer in the trained bands, and as such, on 19 August, he took two hundred men and a cavalry troop over to Lambeth to requisition the archbishop's armoury for Parliament. They came 'about seven of the clock in the evening to my house', Laud wrote in his diary. 'They stayed there all night and searched every room and where any key was not ready, brake open doors. And the next morning, they carried my arms away.' Rawdon was following his orders, but – this was noteworthy to Laud – 'he was towards me and my house very civil in all things'.[42]

Three days later, the king ran up his standard at Nottingham and the country was officially at war with itself. Rawdon, like the vast majority of his compatriots, did not want to pick a side. He did not want to leave his life. He did not want to be buried under an obscure slab in an unknown church in a village miles from home. If he was wondering how it had come to this, he was not alone. 'It is strange,' said Bulstrode Whitelocke in the Commons, 'to note how we have insensibly slid into this beginning of a civil war by one unexpected accident after another, as waves of the sea, which have brought us thus far, and we scarce know how.'[43]

The royalist writer Mercurius Civicus harboured no such doubt. If, he wrote, posterity shall ask who broke down the bounds to those streams of blood that have stained this earth, if they ask who made Liberty captive, Truth criminal, Rapine just, Tyranny and Oppression lawful, who blanched Rebellion with the specious pretence of defence of Laws and Liberties . . . If they ask who would have pulled the crown from the King's head, taken the government off the hinges, dissolved Monarchy, enslaved the Laws and ruined their Country, say: 'Twas the proud, unthankful, schismatical, rebellious, bloody City of London.'[44]

4

Blessed Are the Peacemakers

Robert Devereux, 3rd Earl of Essex, left London on 9 September 1642 in a blaze of glory and a puff of smoke. This proud, popular noble-man, whose father had been loved in the City even as he had rebelled against Elizabeth I, was now the Lord General of the parliamentarian army. At Westminster, he saluted MPs with his hat in one hand and tobacco pipe in the other, then processed through the City with three hundred horsemen. In a macabre demonstration of his commitment, he was trailed by his own coffin, winding sheet and 'funeral scutcheons ready drawn'. The trained bands lined the streets, the pikemen on one side, the musketeers on the other, and cheering crowds waved him out of the City and on to the first terrible battle of the civil war.[1]

The fighting at Edgehill in Warwickshire began on the cold, sunny Sunday afternoon of 23 October 1642 and threatened to resume the fol-lowing day when the frosted survivors raised themselves from the turf and traipsed back to the lines in silent, stupid horror. 'There was a great deal of fear and misery about the field that night,' one trooper wrote to his mother. Sir Adrian Scrope was left for dead and stripped. He used a corpse as a blanket and survived. Most of the men were raw before the battle, unversed in 'the first dry rattle of new-drawn steel', as Rudyard Kipling later put it. They had fought with musket and pike, and cudgel and sword, and tooth and nail, 'and the execution was great on both sides'.[2] The king saw his footman shot in the face. He ordered that the princes, thirteen-year-old Charles and just-nine James, be moved further afield. The Earl of Essex had experienced combat on the Continent, but he was stunned by the cavalry charges that mowed down his wings. He dismounted and fought on the ground with pike in hand, towards his expectant coffin. Afterwards, he was incapable of writing the battle report. His mind and body shut down. The king's

herald arrived at dawn on the 24th and saw 'much trouble and disorder' in the faces of Essex and his officers. At three in the afternoon,
twenty-four hours after the battle's first beat, the parliamentary army
took themselves off the field. Edgehill disabused all who were there of
the notion that this would be a swift and honourable war. Both sides
claimed victory; neither won.

Parliament sued for peace and a great many people prayed for it, but
the prevailing winds were with the 'fiery spirits' in both camps. 'Blessed
are the peace-makers,' Matthew Griffith had preached at St Paul's
Cathedral on 2 October, 'blessed are the peace-takers, too; I mean such
as will readily embrace peace when it is fairly offered.' He asked his
listeners to look at the rest of the world in turmoil, 'whilst this, our
Britain (like the centre), stood unmoved'. But Britain *was* moving:
smiths in the forge, horses in the fields, masons patching up crumbling
walls, cobblers, cutlers, carpenters, sadlers, farriers, armorers, buff-
coat-makers and wheelwrights – all were getting ready.[3]

Mobilisation led to polarisation. Griffith was arrested the day after
Edgehill for his 'scandalous and seditious' sermon, and in truth, his
pacifism was not neutral. He prayed for peace, but blasted 'fanatic sectaries', 'head-strong, brain-sick' sectaries, 'herds, swarms, and shoals of
sectaries' and 'so many sons of Thunder whetting their tongues in pulpits, with cursed and bitter words'. He asked the congregation to pray
for both the king ('who keeps us from temporal and spiritual thral-
dom') and Parliament ('that the spirit of the Lord may rest upon
them . . . even the spirit of wisdom and understanding'). There was no
doubt whose side he was on. Slipped into the end of his sermon was a
little prayer that the good children of Mother Church be prodigal, 'not
only of our time and estates, but even of our dearest blood'.[4]

Around fifty of London's most eminent citizens were also arrested in
the week after Edgehill. Some were taken from their tables, some from
their beds. They were the old guard, 'rich men who are so cold in their
affections to the cause', as the news-sheet that printed their names put it.
'Garway, Whitmore, Cordell, Jacob . . .' Marmaduke Rawdon knew these
men, sat on committees with them, traded with them, borrowed money
from them. They had visited Lord Mayor Gurney in the Tower, as he had
done. They had not contributed to Parliament's war chest, as he had not.
'They do little regard the public good,' the news-sheet announced, 'or
their own private safety.'[5] Here was encouragement for the others.

Parliament's fear, and Charles's hope, of a royalist fifth column in the capital was not without substance. George Benyon's wife was one of several women who had visited the embattled Gurney in the Tower. She was caught the following month with a trunkful of gold for the king. A box of letters en route to Charles five months afterwards contained a pledge signed by 5,000 Londoners 'to maintain the Cavalier army with their lives and estates'.[6] The Venetian ambassador in London, a sympathetic voice for the king, claimed that royalists were 'ever more numerous' after Edgehill, with some being so bold as to wear rose-coloured hatbands as a sign of loyalty.[7]

The siege of London, which was the raison d'être of the Honourable Artillery Company, seemed imminent. The king's army was creeping up the Thames Valley, pressing ever harder on the capital. Londoners were ordered to cease trading and do their bit with pitchfork and spade. 'There is no street,' the Venetian ambassador observed on 7 November 1642, 'however little frequented, that is not barricaded with heavy chains.' Every post was guarded, and at every approach 'they are putting up trenches and small forts of earthwork at which a great number of people are at work, including the women and little children'.[8]

Suspected royalist 'maligants' were stopped, searched and disarmed. Houses and stables were turned over. Chests and trunks were broken up. So many arrests were made that the bishops' palaces were converted into prisons. Royalist propaganda was suppressed, but stories of the cruel intentions of the Cavaliers proliferated: they would rape women in the marketplace and force their 'cuckoldy husbands' to hold up their smocks; they would hang shopkeepers from their signposts; they would beat old ladies to dust and play tennis with their decapitated heads.[9] This is what Londoners were reading.

Charles made conciliatory noises, but his drums sounded louder. Repulsed at Windsor Castle, where Colonel John Venn was in command (unlike Rawdon, he had enlisted with the parliamentary army immediately), the royalists marched to Brentford, ten miles west of London. The cavalry was headed by the king's twenty-two-year-old nephew, Prince Rupert of the Rhine, or 'Prince Robber', as the Roundheads took to calling him. He destroyed two parliamentary regiments and sacked the town. His cannon prelude was 'easily heard' in London.[10]

The following morning, Sunday 13 November, the royalists

descended on Turnham Green in Chiswick, just seven miles from the capital. In their path was Essex's army, reinforced by the trained bands of London. 'Come my boys,' urged Sergeant Major General Skippon, riding between the companies, 'my brave boys, let us pray heartily and fight heartily. I will run the same fortunes and hazards with you. Remember the cause is for God and for the defence of yourselves, your wives and children. Come my honest brave boys, pray heartily and fight heartily and God will bless us.'[11]

Turnham Green might have been one of the great battles of English history. The numbers – 24,000 parliamentarians, 12,000 royalists – are not far behind those for Towton, Worcester and Marston Moor. The armies stood, 500 metres apart, for several hours. There were a few shots, some feints, some 'flurting out' by the royalists, but Essex and the Londoners could not be seduced. As they held their line and sang their psalms, one hundred cartloads of roast meat and 'pies piping hot' were brought to them: a hearty response to the morning sermons asking parishioners to give up their Sunday dinners. There were no meals on wheels for the royalists. Outnumbered, weather-beaten and exhausted, they withdrew to Oxford, Charles's headquarters for the rest of the war. His best chance to take London and be home by Christmas was gone.[12] But no one knew that then. The chains remained, the spadework continued, the watch was doubled, and royalist 'malignants' in the City had a very uncomfortable time.

Marmaduke Rawdon was playing a dangerous game. He had been getting his house in order since the summer. He had taken out large loans, including £500 in July from Sir John Cordell, who was on the richlist of October arrests. He put his plantation in Barbados, valued at £20,000, into a trust, and on 14 October, he conveyed Rawdon House in Hertfordshire to his eldest son for the use of his wife. His trustees were his ever-loyal son-in-law, Edmund Forster, and his old apprentice and business partner, Robert Swinarton. Their sympathies were with the king.[13] Two days later, Rawdon was probably at the Guildhall, taking part in a ceremony designed to reinforce the commitment of the forty captains of the trained bands. 'They all unanimously entered into a solemn resolution to live and die with the Parliament.'[14]

It seems hard to fathom that Rawdon was scoffing hot pies with the trained bands on the parliamentarian line at Turnham Green on 13

November, but it cannot be discounted, since he is listed as lieutenant colonel of the Red Regiment as late as 29 September. He had also been appointed, on 6 September, to an eight-man team tasked with surveying and improving London's defences. Not all the trained bands served at Turnham Green, however. Some stayed behind to guard the City, and according to the Venetian ambassador, a few captains resigned their positions in October. Others were 'put out' at a muster later in the year.[15] If Rawdon was one of them, it is surprising, given his profile and rank, that it was not noted.

Another scenario presents itself if the king's key adviser, Edward Hyde (later Earl of Clarendon), is to be believed. He maintained that he had heard 'many knowing men, and some who were then in the City regiments' say that if the king had charged at Turnham Green, he had 'so great a party in every regiment that they would have made no resistance'.[16] Rawdon could have been one of Clarendon's informants. They had ample opportunity to speak later. It might explain the absence of evidence about him at this stage. His usually reliable nephew, though in this case chronologically vague, wrote that he stayed in post 'till the City, or the most part, began to side with the Parliament, which proceedings he did withstand as much as he durst [dared], but seeing all was to no purpose, rather than obey the Parliament's orders, he laid down his commission and would act no more for them'. They tried to win him over, 'knowing his great abilities and how much he was beloved' by the citizens. They offered him 'what preferment he would be pleased to accept', but finding him 'of too honest principles to be corrupted to do any thing against his conscience or allegiance, they began to suspect him, and he them'.[17]

On 29 November, Parliament introduced a regular assessment on income that would form the basis for direct taxation for the next 140 years. Defaulters risked arrest. Collectors were authorised to break down doors and seize goods. Horses could be taken, too, which would have worried the hippomaniac Rawdon. The tax, which several MPs thought extreme and constitutionally dubious (since only an ordinance), was an assault on property and liberty more severe than anything the king had sanctioned. For some people, this was the last straw. Neutrality was impossible. Those who had tried it had found themselves, in Sir Thomas Roe's phrase, 'as corn between two millstones'.[18]

Christmas was usually 'all in for wines'. The grapes were cut and pressed in September. The delicate malmsey was shipped from Tenerife in November, and in any given year, Marmaduke Rawdon would be buzzing about the wharf in December, sampling his vintage and praying that it hadn't spoiled on the Atlantic wave.[19] Instead, he was drumming up support for peace. A hawkish petition, backed by Hugh Peter and other 'godly' citizens, had been delivered to the Commons on the first of the month calling for the continued prosecution of the war. Rawdon and his allies retaliated with their own petition, written by Archbishop Laud's godson, William Chillingworth. It urged Parliament to find 'a speedy remedy for our present and future evils' and beseeched the Lords and Commons to consider what a long civil war would do to the country: 'the unnatural effusion of blood: fathers against sons, brothers by brothers, friends by friends slain. Then famine and sickness, the followers of a continued war, making way for a general confusion and invasion by a foreign nation, while our treasure is exhausted, our trade lost and the kingdom dispeopled.'

The petition implored Parliament – somewhat awkwardly considering 'Prince Robber' had attacked Brentford during negotiations the previous month – to send the king terms that he might accept 'with honour and safety to the whole kingdom'. The words were not flecked with invective, as Matthew Griffith's sermon had been, but the onus was still on Parliament to be reasonable. Rawdon and his fellow petitioners were compelled, they said, 'after too long patience' and 'pressures hourly growing upon us', to express 'our unwillingness to be longer active in our own unhappiness'.[20]

On 7 December, the petition was confiscated by the new Lord Mayor, Isaac Penington, and the following day one of its promoters was arrested and taken to Haberdashers' Hall. Word soon spread, and by nightfall almost three hundred pro-peace Londoners were holding torches outside the hall, chanting: 'A Petition! A Petition!'[21] Told that it could not be submitted there, they moved down to Penington's house, but there were guards at his gate so they headed up to the Guildhall and had the petition read there. When the trained bands arrived with Captain Edmund Harvey's troop of horse, everyone went home. The petitioners were unarmed, but rowdy.

'The pox on all Roundheads!' shouted one.

'My Lord Mayor, my Lord Fart,' cried another.

'An unjust peace is better than a just war.'

'If this petition die, we die.'[22]

Four days later, they were back at the Guildhall. They needed their text endorsed by the City before it could be forwarded to Parliament. A delegation was invited upstairs to the council chamber to present the petition to the Lord Mayor, the Court of Aldermen and Common Council. The court insisted on amendments. The delegation refused. The court rejected the petition and called for an official City version to be submitted instead. Then there were shouts and bangs from the Great Hall below, followed by 'Murder! Murder!' They barred the chamber door. They heard hooves in the yard, a shot, screams, then cries for help, feet on the stairs, banging at the door. They stayed in the chamber. Carriages were now being wheeled into the yard, more men on the stairs, up the stairs, pressing at the door, begging for protection. The door gave in and the men were in the chamber.

There are two sides to the story of the 'great Hurllyburly' of 12 December 1642, an incident that has largely been forgotten. The parliamentarian version presents the petitioners as Cavaliers masquerading in the wings of a dove. Far from being 'blessed peacemakers', they were papists, atheists, lawyers, monopolists, Custom House men, publicans, actors, 'debauched villains' and 'the whole filth, trash and colluvies of this City'. Their 'saucy petition' was a device to garner support for the king and they were spoiling for a fight at the Guildhall that morning. They jostled some soldiers who were minding their own business and shoved them out of the Great Hall. When the soldiers returned, the petitioners 'closed in upon them', took away their swords and barricaded the doors. Then 'they most cruelly beat, cut and wounded the soldiers, 20 or 30 upon one, kicking them like dogs. After that they fell upon some citizens, calling them "roundhead rogues", beat them black and blue, and abused them in most shameful manner, multitudes on one, with their fists about his ears. The beaten, wounded men cried out "murder murder".'

Captain Harvey and his troopers arrived to appease the rabble. A warning shot was fired, but it was only when two artillery pieces were rolled up to the doors that the occupiers took fright and begged the Lord Mayor for protection. This was granted, but as they left, they muttered darkly about having their way 'by one means or another'.

'Let's go home,' they said, 'and Arm! Arm!'[23]

The petitioners' version was quite different. They came to the Guild-hall that morning 'unweaponed', at the request of the Lord Mayor. Their leaders went upstairs for the meeting and the rest of them waited in the Great Hall. About twenty soldiers suddenly appeared in the hall with their swords drawn, 'as if the petitioners had been destinated to be butchered'. The soldiers herded them into a corner, 'beating, hew-ing and grievously wounding' them, shouting: 'On! On! Strike now or never. Let us destroy these malignant dogs that would have peace, let us cut the throats of these papist rogues.'

The petitioners managed to overpower and disarm the soldiers and barricade the hall doors with tables and stools. Then Captain Harvey rode up with his troopers. One of them shot his gun through the key-hole and blasted a petitioner in the face. Another poleaxed a man who tried to sneak out of the yard, inflicting 'a fearful wound unto death (as is believed)'. The soldiers encircled the building and were ordered to pistol anyone trying to escape.

The stand-off lasted for several hours, until Harvey's troopers threat-ened to blow the hall doors off. The petitioners scrambled upstairs, forced open the chamber door and begged the Lord Mayor for protec-tion. This was granted, and they were allowed to leave the Guildhall, but as soon as they were outside, gangs were waiting for them 'with drawn swords, and bitter execrations'. Others piled in, kicking and beating the petitioners and yelling 'hang them, cut their throats'. Robert Osboldston, who worked at the tollbooth on London Bridge, was chased into the Mitre Tavern, up the stairs, out of the window and onto the roof. As his assailants closed in, he took a long run and jumped, 'leaping from one house top to another'.[24] This conjures an image of a seventeenth-century free-runner, gliding over London's rooftops, but the parliamentarian account is more prosaic and prob-ably more accurate: he was caught on the leads of the Mercers' Chapel, which was at the lower end of Cheapside, close to the Mitre; he can't have got far. Back at street level, other petitioners were taken into custody.

Two days later, on the morning of Wednesday 14 December, about three thousand peace petitioners went to Westminster to present their text to the House of Lords.[25] The Lords refused to receive such a crowd and asked them to return the next day with a small delegation. A small delegation duly appeared, only to be told to come back the following Monday. The following Monday, they were informed that their 'tumultuous petition' had been officially 'damned' by the City, 'both in regard of the matter and the manner of it'. To add insult to injury, those petitioners who had been arrested on the 12th were refused bail and detained for royalist plotting.[26]

The Lords referred the whole matter to a special committee, which was supposed to meet on 3 January 1643. Marmaduke Rawdon represented the petitioners along with an apothecary called William Rosewell, a mercer by the name of Thomas Langley and six others. The Lords did not turn up. The meeting was rescheduled for 5 January, but the Lords could not make the quorum. It was postponed 'until further appointment' and there was no further appointment.[27]

In the end, the only London petition that was accepted by Parliament and sent to Charles in Oxford was the alternative, official version resolved upon by the Lord Mayor and Common Council. It beseeched the king to return to Westminster 'accompanied with Your Royal, not Your Martial, attendance'.[28] Charles replied in equally bad faith, insisting that the City surrender four unpardonable traitors: Isaac Penington, John Fowke, Randall Mainwaring and John Venn. Marmaduke Rawdon knew them all. Penington, 'my Lord Mayor, my Lord Fart', had just arrested his friends and spiked his petition; Alderman Fowke was one of the 'spotted toads' who had denounced his vicar at All Hallows, Barking; Colonel Mainwaring had served under Rawdon in the Red Regiment and was now in command of the trained bands; and John Venn was Rawdon's old rival from the Artillery Company. Rawdon and Venn were so different, so opposed, and yet an exchange of letters the following year suggests a mutual, if grudging, respect. Venn would urge Rawdon to return, 'repenting what you have done'.[29] He knew, even as he could not understand, the conflict of loyalty that tormented Rawdon before he lost his city and chose his king.

On 13 January 1643, Charles's reply to the City petition was read out at the Guildhall. To ensure that there would be no repeat of the previous month's violence, one company of foot, two troops of horse and three pieces of ordnance were stationed in the yard. At least forty soldiers lined the Great Hall. London's liverymen were in attendance, along with a joint committee of Lords and Commons. The king's message received little support, but Thomas Langley bravely shouted 'No Lord Mayor' and railed against the proceedings of the Parliament. 'That shuttle-head' John Pym, the champion of the Long Parliament, was there with his perfectly pointy beard. He gave a thumping speech in support of Venn and the others. When he had finished, the citizens waved their hats and roared: 'We will live and die with them! We will live and die with them!'[30]

Meanwhile, the ghosts of Edgehill were floating back to the field. The shepherds saw them first: strange apparitions fighting a 'game of death' in the sky. The shepherds were frozen to the spot, terrified of being sensed and 'made a prey to these infernal soldiers'. Few believed their story in the village. They must have been mad or drunk, they said, but as the villagers lay in their beds, they too heard horses' hooves, the thunder of cannon and 'the hideous groans of dying men'. Some were crying out for revenge, others for death 'to ease them of their pain'. The next night, trumpets and drums sounded the alarm 'and all the spirit horse and foot appeared and stood in battleray'. They clashed all night in the troubled sky and disappeared, at daybreak, 'in the twinkling of an eye'.[31]

Charles took the reports seriously and sent a team to investigate. They saw the phantoms for themselves and recognised some of their faces. One was the king's standard-bearer, who had been cut down at Edgehill with the flag in his hand. What could it mean? That God was angry with his people was evident. But whose side was he on and what did he want – peace or more blood? Rawdon and his allies had tried peace, but they had failed. They had been besieged at the Guildhall and buried in bureaucracy in the Lords. Now the tax collectors were moving in on their property. If peace really was the answer, they would have to fight for it. So now it was war.

5

The Bell Tolls

They marched out every morning to the beat of the drum. They drew no pay, only food rations. They were 8,000 'lusty men' of the Merchant Taylors' Company. They were 7,000 tuggers of the Watermen's Company. They were 3,000 white-frocked porters, pushing wheelbarrows to Tyburn Fields. They were the Feltmakers and the Fishmongers and the Coopers, filing 'three several ways to three sundry fields'. And they were the women, even on Sundays, 'two and two carrying baskets' with their daughters in tow. One witness saw a thousand oyster-wives striding out of Billingsgate, 'all alone, with drums and flying colours . . . their goddess Bellona leading them in a martial way'.[1] They hacked and packed the turf for long days until, by the late spring of 1643, a chain of forts, ramparts and trenches bounded the suburbs. These were the 'Lines of Communication'. They stretched for eleven miles around Westminster, Shoreditch, Wapping and Southwark, forming one of the largest urban defence schemes in Europe. There were checkpoints along the main routes and armed patrols on the Thames. It is a wonder that anyone made it out, but thankfully for our story, they did.

Robert Amery had transferred from the Musicians' Company to the Vintners in 1630. He was a long-standing member of the Honourable Artillery Company, having joined seven years after Marmaduke Rawdon. He was almost 'torn in pieces by the rude multitude' for backing the king's attempt to arrest the Five Members in January 1642, and he feared for his life again in December as 'chief agent' in taking the peace petition to the Guildhall. 'Forced to hide himself for refusing to take up arms for the Parliament', he left his wife Mary and two boys 'in distress' at home and escaped to Oxford.[2]

For the past seven years, Isaac Rowlett had been renting a house and yard by Holborn Conduit at the junction of Snow Hill and Cow Lane in the parish of St Sepulchre. It was next to the gateway of The George Inn, a cacophonous place where honking, bleating, lowing beasts were driven up the hill to Smithfield Market and equally wretched creatures bypassed them on hurdles down to Tyburn. Rowlett spent over eighty pounds doing up his house, where he lived with his sister Katherine. They had been raised with eight other siblings in a noisy parsonage in Uppingham, Rutland. Rowlett trained with Amery and Rawdon in the Honourable Artillery Company and worked as a scrivener: a scribe who drew up legal documents. He spent his days getting other people's lives in order – conveyancing their land, settling their debts and taking down their wills. He did not think to write his own before he left Katherine at home, at Christmas.[3]

Three doors down from the Rowletts, at the print shop next to the Sun Tavern, lived their younger brother Thomas. He was two-thirds of the way through his apprenticeship with Robert Peake the art dealer.[4] Like his father and grandfather before him, Peake was a venerable member of the Goldsmiths' Company, one of 'the Great Twelve' livery companies of London. His grandfather, Sir Robert Peake ('Peake the Elder'), had been a famous court artist and had given St Sepulchre's church its gilded communion table.[5] As Serjeant-Painter to James I, he had captured the hope and glory of Henry, Prince of Wales, before the boy's death in 1612 left the underwhelming Charles as heir. Peake had also painted their sister, Elizabeth Stuart, in the spring of her life – all coral lips and candyfloss hair – before her marriage to Frederick of the Palatinate, and their acceptance of the crown of Bohemia, had splintered Europe and rendered them 'the Winter King and Queen'.

Robert Peake did not inherit his grandfather's talent, but he had an eye for good art and he knew what sold. Displayed in his shop in the early 1640s were images of English monarchs, European warriors and the stars of the Stuart court. Ordinary men and women, who had little hope of visiting the royal palaces, could gaze upon Peake's prints and put faces to names. Those looking for culture could stroke their chins at architectural plans and ornamental frieze designs. Others, seeking style or merely titillation, could admire Wenceslaus Hollar's feathery etchings of fashionable women. There were maps of the world and screaming broadsheets like *Rome's Monster on his Monstrous Beast*, which depicted the Pope riding the seven-headed beast of Revelation.[6]

Inside the shop, beyond the gallery and catering to an exclusive clientele, were the illustrated Bibles. They contained religious images copied and re-engraved from a Jesuit devotional book. They were popular with the crypto-Catholics at court. To Puritans, they were perfect idolatry, an open-and-shut case of graven-image worship: 'horrible impiety stares through them', wrote one. Archbishop Laud quietly licensed them. He called them 'the Bishop of Canterbury's Bibles', but advised Peake to keep them under the counter.[7]

One of Peake's neighbours was Hugh Peter, the Puritan preacher who had caused such a stir in the parish in the 1620s. He had returned from Salem, Massachusetts, in September 1641 and gone on to Ireland to serve as chaplain to the forces sent against the Catholic insurgents. He was back in London the following September, reigniting congregations with his frenetic Puritan zeal. Royalists loathed the crass, rattish, grossly popular Peter and he enjoyed offending them. 'An Irish rebel and an English Cavalier', he pronounced, is 'as unlike as an egg is to an egg'.[8] In one previously unrecorded sermon, he told Londoners that the 'cursed and damned Cavaliers' were on their way to 'suck your blood, rape your handsome wives and deflower your sweet virgins'. The men with 'ugly wives and daughters', he gibed, 'shall escape better'.

While moderates in both camps pleaded for peace, Peter insisted on war:

> The Lord's battle is begun in your land, fight courageously, go on victoriously, lend more moneys, send your servants and comfort one another with these words: Puritan, Rebel, Roundhead, for at the general day when ye shall be called by these names, be sure to make answer and ye shall be sure to go to heaven.[9]

As Hugh Peter galvanised the neighbourhood, the view from Robert Peake's window was bleak. He could see soldiers converging on the muster point at Holborn Conduit. These were not hardened warriors, but local members of the Orange trained band. They were drawn from the same streets as him, and wheezed up the same hill to church. It's quite likely that Peake, an Artillery Company man, had mustered with them himself in the past. Their captain, Nathaniel Camfield, was the draper who lived at the King's Head on Snow Hill: 'a fellow that looks as if he had changed his face with his place', jeered one unkind source. And there was Miles Pettitt, who lived four doors up from Peake and seemed to enjoy the feasting side of the Artillery Company more than the training. The sight of him, remarked the same hostile source, 'makes me remember my Aunt Basset swill tub'.[10]

Whatever *campanilismo* these men might have shared, and however discreet Peake might have been with his popish Bibles, the parish was too hot for him now. The vicar of St Sepulchre's was a reformer, and while there were plenty of traditionalists still in the neighourhood, Peake knew that they would come for him when it came to it, for he had not paid Parliament's levy. He had squirrelled away much of his estate by the time tubby Pettitt and the other assessors of the Committee for the Advance of Money stopped at his door in February 1643. They submitted their report on the 17th. Peake was to pay 5 per cent of his estate: 20 pounds. He had paid: 0. He was allowed on loans: 0. He was abated: 0. He was 'with the king'.[11]

Peake had two apprentices living with him at the time: Thomas Rowlett, the scrivener's brother, and William Faithorne, who was twenty-one. He had been with the Peakes since the age of fourteen and had lost his father, a Whitehapel loriner (a maker of horse bits), when he was a small child. He had a gift for capturing the features of a face: in paint, lead, crayon and especially with his burin on a copper plate. The Peakes recognised and nurtured his talent, selling his engravings during his apprenticeship and employing the hard-drinking John Payne as his tutor.[12] Payne had engraved the frontispiece of Thomas Johnson's *Herball*, and it is not difficult to imagine the apothecary, a keen draughtsman, bounding down Snow Hill to check out the latest prints in the shop that was known to have 'the most choice' in town.[13]

It was rare for contemporaries, especially apprentices, to give precise reasons for their allegiance in the civil war. Most, if they said anything at all, spoke in woolly terms of 'religion', 'liberty', 'loyalty', 'law'. It is no surprise, though, that Robert Peake, with his family tradition of service to the crown, a brother in the Church, and his own discreet work for Archbishop Laud, chose the king. Nor that the Rowlett brothers, sons of a parson, might have had the Church of England in their bones. Thomas Johnson, on the other hand, left no clues beyond a few courtly contacts and a single expression of 'delight' at 'the wonderful artistry and taste of the stained glass windows' in Canterbury Cathedral. This would have been an unlikely comment for a Puritan to make, so perhaps Johnson veered towards the beauty-of-holiness end of the religious spectrum. Perhaps. But royalism was a complicated, fidgety beast that tended to defy explanatory moulds. Then there were the dependants – the servants, siblings, wives, children and elders – who had little say in the matter, or who might have had a great deal to say, but we strain now to hear them. We see through a glass darkly, but with William Faithorne, whose languid eyes gaze out of his self-portrait, it is face to face. 'When the service of the king challenged the duty of his subjects,' he reminded Peake years later, 'you then prompted me unto loyalty.'[14] Whatever doubts he might have harboured about the king, in the end William Faithorne followed his master.

Peake, Faithorne and the Rowlett brothers would have travelled together.[15] Thomas Johnson, who was last noted in Apothecaries' Hall in December,[16] might have joined them, along with his colleague, William Rosewell, who had been an apprentice at the same time as Johnson and lived nearby at the Old Bailey. Rosewell was very well connected. His father-in-law had been an auditor of the Royal Exchequer for over forty years, handling the accounts of the unpopular renovation of St Paul's Cathedral, while Rosewell himself had attended to Archbishop Laud's great ally and patron, Richard Neile, the hardline Archbishop of York, who had died just before the opening of the Long Parliament. The king had even recommended Rosewell's skill and 'sober conversation' to the governors of St Thomas' Hospital. Rosewell was part of the nine-man peace delegation at the Lords with Rawdon and Langley. The following month, on 17 February 1643, he was assessed by the Committee for the Advance of Money. Sums unpaid: 30 pounds. Sums abated: 0. 'Gone.'[17]

They slipped out just in time. The defences were still going up, so the City was seamy, but it would not have been easy. Soldiers patrolled Holborn Conduit day and night and without prejudice, as the earls of Carlisle and Suffolk had found to their fury when they were detained at one in the morning after riding down from Smithfield.[18] It would have helped the fugitives that The George was a place of 'considerable trade'. Wednesdays, Thursdays or Fridays would have been best, when the carriers of Buckingham, Brackley and Banbury all stayed at the inn. Robert Peake owned the middle yard with its warehouses and stables, and there was a passage into the inn from Cow Lane, where Isaac Rowlett lived.[19] It had been another bitter winter, so they would have packed their warmest clothes and provisions for the journey. Johnson might have taken his books and apothecary's travelling chest, Faithorne his engraving tools. Peake somehow managed to smuggle out a box of jewels and £500 worth of gold and silver plate.[20]

If they took the obvious route along the Oxford road, they would have set off on the highway of the condemned – down Snow Hill ridge, over Holborn Bridge, up Holborn Hill where the road widened, through Holborn Bars where more soldiers mustered, and out into the countryside past Crabtree Fort and Tyburn Tree.*

Marmaduke Rawdon's last recorded appearance at Clothworkers' Hall was on 18 January 1643. He had been assessed at £300 for the parliamentary levy. 'To secure himself from being seized,' writes his nephew, 'he went from London to Hoddesdon where he had a fair house.'[21] He probably took the old north road from Islington to Hertfordshire. The Lines of Communication would have posed no great obstacle, since Rawdon had been on the September committee advising on the first phase of works. He knew which passages out of the City had gates and chains and which had not yet been 'stopped up'. He knew how to avoid the watch-houses and the forts at Hoxton, Holloway Road and Newington Green.[22] He would have ridden roughly along the path of today's A10: Islington – Edmonton – Enfield – Waltham Cross – Cheshunt – Broxbourne – Hoddesdon.[23]

The Hertfordshire militia had come out for Parliament. Local royalists like the Fanshawes of Ware and the Harrisons of Balls Park were being targeted. Sir John Harrison, a prominent customs farmer, had been arrested in London, but 'under pretence to fetch some writings' had managed to escape to Oxford. His seventeen-year-old daughter

---

* It shows how far the City has shifted west over the centuries to consider that Oxford Street, once countryside, is now in central London. The site of Tyburn Tree gallows is at Marble Arch.

Ann recalled her hustled flight from Hertfordshire to join her father at the king's new court. She and her little sister Margaret took only what a man or two could stuff into their cloak bags: 'We that had, till that hour, lived in great plenty and great order, found ourselves like fishes out of the water.'[24]

Rawdon spent a few days with Elizabeth and the children. It was agreed that their eldest daughter, also Elizabeth, and her husband, Edmund Forster, would stay behind to manage the business. A substantial portion of the family silver seems to have been deposited with Elizabeth's stepmother Martha, the beloved matriarch who loved the Rawdons 'as if they were my own'. Indeed, by 'bonds, specialties and otherwise', she lent Rawdon over £4,000. The best furniture and paintings were shipped out to the plantation in Barbados. Rawdon's second son and nephew were to stay in the Canary Islands to oversee the factory. His eldest son Thomas, who was newly married, would lie low at Rawdon House. This, Rawdon's nephew explained, was 'according to the policy of the great and wise men of those times, thinking to have two strings to their bow, that if the king should chance to have the worst, their eldest son remaining in the Parliament's quarters without acting might preserve their estate'.[25]

And so it was decided. And so it was time. Marmaduke and Elizabeth were no longer young. In another world they might have been happily retired, surrounded by the grandchildren, playing backgammon and bowls and preparing, in March 1643, for Marmaduke's sixtieth birthday.[26]

Rawdon left Hoddesdon on 9 March with an entourage that included his chaplain and French caterer. The sixty-mile ride over the Chiltern Hills would have taken about three days. At Oxford, he presented himself to the king, 'who knew him well and was very glad to see him'. According to Rawdon's nephew, Charles was hopeful that Rawdon, 'a popular man', would bring in more Londoners, and 'indeed many honest citizens did come and serve under him'.[27] What the nephew neglects to mention here is that on 16 March, about four days after Rawdon's arrival, Charles drew up a secret commission authorising seventeen prominent Londoners to organise an armed rising in the capital. Rawdon was sixth on the list. His son-in-law, Edmund Forster – who, like Rawdon, had been a lieutenant colonel in the trained bands – was sixteenth. His fellow peace delegate, Robert Abbot, was also named. Sir Nicholas Crisp, another peace petitioner and Rawdon's friend from the Honourable Artillery Company, was first on the list. He had been rumbled in January 'for secret service done for His Majesty' and had managed to escape the City disguised as 'a butter-woman'.[28]

The plan, reading between the lines of subsequent parliamentary outrage and royalist back-pedalling, was for this seventeen-man 'council of war' to arrange for a covert force to be ready to rise in the City when the time was right. A poll would be taken to find out who in London was for the king ('right men'), who for Parliament ('averse men') and who wanted to remain neutral ('moderate men'). At the appointed hour, 3,000 troops would be deployed to within fifteen miles of London, ready, upon notice, to advance.

No such force materialised in the Thames Valley when the plot was reportedly activated in May, and by the end of the month it was all over. John Pym, having sat on the intelligence for a few days, exposed the 'treacherous and horrid design' with impeccable timing on the fast day of 31 May. It was framed as a plot 'raised out of the ashes of the late petition of London for peace'. The king's commission had been discovered in a cellar, having been smuggled into London in the hair of Lady d'Aubigny (seventeenth-century up-dos were elaborate enough for this not to be implausible). The owner of the cellar was Nathaniel Tompkins, a servant of the queen and the brother-in-law of Edmund Waller, after whom the plot was subsequently named. Waller was a poet and moderate MP who had just been in Oxford as a parliamentary peace commissioner. He bought his life for £10,000, a 'free and ingenuous confession' and a list of his accomplices, which included several peers. 'I made not this business,' he protested, 'but found it. It was in other men's hands long before it was brought to me.'

Tompkins was hanged outside his house in Holborn on 5 July, and another plotter, Richard Chaloner, was strung up at the Old Exchange. Hugh Peter, who had a habit of cropping up at key moments, urged Chaloner at the gibbet to confess. Chaloner replied that Waller had persuaded him that 'if we could make a moderate party here in London to stand betwixt the gap, and in the gap, to unite the king and the Parliament, it would be a very acceptable work'. If he was telling the truth, it is possible that two movements – a peace party seeking to pressurise Parliament into a negotiated settlement and the more bullish, militant option proffered by Crisp and spurred by Rawdon's arrival in Oxford – dovetailed (or, according to Clarendon, was 'kneaded') in May to produce 'Waller's Plot'. The whole affair was murky, both to royalists, who appeared mendacious, and to parliamentarians, whose divisions were exposed. In the short term, however, it enabled the hawks in Parliament to discredit the peace movement and crack on with arrests, levies, distraints and, on 9 June, a loyalty oath for 'all who are true-hearted and lovers of their country'.[29]

If the purpose of Waller's Plot was to end the war and unite the realm, it had the opposite effect. The next time there was a push for peace in the capital, it was fronted by women with children in their arms. Most men, apart from a few disguised as women, were too scared of the mark of malignancy to appear.*[30]

In Oxford, meanwhile, Rawdon was forming an infantry regiment. He received a commission on 21 March to raise 1,100 volunteers in the king's service.[31] He already had his senior officers – Robert Peake and Robert Amery of the Artillery Company; Thomas Langley and William Rosewell from the peace delegation; and Thomas Johnson, the apothecary of Snow Hill, whose acquaintance he may have made via the apothecary Rosewell, or Johnson's near-neighbour Peake, or indeed, much earlier (both Rawdon's son-in-law and his accountant had witnessed the will of a great friend of Johnson in 1640).[32] There was a certain amount of crossover: Amery was also involved in the peace petition, Langley was also a member of the Clothworkers' Company.[33] These were men Rawdon knew and trusted.

The regiment had three officers of field rank – Colonel Rawdon, Lieutenant Colonel Peake and Sergeant Major Johnson, who was made

* The 'humble petition of many civilly disposed women' was backed, on 9 August, by around 5,000 women. It was well organised, with petitioners wearing white ribbons in their hats. Some carried their children and were peaceful. Others blocked the entrance to the Commons and allegedly threw stones and brickbats. The parliamentary press attempted to denigrate them as 'whores, bawds, oyster-women, kitchen-stuff women, beggar women and the very scum of the suburbs, besides a number of Irish women'. One apparent leader was described as 'a most deformed Medusa or Hecuba with an old rusty blade by her side'. The petitioners were dispersed by the trained bands. According to the Venetian ambassador, ten were killed and over one hundred injured. 'Swords in the hands of women do desperate things,' the *Parliament Scout* informed its readers, 'this is begotten in the distractions of Civil War.'

an honorary doctor of physic on 9 May. This would have pleased him as much as it would have infuriated the predominantly parliamentarian College of Physicians.[34] Rawdon raised the regiment 'at his own charge', though at least two of his captains, Langley and Amery, assumed the cost of equipping their own companies.[35] Another captain, William Rosewell, received his commission on 16 July. The king authorised him to raise and train 'such as will willingly and voluntarily serve us for our pay and for the defence of our Royal Person, the two Houses of Parliament, the Protestant Religion, the Law of the Land, the Liberty and Prosperity of the Subject and Privileges of Parliament'. Rosewell was to follow orders 'from ourself, our General of Horse, our Lieutenant General, your Colonel or other your superior officers, according to occasion and the discipline of war'.[36] This seemed, at first, straightforward.

The rank and file were drawn from the local area, the Sheriff of Oxford being required to summon about three hundred 'unmarried, fit and willing' men to enlist under Rawdon. Their pay seems to have been three shillings a week, with an additional twelvepence in bread and cheese. Uniforms were cut out in the Schools of Music and Astronomy. The choice was red coats, breeches and caps, or blue. Rawdon of the red-coated Honourable Artillery Company and the Red Regiment of trained bands, as well as the proud bearer of a *fess gules* (red band) in his coat of arms, surely went for the former.[37]

More important than uniforms were the 'colours'. These were military banners that were carried high into combat by the ensign of each foot company and the cornet of each troop of horse. Ensign colours measured about six and a half feet square, while the mounted cornets necessarily carried smaller flags. They were commonly made of taffeta and usually displayed an emblem and a Latin motto. Colours identified and rallied units on the field and were a matter of pride and, if lost, terrible shame. Victorious armies would parade captured colours like trophies, while anyone caught abandoning his colours faced capital punishment. Roundheads tended to deploy more religious imagery; Cavaliers more satire. Five royalist colours explicitly derided the cuckoldry of Lord General Essex, whose wife's infidelities were notorious. Some colours were cruel, some playful, some self-righteous, some pornographic. One royalist banner depicted a soldier with a naked sword, erect penis and the words: 'Ready to use both'. Marmaduke Rawdon chose a stoat for one of his devices. This was a symbol of moral purity, since it was believed that stoats would give themselves up in the hunt before besmirching their ermine fur. The accompanying motto was *'Mallem mori quam foedari'* – 'I would rather die than be defiled'.[38]

Munitions came from the magazine at New College. Rawdon received the first batch – 25 pikes, 6 halberds, 10 barrels of gunpowder and 3 skeins of match – on 21 April. Six days later, Thomas Johnson, who was staying with a bookseller behind All Hallows Church (now Lincoln College Library), signed for 12 pikes and 12 bandoliers, followed by 83 pikes and 3 skeins of match on 19 May. A week later, Rawdon collected 60 brown bills and 40 musket rests.[39] A skein of match was a coil of cord dipped in saltpetre and used on a slow burn to light the priming powder in a musket pan. Timing was crucial, since muskets fired neither long nor straight, so the best chance of hitting a target was to shoot in rank, in range and on time. Muskets were about four feet long and weighed around twelve pounds, hence the need for forked rests.[40] Bandoliers were belts worn over the left shoulder and across the musketeer's breast. Hanging from them were around twelve wooden or pewter containers containing pre-measured charges of powder. Halberds were spiked staffs with hooked axeheads. Bills were similar and derived from agricultural billhooks. Pikes were trailed by about one-third of the infantry and were considered a prestige weapon. They were sixteen-foot ash poles with steel spearheads. When handled in close formation, they presented porcupines of defence against cavalry charges. At 'push of pike', opposing blocks would scrummage for ground on the field.

Colonel Rawdon, Lieutenant Colonel Peake and the other members of the Honourable Artillery Company had read the books, studied the figures and drilled countless times in Spitalfields and Moorfields. It remained to be seen if they could handle actual combat, or train three hundred raw recruits in four months, but they set to work in the groves and meadows of the old university. Rawdon's neighbour, Ann Harrison, leaning against a tree and watching another regiment march past, was almost hit by a gun salute: a spray of musket fire entered the tree trunk two inches from her head. To an adventurous 'hoyting girl' like Ann, there was a romantic thrill in all this. She would fall in love in wartime Oxford and marry the dashing Richard Fanshawe, but she would also bury her brother there, and her baby, and her old life. 'From as good a house as any gentleman of England had,' she wailed, 'we came to a baker's house in an obscure street' with 'a very bad bed in a garret' and 'one dish of meat *and that not the best ordered*'.[41]

Captain Amery, who came not from such privilege, would always remember the 'great charge' of staying in the garrison town. There were too many people in too few rooms, with not enough food or beer.[42] Even the king had to share his quad in Christ Church with a herd of cattle. The street cleaners were overwhelmed. Dunghills sprang up like molehills. The 'water poet' John Taylor had the impossible job of keeping the rivers clean. He found them clogged with

> Dead hogs, dogs, cats and well-flayed carrion horses,
> Their noisome corpses soiled the water courses:
> Both swines and stable dung, beasts guts and garbage,
> Street dirt, with gardeners' weeds and rotten herbage.
> And from those waters filthy putrefaction,
> Our meat and drink were made, which bred infection.[43]

The plague visited at the end of April, just as Rawdon was getting up his regiment. By 10 July, forty people a week were succumbing to disease. The following month, one of the queen's ladies died in the room next to her bedchamber. 'We had the perpetual discourse of losing and gaining towns and men,' recalled Ann Fanshawe, and 'at the windows the sad spectacle of war, sometimes plague, sometimes sicknesses of other kind by reason of so many people being packed together'.

News arrived uncertainly. 'I hope you will not be so severe to expect truth in every circumstance,' began one periodical, 'for all mercuries, having the planet Mercury predominant at their nativities, cannot but retain a twang of lying.'[44] One unlikely story, which turned out to be true, was the felling of Cheapside Cross in London. The iconic monument had been put up by Edward I in the 1290s to commemorate his queen. It was a London landmark: a place to meet, hear news and recruit the chimney sweeps who clustered there in the half-light. It was pulled down in May 1643 by order of the Committee for the Demolition of Monuments of Superstition and Idolatry. Very soon, even the display of plain crosses was outlawed. This marked a hard drift from

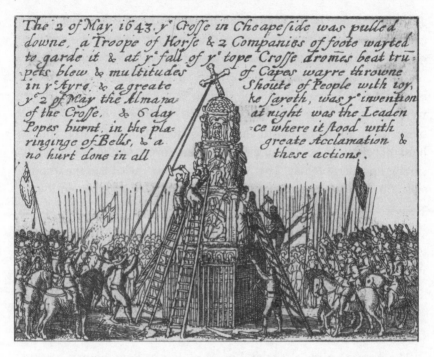

The destruction of Cheapside Cross, 2 May 1643: 'drums beat, trumpets blew and multitudes of caps were thrown in the air'.

anti-Laudian protest to Puritan iconoclasm, and heralded the defor-estation of London's steeple-crossed skyline.[45]

Both sides traded in atrocity stories. The royalist newsbook *Mercu-rius Rusticus*, first published in Oxford in May 1643, produced a weekly drip-feed of 'murders, robberies, plunderings and other outrages com-mitted by the rebels on His Majesty's faithful subjects'. The second issue brought the story of an Essex woman who had refused to hand over the possessions of her parson's children. She was clubbed 'with such violence that her brains came out at her nostrils'.[46] The fourth issue, published on 10 June, told the sorry tale of Sir Richard Mynshull, who had left his estate in Buckingham to join the king. His cellars were smashed up, his manuscripts were burned and the lead was stripped from his roof.

They tear down the walls of the house with spades and mattocks. They dig up the lower rooms, hoping there to find more treasure. They break the windows, doors, wainscot, ceilings, glass. They take away all iron bars, casements, locks, keys and hinges. They break open his wool-house and barns and empty all. They enter the dove-house and, like vermin, destroy the pigeons.

The parliamentarians put a guard on his wife and refused her a bed. They threatened his children, who hid for twenty hours in a hemp field. They vowed to catch up with Sir Richard himself and chop him up 'as small as herbs to the pot'.[47]

The news from home was grim enough without the pages of *Rusticus*. Isaac Rowlett's house in Holborn was raided and his sister Katherine, 'in no ways concerned in the delinquency of her brother', was evicted. Robert Amery's wife and children were also 'plundered and turned out'. All their money was taken and they were harried 'so violently' from place to place that 'they suffered exceedingly by abuses and want of maintenance'.[48] Marmaduke Rawdon's house in Water Lane was sequestered; the *Marmaduke*, along with its cargo of currants, aniseed, quicksilver and silk, was impounded; and his warehouses were emptied. His estate was 'torn in pieces', but at least some of it was offshore and a proportion of the Hertfordshire property was in trust for his son, Thomas, who was lying low there.[49] Or so Rawdon thought.

In the middle of June, Thomas pitched up in Oxford. 'He was too much the son of his father to be a looker-on and no actor when the royal game was up and a playing,' wrote his cousin with the jaunty detachment of a quarter-century's hindsight. This was all very well for young Thomas, but it would have dismayed his father, whose careful plans were upended. Marmaduke had no choice but to present his son to the king, who was apparently glad to see him, 'being a gallant, comely soldier-like gentleman'. He was appointed captain of a troop of horse in the regiment of Nicholas Crisp, Rawdon's ally in the plot to take back London.[50]

Rawdon had read of his own arrest at the end of April, 'which was strange news to us at Oxford', another royalist newsbook, *Mercurius Aulicus*, noted wryly. Thomas Johnson read about himself too, in the parliament-supporting *Wednesday's Mercury* on 28 July. 'The malignant apothecary,' it announced, 'a man formerly of great esteem and eminency in the City of London, shall be made President of the Physicians' Garden, a great place and of small profit considering the estimation which he hath lost in this city by professing himself so open an enemy to the liberty of his country.'[51] Johnson the apothecary-botanist would have loved that role, but it was not to be. Four days later, Sergeant Major Johnson collected 75 powder bags and 25 bandoliers from New College magazine.[52]

The good news for the royalists was that they were winning the war, or so it seemed in Oxford in the high summer of 1643. Since neither Edgehill nor Turnham Green had proved decisive, the conflict had turned into a series of regional contests. In the north, the Earl of New-castle won an emphatic victory over Ferdinando, Lord Fairfax, at the battle of Adwalton Moor on 30 June. This gave the king dominance of Yorkshire, but ultimately brought the Scots back into play. In the south-west the following month, Prince Rupert stormed the crucial port of Bristol, capping a successful campaign for the royalist Ralph Hopton against William 'the Conqueror' Waller (so called because of his early successes at Portsmouth, Farnham, Winchester, Arundel and Chiches-ter). Hopton had forced a furtive retreat from Waller at the battle of Lansdown near Bath on 5 July, but was temporarily blinded – and 'his horse singed like parched leather'[53] – when a carelessly lit tobacco pipe exploded a powder wagon. The royalist cavalry broke out of Waller's attempted siege of Devizes in Wiltshire a few days later, Hopton hav-ing parleyed for time and taken the town's bed-cords and bell-ropes to augment his dwindling match supply.

On 13 July, the royalist horse, which had been reinforced from Oxford, bettered Waller's out-of-condition cavalry at the battle of Roundway Down. They harried his close formations as nimbly, one captain noted, as English ships against the Spanish Armada. Sir Arthur Hesilrige's 'lobsters' – so called because they were shelled in three-quarter armour – 'were turned into crabs and crawled backwards'. Other runners and riders crashed down the steep slopes of Roundway Down into a broth of metal, bone, leather and flesh. The battle was rechristened 'Runaway Down', and William the Conqueror became 'William the Con – so fast did he run / That he left half his name behind him.'*[54]

---

* The author of this lampoon was Sir John Denham, who reportedly begged the king not to hang his parliamentarian rival George Wither, 'for that whilst George Wither lived, he should not be the worst poet in England'. (Aubrey, *Brief Lives*, ed. Kate Ben-nett, I, 351–2.)

Hopton and Waller were old friends. They had fought together on the Continent in the lifeguard of Charles's sister Elizabeth, and had helped her (and her infant son Prince Rupert) escape from Prague after her husband's defeat at the battle of White Mountain in 1620. According to one account, the snowfall had been so heavy, and the pursuing Cossacks so swift, that the pregnant Elizabeth had had to step out of her carriage and ride pillion behind Hopton. It was a totemic, bond-forging event for the two young soldiers. Now, over two decades later, they commanded opposing armies in the south of England.

The royalist Hopton had reached out to parliamentarian Waller at the beginning of the campaign, asking if they could meet. 'Sir,' Waller had replied, 'the experience I have had of your worth, and the happiness I have enjoyed in your friendship, are wounding considerations when I look upon this present distance between us.' His affections were 'unchangeable', he assured his old friend, 'but I must be true to the cause wherein I serve':

> That great God, which is the searcher of my heart, knows with what a sad sense I go upon this service and with what a perfect hatred I detest this war without an enemy, but I look upon it as *opus Domini* [the Lord's work], which is enough to silence all passion in me. The God of peace, in his good time, send us peace and, in the meantime, fit us to receive it. We are both upon the stage and must act those parts that are assigned us in this tragedy. Let us do it in a way of honour and without personal animosities.[55]

It has been called 'one of the most moving communications in the history of warfare'.[56] It is also an acknowledgement that when the god of war is in the ascendant, sentiment is secondary. The Iron Century required an iron resolution.

It was time for Marmaduke Rawdon's regiment to step out of the wings. Captain Thomas Langley left New College magazine on 27 July with one hundredweight of powder, shot and match. This was one pound per man for a hundred musketeers. Soldiers usually carried only half a pound, with the other half to come later in reserve, but there were to be no noisy wagons on this march.[57] The Marquess of Winchester had been in town, requesting urgent assistance at his seat in

Hampshire. It had been attacked in December with the marchioness and the children inside: 'some men were shot' and they 'nightly and daily keep a watch'.[58]

Another assault had been repulsed with just six muskets, but with the parliamentarians ensconced at Farnham, Winchester and Reading, a third attempt was imminent. 'If this house be anyways considerable for Your Majesty's service and advantage,' the marquess had implored Charles before Christmas, 'be pleased to take it into your consideration and protection, lest I be necessitated to leave it to the will of the enemy.'[59] The house's position near the main road between London and the west made it useful to the king. He turned to Colonel Rawdon, who sent Lieutenant Colonel Peake and Captain Langley down with an advance party of a hundred musketeers. 'Speed and secrecy' were vital, they were told. They left Oxford on a quick march at the end of July. Their destination was forty miles south of Oxford, near the market town of Basingstoke on the south bank of the River Loddon. It was said to be 'the greatest of any subject's house in England', as big as a palace, as big as the Tower.[60] Its name was Basing House.

PART TWO

THE AUTUMN ASSAULT

Our army being raised, the trumpet sounds;
The colours are displayed, the drums do beat:
To make a passage, through blood and wounds,
For Justice, Truth, and Peace, we forward set:
And, while we marched, my heart, with thoughts confused,
Was over-filled; and this I sadly mused.
Those dreadful tragedies, must I, O Lord!
Must I, not only now survive to see;
Which were so long time feared, and so abhorred?
But live, in them, as actor too, to be?

George Wither, *Campo-Musae* (1643)

6

Stone Fidelity

Colonel Richard Norton expected 'much spoil and little opposition' from Basing House. He knew that there was no garrison there, just some servants and a handful of muskets. It had been a simple task to break through the park paling, and now, on Monday 31 July 1643, his men were ready to attack. Alongside his regiment were Captain Cole's 'ragged rabble of dragoons' and Colonel Edmund Harvey's troopers, last seen menacing peace petitioners at the Guildhall. Suddenly, a crack of musket fire came from the house, followed by an avalanche of men who fell upon the besiegers with indecent fury.

Robert Peake and his musketeers had made it just in time. Hours earlier, they had quietly cleared the village and 'thrust' themselves into Basing House. The parliamentarians were taken completely by surprise: 'They were so bravely driven back by the foot that they ran all quite away.' Then the royalist cavalry arrived under the command of Colonel Henry Bard. He had been sent to assist Peake, but, according to the royalist newsbook *Mercurius Aulicus*, he needn't have bothered: 'Lieutenant Colonel Peake had cleared the town and gained the castle as soon almost as he appeared.'[1]

With the attackers beaten off and Bard returning to Oxford, Peake had time to familiarise himself with the house and grounds. It was not a short survey. Basing House was, in fact, two houses: a castle fronted by an imposing Tudor gatehouse, and next to it, the Marquess of Winchester's stately pleasure palace. It was 'seated and built as if for royalty', recorded an anonymous diarist inside the house.[2] The high towers of the gatehouse commanded a panoramic view of the market town of Basingstoke a couple of miles to the west, right across the Loddon valley with its meads and rivulets, and over to the village of

Basing and the church of St Mary, where Winchester's ancestors were interred.

In front of the gatehouse was the bailey, a curtain wall, a public lane and then the Grange, with about twenty farm buildings, a large barn and three brick-lined fishponds. Beyond was the river, high ground known as Cowdery's Down, and a chalk pit. This, Peake would have realised, was the obvious place for besiegers to mount artillery and shelter a camp.

Stone Age flints have been found just south of Basing House, and there are traces of Iron Age activity across the site. The marquess might have told Peake about the children of Basa, a legendary Saxon tribe after whom the house, village and town were named. War had scorched this earth before: at the battle of Basing in 871, the Vikings defeated King Aethelred of Wessex and his younger brother, the future Alfred the Great. Then came the Conqueror and the de Port family, who raised a timber ringwork castle sometime in the mid twelfth century. A licence to erect battlements was granted by Henry III in 1261 and another was issued by Henry VIII in 1531, permitting the then owner, Sir William Paulet, to rebuild 'the Old House' – as it was later known – and add a new one.

Walking through the gatehouse, Peake would have entered a courtyard that fanned out to buildings and courts ranging along the curves of the Old House. Still traceable today amidst the ruins are kitchens, bread ovens, a cellar, a communal lavatory and a drain that ran out under the citadel. The house's best defence was its thick brick rampart and a deep dry ditch measuring thirty-six feet from its base to the crest of the wall.

The south side of the house overlooked the deer park (now Basingstoke Common), and beyond it was the London to Exeter road. To the west of the Old House, close to the lane but protected by marshland, lay gardens and orchards. To the east stood the New House, a magnificent mellow red-brick complex set around two large courtyards, like an Oxbridge college. It was connected to the Old House by two bridges – one made of stone, one of wood – and reportedly surpassed it 'in beauty and stateliness'. The Winchesters' chambers were here, as well as stabling for the finer horses. A sixty-foot-deep well supplied the water, which was raised to a tank by animal power and piped around the house.

Although the current marquess's great-great grandfather, Sir William Paulet, had emparked three hundred acres of land and made the most of his licence 'to fortify the manor of Basing', he had put up these buildings for entertainment, not defence.[3] Henry VIII and Anne Boleyn had stayed in 1535 on a western progress that also took in Wolf Hall in Wiltshire. Fourteen-year-old Edward VI had followed in 1552, a year after Paulet's elevation to the marquessate of Winchester, and then Mary I in 1554, on her honeymoon with Philip of Spain. Elizabeth I, having confirmed Winchester as Lord Treasurer, was his guest several times at Basing House. 'By my troth,' she once exclaimed, 'if my Lord Treasurer were a young man, I could find in my heart to have him to my husband before any man in England.'[4] He had weathered the buffeting Tudor storms by making himself indispensible in government and by bending to the political and religious winds. When asked the secret to a long life, he declared:

> Late supping I forbear;
> Wine and women I forswear;
> My neck and feet I keep from cold;
> No marvel then though I be old.
> I am a willow, not an oak;
> I chide, but never hurt with stroke.[5]

He lived to be ninety-seven, having seen the reigns of six kings and two queens. Prominent on his hearse in 1572 was the motto: *'Aymes Loyalte'* – 'Love Loyalty'.[6]

Loyalty was rewarded – Winchester had scooped up the assets of fallen ministers, including Thomas More's house in Chelsea and Thomas Cromwell's at Austin Friars – but it was also expensive. Beyond the thrill of entertaining royalty, the costs of catering, cleaning and heating Basing House threatened to overwhelm Winchester's heirs. Elizabeth's final visit, in 1601, was hosted by the 4th marquess and lasted thirteen days. Six years later, the house was said to be 'overpowered by its own weight'.[7]

The 4th marquess was rumoured to be a 'fool'. The gossip was that on his marriage night to Lucy Cecil, he had not known 'at which end to begin'.[8] He also had to fight a long-running inheritance dispute with his father's mistress and children – 'Mrs Lambert and the bastards'.[9] He pulled down a wing of the house and moved to a hunting lodge two miles away. In 1635, six years after his son John – the 5th marquess – inherited Basing, the New House was apparently 'forsaken', but the Old was still quite grand.[10] When Basing shuddered to war the following decade, its rooms were 'all completely furnished', the chapel was full of elaborate vestments and the marquess's best bed was worth £1,300. 'In truth,' remarked one hostile observer, 'the house stood in its full pride.'[11]

John Paulet, the 5th marquess, was forty-five in 1643, seven years older than Robert Peake. He was somewhat jowly, the art dealer might have noticed, and splendidly moustachioed. His eyes were lively and happily creased at the outer corners. He was not ambitious and would have preferred to have been a private man. He was interested in farming and French devotional literature. As a teenager, he had attended the riding school at Angers in the Loire Valley. His contributions in the House of Commons, and subsequently the Lords, were unremarkable, except for one intervention during a debate in 1621 when he exposed a corrupt commissioner for threatening to arrest any 'pretty wench' who resisted his advances.[12]

The marquess had a powerful sense of honour and a deep attachment to the family motto. When Charles had issued a last-minute call to arms for his Bishops' War against the Covenanter Scots in 1639, Winchester had responded 'with alacrity of heart and in the best equipage my fortunes will permit'. He was close to the king, close enough not only to play chess with him frequently in York in October 1640, but also to give him a proper game and to 'blurt' out, during one such game, 'See, Sir, how troublesome these bishops are.' Charles had said nothing, 'but looked very grum'.[13]

As a Catholic, Winchester was required to break up his large armoury in 1641. This had been ordered as early as 1626, when weapons for 2,000 men were moved from Basing House to the Bishop's Palace at Winchester. In 1630, they were transferred to Winchester Cathedral, but by the end of the year they were back at Basing, on the condition that the marquess sell them off. He had clearly not done so, since an inventory in January 1639 reveals that 'Basing Armoury' was stocked with 188 pikes, 250 firearms, 300 suits of German armour and 650 headpieces. It also housed weapons from an earlier, pre-powder age – longbows, javelins and 70 demilances ('not serviceable'). Basing's armoury, like the house and England itself, was half in the old world and half in the new.[14]

In November 1641, in the very different political climate of the Long Parliament, Winchester had bowed to the inevitable and sold off all but six muskets. An anonymous siege diary written by someone inside the house claimed that the marquess had wanted no part in the conflict, 'hoping integrity and privacy might have preserved his quiet', but a big house was a weapon in war. Parliamentarians complained that Basing House was hostile – giving shelter to royalist troops, its occupants seizing horses on the road and shooting from the windows – long before it was a garrison for the king.[15]

The marchioness, Honora, was Winchester's second wife; his first, Jane, had died after giving birth to a stillborn boy. The only surviving child of the first marriage was Winchester's heir, Charles, who plays no part in this story. Nor does Jane, except to note that she was an impossible act for Honora to follow. Hailed as 'an exact model of female perfection', she was mourned by a galaxy of poets that included Ben Jonson and a young Cambridge graduate called John Milton: 'This rich marble doth inter / The honoured wife of Winchester.' (The elegy improves, as did the poet.)[16] In his grief in 1631, the marquess commissioned a stunning posthumous portrait of Jane, but two years later he was married to Honora Burke, and it is with her that he now lies, in stone fidelity.

Like Philip Larkin's Arundels, 'time has transfigured them into untruth'. Honora was not exactly smitten with John. She had wanted to marry the Ulsterman Randal MacDonnell (later Marquess of Antrim), 'a tall, clean-limbed, handsome man with red hair', but he was the grandson of Tyrone the rebel and her parents had forbidden it. (Her mother intimated that there were other reasons for the rejection, 'fitter for discourse than letters'.) Honora told her half-brother, the 3rd Earl of Essex, that if a fit husband could be found for her, 'and one that I could affect, I would give way'. No fit husband was forthcoming, and at the end of 1629, Honora's other brother, Ulick, despaired that she was 'growing to years rather of declining than bettering'. She was nineteen. Then along came the widowed Marquess of Winchester (who was also Essex's wife's uncle), and in August 1633, with Honora's 'good liking' and a £10,000 dowry, they were betrothed.[17]

She was exquisitely beautiful, with delicate features and a face unscarred by the smallpox that had once caught her. She inherited her looks from her mother, Frances, the daughter of Francis Walsingham, Elizabeth I's spymaster. As a five-year-old in Paris in 1572, Frances had witnessed the Massacre of St Bartholomew's Day, one of the worst Catholic-on-Protestant atrocities of the period, and while still a teenager, she was married – and widowed – to the poet and Protestant champion Sir Philip Sidney. Soon afterwards she secretly wed the queen's erstwhile favourite, the playboy rebel Robert Devereux, 2nd Earl of Essex. She watched him burn his papers in Essex House at the end of his failed rebellion against Elizabeth in 1601. After Essex's execution, Frances found peace with her lover, Richard Burke, Earl of Clanricarde, Honora's father. He was from an 'Old English' family that had settled centuries earlier in the west of Ireland. He was president of Connacht and owned tracts of Galway, but he also held several English lordships, and Honora grew up in Kent with her older brother Ulick. It was a Catholic household, Frances's conversion to Rome being the cause of much mirth in recusant circles, where the name of Walsingham inspired fear and loathing.[18]

The 3rd Earl of Essex was nineteen years older than his half-sister and avuncular in his concern for her. Their mother kept him updated on her smallpox – 'her only trouble now is that she is so sore that she cannot put on her clothes' – and confided her fear that 'your poor sister Honora' was 'to be named to many matches and yet concluded of none'.[19]

Honora's claret-loving brother Ulick, later Marquess of Clanricarde, was also close to Essex, 'both in blood and friendship', and to their other half-sibling, Frances, who married William Seymour, Marquess of Hertford.[20] To read their letters after they had hunted and bowled and played 'cribitts' and 'baggamen' together is to inhale rarefied air. 'You have so infected us with the game of slamm that we have scarce forborne it a night since your departure,' Hertford told Essex on 25 April 1630. 'I must now only apply myself to bowls and such kind of exercises till I see you and then I doubt not but I shall find your hounds perfect in their work,' wrote Ulick to Essex on another occasion. In August 1633, an underwhelmed Honora sought her half-brother's blessing for her marriage to the Marquess of Winchester: 'I will not trouble you with rehearsing any particulars concerning it. Most think it a good match in respect that there is not now a better, all things considered.'[21]

A decade on and Honora had given birth to seven children, her parents were dead and her home, Basing House, was a garrison for the king. Ulick was in Ireland, having moved to Galway in September 1641, a month before the uprising. 'For some few days after my arrival here,' he wrote, 'I thought myself a most happy man, being retired to this most quiet corner of my own, when on a sudden I was surprised with the most fatal news of a most wicked and dangerous attempt upon Dublin Castle, a desperate rebellion in the north and a rumour of a general combination and conspiracy throughout the kingdom.' He upheld his father's dying wish for him to be loyal to king and crown,* and for the next few years he tried to broker a peace between the Irish Catholic confederates and the English Protestant royalists. It was a thankless task. He was, he complained from Dublin in February 1644, 'forgotten by my friends in England, suspected and discountenanced formally by the state here, hated and scorned by the natives for my opposition to their ways and nothing regarded for it by others'. Without a settled government, he warned, Ireland would be 'the stage of much more confusion and bloody actions than has been hitherto, even Irish against Irish and English against English, and all in a confused opposition to each other'.[22]

Ulick and Honora's half-brother-in-law Hertford, meanwhile, was with the king's court in Oxford. He had been one of the twelve peers who had petitioned Charles for a Parliament in 1640, hoping to reconcile him to the rule of law, but when civil war had broken out two years later, he had rallied to the royal standard. He would prove a useful ally to Honora.

And then there was Essex – 'dearest', 'loving', 'faithful', pipe-smoking, pockmarked Essex, who had aligned himself with the Earl of Warwick and other members of the so-called 'Junto cousinage' on his father's side of the family.[23] He was now commander-in-chief of the

---

* This despite Ulick being a bitter enemy of the king's Lord Deputy, Strafford, whom he accused of hounding his father to his death in 1635. Strafford denied any such thing – 'the calumny hath flown up and down in the air like a bird of paradise, yet resting nowhere'. (TNA SP 63/255/81.) Ulick colluded with Essex in getting rid of Strafford in 1641. Like many royalists, he did not back the king unreservedly.

parliamentarian army, though doubts were being raised in London about his commitment. He tried to safeguard his royalist siblings' estates and keep in touch through various back channels, but there was an inevitable drift. Ulick insisted that he could not correspond with someone, 'though near me in blood, that continues in so high an opposition to His Majesty'.[24]

'Thou wouldest think it strange,' one royalist wrote in his commonplace book, 'if I should tell thee there was a time in England when brothers killed brothers, cousins cousins, and friends their friends.'[25] Not all families could afford the luxury of choice, and very few brothers actually killed one another, but many once-beloveds in Charles's kingdoms found themselves, like Honora and Essex, on opposite sides in the violent referendum that was civil war. It was 'so strange a separation', wrote Ulick, and it led to a withdrawal of empathy and a hardening of hearts.[26]

The Marquess of Winchester's first act after the repulse of the Roundheads on 31 July 1643 was to poach Lieutenant Colonel Robert Peake's company from Marmaduke Rawdon's regiment. Peake, whose grandfather had painted Honora's mother and brother, and whose 'popish Bibles' made him at least sympatico to their faith, was evidently amenable to the transfer. When, in late August, Colonel Rawdon came down from Oxford with the rest of the regiment, he found himself challenged by Winchester, who had procured commissions for himself as governor of the garrison and colonel of a new regiment of foot and two troops of horse. Winchester drew off Peake 'without my knowledge', Rawdon complained, and fifty armed men 'without my consent'. When Rawdon questioned Peake about the men's maintenance money, he 'refused to give me any account'.[27] Around the same time, three small pieces of artillery with proportional powder, shot and match were delivered to Basing House from the king's magazine. Winchester signed the receipt.[28]

Basing House effectively had two leaders now: Catholic, aristocratic Winchester, the forty-five-year-old owner-governor, whose responsibilities extended to his wife, children, servants, tenants and the very bricks of his ancestral home; and the sixty-year-old military governor Rawdon: a self-made merchant and 'true son of the Church of

England', who had raised his regiment at his own charge and in the king's name and would take orders from none other.[29]

Peake's apprentices, William Faithorne and Thomas Rowlett, followed him into Winchester's regiment, but Thomas's older brother Isaac, the scrivener, remained with Rawdon, as did Captains Langley, Amery, Rosewell and Sergeant Major Johnson, who replaced Peake as Rawdon's lieutenant colonel. They were known as 'the London Regiment' and they had in Rawdon a colonel with thirty years' experience of drilling and mustering in the Honourable Artillery Company. Thirty-eight-year-old Robert Peake, by contrast, had been a member for just seven years.

The numbers for both regiments were low, not even close to the figure of 1,100 that Rawdon had initially been commissioned to raise. He brought 150 men over from Oxford to reinforce the 100 musketeers who had gone on ahead with Peake and Langley. Winchester would have been able to call on a few dozen more from his household and tenantry. By November, the garrison was 400 strong, the extra men coming in by impressment – forcible recruitment. Rawdon had a royal warrant to the sheriff of Hampshire ordering him to round up able-bodied men for the king's service, but again, Rawdon complained, Winchester behaved badly and diverted several of them, 'against my will', into his own regiment.[30]

Another immediate source of friction was the camp followers. These were the wives, children, old people and other dependants, who might help with cooking, cleaning, nursing, morale-boosting and so on but were a liability to a garrison on short rations. Some 'useless mouths', as they were known, followed armies by choice, seeking adventure and opportunity in war. Others couldn't bear the pain of separation from loved ones. Most simply had nowhere else to go. After Robert Amery left his wife and children in London, they were turned out of their house and hounded 'violently' from place to place. They lost all their money and 'suffered exceedingly by abuses'. They finally managed to get out of the city and ran for 'their lives and liberty' to Basing.[31] They needed food and shelter, as did all the others. Winchester complained that Rawdon had too many women attached to his regiment. Rawdon retorted that Winchester had 'at least three for one in his'.[32]

Basing House also attracted refugees from cramped, disease-ridden Oxford as well as local royalists threatened with sequestration and plunder. Just a week after the house had become a garrison, a parliamentarian spy sent word that 'there are 500 households gotten into Basing House where they are fortifying themselves'.[33] Winchester's seat gained a reputation as a Catholic haven, and this was self-fulfilling to some extent as more and more came in. One parliamentarian described the house as 'the only rendezvous for the Cavaliers and papists thereabout'. They were all 'in a manner papists, with their wives and children and great store of wealth and treasure, which they, together with the malignants of those parts, have brought thither for safety'.[34]

This writer had the grace to distinguish between 'papists' (Catholics) and 'malignants' (Cavaliers), but many Roundhead reporters deliberately conflated the two. Not only was it offensive to the Protestants in the house (and indeed the Catholics) to be labelled papist, but it also had practical repercussions, since it made them vulnerable to especially cruel treatment should they be captured or cut off from their comrades. On a day-to-day basis, it was wearying and made recruitment, collections, foraging, scouting and the many other tasks usually facilitated by local cooperation that much harder.

Within the house, the religious differences between the rival regiments soon threatened the integrity of the garrison. It could hardly be otherwise when the hand of God determined victory and soldiers fought as God's instruments. Sermons and prayers were key to a soldier's identity and preparation for battle, but the London Regiment, which had its own chapel and chaplain at Basing House, heard different sermons and said different prayers to the marquess's men. The 'True Church' in this period was often depicted emblematically as a castle. This castle had two churches.

The priority was to fortify the house and bring in men, money and supplies before the next, inevitable attack. The town of Winchester, which was about twenty miles south-west of Basing, was retaken by the royalists in October, but most of the rest of Hampshire, including Basingstoke, favoured Parliament. Raiding parties sallied out of Basing House to intercept convoys and plunder Roundhead homes. They returned with horses, cattle, wheat, barley, peas, cheese, corn, malt, fodder, linen, plate, weapons and anything else of use or value that was portable. George Long, who had the misfortune to live at Preston Candover, halfway between Basing and Winchester, returned from London to find his house 'almost utterly ruined and his land laid waste by means of the said garrisons'. Sir Thomas Jervoise of Herriard, whose estate was even closer to Basing, reckoned on thousands of pounds' worth of losses, including 350 acres of crops, 200 bales of hay, 'and wood and timber cut by order of the garrison'.[35]

The royalists also collected weekly contribution money demanded by the king for the war effort. Winchester issued a warrant in October, which was intercepted and read out in the House of Commons, prompting calls for his arrest for high treason. Soon afterwards, Parliament established a committee for Hampshire charged with raising men for a new army – the Southern Association of Hampshire, Surrey, Sussex and Kent – under the generalship of Sir William Waller.[36]

Local people found themselves squeezed by both sides, 'as between Scylla and Charybdis', lamented Edward Pitt of Stratfield Saye, just north of Basing. He had private royalist sympathies, possible Catholic leanings and a wife related to Colonel Ralph Hopton, but he tried to navigate 'that narrow path between His Majesty and Parliament'.[37] He did not offer to pay Parliament's 'voluntary' assessment, but nor, privately, did he back the king's levy 'for the payment of the soldiers that are quartered in and about Basing'. In an unsent letter to Winchester, he stressed 'the vastness of the charge and the disability of the country to bear so great a burden'. The king's levy 'doth more than double the weekly proportion laid by the Ordinance of Parliament', he wrote. He counselled moderation lest it 'may rather retard than advance his Majesty's service'.[38]

Pitt drafted his letter from prison in Windsor Castle. He had been arrested in January 1643 for the crime of 'not doing' – not volunteering for the parliamentary loan – and for being the father of a son who had gone over to the king in Oxford. His house was pillaged, his wife and children were 'affrighted' and his plate was melted down. The governor at Windsor was John Venn, Marmaduke Rawdon's nemesis from the Honourable Artillery Company and one of the key movers in the Puritan takeover of London. When Pitt requested permission to take exercise in the town, Venn informed him that 'there was but one way to purchase liberty'.[39]

Halfway through the year, Pitt's son Will died in Oxford. The boy had ordered his armour but succumbed to disease before he could try it out. 'Oh my dear and sweet heart,' Pitt wrote to his wife Rachel, 'sweet soul, he is with God.' He asked her to visit him at Windsor, 'that we may yield each other the best comfort we can and our sad condition will permit'. Rachel did visit, but then, and probably there, she caught the fever that killed her. Pitt never forgave Venn for withholding permission for him to visit her on her deathbed. His seemingly sensible strategy of being 'merely passive in this great difference' had reduced him, within one year, from a proud and respected landowner to a plundered, imprisoned, grieving father of 'eleven motherless children'.[40]

His sister-in-law, Abigail, who had nursed Rachel in her sickness, came to the rescue and took care of the children. She was married to Pitt's brother, a parliamentarian who had friends on the Hampshire committee. She updated Pitt on the children's progress and managed to sneak Rachel's last letter out to him. Finally, after ten months' imprisonment without charge, Edward Pitt was released. Days later, he too died.

Abigail's compassion showed that tragedy could heal family division, but she herself was made to feel the full hostility of the Marquess and Marchioness of Winchester. Before the war, the marquess had humbly apologised to her for his brother Charles's unmannerly behaviour in a fishing dispute. Now, in September 1643, when she challenged him about the seizure of her tenant's horses, he was not sorry. Indeed, he asked why his men had not also taken her corn. The marchioness pointed out that Abigail's husband supported Parliament and had been in the enemy's quarters for the past half-year. 'Truly,' wrote Abigail, 'I did receive such language from my lord and so much of his mind as I was bold to tell his lordship I should not have believed it could have come from him had I heard it from another. The Lord mend what is amiss and teach us all patience.'[41]

There was no time. The royalist summer was over. The advantage had been squandered by failed sieges in the north and south, giving Parliament space to breathe and regroup. The king raised the siege of

Gloucester upon the approach of Essex's main field army, and on 20 September 1643, there was another big battle, at Newbury, fifteen miles north-west of Basing. As at Edgehill, it proved to be lengthy – the fighting lasted from six in the morning till past midnight – costly and inconclusive. It pitted Marmduke Rawdon's old London regiment, the Red Regiment fighting for Parliament, against his eldest son, Thomas, in the royalist cavalry. Thomas's horse was slain under him, but he survived to tell the tale.[42] Rawdon's old commanding officer, 'that shitten fool Atkins', who had let himself down at the trained band muster the previous year, now held his nerve as his men were pounded at close range by the king's artillery. They stood 'like so many stakes against the shot', even as their fellows were blasted off the line, even when a whole file, six deep, was beheaded by a single ball. It was 'somewhat dreadful', a survivor wrote, 'when men's bowels and brains flew in our faces'.[43]

Newbury was a draw, like Edgehill, but this time it was the king who quit the field. Low on powder, he abandoned any design on London and withdrew to Oxford. It was a blow to royalist morale. Writing from the university town on 3 November, Rawdon's old friend Endymion Porter, of the King's Bedchamber, despaired of the 'many mistakes' recently made by Charles's fractious council. Royalist affairs, he wrote, were 'slubberd', and 'the rebels have ever since increased in power and insolency'.[44]

The previous day, Winchester wrote to Lord Percy of the Ordnance Office, chasing up an order for ten barrels of powder and a double proportion of match. He requested an additional hundred muskets and stressed the need for speed, 'this garrison standing not only in great want' of powder, 'but also daily expecting the enemy's approach'.[45]

The defenders of Basing House were now busying themselves on the walls. A decade earlier, on one of his herborising trips to Kent, Thomas Johnson had looked out from Canterbury Cathedral and noticed the inadequacy of the city's defences. 'Our people,' he wrote, 'like the Spartans of old, set more store upon arms than upon walls for protection.' In the little time they had, and 'according to the quantity of men now added', Basing House was fortified.[46] Trenches were dug and the clay subsoil banked against walls and gates. 'Half-moon' outworks were thrown up in front of the walls. Holes were cut into the masonry for muskets. Trees and hedges were chopped down to deprive the enemy of cover. The garrison's three 'drake' artillery pieces – two six-pounders and one that fired three-pound balls – were mounted and manned by expert gunners. Each piece was apportioned twenty-five iron roundshot and five case shot (tins filled with lead musket balls).[47]

All hands were required. It took a foot of packed earth to catch a musket ball and over twenty feet to stop a roundshot. If an earth-packed wall was half as high as it was deep, this meant there was a lot of ground to move – more than a thousand barrowloads for just twenty feet of artillery-proof banking.[48] It was a royalist article of war that 'no common soldier shall think himself too good or refuse to work upon any piece of fortification'.[49] It was also assumed, as in London, that women and children would take up barrow and spade.

The soldiers checked their equipment and cleaned their muskets, rodding the barrels and clearing the pans upon which the fine priming powder would be sprinkled and lit by the slow match. This would create a flash of flame that would fly through the touch-hole to ignite the charge inside the barrel behind the musket ball. Muskets were notoriously unreliable – hence the saying 'a flash in the pan' – and Rawdon had sent over a dozen back for repair while still in Oxford.[50] The 'postures of a musket' were also fiddly and time-consuming, but could be learned in steps and mastered with practice. 'No man is born a soldier,' William Barriffe assured his readers in the introduction to his popular drill manual *Military Discipline*. He dedicated it to Marmaduke Rawdon and the other Artillery Company captains, 'unto whom I was first beholding for the rules and rudiments of my military instruction'. The garrison at Basing House was in good hands:

> Open your pan.
> Clear your pan.
> Prime your pan.
> Shut your pan.
> Cast off your loose corns.
> Blow off your loose corns and bring about your musket
>   to the left side.
> Trail your rest and balance your musket in your left hand.
> Charge with powder.
> Draw forth your scouring stick.

Shorten your scouring stick.
Charge with bullet.
Put your scouring stick into your musket.
Ram home your charge.
Withdraw your scouring stick.
Shorten your scouring stick.
Return your scouring stick.
Bring forward your musket and rest.
Poise your musket and recover your rest.

'By practice is gained knowledge,' Barriffe continued in his opener, 'knowledge begets courage and confidence.'

Join your rest to the outside of your musket.
Draw forth your match.
Blow your coal.
Cock your match.
Fit your match.
Guard your pan.
Blow the ash from your coal.
Open your pan.
Present upon your rest.
Give fire, breast high.[51]

The snow began to fall on Saturday 4 November, in squalls that saturated powder and match. There would be no attack that day. Sunday was clearer. It was the fifth of November, a day of bonfires and bells back home and sermons celebrating the blessed deliverance of the king and Parliament from the Gunpowder Plot. At Basing House, the garrison waited that frosty night, and they prayed in their separate chapels.

The following morning, ten miles away in the fields outside the village of Chilton Candover, five thousand bodies started to shift on the ground. Major General William Waller's army had bivouacked under the stars. 'This was a very cold night,' Lieutenant Elias Archer of the Tower Hamlets Yellow Auxiliaries remembered, 'and very tedious to many of our men which never were accustomed to such lodging.'[52] The reveille sounded while it was still dark. The men shook the cold from their limbs. Archer's fellow musketeers pulled up their woollen stockings, slung on their bandoliers and secured their powder horns, match skeins, shot bags and rests. About an hour before daybreak, they shouldered their muskets and began to march.

They'd been heading in the direction of Winchester for Waller's much-anticipated showdown with his old comrade Ralph (now Baron) Hopton. But the previous evening, just beyond Alton, Waller, who was known as 'the night owl' for his evening manoeuvres, had called a halt and changed the order. His army had wheeled to the right, towards Basing House. 'If I could carry it', he wrote, it would be 'a great encouragement to the soldier'. It was, everyone told him, 'but a slight piece'.[53]

7

A Slight Piece

'Most dear and loving husband,' she began,

> my king love, remember unto you, hoping that you are [in] good
> health as I am at the writing hereof. My little Willie have been sick
> this fortnight. I pray you to come home if you can come safely. I
> do marvel that I cannot hear from you as well [as] other neigh-
> bours do. I do desire to hear from you as soon as you can. I pray
> you to send me word when you do think you shalt return. You do
> not consider I am a lone woman. I thought you would never have
> leave me thus long together. So I rest, ever praying for your safe
> return,
> Your loving wife,
> Susan Rodway,
> ever praying for you till death I depart.[1]

Robert Rodway belonged to the foot company of Captain George
Warren in the Westminster Liberty Trained Band. He was one of the
five thousand men who had spent Bonfire Night on the fields of Chilton Candover, and was now crunching through frozen snow towards
Basing House. It was Monday morning, 6 November 1643.

Marching alongside the Westminster band were two other London
regiments: the Tower Hamlets Yellow Auxiliaries and the City Green
Auxiliaries. They had been selected by lot just over a month earlier and
had mustered at the new artillery ground in Bunhill Fields. The Yellow
Auxiliaries had set off from Smithfield, just above Snow Hill, while
Rodway's Westminster men had rendezvoused at Holborn 'and down
towards Newgate'. Quite possibly they had been watched by the

friends and families of the apothecary, print-seller, engraver and scrivener now waiting in Basing House.

The Green Auxiliaries had briefly fought in Kent in July, but the rest
of the London brigade had no combat experience. They were young
men – many still apprentices – who had volunteered to man the City
defences. Once ordered to serve beyond the Lines of Communication,
some had paid 'hirelings' to take their place.[2] Others had deserted
along the way, but Rodway, a twenty-eight-year-old tallow chandler
from Bell Yard off Fleet Street, had followed the drum into Hampshire.
He left behind Susan, the now-sick Willie and a baby girl called
Hester.[3]

The garrison could hear them before they could see them. The fog was
thick and enveloped the house. A lone trumpeter emerged with a summons for the Marquess of Winchester. According to siege etiquette, if
he agreed to surrender now, he could lead his men out of the house,
fully armed and with flying colours, but to his own disgrace and a
probable court martial for cowardice. The summons was rejected. The
trumpeter receded into the mist.

At about 1 p.m., the sun finally punched through the fog and Waller's
army was revealed like a peacock in the park – sixteen troops of horse,
eight companies of dragoons and thirty-six foot companies, including
Colonel Samuel Jones's Greencoats from Farnham and a blue-coated
company carrying firelock muskets that guarded the ten-gun artillery
train.[4] The Tower Hamlets auxiliaries stood under their yellow colours, the City auxiliaries under their green, and Robert Rodway waited
under a red flag with silver stars. Above Major General Waller, who
was 'little in person', fluttered a taffeta flag depicting a walnut tree,
three gold fleurs-de-lis and the motto 'The fruit of virtue'.[5]

Waller detached a 'forlorn hope' – an advance party selected for
high-risk work – and sent it right up to the lane between the Grange
outbuildings and the north front of the Old House. This was 'fittest to
batter', he recalled, but 'I found that the enemy had fortified most
strongly on that side with diverse retrenchments one under the command of another.'[6] A firefight commenced, with the garrison defending
the lower wall until the forlorn hope ran out of ammunition. Waller's
dragoons took over and maintained pressure on the defenders till the
edge of the evening.

Meanwhile, the rest of his army marched round the house through Basingstoke and up onto Cowdery's Down, the hill beyond the river to the north-west. Here Waller planted his artillery, including two demi-cannon that hurled thirty-pound shot. The first great gun sounded at four in the afternoon and was followed by ten more mighty roars. Having bared his teeth, Waller signalled a parley and sent his trumpeter back with a fresh demand for Basing House to be rendered 'for the use of the king and Parliament'. He offered fair quarter to all within. As Winchester prepared his response, two of Waller's drakes were let off 'by reason of an unfortunate accident of scattering powder'. Winchester detained the trumpeter and sent a message demanding an explanation for this breach of etiquette. 'He understood very well the words *king and Parliament*,' he wrote, 'that, as they were now taken, the *king* was one thing, and the *"king and Parliament"* was another; that Basing was his own house which the law told him he might keep against any man; that it was now more particularly commanded by His Majesty (who had put a garrison into it) beyond which command he knew no obligation.'

After two hours, Waller returned Winchester's messenger with an apology for 'the rudeness of his disorderly guns during the parley' and an offer to the marchioness, 'being sister to his General the Earl of Essex, whom he entirely honours', to depart freely with her children and all the women. Honora turned it down. She thanked God that she was 'not yet in that condition to accept fair quarter at Sir William Waller's hands'. She was 'resolved', she said, 'to run the same fortune' as her husband, 'knowing that there was a just and all-seeing judge above, who she hoped would have an especial hand in this business' and from whom Waller 'could pretend no commission'. Whatever might befall her, she added, she was 'not unprovided to bear it'.

The formalities dispensed with, Waller's trumpeter was dismissed into the darkness through 'a little brook', which the Cavaliers assured him would be a small, safe leap for his horse. It turned out to be so mirey that the mount, 'although a very stout one', was stuck in the mud. The trumpeter had to abandon it and make his way back on foot. When he eventually returned to camp, Waller issued orders for an assault at daybreak.

The parliamentarian guns pounded Basing House for most of the night, rowelling the ears of all inside. Few would have heard anything like it before. The loudest sounds they knew were cathedral bells and thunderstorms. Contemporaries struggled to articulate 'the fury of the ordnance', grasping for comparisons with the weather and wild beasts, or both: 'the thundering cannons roaring'.[7]

The bombardment stopped at 4 a.m. and resumed at first light, the guns 'playing very fiercely upon the castle'. The garrison replied with one piece, 'which notwithstanding was so well bestowed that it extremely annoyed the rebels in their works'. The soldiers in Waller's camp saw fires dotted around the house that morning. The defenders had torched the surrounding cottages to deny the besiegers shelter.

Waller now sent a party down the hill towards the great barn and the twenty-odd outbuildings that made up the Grange. Located on the other side of the lane to the house, the Grange was extremely vulnerable to attack. Winchester should perhaps have razed it with the cottages, but it contained precious livestock and stores. The garrison shot at the attackers through the loopholes in the curtain wall, but the numbers were overwhelming. The Grange was taken and its contents seized: 'bread, beer, bacon, pork, milk, cream, peas, wheat, oats, hay and such like, besides pigs and poultry and diverse sorts of household goods, as brass, pewter, feather beds'. After their hard march into Hampshire and two long nights in the field, this abundance was too good for the Roundheads to resist. Some stuffed their faces, others their pockets, but the fighting never ceased, 'and when one party was weary, another party relieved them'.

With the Grange taken, it seemed only a matter of time before the house itself would be breached. The royalists had to come up with something fast. Lieutenant Colonels Robert Peake and Thomas Johnson decided to lead a sortie across the lane to set fire to the Grange. They targeted the corn stores, which immediately flared up, and soon the precinct was a maze of flames and falling timber. As the smoke filled their lungs, the Roundheads floundered out of the buildings into the yard. With barely time to draw breath, they were attacked by Thomas Johnson and just twenty-five Cavaliers, who 'courageously ventured' into the jellied heat. There was no time to load a musket. The men fought hand to hand for their lives. The apothecary grappled with Captain Clinson, an officer in Waller's own company and reportedly 'a man of great courage and resolution'. Johnson was overpowered and 'too far engaged'. His war would end here, it seemed, in a farmyard full of squealing pigs and howling men. Suddenly 'two or three stout fellows of the garrison' were at his side. They piled into his opponent and beat him to death.

Further along the lane, the Roundheads were continuing to put pressure on the north front of the house, 'the great guns all the while thundering'. Colonel Marmaduke Rawdon was everywhere, directing the defenders with 'exceeding diligence and courage' and bellowing that Waller would 'not stay it out'. This might have been the moment, later mentioned by his nephew, that Rawdon was nearly hit by a cannonball. One of his captains, James Freeman, tackled him out of the way, the shot 'just passing by where he stood'.

Back at the Grange, night fell and the flames rose. The parliamentarians had no choice but to retreat, 'leaving all their arms and many of their fellows behind them, some dead, others in the barn wounded, shortly to end their lives by fire'. For the third consecutive night, they bivouacked in the field. 'Our lodging and our service did not well agree,' wrote Lieutenant Elias Archer, 'the one being so hot and the other so cold.'

It was another 'foul' night, agreed his general, 'a great discouragement to the London regiments who were not used to this hardness'. Waller was nonetheless shocked when the officers asked to be drawn off. 'Many of the soldiers were hirelings,' he reported, 'and their money being spent, they began to think of their return.' Waller was a hard but fair taskmaster, as tough on mutineers as he was on looters.[8] Five days earlier, he had hanged an insubordinate from a tree in Farnham Park. But the London brigade comprised almost half his army. 'The weakness of my condition without them,' he wrote, 'enforced me to yield.' He dismounted the great guns and withdrew to Basingstoke.

I found four dead soldiers and three which were leaning against the wall, their faces wholly disfigured, and neither saw, nor heard, nor spoke, and their clothes did yet flame with the gunpowder which had burnt them. Beholding them with pity, there happened to come an old soldier who asked me if there were any possible means to cure them. I told him no. He presently approached them, and gently cut their throats without choler [anger]. Seeing this great cruelty, I told him he was a wicked man. He answered me that he prayed to God that whensoever he should be in such a case, he might find someone that would do as much to him, to the end he might not miserably languish.[9]

When Thomas Johnson published those words in 1634, they were not of his composition, nor even his experience. He was compiling a translation of the works of the war doctor Ambrose Paré, who had written about his campaigns with the French army in Piedmont the previous century. Paré was a pioneering surgeon whose techniques were invaluable to Johnson and his medical colleagues. He was best known for using ligature to arrest haemorrhage, rather than cauterisation with a red-hot iron, and he was concerned not only to cure his patients, but also to alleviate their suffering. In that stable in the Alpine foothills where he had found men smouldering, he had realised that it was sometimes more humane to withhold treatment.

We cannot know if Lieutenant Colonel Johnson was confronted by a similar scene or performed like mercies on any of the survivors of the Grange fire. All that is recorded is that both dead and wounded bodies were carried from the charred remains and returned the following morning by cart to Waller. The royalist newsbook *Mercurius Aulicus*, which always imputed the worst faith to its enemy, claimed that Waller was smarting so badly from his repulse that he imprisoned the carter and kept his horses. Basingstoke was reportedly 'so full of wounded men that one surgeon was fain to take four score under his cure'.

As with almost every civil war engagement, the casualty figures were disputed. 'In this act of the Grange alone,' Rawdon's nephew would write over twenty years later, 'they killed and burned about 300 of Waller's men and wounded and maimed above 500 more.' *Mercurius Aulicus* reported 150 dead and as many wounded. Waller himself claimed that he had lost 'twelve or thirteen men' in the Grange 'and as many more hurt'. The parliamentarian *Scottish Dove* heard that it was fifty – 'we hope not so many'. Lieutenant Elias Archer of the Tower Hamlets Yellow Auxiliaries was vague: 'diverse were wounded and some slain, as in such cases it cannot likely be avoided'. What was clear to all, and especially to a reflective Puritan like Waller, was that God had not favoured Parliament. Basing House was 'a difficult work', *The Scottish Dove* conceded, 'and cannot be gained without loss, but a sparrow falls not to the ground without God's providence'.[10]

Mercurius Aulicus was gleeful, noting the 'busy' Waller's rocketing confidence before the royalists had 'sent this Conqueror packing into Basingstoke'. The Marquess of Winchester, meanwhile, reported to the king's secretary Sir Edward Nicholas that he had suffered only one death and one injury. He still had four hundred men, and, despite the fire at the Grange, provisions for three weeks. He expected Waller to return and was hopeful of relief from Lord Hopton's gathering force. His powder was low, though. The ten barrels that he had been chasing from Oxford had been diverted upon sight of Waller's army.[11] On 10 November, Nicholas sent news of Basing's resistance to the Marquess of Ormond, the king's commander in Ireland. 'If His Majesty's forces shall (by God's blessing) defeat Waller's forces now, it will secure to His Majesty all the west.'[12]

The Conqueror did not lick his wounds for long. He occupied The Vyne, a grand mansion five miles north of Basing, in order to 'bridle' the garrison and cut off its supplies from the north. His governor in Farnham sent menacing letters to Winchester's tenants, demanding wheat, malt and barley upon pain of 'the same penalty . . . [with] which the Marquess of Winchester threatens you, there being more reason that you should serve a Protestant before a Papist'.[13] And he sent for scaling ladders, petards and granadoes – instruments for a storm. A petard was a bell-shaped bomb used for blowing open gates. It had to be clamped onto its target and the fuse lit by a nimble engineer, who then had to run for it or be hoist with his own petard.

Granadoes (from the Spanish for pomegranate) looked like super-sized grenades. They were metal shells filled with powder, plugged with a fuse and fired from squat, wide-bored mortars that belched them out slow and high. The mortar was manned by a specialist fireworker, who had to light both ends – the granado fuse in the mortar mouth followed by the propellant in its backside. The powder inside the shell could be mixed with nails, stones, pitch 'and other things combustible and violent'. Granadoes crashed through roofs and floors, bouncing and scudding before exploding. Sometimes they tore into the ground 'as if a bear had been rooting up the earth'. Because of their unpredictable trajectory, their pyrotechnic energy and their ability to surmount even Basing's heights, they were feared more than anything

Petard

Granado

else in the siege train. 'It is,' wrote an observer, 'of all hands acknowledged that no engine or instrument of war doth more mischief, nor
imprints a greater or a juster terror.'[14]

In Southampton on Thursday 9 November 1643, a fast was held for
the good success of Sir William Waller. At the House of Commons the
following day, an ordinance was proposed to protect manuscripts and
deeds 'taken by distress' from royalist properties. The day after that,
the parliamentarian newsbook *A Perfect Diurnall* was informed by its
sources of the 'great probability' that Basing House would fall. From
the garrison itself, a man stole out and headed for Waller's quarters.
He had been captured by the royalists at the battle of Roundway Down
in July and had presumably turned his coat for his freedom. Now he
changed sides again, telling his old general where the wall was weakest
and offering to lead him there. 'Upon an information I had received of
a place that might give me some advantage', Waller wrote, and 'the
army being sufficiently refreshed, I resolved to have another fling at
Basing'.[15]

8

Another Fling

'Sabbath day, November 12,' began Lieutenant Elias Archer in his journal. 'In the morning we were all drawn out against the house, on the other side of it, Sir William intending desperately to storm it and scale the walls.'[1]

'Our army had no shelter,' continued another parliamentarian in the park, 'not so much as any village hovel.' Apart from some thin young trees, it was open country – 'a champion place' – but they were 'nothing at all' daunted. This anonymous writer, whose *Souldiers Report* was published five days afterwards, reckoned that Waller had 8,000 men, 'some say, 6,000' with ten pieces of ordnance and scaling ladders, petards and granadoes. He'd heard that Basing House was full of 'papists', women, children and treasure.

The garrison saw them clearly this time, and they heard their psalms and endured their taunts:

'Where's your Hopton?'

'Prince Rupert hath but three men!'

The first cannonball hit them loud and low. Basing's clay banking swallowed it up, and, as if disgorging an alien invader, rattled a blast of case shot out of its drake on the roof. 'We played upon them and they upon us very hot,' wrote the anonymous parliamentarian, 'and about noon some of our men got to the wall.'

Waller had planned a two-pronged attack. His own regiment, Major Strachan's dragoons and Colonel Jones's Greencoats would fall on the New House from Basing village in the east. The London brigade would storm the Old House from the park in the south. Observing the deployment of the Londoners, Winchester and Rawdon sent some 'choice men' out from the south-west walls to disrupt them. As at the Grange, Lieutenant Colonel Johnson led the operation. He sallied out of the

Old House with a brave band of thirty musketeers and lured the besieg-ers up towards the garrison's half-moon outwork. As they drew close, he gave fire and retreated to a winding hedge. The besiegers' blood was now up and they pursued their quarry oblivious to the bigger beast lying in wait. As Johnson crouched behind the hedge ready to defend himself with his musket butt, his hunters ran into a wall of case shot. 'Three several times' he executed this move – 'most strange, but most true', observed the not always truthful *Aulicus*.

Waller ordered the rest of the London brigade to fall on to the Old House. Five hundred men charged with scaling ladders. But here was the second drake, hidden on the rampart and loaded with a tin of case shot. The garrison gunner 'spied his time', put his match to the touch hole and discharged his piece. The oncoming battle-cry curdled to a scream as the buff-coated Londoners were sprayed at close range. Some were slain, many were wounded, and the charge faltered. 'On or die!' cried their officers, but the gunner reloaded and blasted them again, and those that had not melted like wax into the ground, fled so swiftly 'that it was not in the power of their commanders to drive them on the third time'.

According to Elias Archer of the Yellow Auxiliaries, it was the West-minster Trained Band, the one containing Robert Rodway (father to a sick son, husband to an anxious wife), that bore 'the greatest share' of the slaughter. Whether the fault lay with their colonel, 'either through want of courage or discretion I know not', Archer wrote, but the men panicked. All training forgotten, all discipline lost, the first rank of musketeers fired too soon, 'and for want of intervals to turn away speedily, the second and third ranks fired upon them, and so, conse-quently, the rear fired upon their own front and slew and wounded many of their own men'. Seeing the soldiers collapse like so many dominoes, the garrison gunner coolly adjusted his drake and added his case shot to the party. 'Much injury,' noted Archer, 'a lamentable spec-tacle.' One of the surviving captains later told him that seventy to eighty men were killed or hurt in a few disordered minutes.

Waller was faring better against the New House in the east, where his men had greater numbers and firepower and some protection from a wood near the village. His spy had pointed out the weakest point of the wall, beyond the lower half-moon outwork there, and this was

where he concentrated his fire: 2,000 musketeers reinforcing his ordnance and producing – with replies from the garrison – 'such a loud
and continual thunder for two full hours that the like, as soldiers affirm,
hath never or very rarely been heard'. The livestock in the precinct
added to the racket. One cow was so distressed that it broke out of its
pen and tried to jump over the wall.

The dragoons fell on with extraordinary courage, storming the outwork, driving off the defenders and planting their flag into the ditch as
if they had conquered a mountain. Some put their ladders to the wall
and started climbing, but were beaten off by bricks and stones hurled
by the women on the roof. 'Come up Roundheads if ye dare!' they
shouted. Elsewhere on the turrets, the marchioness was hectic with
her maids, stripping off lead and casting it into shot to replenish the
garrison supplies. Everyone in the house, we are told by the royalist
Aulicus, 'from the noble marquess himself to the meanest soldier',
played their part bravely, Rawdon and the rest of the officers 'animating and directing their men' and firing alongside them with muskets.

Still, though, Waller's thousands rolled into the ditch and crashed
upon the walls 'in the fury of the most violent assault that ever was'.
'All is our own!' they cried, shooting into loopholes and hazarding
themselves 'upon the mouths of their enemies' muskets'. The petard-
ier now advanced with a bomb in his arms. He clamped it into position,
lit the fuse and ran for it. 'Unluckily', wrote Waller, he 'mistook the
place, for whereas he should have applied [it] to a place in the old wall
which was but a brick and a half thick, he set it against a door that was
bricked up and lined with earth, so that it took no effect'.

Inside the house was a foreign sniper, 'an ingenious and vigilant
man' and probably a veteran of the war on the Continent. Watching
the parliamentarians take the outwork and surge over the ditch, he
calculated that a building that jutted out towards the north end of the
New House would give him a good shot at them. He 'beat a hole
through the wall and, with a few muskets at hand, gave fire'. He
took down three or four men instantly and scattered the rest. 'This
unexpected execution so awaked the rebels,' reported *Aulicus*, 'that
finding no safety to stay, nor any way to enter the house, the petard
failing, they quickly began to run.' This, along with the news of the
parliamentarian collapse in the park, boosted the garrison. They redoubled their efforts, taking back the outwork and plying the enemy with

shot, 'the ladies and gentlewomen as earnest as any in melting lead to set forward the work'.

At three in the afternoon, the wind began to rise and the rain began to fall. An hour later, darkness crept in and 'we could not see their loop-holes'. Waller had no choice but to retreat. 'That night fell out so foul,' he wrote, 'that I could not possibly keep my men upon their guards.' He drew them back to surrounding fields and meadows. They left their ladders and their guns, their powder and their shot, even their flag, which stood in the ditch, slapped about by the wind and the rain. The royalists wanted to carry it inside in triumph, but the marquess forbade them, 'being loath in a little vanity to hazard those men's lives, which in all the fierce assault had been so blessedly preserved'.

At 10 p.m., there was more shooting as 'the London youths' of the City Green Auxiliaries ventured through the sucking mud to retrieve their field pieces. Roundhead reports claim that they dragged them away without loss. Cavalier sources said that it cost them twenty men. The rest of the night they harvested the dead, 'except some thirty bod-ies, which lay so near the works that they durst not fetch them off to give them burial'. Amongst the corpses was Waller's informant, lying where he had directed the assault. Nearby was a man who was still alive. His leg was shattered and he cried out 'piteously'. What, replied the royalists, had the king ever done to him to make him rebel? 'At which question,' reports *Aulicus*, 'this desperate wretch pulled out his knife and cut his own throat.'

9

The Strongest Place in England

In the first half of his hitherto forty-five years, Major General Sir William Waller had escaped from a bullet over his cradle, a near-drowning in a pond, a fall from a horse, pleurisy, smallpox, pirates, shipwreck, the Roman Inquisition and – alongside 'my old friend' Ralph Hopton – pursuing Cossacks after the battle of White Mountain in Prague. Understandably perhaps, he believed that God had preserved him for a higher hidden purpose. He detested civil war, but, as he had explained to Hopton, he regarded it as the work of the Lord, 'which is enough to silence all passion in me'.[1] As he lay out that night in a sodden Hampshire field thinking about the distance between himself and his erstwhile comrade, he must have wondered, also, at the mysteries of God's will. The 'fireworks from London' had not arrived in time, the petard had failed, the ladders (at least according to Lieutenant Archer) were the wrong type and God had not helped with the weather.[2] If Waller had any doubts, though, he kept them to himself. According to the author of *The Souldiers Report*, the general was an inspiration, 'fearing no danger' during the day and, 'although it grew dark and the rain fell and the cold winds blew', lying out with his men 'all night on a bundle of straw in the open meadow'. He hoped for a break in the clouds, but the rain 'ceased not'.[3]

'A very tempestuous morning of wind, rain and snow', recorded Archer in his entry the following day, Monday 13 November 1643. Waller's scouts came in early with news of Hopton's advance. He was six miles away, at full strength and about to link up with a considerable force from Reading. Waller quickly drew his army into the field. 'As I was riding about to give orders,' he wrote, 'I was saluted with a mutinous cry amongst the City regiments of "Home! Home!" so that I was forced to threaten to pistol any of them that should use that base language.' He called a council of war and offered three options: fight Hopton in the field, retake the town of Winchester or retire to Farnham. The first proposition was carried clear, but when the field officers returned to their men, 'those of the City would not march one foot further'. And so that was that, again. Waller withdrew first to Basingstoke, where scaling ladders, granadoes and powder had just arrived from London, and thence to Farnham, 'where I now am', he reported on 16 November. Some of the Londoners had already left, 'and the rest threaten to follow immediately, so that I am in a deserted condition'.

Waller's providentialism made for dismal reading. 'Pardon my many failings in this service,' he beseeched Parliament, 'which are not only my fault, but my punishment.' Yet if he acknowledged God's chastising hand in his beating, he also reminded Parliament of its responsibility to pay his men – 'we are all in a most wretched degree of want'. Mainly, though, he blamed London's hirelings: 'I have reason to suspect there [were] malignants that put themselves upon this service only to overthrow it and they are the men that have blown these coals.'[4]

The newsbooks also blamed the City brigade, in particular the Westminster Trained Band. Had they backed Waller up as they should have done, *The True Informer* insisted, Basing House would 'questionless' have been taken. 'Undoubtedly,' agreed *The Parliament Scout*, 'for his other soldiers did bravely . . . but the Westminsterians failed and could not be got on.' One of their captains, Christopher White, the Keeper of Petre House, where Catholics were imprisoned, was accused of holding back his company 'for fear of displeasing his prisoners'. Other commentators repeated the general suspicion that the Westminster men were sympathisers of the king, 'whom they expected to come shortly and be their neighbour again'. One newsbook, *The Scottish Dove*, also blamed the Tower Hamlets Yellow Auxiliaries, 'especially the officers'.[5]

Both the royalist *Aulicus* (writing at the time) and Colonel Rawdon's nephew Duke (twenty-four years later) claimed that 'the Green regiment', that is, the City Green Auxiliaries, who had fought commendably in the assault, had been Rawdon's old trained band unit in London. Before November, Duke wrote, they 'never knew what it was to fight against him'. Afterwards, many 'could never be persuaded to fight any more against the colonel'.[6] Rawdon's old regiment was the Red Regiment, though; the Green Auxiliaries were formed only after he had left

London. It is possible that a few of his old regiment made their way into the Greens in 1643, and perhaps too some officers in the London brigade knew Rawdon from their peacetime drills in the Artillery Garden. Robert Rodway's Westminster captain, George Warren, for example, was a long-standing member of the Honourable Artillery Company.[7]

Ultimately, though, the issue had not been whom the auxiliaries were fighting so much as what they were fighting. The author of *The Souldiers Report* prefaced his account with an awed description of Basing House. It was 'as large and as spacious as the Tower of London', he wrote, 'and strongly walled about with earth raised against the wall of such a thickness that it is able to dead the greatest cannon bullet'. Waller's trained bands 'offered their lives to him in any service against men', concluded *The Compleate Intelligencer*, 'but were loath to venture further against walls. We must excuse them, they being young and raw soldiers and not as yet frosted abroad.'[8]

Naturally, the casualty figures were disputed. Waller counted 30 fatalities amongst his men 'and near upon 100 hurt'. *The Souldiers Report* gave 40 wounded, but pointed out that the number of deaths was unknowable since most bodies had been buried overnight. Lieutenant Archer of the Yellow Auxiliaries allowed for 250–300 parliamentarian losses 'at the most' over all three days of action. In response to one newsbook's claim that Waller had lost only three men on the 12th, the royalist organ *Mercurius Aulicus* wondered: 'Were all the rest apes?'

Aulicus played the game too, though, claiming that over 1,000 parliamentarians were killed and wounded, but not a single royalist 'so much as hurt'. This was incredible even to his own side. The royalist lawyer Orlando Bridgeman didn't believe a word until the king's secretary wrote to confirm 'that 500 of Waller's men (really) were killed before Basing'.[9] The Marquess of Ormond forwarded the news to Honora's brother Ulick in Ireland, adding that he could find a fuller relation, 'though I cannot absolutely say the truer', in *Mercurius Aulicus*.[10]

Basing House was quiet the day afterwards, apart from the near-blizzard outside. The garrison buried two of their own and tended to the wounded. They sifted through the rubble and hauled off the cow carcass. They piled up discarded guns, pikes and ladders. They salvaged the musket balls that had fallen short and they began to patch up the fortifications, which had received 'some little injury'.

Winchester and Rawdon sent express reports to a jubilant Oxford. The queen gave Rawdon's messenger 'a golden reward' and Charles summoned him to give a further account in person.[11] Winchester continued to liaise with Hopton's army via an unnamed female messenger. He 'earnestly pressed for relief', but was told to hold tight.

Hopton had been slow getting his army together and it had been 'very convenient' for him to have Waller held up at Basing House.[12] The parliamentary press claimed that he didn't have the nerve to take Waller on. On Wednesday 15 November, wagers were laid in the Royal Exchange that Basing House had fallen, but even when the rumour was scotched and the bets lost, it was assumed that 'if relief come not', Waller would have yet another fling. 'There are in it divers ladies and gentlemen and many citizens,' reported *The Parliament Scout*, 'and it's conceived much wealth. We do not hear that the enemy advances to their relief.'

'We cannot hear as yet of any assistance coming into them,' echoed *The True Informer*. 'Much talk hath been of the Lord Hopton's approach that way, but as yet we cannot be ascertained of any such thing.'[13]

Rawdon tried to prepare the shocked garrison for another onslaught. Few of them would have experienced anything like what they had just been through – not in the Honourable Artillery Company, or during the hurly-burly at the Guildhall, or the repulse of Norton and Harvey in the summer. Most of the city tradesmen and the pressed men from Oxfordshire and Hampshire had been, to use the contemporary phrase, fresh-water soldiers. 'If an army,' wrote the clergyman Richard Ward, 'consists of raw, young and fresh-water soldiers, who seldom or never saw men wounded or slain, when they come to see such sights, they will tremble and be confounded with fear.'[14]

Thomas Johnson had dedicated his life to healing, to quickening pulses, to finding God's gifts in the native soil. In the past week, though, he had reduced men and animals to cinders. He had felt a living force dissolve in his arms. He had lured young men into an ambush and watched others, who lived not far from his home, destroy each other. We cannot know how he felt about any of this, but according to *Mercurius Aulicus*, he performed 'excellently'. He led sallies as urgently as he had hurried out to find plants. He confronted the enemy as vigorously as he had tackled Mount Snowdon. Whether Thomas Johnson had taken to war or not, war had taken to Thomas Johnson.

On Friday, 17 November, Hopton and his army of three thousand foot and two thousand horse finally arrived at Basing House. They reprovisioned and refortified the place ('as time and number would permit')[15] and Rawdon had the brief joy of seeing his eldest son Thomas, now a captain of horse in the regiment of his old London ally, Sir Nicholas Crisp. Then they were off again to take the fight to Waller, accompanied, it was reported in London, by most of the garrison.[16] They were billeted in and around Odiham, between Basing and Farnham, and there were skirmishes almost every day until 28 November, when Hopton's 'handsome little army' presented itself on a heath outside Farnham Castle and tried to lure Waller out of his stronghold.

Farnham was shrouded in cloud all that morning, just as Basing House had been for Waller's first assault. This time, he saw it as God's protective mist. A few guns were fired, but it was not the day. These were long, cold nights to be out on duty, especially for the horses, which were out of condition.[17] Hopton made the decision to put his troops into winter quarters – at Winchester, Alton, Alresford and Petersfield – though he sent a detachment from Petersfield on a quick march over the hard ground to take Arundel Castle in Sussex.

Three days later, on Tuesday 12 December, a reinforced Waller sensed an opportunity to beat up the royalist billet at Alton. He put it to the Londoners who were still with him at Farnham that they could go home the next day, as he had promised, or erase the stain of Basing with one more piece of service. They chose to fight and saw Waller 'the night owl' at his very best: a midnight march, a feint towards Basing House, a stealthy approach cross-country and a lightning strike on Alton in the morning. Here the Cavaliers were on the back foot until they ran out of ground. From the churchyard, they retreated into the church, where they barricaded themselves behind a heap of dead horses. Finally – the story goes – Colonel Richard Boles was backed into the pulpit, where he waved his sword and vowed 'God damn his soul!' to run it through the heart of the first man who dared to ask for quarter. Then he was cut down and his men gave up.

'This is the first evident ill success I have had,' Hopton admitted to

Waller in a letter asking for the return of Boles's body. 'I must acknowledge that I have lost many brave and gallant men.' The church and
yard were strewn with mangled bodies. Most had fallen to the axehead
of the halberd or the butt of the musket. 'God give a sudden stop to
this issue of English blood,' Hopton concluded, 'which is the desire,
Sir, of your faithful friend to serve you.'[18] Three weeks later, on 6 January 1644, Waller retook Arundel Castle, denying Hopton a Sussex
springboard into Kent and consigning the beleaguered inhabitants of
Hampshire to more war.

The three London regiments that had served at Basing House were
home for Christmas. At the church of St Giles-in-the-Fields, where a
window pane honoured Marmaduke Rawdon's generosity, the bells
were rung for the safe return of its parishioner, Captain Walter Bigg.
Over Holborn Bridge, up the hill and along Newgate Street to Christ
Church, a solemn thanksgiving service was held for the three regiments on 2 January. 'How safe they came back,' sniped *Mercurius
Aulicus*, 'let the London widows and orphans manifest.'[19]

Oxford-based *Aulicus*, which had first appeared the previous January,
was the royalist counterblast to the parliamentary periodicals that had
been mushrooming in London since the collapse of censorship at the
end of 1641. As the war progressed, the rival papers regularly, and
increasingly effectively, strafed each other with 'paper bullets'. The
writing was smart, caustic, economical with the truth and ethically
questionable. It was the beginning of popular journalism in England.

The man behind *Mercurius Aulicus* was a slick young journalist called
John Berkenhead. He was sometimes funny, frequently cruel and had
the full force of the royal court behind him. In December 1643, he
chose to print a private letter from a London wife to her soldier husband. It had been intercepted in Hampshire by the royalists. Berkenhead
published it in full (with a snide aside on the bad spelling) in order to
lecture allegedly hawkish wives, 'the Lady Waller for one', on the virtues of goodwifery and the importance of the home. 'Most dear and
loving husband,' Susan Rodway began, 'my king love, remember unto
you, hoping that you are [in] good health as I am at the writing hereof.
My little Willie have been sick this fortnight. I pray you to come home
if you can come safely . . . '[20]

It is often assumed that Robert Rodway perished with the

Westminster musketeers in Basing Park. In fact, he made it back to Susan and the children in Bell Yard. He was to live for many more years, have several more children and rise to the top of the Tallow Chandlers' Company. Sick 'little Willie' also survived, but only for three more years. Baby Hester succumbed to 'rising lights' (croup) in June 1644. They were buried in the churchyard of St Dunstan-in-the-West.[21]

If the December tumults of 1641 had been the 'maddest' Christmas that had ever been, and the 'great hurllyburly' at the Guildhall the following year had been the most desperate, in 1643 Christmas itself came under the cosh. Christ's nativity was a popular feast in the English ritual year, but no date was specified in the Bible and no observation was commanded. Puritans deemed it more than a little popish and were alarmed by the licence Christmas gave to 'carnal and sensual delights'. On 25 December 1643, a group of 'holy Londoners' opened their shops for business as if it was just an ordinary day. The apprentices of Cheapside were not at all keen on losing a holiday and forced them to close.*[22]

Further reformation was a hot topic at the close of 1643 because it was a condition of Parliament's new alliance with the Scots. By the terms of the Solemn League and Covenant, and in return for Scottish military assistance, Parliament bound itself to religious uniformity throughout the three kingdoms and the extirpation of popery and prelacy. In order to bind the people with one another and with God, Parliament insisted on subscriptions to the Covenant. One clause contained a promise not to fall into 'detestable indifferency or neutrality'. Another expected subscribers to denounce the 'malignants' in their midst.[23] As one newsbook explained, those who were lukewarm, like half-baked pies, must be brought 'to the oven to make them hard and stiff for religion'.[24]

Around the same time, Charles made a deal of his own – the 'Cessation', by which the fighting in Ireland between the Catholic confederates and Protestant royalists was suspended in order to free up the king's troops to serve him over in England. Perhaps 2,000 of the 9,000 soldiers

---

* The following year, 1644, Christmas clashed with the monthly fast day designated by Parliament for prayers to end the Irish rebellion. MPs privileged the fast over the feast and thenceforth Christmas was cancelled.

who crossed the Irish Sea between October 1643 and the end of the war were Irish born, but the majority were native Englishmen.[25] Parliament depicted Charles as a craven appeaser of the Irish rebels, garbed in ever more popish robes. The troops from Ireland were not particularly effective, however. The main reason Hopton had been slow to relieve Basing House in November was because he was dealing with mutiny in their ranks. The Scots came in greater numbers and fared better. As 1643 came to a close, over 20,000 Scottish soldiers prepared to cross the border to fight their king.

And so the year ended with little hope of resolution. When John Piggott gave a sermon at St Sepulchre's on the text 'Shall the sword devour forever?', he was derided, 'as if a sermon of peace in these times of wilful distraction were like snow in summer'.[26] The war had widened and intensified. The Solemn League and Covenant was championed in the pulpits in the language of holy war. 'God's sword,' preached Thomas Coleman, 'hath not eaten flesh enough.' It was no time for mercy – 'not now', warned *The Souldiers Catechisme*, 'to look at our enemies as countrymen, or kinsmen, or fellow Protestants, but as enemies of God, and our Religion, and siders with Antichrist, and so our eye is not to pity them, nor our sword to spare them'.[27]

The deliveries to Basing House arrived just after Christmas. They came in four carts at the rate of sixpence per mile. They contained ten barrels of powder, twenty hundredweight of match, sixty iron roundshot and two new pieces of ordnance known as 'minions' (from the French for 'cute').[28] Marmaduke Rawdon probably placed the order, since he was in Oxford around that time. According to his nephew, the king offered his hand to kiss and said to him, 'Oh my honest citizen, I give you thanks for the good service you have done me.' He asked Rawdon to draw out his sword, and in front of all those present took it in his hand and announced, 'This sword hath got you honour and shall give it you.' He bade Rawdon kneel and 'gave him the honour of knighthood'.[29]

'The principal marks whereat every man's endeavour in this life aimeth are either profits or honour,' Rawdon had written before the war. 'The one proper to vulgar people and men of inferior fortune; the other due to persons of better birth and generous disposition. For as the former by pain and parsimony do only labour to become rich, so the other by military skill, or knowledge in civil government, aspire to honour and human glory.'[30] The City trader, plantation owner, cartel runner and privateer had spent a lot of money to slide into the elite. He had all the trappings of a 'generous disposition'– the country house and bowling green, the fine horses and furniture, the church windows, and even the statue of the Samaritan woman in Hoddesdon market-place. But to the nobility and gentry clustered around the king at Oxford, and no doubt also to the Marquess and Marchioness of Winchester at Basing House, Marmaduke Rawdon was a somewhat vulgar man. *Sir* Marmaduke Rawdon, on the other hand, was a man of honour, accredited by the sword and not the coin.

A commemorative portrait followed (see plates). It might have been painted at Oxford, though not by the remarkable William Dobson, or back at Basing House, where Ensign William Faithorne had the ability to do it, if not perhaps the inclination. (Faithorne had followed his master Peake out of Rawdon's regiment and into Winchester's in July.) Rawdon appears in the picture in perfectly riveted armour, straight-backed, stout and proud.[31] He stares directly out of the canvas, as if daring Sir William Waller to have another fling. Over sixty, he looks a decade younger, his hair still thick and lustrous. The colours are muted apart from the gleam of the sitter's armour and a great gold chain around his neck. Suspended from it is a medallion of pure gold bearing a profile of Charles I.

It was African gold, delivered in person by Rawdon's second son, twenty-two-year-old Marmaduke. He had shipped it over from the Canary Islands with a cargo of wine 'and other goods', possibly arms. According to the family history, he was conducted from Basingstoke to Basing House by ten files of Rawdon's musketeers. Inside the house, he presented his father with the chain, 'a rich hatband of goldsmith's work' and £500 worth of gold.

'Let me see your gold,' said the colonel. His son emptied a silk purse onto the table. Rawdon asked him to select ten of the best pieces. 'This,' he said, 'I take to make the king's picture to wear with the chain of gold.' He returned the rest to Marmaduke junior, who, he said, would need it more.[32]

Young Marmaduke stayed at Basing House for about a fortnight and was 'very nobly entertained'. Then he travelled to Oxford, escorted by Captain Robert Amery. He kissed the king's hand and delivered a message from his father. The Rawdon family history records numerous subsequent adventures. Young Marmaduke evades capture in Surrey and sends more wine and armaments to Basing House. He visits his mother but cannot stay because the family home has been stripped so completely that only one bed and a little furniture remain – 'though before the plunder few houses in Hertfordshire were better furnished'. He proceeds to London to fit a ship for Spain and is about to embark from the Downs when a postmaster, 'knowing him to be son to Sir Marmaduke Rawdon', alerts the port. He is imprisoned in the Counter in Southwark and hears a hawker cry the news 'young Rawdon taken prisoner'. He asks the man what will become of the lad and is told that it will 'go very hard with him'. He is released in the end because he has contacts and money and is soon back on the high seas.

There is a picaresque quality to all this, but it is telling that both on Marmaduke's journey to Basing from the Cornish coast and later as a prisoner in Southwark, the Rawdon name was recognised. Throughout the West Country, 'the innkeepers and all others, knowing whose son he was, did treat him with extraordinary civility'. In Southwark, 'the common people did so flock together to see him, pressing upon him, that the soldiers had much ado to beat them off'.

Basing House appealed to the public imagination. It was alluring and dangerous, charmed and damned. It was 'that invincible garrison, that nest of unclean birds', full of treasure, fair maidens and Irish rebels. 'In old times,' began a satirical newsbook, 'mighty giants lived in enchanted castles', and now 'a great company of malignants live so strongly fortified in Basing House' that even Sir William Waller has had to withdraw. 'The walls,' it adds, 'be as thick as those of Pluto's Court [Hades], where he doth live with his malignant Queen Proserpine.' The writer was stirred by the image of the 'many malignant ladies and other women within the castle' throwing stones from the parapet and taunting the soldiers, 'Come up Roundheads if ye dare!' Undoubtedly, the writer prophesied, the Roundheads would come up, to take away all the gold and silver 'that doth lie buried in the ground [and] in the sheets'.[33]

Other contemporaries searched for biblical analogies. Colonel Robert Titchburne prayed that Basing's defences would collapse 'like the walls of Jericho'.[34] Mystique bred rumour: that King Charles and Prince

Rupert had visited with thousands of troops, that the house would be the launchpad for a new attack on London, and that – this one had some substance to it – Inigo Jones the great architect had been brought in to design ever more fearsome fortifications.[35]

How to win the prize? If Basing House could not be battered or scaled, its inhabitants might be tricked or poisoned or starved. 'Some think the only way of taking it will be by mining,' noted *The True Informer*.[36] 'It is absolutely the strongest place in England,' despaired a lieutenant on the ground, 'and requires a summer siege.'[37]

PART THREE

THE SUMMER SIEGE

10

Paulet the Hangman

Antigonnus King of Macedonia was wont to say that the strongest
hold in the world might be reduced if, by the gate of it, a mule laden
with gold might enter therein.

David Papillon, *A Practicall Abstract of the
Arts of Fortification and Assailing* (1645)

On 15 January 1644, Sir Marmaduke Rawdon wrote to his old London
enemy John Venn. Their battle over the leadership of the Honourable
Artillery Company was over a decade in the past, but their enmity was
raw. Venn was now the governor of Windsor Castle and he had in his
hold Rawdon's servant Robert Baites.

Civil war prisoners could not expect good treatment. There were
horror stories from both camps, and some guards, most notoriously
the Cavalier in charge of Oxford Castle, were sadists. Venn was not
demonstrably cruel, but nor did he have any discernible sense of compassion. One of his prisoners, Edward Pitt, whom Venn had refused
parole to see his dying wife, thought him 'the most uncharitable and
unchristian-like wretch that breathes upon the face of the earth'.[1]

In his letter of 15 January, Rawdon asked Venn to release his servant
Baites in exchange for a prisoner at Basing House. Venn replied two
weeks later, granting Rawdon his request and offering to do the same
for forty or four hundred more, should Rawdon ever capture so many.
'Our prisons are all full of your soldiers,' he gloated, 'we know not what
to do with them, besides those that run away from your garrisons.'

'I hope,' the Puritan continued, 'you yourself will so understand
yourself and your bad cause that you will return, repenting what you
have done.' He would leave it to God to turn Rawdon's heart. And yet,
he wondered 'how you, that have been bred up in a Protestant religion,

can draw a sword in the papist cause and abide in such a popish garrison'. Venn concluded with prayers 'that the kingdom of Christ may
be set up in power and purity of worship, and that the kingdom of
Antichrist, which is the Pope, may fall to the ground'.

Rawdon replied on 6 February, thanking Venn for the release of
Baites and promising to honour any similar request, 'for I hate ingrati-
tude'. The truth, he admitted, was that 'we have not at present so many
prisoners to exchange as you vainly boast of, although we have had far
more, and when God pleaseth may have again, whereof will be no
bragging, being things rather to be pitied. And for any that run from
our garrison to yours, I dare boldly say there come ten from yours to
us for one of ours that goes to your army.'

Far from repenting, Rawdon was resolute: 'Had I ten thousand lives,
I would spend them to the last drop of blood in the cause.' He had 'no
such thought' of defending popery: 'It's the true Protestant religion
established by king and Parliament I draw my sword for, joined with
obedience and duty I owe to our most gracious sovereign, the best of
kings.' Venn had 'no spark of charity' in him, wrote Rawdon, if he
refused to believe the king's many promises to uphold the Protestant
faith.

'And whereas you,' he continued, 'would scandalise me with staying
in a popish garrison, it's well known to all the world we have liberty of
conscience, preaching, and daily reading of the Book of Common
Prayer and, although the castle belongs to my much honoured Lord,
the Marquess of Winchester, yet *as it is a garrison*, it appertains to His
Majesty by whose command I am here with my regiment.' Rawdon
thus made a distinction between the pre-war civilian house and the
royalist military garrison.

Finally, he too offered prayers, that his 'old acquaintance' might see
'the abominable, horrid and infested treason' he was living in, and
understand the scriptural injunction to obey kings. This held even for
tyrants, wrote Rawdon, so much more, therefore, for 'this merciful
benign King Charles, who so often hath tendered his pardon to all you
rebels'.

Rawdon was a moderate sort of Protestant. He loathed sectarianism, not least because it was bad for business. He imported French
claret, Portuguese Madeira and Spanish Canary and maintained fruitful contacts with Catholic merchants and vintners. For a week in 1639

he had even hosted the Spanish governor of the Canary Islands at his house in Hertfordshire. The recusant writer John Hawkins had dedicated a biography of the Catholic hero Sir Thomas More to Rawdon, 'that worshipful and worthy lover of learning and arts'.[2] But trading with, befriending and even admiring Catholics was a world apart from upholding 'popery'. Rawdon was offended – 'scandalised' – by the notion that he could serve in a popish garrison. As he made clear to Venn, his service was to his Protestant king, not the Catholic marquess. But in stoking Rawdon's outrage, Venn had exposed the fault line between the two colonels of Basing House.

Winchester could never think of his home simply as a garrison. The damage was personal, and strategic decisions such as felling ancient trees and torching cottages to provide field of fire had long-term implications for his tenants and neighbours. Rawdon might try to undermine Winchester's jurisdiction in the garrison, but ultimately, as Rawdon's nephew later wrote, 'the marquess was not pleased to have any governor of his own house but himself'.[3]

On 8 January 1644, Thomas Roberts of Basing died of 'the sickness'. He just had time to make an oral will. It was witnessed by the Marquess of Winchester's ensign, which makes it likely that Roberts was a soldier in the garrison. He left some money for the maintenance of his two daughters and a twenty-pound annuity to his wife Elizabeth, who had previously provided 'good service' to the Winchester family. The sum was to be paid by the marquess out of the 'Farm Grange' – now a bed of ashes.[4]

A few days later, Winchester received a letter on behalf of Mistress Zouch, the 'unhappy' widow of a royalist colonel who had died at Reading. She lived in Odiham, a town between Basing and Farnham, and could no longer pay the contribution money demanded for the upkeep of the garrison.[5]

Other neighbours were also blighted by the conflict. Thomas Pile had given Sir William Waller corn to the value of £300 'during the late siege of Basing House'. After the parliamentary withdrawal, the royalists exacted double the tribute.[6] The destruction of vital documents could be devastating, too. Before the war, John Atfield of Basingstoke had leased a plot of land in Kingsclere from the Marquess of Winchester. It wasn't worth £3 a year, he said, but he paid twice as much for a term of 99 years. He had built 'two new substantial mills' on the land, and a maltmill, 'all new stones'. But 'it so happened that in the time of the garrison at Basing, my house being burnt with all my goods and writings, amongst the rest (I suppose) the lease of the mills was consumed'. So now Atfield had no proof of his interest in the property or, indeed, of the £200 he had sunk into the mills. 'All these times,' he added in his petition, he'd paid his rent, the marquess 'never favoured me a farthing'.[7]

The almsfolk at the hospital of St Mary Magdalen near Winchester lost thirty-six sheep to Ralph Hopton's troops over Christmas. They didn't complain at the time, but the following March they were forced to petition him after royalists had broken in and taken all their seed barley and every bit of wood – the gates, doors, wainscot, tables, cupboards, even the pews and communion table in their chapel. 'Your poor petitioners,' they wrote, 'being very aged and impotent persons', are 'thereby made destitute of the means of having either temporal or spiritual food'. Hopton signed a protection order, but by then there wasn't even a stable door left to close.[8]

And so it went on, relentlessly, for many months. Winchester and Rawdon both added horse regiments to their original foot regiments, thereby extending their range for intelligence and provisions, but also their capacity for damage. 'The king's cormorants at Basing House', as one contemporary called them, were bad neighbours. They levied taxes, disrupted markets, held up the clothiers on the London Road and raided homes, farms and fields.[9] They were not uniquely cruel or violent in this cruel and violent conflict, but because they were seen as 'such a popish garrison', as Venn had put it, they were often portrayed as such.

Conscription too was deeply unpopular. Men between the ages of sixteen and sixty were forcibly recruited by both sides, for there weren't enough volunteers for the rank and file. 'My countrymen love their pudding at home better than a musket or pike abroad,' observed one contemporary, 'and if they could have peace, care not what side had the better.'[10] If they could afford it, they would sometimes hire more desperate men to take their place. These hirelings' loyalties were to the coin that put clothes on their backs and food on the table.

As Venn's correspondence with Rawdon reveals, the battle lines were porous. On 11 January 1644, a group of troopers slipped out of Basing House, claiming that they had been forced to take up arms for the king. A few months later, a soldier called Richard Kiddle, drinking in Alton with some fellow Roundheads, was persuaded to slope off with them to Basing House. He was caught, returned to barracks and court-martialled. Found guilty of running from his colours, he was sentenced to be 'hanged by the neck until he be dead'.[11]

Garrisons close to main roads were vital for communications. Basing House channelled information in and out of the west and also between Oxford and London, to which it was closer than any other permanent royalist garrison. Before the war, Basing's bullet-maker, Tobias Baisly, had been a porter at the Ram Inn in Smithfield. He now earned five shillings a week to cast lead for the garrison and a fair bit more scouting about on the roads, talking to carters, carriers and post-boys. Throughout 1644, he also made trips back to London to pick up intelligence from his old friends in the porter community. His luck ran out early the following year, when he was arrested and hanged as a spy. He was defiant to the last, refusing to pray with the minister, and reportedly showing 'much unwillingness to go off the ladder'.[12]

Some agents employed ingenious methods to convey information. An old woman and a 'ragged man' swallowed messages encased in bullets and acted as mules for the royalist garrison at Newark. Another royalist courier smuggled letters between Oxford and London in a hollowed-out walking stick. He was caught when he thumped the cane too vigorously on the ground and some rolls of paper dropped out. There was even, if we are to believe an eighteenth-century account, a royalist spy dog in Lancashire who leapt in and out of Lathom House with notes attached to his collar.[13]

Some women found espionage a thrilling outlet from a patriarchal world. 'I know you prefer that so much before the lazy quiet most here place their happiness in,' one noblewoman was told, but for many 'she-intelligencers', the work was born of necessity. The woman who carried messages between Hopton and Winchester at the time of Waller's attempt on Basing House was not named in their correspondence, but she might have been Katherine Haswell, who had lost her father to a parliamentary prison and her brother at the battle of Edge-hill. 'And herself,' she added in a later petition, 'after many services

upon a royal account in carrying of letters and the like, was dangerously wounded by the rebels at Basing House, whereby she is utterly
disabled from a livelihood.'[14]

Another candidate is Katherine de Luke of the New Forest, who
claimed to have carried information for the royalists 'when none else
durst adventure to do it'. Her husband was an officer under Hopton
and 'received such wounds . . . as shortened his days in misery'. The
parliamentarians eventually caught her, whipped her, burned her with
lit matches and 'cruelly tormented' her 'to make her betray her trust'.
High-ranking royalists later vouched that she was 'a great sufferer for
her loyalty and service'.[15]

The renumeration, at least, could be generous. The Earl of Essex's
Scoutmaster General, Sir Samuel Luke, received £7 a day to watch the
royalists in and around Oxford. He employed twenty regular scouts at
five shillings a day, and each had his own web of informants, including
'two men that live in Basing House'. Luke's journal provides a running
commentary, though not always an accurate one, of the strength and
condition of the king's garrisons. He knew from Ralph Norton about
six deserters hanged within Basing's walls in January 1644, and from
William Blewett about the contents of three carts wheeled into the
house the following month: 'a load of powder and bullets, one load of
match, a load of muskets and pikes and 2 pieces of ordnance'. His journal entry for this date, Friday 23 February 1644, adds that 'they have
sent for all the trained bands thereabouts to come to their assistance,
being in continual fear of Sir William Waller's coming to besiege the
house'.[16]

Luke also managed to infiltrate the king's army. Reportedly, one
colonel of the council of war, one lieutenant colonel, one captain,
one ensign and several sergeants and corporals were on the parliamentary payroll. Apparently they knew nothing of 'each other's being so
employed'. They smuggled their letters out of Oxford by slotting them
through holes in the windows of houses against which they urinated
(peeing in the street was a common enough practice for it not to warrant a second glance). The messages were then retrieved and passed on
to men disguised as town gardeners, who hid them in their barrows
and dropped them two miles out of town by a ditch. Luke's scouts collected them and took them up to him in Newport Pagnell. One
parliamentarian newsbook gloated that Luke watched the royalists 'so

industriously that they eat, sleep, drink not, whisper not, but he can give us an account of their darkest proceedings'.[17] Perhaps, then, he already knew about the plot to betray Basing House.

By late February 1644, there was a feeling in Hampshire that a big battle was coming that might decide if not the war, then at least the contest between Waller and Hopton in the south. On the 23rd, the same day that Luke's journal records the cartloads of arms going into Basing House, it also notes a build-up of royalist troops around Winchester. 'There is great boasting,' he wrote, 'that within one month they will rout and destroy all Sir William Waller's forces, who they conceive to be very weak.'[18]

Eleven days later, on Tuesday 5 March, the king's Secretary of State, Sir Edward Nicholas, reported from Oxford that 'Sir Richard Grenville came Sunday last with thirty horse to serve His Majesty'.[19]

Grenville was a Cornishman and an old campaigner whose boots had collected the mud of the Low Countries, Germany and most recently Ireland, where he had fought the insurgents and picked up a reputation for brutality. At the cessation of arms, he crossed the Irish Sea, was captured by Parliament and promptly defected. His new allies were sure of his good faith because he took a loyalty oath and pledged in the Commons to fight for Parliament to his 'last drop of blood'. They appointed him lieutenant general of Waller's horse and gave him men, money and a seat on the war council. At the beginning of March, having pocketed the minutes of the latest meeting, he sped to Oxford with his troopers, trumpeters and £600 in cash. The Roundheads were left red-faced and raging. They proclaimed Grenville a 'traitor, rogue, villain and skellum' (from the Dutch *schelm*, rascal) and nailed the proclamation to gibbets at Palace Yard and the Royal Exchange. In the London press, he was branded a 'Turk', 'Infidel', 'Judas' and 'a scabbed sheep'. *The Spie* predicted that 'when the terrors of death shall seize upon his body, his affrighted soul will be Covenant-shaken, and the Devil raise an earthquake in his conscience'. Until that happy day, he was hanged in effigy in the streets.[20]

Grenville had all sorts of interesting things to tell the king about Parliament's plans for the coming campaign. 'And in addition,' Prince Rupert's informant wrote on 8 March, 'the schemes by which Lord Charles Paulet was planning to betray Basing House.'[21]

Winchester's younger brother Charles was an intemperate man. In the spring of 1642, he had fallen out with a family friend over fishing rights and sent him an abusive letter. The friend's wife had complained to Winchester, who immediately smoothed things over, apologising for his brother's 'sudden and extraordinary passion'.[22]

Since the outbreak of the civil war, Paulet had been living in Basing House with his wife and children, 'as unsuspected as a brother ought to be'. Early in 1644, when the marquess was summoned to Oxford to attend the king's new parliament – a fractious and ultimately failed attempt to replace the Westminster assembly – he had left his brother in charge. It was during this interval that Paulet and Sir William Waller made contact.

According to the Venetian secretary in London, 'Waller had come to an understanding with the brother of the Marquess of Winchester, for a heavy bribe, to put into his hands Basing House'. In his next dispatch, the Venetian added a rumour that further plots had been primed against royalist Reading 'and in Oxford itself and against the king's own person'.[23]

Edward Hyde (later Earl of Clarendon), who was in Oxford at the time, recalled in his *History of the Rebellion* that the king, upon hearing of Paulet's treachery, sent an express messenger to Winchester 'with all the particular informations'. The marquess seized his brother and several accomplices, who immediately 'confessed all, with all the circumstances of the correspondence and combination'. Clarendon was of the opinion that, had it not been for Grenville's timely revelation, Basing House would have been lost in a matter of days.[24]

Paulet, his wife and co-conspirators were first taken to Reading and then, on Friday 22 March, to Oxford, where they were spotted by a Roundhead spy. 'It is thought he will lose his head for it,' the spy reported.[25]

Paulet was imprisoned in Oxford Castle for six weeks and then sent for trial to the army camp in Wantage. All the evidence against him and his accomplices was forwarded, along with a book of the latest military orders. The Advocate General arrived. The court martial was ready.

Winchester, meanwhile, was begging the king to spare his brother. According to Clarendon, Charles finally agreed that Winchester 'might only turn his brother out of the garrison, after justice was done upon his complices'. The order was sent down to Wantage on 7 May: 'His royal pleasure is that his lordship shall have his gracious pardon.' Paulet was bailed and the court was discharged.[26]

The whole affair is murky, not least because nearly all the records from both Basing House and Oxford were destroyed at the end of the civil war. There is even some confusion over the identity of the traitor, or traitors. At the time, Sir Samuel Luke, Sir Edward Nicholas and Rupert's informant, Arthur Trevor, all named Lord Charles Paulet, but Clarendon, writing a few years later, fingered the youngest Paulet brother, Edward. 'The name of Edward has never since been borne by any of his family,' declared Reverend George Godwin, the Edwardian historian of Hampshire. Godwin also proffered a theory that has since become legend: that the traitor Paulet's punishment was 'to act as the executioner of his accomplices and of all criminals belonging to the garrison'.[27]

There was indeed a seventeenth-century custom whereby felons might escape the rope if they agreed to act as the town executioner. It happened in York in 1658, for example.[28] If it was the fate of Edward Paulet at Basing House, there is only one piece of evidence to suggest it. It is inconclusive, but certainly curious. In a list of people inside the house in October 1645, the final entry reads: 'Edward Pawlet the hangman'.[29]

11

Worthies

The alarm was raised at one in the morning on Saturday 30 March and soon they were piling in: Colonel Fielding with the artillery train, Lord Hopton with the foot, and Lord Forth covering the retreat with the horse. Marmaduke Rawdon would have been looking out for his son, Thomas, as the riders came in on their steaming white-eyed chargers. They probably reeked of smoke, as they had set fire to the town of Alresford on their way out.

The day had started so well for them. Hopton had won the race to Alresford and secured the town. He'd positioned his army on high ground with Cheriton Wood to his left. Waller's night owls had crept into the wood on Thursday 28 March, but when the mist cleared on Friday morning, the royalist musketeers beat them out. One Londoner allegedly ran out, wringing his hands and crying that the day was lost, 'like a great booby'.[1]

Hopton had perhaps six thousand men to Waller's ten thousand. Both armies were a hastily stitched patchwork of different militias, brigades and associations – old and new, city and county, English, Irish, Scottish and a fair few Frenchmen in the Queen's Regiment. The embarrassment of Alton had inflicted a wound that bled 'inward' for Hopton. The scars of Roundway Down and Basing House had not faded for Waller. This was the showdown.[2]

There were some notable units on the field. For Parliament these included the Hampshire horse regiment of Richard Norton, the governor of Southampton, whose failed assault on Basing House the previous July had turned it into a garrison; Samuel Jones's Farnham Greencoats, who had taken part in Waller's November assaults; and Sir Arthur Hesilrige's mounted 'lobsters', last seen scuttling away from

Roundway Down. On the parliamentarian right wing was a detach-
ment from Essex's field army commanded by Sir William Balfour, a
Scot whose troopers were full of beef and bacon taken from a Basing
House raiding party earlier in the month.[3]

Facing them for the king was the Lord General, the Earl of Forth, a
gnarly veteran of the continental wars who had won the admiration of
the great Gustavus Adolphus of Sweden. Forth had marshalled the
royalists at Edgehill and had been shot in the head at Gloucester. He
was a gouty, half-deaf Scot, puckered with scars and practically pick-
led. They called him 'Pater Rotwein' (Father Red Wine), since he drank
as hard as he fought.[4]

Lieutenant Colonel Thomas Rawdon was in command of a regiment of horse in the brigade of Lord John Stuart.[5] He had just turned
thirty-two. Stuart, who was the king's third cousin, was a decade
younger. He had fought, and lost a brother, at Edgehill. Another veteran of that first battle now lining up to face the Roundheads at
Cheriton was Major General Sir John Smith. Described as a man of
stern aspect 'rather formed to command armies than allure ladies', he
had won fame – and his knighthood – by rescuing the king's stolen
standard on the battlefield.

If, at Cheriton on 29 March 1644, Smith was the trump card in the
royalist pack, the joker proved to be Colonel Sir Henry Bard, a maverick adventurer and future envoy to the Shah of Persia. He had ridden
to Basing House back in July to help Peake repulse Norton. He 'lived
high', but the coming battle would be his nadir.[6]

Just before noon, 'with more youthful courage than soldier-like discretion', Bard reportedly broke ranks and charged the parliamentarian
line. Hopton and Forth sent the cavalry in support, but Waller's men
stood to it, resisting each disjointed charge and gradually driving the
royalists back in a battle marked by one of the longest cavalry engage-
ments of the war.

The fighting was a messy affair. There was no standard uniform yet,
so soldiers distinguished friend from foe by colours, field signs and
passwords. At Cheriton that day, the parliamentarians chose to wear
something white in their hats and use the password 'God with us'. So
too did the royalists. All was chaos, each man slashing and straining
on uneven terrain along hedged lanes that caught the cavalry in

bottlenecks. Attempting to describe it later, Robert Harley, a captain of Waller's horse, apologised for scribbling 'nothing else but a confused thing patched up by a short memory'.[7]

For four hours the carnage unspooled on the Hampshire field. Henry Bard, the first charger, lost an arm, George Thompson a leg. Raoul Fleury's foot was ripped off by a cannonball, 'whereof he shortly after died'. Ralph Hopton's horse took a musket ball to the shoulder. Other mounts were pocked with shot and collapsed under their riders. Sir John Smith, his horse rearing, was shot in the belly by one of Hesilrige's 'lobsters'. His lieutenant ran down the 'armed monster' and put a bullet in his eye, but Smith did not survive. He was one of 'the excellent men,' his elegist would write, unlike 'those windy gallants whose chiefest eminence doth consist in vapouring bravely'.[8]

Lord John Stuart was mortally wounded in another charge. He had posed for Van Dyck before the war in flouncy silks with his brother Bernard, who would die at the battle of Rowton Heath, also aged twenty-two.

By four in the afternoon, with so many royalist officers down, their horse in disorder and their foot driven 'from hedge to hedge', Hopton and Forth agreed to withdraw. The cavalry formed a shield on the ridge to cover the retreat. It was terrifying service under 'very hot' fire. Thomas Rawdon's troop began to panic. 'Stay but a little with me,' he roared, 'and be not afraid and I shall look upon you as men as long as I live, and I will shelter you the best I can.' Smiling, reportedly, he stood his ground, and his men stayed with him, 'till the foot all drew off and then, with his horse, he brought up the rear and made a very safe and honourable retreat'.[9]

The parliamentarians were sluggish in pursuit, but close enough to put out the cover fires the royalists had started in Alresford. It was another sixteen miles through the woods to Basing House. Lord Forth – 'Father Red Wine' – earned a glass of the marquess's finest that night. 'With admirable conduct and gallantry', Hopton tells us, Forth and his page were the last upon the ground and were 'forced to face about at every pass for the first 2 or 3 miles, and many of his horse brake from him; yet it pleased God that all, both horse and foot, cannon and carriages came safe to Basing that night'. Here the royalist army rested for a day, but 'fearing to be besieged there', moved on to Reading and then Oxford to face the king.[10]

Marmaduke Rawdon would have been relieved to find his son unscathed. Thomas had lost a scarf, 'shot with a musket bullet from about his neck', and his horse was wounded, 'but he himself had no other hurt'. Soon afterwards, he was sent to Lisbon to petition John IV of Portugal for aid. He left Bristol in a merchant vessel 'and with some difficulty passed eight sails of Parliament's ships'. He arrived in June accompanied by his domestic servant, Robert Baites, the same man whose release from prison his father had arranged with Colonel Venn at the beginning of the year.

The Portuguese king – father of Catherine of Braganza, future queen consort of England – assured Rawdon that if he was a private man, he would volunteer to fight for Charles I 'sooner than any prince in Christendom'. Rawdon would return to England in October 1644 with a frigate full of soldiers and large quantities of saltpetre, an essential ingredient for gunpowder and increasingly scarce in England. Charles would inform him that 'he came home in a very good time to help relieve his father, who was there besieged in Basing'.[11] By then, in autumn's crepusculum, Sir Marmaduke Rawdon and Basing House both looked very different.

The royalists' disciplined withdrawal from Cheriton had saved them from a rout, but it was a comprehensive defeat and a turning point in the war. After the battle, there could be no more serious talk of a royalist advance on London. Hopton's forces were absorbed into the king's field army and he was shunted into western sidings.

Sir William Waller took the town (though not the castle) of Winchester and marched on to Basing House on 21 May. The garrison 'welcomed us with two or three pieces of ordnance', wrote one of the Roundheads, but did no damage, 'only scared our under-marshal, the blast blowing off his hat'. Waller's horse went round to face the house. They picked off two sentries from the breastworks and hovered for a few hours. The garrison anticipated a long siege and burned 'all the houses and two mills' close to Basingstoke, where Waller's army was quartering.[12]

This time, though, the knight was after the king. Three days later, Waller moved his men up and out of Hampshire to converge with the Earl of Essex on Oxford. Charles escaped at the head of a flying column in June. Queen Henrietta Maria, who was pregnant, had already left town in April. They would never see each other again. The battle of Cheriton, wrote Clarendon, 'broke all the measures and altered the whole scheme of the king's counsels, for whereas before he hoped to have entered the field early, and to have acted an offensive part, he now discerned he was wholly to be upon the defensive part; and that was like to be a very hard part too'.[13]

The Loddon lily comes to the valley at the end of spring and the woods lay out their bluebell carpets. Not all the trees were gone at Basing. Not all the earth was scorched. But not even the quickening light and the darling buds of May could leaven the mood inside the garrison house.

Lord Paulet's betrayal, and subsequent reprieve, had widened the divide between the two governors. The old, unspecified 'sickness' and the new wounded kept the place stale in the reek of defeat. The garrison was isolated, twitchy and hungry. Provisions were not getting through. One thousand sheep 'and much fat cattle' were intercepted by the parliamentarians on 24 April, for example, and each failed foray cost the garrison men, money and morale.[14] When Waller left Hampshire, the local Roundheads stayed, and in ever-constricting circles they closed in on Basing House.

And yet, amidst the funerals, there was a wedding. We don't know the names of the bride and groom, the date, or even if it was a wartime romance or a long-standing betrothal.[15] All we know is that the groom was one of Rawdon's officers, the venue was 'a town near Basing' and a massacre was averted. According to the Rawdon family history, the bridegroom invited his colonel to the marriage feast and asked him to let several other officers attend. Rawdon gave his permission and said that he would try to come too, but that they should not wait for him. He anticipated trouble, 'the enemy lying not above five miles from the place'. After the groom and his guests departed, Rawdon gathered a discreet force of horse and foot and marched beyond the venue to a thick quickset hedge that the

Roundheads would have to pass if they advanced. He lined it with his men and told them to hold fire till the order:

> According to his imagination, it fell out, that about noon the enemy came with a party of horse. His soldiers did as he commanded them, lay close till most of them were passed by, and then discharged upon them. Some they killed, some they took and the rest, with much ado, escaped. This being done, away he went to the town to the wedding and told them that now, having secured their good cheer, he would venture to stay and dine with them, which he did, and was very merry amongst them.

Another welcome distraction came in the portly frame of Hopton's thirty-five-year-old chaplain, Thomas Fuller. 'The great Tom Fuller', as Samuel Pepys would call him, was the minister of the Savoy Chapel in London, the author of a history of the crusades, a 'biographist' (his word) and a man with a remarkable memory. His party trick was to recite all the shop and tavern signs from Temple Bar to Cheapside Conduit, on both sides of the road, forwards and backwards. 'He was a perfect walking library,' his biographer recalled.[16] Fuller was a big man, round and ruddy. 'They say that he looks like a butcher,' sneered an enemy. His hair was fair and curly and his disregard for clothes bordered on contempt: 'it was with some trouble to himself to be either neat or decent'. He fizzed with curiosity and overflowed with pithy apothegms. 'They that marry where they do not love,' for instance, 'will love where they do not marry.'[17]

Fuller disapproved of sectarianism and favoured moderation, which he described as 'a mixture of discretion and charity in one's judgment'. On the subject of Christmas, for example, he suggested that adults should observe the fast, but allow the young 'their toys and Christmas sports'. Like Rawdon and some of his officers, he had campaigned for peace. 'War makes a land more wicked,' he had preached in December 1642, 'makes a land more woeful, is bad in itself, is worse in its train, destroys Christian people.' He knew that moderates were 'commonly crushed betwixt the extreme parties on both sides', but he had kept his mind open and his manner mild, staying on in London when the others had gone to the wars.[18] In the wake of the royalist plot to retake the City – the one that had involved Rawdon and his son-in-law – a hawkish new loyalty oath had been introduced in the summer of 1643. Fuller could not take it without reservation. Then tragedy struck. On 21 August, he christened his baby girl Ellinor; the next day, he buried her. On 26 August, he buried his wife. Personally and publicly devastated, he left for Oxford.[19]

Like many reluctant royalists, Fuller was critical of his own side, which he blamed in no small part for the war. He believed that a monarch should be checked and balanced by an active Parliament in order to safeguard the ancient constitution and the liberties of the people. The roots of the conflict, he thought, lay in 'the church history of Britain', particularly the recent authoritarianism of Archbishop Laud, who had used 'more vinegar than oil' in dealing with nonconformists (Fuller disliked the pejorative term 'Puritan'). In Fuller's opinion, Laud was guilty of 'over-meddling in state matters' and overshooting himself in Scotland. The reaction from Parliament and the public was understandable, therefore, if ultimately out of control.[20] In the end, though, Fuller sensed that the greater threat came from Parliament, with its unlawful ordinances, arbitrary taxation and radical drive to dismantle the Mother Church. Whatever her flaws, he argued, the Church was a pillar of the commonwealth: 'my hoary hairs will go down to the grave in sorrow for her sufferings'.[21]

Fuller had arrived in Oxford in September 1643, just after Rawdon's regiment had moved out to Basing House. He had stayed at Lincoln College, 'where seventeen weeks cost me more than seventeen years in Cambridge'.[22] Then he had joined Hopton's army as a chaplain and concentrated, he quipped, not so much on studying history as not becoming a history. But he never stopped his scholarly pursuits. 'With the progress of the war,' wrote his biographer, 'he marched from place to place, and wherever there happened for the better accommodation of the army any reasonable stay, he allotted it with great satisfaction to his beloved studies.' He talked to every 'superannuated' person, patiently listening to their peeves and 'circular rambles' until he found gold in the pan.

After the battle of Cheriton, he clattered into Basing House with the rest of Hopton's sunken army and stayed for over a month. He was working on a big new book. The 'horror and rigidness of the war' could not 'stiffen him in such a stupidity which generally possessed all learned men', gushed his biographer, but he was sorely tested at Basing, where Sir William Waller 'came to besiege the doctor's sanctuary', albeit briefly, in May. This was the culmination of a miserable month for the garrison, with the parliamentarians pressing in from Odiham, Greywell and Basingstoke, and 'harrowing the country about'.[23] Fuller was undaunted by the Roundhead presence, we are told, but 'the noise of the cannon playing from the enemy's leaguer interrupted the prosecution of digesting his notes'. He got his own back, apparently, with motivational sermons inspiring the defendants to sally out, 'suffering the besiegers scarce to eat or sleep'. Once Waller's forces had marched away, Fuller returned to his notes.[24]

The book he was working on would be known to later generations as *Fuller's Worthies*. It was the first dictionary of English biography, and because of the way he structured it, situating his subjects within their counties and alongside their 'native commodities and rarities', it was a landscape as well as a portrait. Fuller wrote about Cornish tin mines and Sussex foundries, Kent cherries and Cheshire cheese. He worried about the state of the cloth trade and competition from abroad. He digressed on the moles in Hampshire ('malignant pioneers, mischievous to grass, more to grain, most to gardens'), and the small dogs from Portsmouth that hunted them.[25] He burrowed deep through the strata of memory, sniffing out local stories and proverbs, such as 'England is the paradise of women, hell of horses, purgatory of servants'. Or: 'From Hell, Hull, and Halifax deliver us' (this was in reference to Yorkshire's treatment of its vagrants; 'they least fear the first', he wrote).[26]

Fuller's Hampshire was 'a happy country' with good firewood, fertile ground, piercing air and 'troutful water'. It was known for red deer, honey and the hogs that nibbled on New Forest acorns and were universally acknowledged to provide the best bacon. In a section on 'the wonders' of the county, Fuller wrote of an oak tree near Lyndhurst that reportedly grew green leaves every Christmas. 'I could point more exactly at the position thereof,' he wrote, 'but am loath to direct some ignorant zealot, lest he cut it down under the notion of superstition, and make timber of this oak, as some lately have made fuel of the hawthorn at Glassenburie.'*

---

* The Christmas-flowering 'holy thorn' at Glastonbury was associated with the legend of Joseph of Arimathea and the early Christians. It survived the dissolution of the Abbey, but was cut down and burned by a Roundhead soldier in the civil war. When Wenceslaus Hollar engraved Glastonbury after the war, he put the holy hawthorn back in the picture. One descendant from a rescued cutting grows in the Abbey grounds today and another is in the nearby church of St John. The queen receives a sprig every Christmas.

Of Hampshire's buildings, Fuller thought that Winchester Cathedral 'yieldeth to none in England for venerable magnificence'. As for civil structures, 'Basing, built by the first Marquess of Winchester, was the greatest of any subject's house in England, yea larger than most – (eagles have not the biggest nests of all birds) – of the king's palaces. The motto *Love Loyaltie* was often written in every window thereof, and was well practised in it.'[27] According to his biographer, Fuller regarded Basing House as 'the chiefest fabric in Hampshire' and his fondness for 'the place of his refuge' was due to 'some more peculiar obliging regards and respects [that] he found during his abode there'.[28]

The men – and a few women – who illuminated Fuller's counties were warriors, statesmen and prelates, naturally, but also unlikely heroes – lawyers, librarians, musicians, inventors, the founders of free schools and almshouses, the builders of bridges and conduits, 'memorable persons' who were simply exceptional ('this last topic is like a public inn, admitting all comers') and 'all such mechanics who in any manual trade have reached a clear note above others'.[29] He wrote about James Yorke, a Lincolnshire blacksmith whose horseshoes were so thin and light that 'if Pegasus himself would wear shoes, this man alone is fit to make them'. He introduces us to Edward Bone, a deaf mute from Cornwall who taught himself how to lip-read and sign. And to Thomas James, the first librarian of the Bodleian in Oxford: 'Some men live like moths in libraries . . . not so Dr James, who made use of books for his own and the public good.' Fuller included Joan Tuckvile, who made sure that hanged criminals were decently buried in Exeter, and Thomas Johnson, a doctor born 'not far from Hull', who was 'bred an apothecary in London, where he attained to be the best herbalist of his age in England'.

Johnson, Fuller continues, was 'a man of such modesty that, knowing so much, he would own the knowledge of nothing'. Oxford gave him an honorary doctorate and his loyalty adhered him to the king. 'When, in Basing House, a dangerous piece of service was to be done, this doctor (who publicly pretended not to valour) understood and performed it.'[30]

Another personality for Thomas Fuller to observe at Basing House was Inigo Jones, the Surveyor of the King's Works and architect of the Banqueting House at Whitehall. He was now in his eighth decade. He had been thirty at the death of Elizabeth I. One imagines that he would have been given the best room and the finest wine at Basing House, but for a 'Dominus Do-All' and 'Marquis Would-Be', as Ben Jonson had called him, it can't have been easy.[31]

Jones was an extraordinary, avant-garde talent, a designer of costumes, stage sets and controversial buildings like St Paul's, Covent Garden, which was the first church built on a new site since the Reformation and looked like a Roman temple. The times, though, had turned against him. No longer a rule-breaker from Smithfield, but a regulator at the heart of the establishment, he was seen as a propper-upper of the queen's Catholicism and the man who had turned the king's exalted sense of majesty into an intoxicating imperial aesthetic.[32]

When the war began, the works stopped. The Catholic chapel that Jones had built for Henrietta Maria at Somerset House was violently attacked and the art inside desecrated. A statue of the Virgin and Child was toppled, their smooth faces stamped on by soldiers. An altarpiece of the Crucifixion by Rubens was hoiked off the wall, ripped up and dumped in the Thames.[33] Jones was derided in the press as the 'Contriver of Scenes for the Queen's Dancing Barn' and the 'great enemy to St Gregory'.[34] The latter was a reference to his destruction of the church adjoining St Paul's Cathedral during his refurbishment work there. The Long Parliament had impeached him for it.

We know frustratingly little about Jones's time at Basing House. We don't know how or when he arrived, though he probably came from Oxford, where William Dobson had painted him with a white beard and haunted eyes (see plates). Like so many survivors of wartime trauma, he never spoke, at least on extant record, about his experience: better nothing than bland platitude. He was 'a very aged, infirm man' at this stage, troubled by kidney stones and 'scarce able to walk abroad'.[35] His house had been 'spoiled' and he had no immediate family.

One newsbook claimed that Jones had gone to Basing House to secure his treasure, another that he was brought in to help with the defences. Both claims are plausible and compatible. He had some experience of fortifications, having reinforced the Tower of London in the 1630s.[36] He had also seen the impact of gunpowder on the European landscape. During the so-called 'military revolution' of the sixteenth and seventeenth centuries, stone castles and high towers had been replaced with thick, squat walls and star-shaped forts. These enabled defenders to protect their flanks against the increasingly powerful artillery of the Iron Century.[37] Jones had travelled extensively in Italy, where the starry *trace italienne* forts were pioneered, and also through the Netherlands, where the siege defences were state-of-the-art. He owned several books on the subject and had scribbled in the margins of a few of them. In Gabriello Busca's *L'Architettura Militare*, he had highlighted a passage on hill-site defences. He also had his mathematical instruments with him, 'and other things of that nature belonging to my profession'.[38]

Since the words genius and engine share the same root (*gignere*: to beget), it is hardly surprising that art and engineering elide, but the lines were never so blurred as they were in the early modern period, when war was a constant cloud. Michelangelo had been in charge of Florence's fortifications in 1529, while Leonardo da Vinci's ten-point CV to Ludovico Sforza of Milan was basically a manifesto on how he could help him win his wars. He could advise on bridge design, he wrote, or secret passages, prototype tanks, cannon, catapults, granadoes and 'other engines of wonderful efficacy'. Only his tenth and final point mentioned that, by the way, he could also sculpt and paint.[39]

The skills required to erect a bastioned defensive scheme – a mastery of geometry and mathematics, a sense of perspective and proportion, an ability to draw to scale and handle materials, equipment and a workforce – were the transferrable skills of the architect. 'This art of military architecture,' lectured Jones's rival Balthazar Gerbier, is 'properly termed architecture, by reason that it serves for a rule to the building of forts, castles and towns, though their besiegers batter and ruin them faster than they were first erected by the same art.'[40] Basing's defences were well within Jones's remit, therefore, and he certainly would have been ruthless enough to insist on the clearance of properties that impeded his vision.

The works could only progress 'as time and number would permit', though, and were 'rather strong than regular', according to the anonymous siege diarist. Soldiers were not keen on digging, and Basing's clay subsoil would have been hard work, if also its greatest asset. Clay was the best material for fortifications, argued Gerbier, 'because it is maniable, groweth hard, and needs no great slope'. It didn't require a thick facing, either, and could be mixed with wood, rendering it, in Gerbier's opinion, 'a grave to cannon balls'. Basing's bastions withstood many poundings, and although some would fall to the cutting of Basingstoke Canal at the end of the eighteenth century, a few have weathered every change of season and coat so that they are still visible on the ground and magnificent from the air.[41]

As his surviving sketchbooks show, Jones 'the great ingeneere' was an outstanding draughtsman.[42] He was also a connoisseur. One of the most vivid stories about him (and indeed about Charles I) comes from the papal envoy Gregorio Panzani, who told of the pair's excitement over a shipment of paintings from Rome. 'As soon as the king heard of their arrival,' wrote Panzani, 'he rushed to see them', calling Jones to his side. 'The very moment Jones saw the pictures, he greatly approved of them and, in order to be able to study them better, threw off his coat, put on his eyeglasses, took a candle and, together with the king, began to examine them very closely, admiring them very much.' According to Panzani, the *'vanissimo'* Jones bragged a few days later that when Charles had playfully removed the labels from each painting, he had managed to get nearly all of the attributions right.[43]

There were no Italian masters at Basing House, but it bristled with talent. There was Isaac Rowlett the scrivener, who could write exquisitely – an appreciated skill at the time. There was Johnson the apothecary, who sketched his plants, and Robert Peake, who was better at selling art than making it, but could engrave for the Goldsmiths and turn a paintbrush well enough. And there was William Faithorne, who turned out to be the best of the lot, and might well have prompted Jones to fetch his eyeglasses and candle.

One particular story involving Faithorne shows what we might have lost. He was in a tavern with some hard-drinking artist friends, including the corpulent Francis Le Piper, who picked up a piece of coal and ran up a quick portrait on his wooden trencher plate. He passed it to Faithorne, 'who touched upon it'. 'In the meantime, Mr Le Piper drew another on another trencher, and exchanged it with Mr Faithorne for that which he had touched. They did thus ten times and between them wrought up the heads to such a height of force that nothing could be better done in the kind.'[44]

The thought of Faithorne and Inigo Jones doing something similar at Basing House, perhaps even collaborating on a gallery of garrison-ers, is tantalising. So too is the 'box of brass graven plates' that we know Robert Peake had with him in the house.[45] In reality, though, no good art has survived of the siege. There is no Faithorne, no Jones, not even a Johnson sketch of a Loddon lily that can take us there.

There is only one surviving picture of the house as it stood at the time (see plates and endpapers). It is sometimes attributed to the Bohe-mian etcher Wenceslaus Hollar, but it is not his style and he is unlikely to have been there.[46] Indeed, it is some kind of Puritan irony that the only drawings that did survive the siege were scrawls on cellar walls made by parliamentarian prisoners of war. During excavation work on the Old House at the turn of the twentieth century, rough charcoal sketches were found of civil war soldiers, ships, a head with a pointy beard and a man on a gibbet. The prison graffiti, as it was assumed to be (it was too high up to have been drawn by a child), was covered by a temporary lean-to roof. In April 1908, a freak snowstorm hit the south of England and heavy drifts banked the cellar walls. When the snow melted, the pictures were gone.[47]

The archaeology of Basing House compensates, to some extent, for the loss of art. There have been some intriguing finds over the years, including a Yoruba ivory cup from Owo, West Africa, discovered in a nearby field; and on the site itself, drinking glasses from Venice, apoth-ecary jars from Delft, and fragments of a Chinese porcelain bowl decorated with lines from an eleventh-century poem on the battle of Red Cliffs. This work by Su Shi observes the eternal dance between man and nature, in this case on a stretch of the Yangtze downstream of Wuhan:

> The Great River flows east
> Washing away
> A thousand ages of great men.
> West of the ramparts –
> People say –
> Are the fabled Red Cliffs of young Zhou of the Three Kingdoms.
> Rebellious rocks pierce the sky

Frightening waves rip the bank
The backwash churns vast snowy swells –
River and mountains like a painting
How many heroes passed them, once . . .

Think back to those years, Zhou Yu –
Just married to the younger Qiao –
Brave, brilliant
With plumed fan, silk kerchief
Laughing and talking
While masts and oars vanished to flying ash and smoke.
I roam through ancient realms
Absurdly moved
Turning grey too soon –
A man's life passes like a dream –
Pour out a cup, then, to the river and the moon.[48]

Also roused from Basing's underworld were flagons, bottle stoppers, musket rests and bandolier caps. There is a lead bird-feeder marked with Winchester's arms and a flowerpot stamped with his crest. There are shards of glass painted with lettering, possibly the family motto. There are keys and coins, teeth and nails, buckles, bells and oyster shells. There is a chamber pot and the leather sole of a child's right shoe. There are iron shackles and a copper alloy syringe. There are tiles depicting hunting scenes and a brick indented with the pawprint of a large dog. There are scissors, thimbles and combs. There are clay tobacco pipes, including a gauntlet pipe from Wiltshire, which, Fuller informs us, was the best type.[49] There is shot, great and small, in iron, lead and stone. There are granado shells and two bullets fused together. There is the severed skull of a young man with a broad face, narrow nose and prominent brow. (We can tell that he suffered from anaemia and toothache.) And there are the busted-up stone heads of ancient worthies, who watched it all, agape, from Basing's proud towers.[50]

Thomas Fuller's new *Worthies*, part-written in the house, was his attempt to preserve the nation's memory and to do so carefully, through keen observation and diligent research. He feared that 'the pamphlets of this age may pass for records with the next' and that 'what we laugh at, our children may believe'.[51] Old archives were being destroyed. Soldiers were using ancient manuscripts to scour their guns and were stabling their horses in the churches. Monuments were desecrated and registers lost. The civil war created an urgency – manifested, too, in the work of antiquaries like John Aubrey – to pick up the pieces of the past and reassemble them before they ran up 'like paper in the fire'.[52]

When Sir William Waller's men had ridden into Winchester Cathedral in December 1642, they had shot at the statues of James and Charles on the Inigo Jones choir screen and broken up the mortuary chests of their Saxon forebears (allegedly using the bones to smash the windows).*[53] Moving on to the muniment room, they scattered all the books and papers. When they were gone, the chapter clerk, John Chase, devotedly reorganised them. Four years later, more Roundheads came, 'and all my ledger register books [were] taken away', lamented Chase, 'the records, charters, deeds, writings and muniments lost, the foundation of the church cancelled, the common seal taken away and diverse of the writings and charters burned, diverse thrown into the river, diverse large parchments they made kites withal to fly in the air'.[54]

Chase and his colleagues could be seen afterwards trying to catch the kites and retrieve the wet manuscripts from the river. Four years later, a butcher found one on Winchester High Street, 'all soiled'.[55]

Thomas Fuller lamented the desecration of Winchester Cathedral. He couldn't understand how soldiers could behave so 'barbarously' towards innocent tombs. 'Why malice should scratch out that which did not bite it is to me unknown.'[56] His book of *Worthies*, forged under fire at Basing House, was a salvage effort, his attempt to reclaim the land that he loved and return colour to memories blanched by trauma.

---

* The Roundheads took away the bronze statues of James and Charles. A Hampshire man called Benjamin Newland paid £125 for the pair and buried them in his garden in the Isle of Wight. Two decades later, when it was safe, they were unearthed and returned to the cathedral. They can be seen today inside the west door. There are holes in the statue of Charles from musket balls, and conservators have found soil in the cavity.

It is a testament to deep roots and superannuated guardians – to the strength of the landscape and the poetry of history to catch a memory, a moment, a *genius*, and keep it alive: 'Pour out a cup, then, to the river and the moon.'

12

Dog, Cat or Rat

The plan was to march to Odiham, 'a pretty market town', and burn it to the ground. It would be a pre-emptive strike to prevent the place from becoming a permanent enemy outpost. It would happen at night. The soldiers would follow two local guides carrying a dim lantern. They would get an extra week's wage and 'all the plunder of the town'. They would give no quarter to any Roundheads there, 'but put all to the sword'. It was ruthless. They were desperate. The password was 'Honour'.[1]

All the horse and most of the foot left Basing House at 11 p.m. on Saturday 1 June 1644. Only the soldiers on the watch and those too sick to march stayed behind with the civilians. The Marquess of Winchester rode some of the way with them before giving each man five shillings and heading back. The garrison couldn't afford to lose any more key men. One of their most popular officers, Captain William Rosewell, had been captured in May with a dozen riders collecting contribution money. An apothecary, like Thomas Johnson, he had lived by the bells of Old Bailey and campaigned for peace alongside Marmaduke Rawdon. He was taken to Farnham Castle, where, if *Mercurius Aulicus* is to be believed, he was thrown into 'so noisome a hole (the rebels made it so) as tis not conceivable how a man should breathe in it above two hours'. His treatment was especially harsh, thought *Aulicus*, 'because he belonged to the garrison of Basing'.[2]

The war was becoming ever more cruel. Four days before the strike on Odiham, Prince Rupert, riled by the hanging of one of his 'Irish papist' soldiers, had ruthlessly sacked the town of Bolton, near Manchester. 'Long wars,' observed the author of *The Anatomy of Warre*, 'make men inhumane . . . that is, at first sin seems to us loathing, but often sinning makes sin seem nothing . . . where before [a man] ever truly entered into the wars, he thought he could never be so cruel as to dash the children's brains against the stones . . . but afterwards, when he was inured with war, he did it.'³ The royalists of Basing House were becoming 'inured with war' too. Parliamentarian prisoners claimed that they were being treated 'barbarously' and had been 'stripped naked to their very shirts from their backs'.⁴

Odiham was about six miles from Basing House. The eighty horse and two hundred foot marching in the moonlight along uneven lanes made slow progress. At about two in the morning, they came to Warnborough Mill, a mile outside the town. A sentry guard sounded the alarm. Soon the rest of the parliamentarian watch came out and there was a skirmish before the royalists forced their way through. Then, out of the darkness, a wave of horse crashed upon them. It was Colonel Richard Norton's troopers. The royalists had been ambushed.

It may have been at this moment that the bit of Rawdon's horse snapped in half. He was mounted upon 'an unruly stone horse' (uncastrated) and completely lost control. Quick-thinking Henry Henn, who was riding 'a lusty mare', spurred her ahead. Rawdon's stallion, seeing the mare, gave chase 'and so they both escaped out of the danger'. Luckily for Rawdon, Henn knew a thing or two about horses, having been sergeant of the king's carriage horse before the war.⁵

When Rawdon returned to Basing House, he took stock of the situation. It was a catastrophe. Three gentlemen of arms, three sergeants, three drummers, one quartermaster and seventy-five common soldiers had been captured. Some were parliamentarian deserters and were 'likely to receive their just reward', according to a Roundhead pamphlet.

One hundred arms and several horses had been seized. Four men were dead on the ground and many more were wounded, 'some very dangerously'. The marquess's surgeon had been forced to surrender, as had his ensign, Roger Coram, a Catholic from Winchester. The Rowlett brothers were both taken. So was Lieutenant Amery, son of Captain Robert Amery the vintner, and Ensign Nathaniel Lucas, a silk dyer from the Old Bailey.⁶

The highest-ranking royalist prisoner was Major Thomas Langley, the mercer of Paternoster Row who had been one of the first to garrison Basing House for the king. Before the war, he had campaigned vociferously for peace with Rawdon and Rosewell. He was soon back at Basing, though. He had been dressed so shabbily, 'more like a tinker than a gentleman', that the Roundheads had let him go. That was the story, in any case, although one London newsbook claimed that Langley had actually escaped. Some inside Basing House began to wonder if he could be trusted. Someone, after all, had leaked the plan to the enemy.

Colonel Norton sent his prisoners to Southampton, then London. The distress of their families can be imagined. Some, like the Amerys, were inside Basing House. They knew about the sufferings of poor Captain Rosewell, chained in the hole at Farnham. To add insult to injury, ten of the seventeen inmates in the garrison's own jail had escaped while the soldiers were out on the raid. They had torn up a hop bag in their cell, knotted the strips together and lowered themselves down from a window. 'This is such a shake to the garrison,' crowed the Roundheads, 'that it is believed there are scarce so many more in Basing House to keep [it].'

At about four o'clock on Sunday 2 June, Colonel Norton appeared before the house with his troopers. Some were on their new prize mounts. Their trumpets tooted a challenge, followed by two or three taunting levets. The house was silent. 'By this time,' reported a London pamphlet on 5 June, 'if the Surrey and Sussex forces be come up to Colonel Norton, Basing is besieged.'

Richard Norton was not yet thirty when he received the order to lay siege to Basing House. He had failed to take it the previous summer, but otherwise he had had a successful war as governor of Southampton and at the battle of Cheriton in March, when his knowledge of the terrain had helped steer Sir William Waller to victory. He came from a wealthy Puritan family and was respected by his men, who were paid more regularly than most units. His mother, 'the zealous Lady Norton', was a trenchant parliamentarian who had helped dig the defences at Portsmouth. His younger brother Edward was a royalist. Norton's friend Oliver Cromwell would later call him Idle Dick, which was an affectionate dig at his provincialism; Cromwell always hoped he would do more on the national stage. In Hampshire, though, Dick was anything but idle, and he had unfinished business with Basing House.[7]

'This house,' wrote one of his men, 'hath not only been a great annoyance to all the country round about it, but hath been a means to stop the trading out of the west to London by robbing and pillaging the carriers and clothiers.'[8] As both a parliamentarian colonel and sheriff of Hampshire, Norton relished the prospect of taking out Winchester's seat.

He returned on 4 June with a regiment of horse and dragoons. He posted patrols on the lanes and set up camp in Basingstoke. A week later, the deer park became a sea of red, white and blue as Colonel Herbert Morley arrived with six blue colours from Sussex, Colonel Richard Onslow with five companies of red from Surrey, and Colonel Jones with two companies of white from Farnham. Norton also secured three fresh troops of horse. His force totalled around two thousand men and was quartered in the nearby villages. There were several skirmishes with the garrison over the first few weeks. 'We hear that they want men in the house and that there is not above two hundred in it,' read a report from Basingstoke on 15 June.[9] 'No relief can pass unto them,' added another, and 'they want a mill to grind their corn, being in a great strait likewise for salt and other necessaries'.[10]

On 17 June, the parliamentarians moved into Basing village and took over the church where the past marquesses were buried. Each side accused the other of desecrating the building and stripping lead from the roof for bullets. According to *Aulicus*, the Roundheads imprisoned captured royalists in a vault, 'where there's no light, nor anything else, but souls of dead men and rotten bones underground'. The prisoners were allegedly given just enough bread and water to make them 'sensible of their misery'.[11]

On 19 June, smoke was in the wind as the garrison torched all the buildings between the house and the church. The air rang with bells and shot. 'Continual firing,' noted the anonymous Siege Diary. One sentry was killed that day, another hurt.[12]

The garrison was spread so thin that it resorted to rotating watches, as on a ship. The house was divided into four, and within each quarter, two watches assumed guard duty while a third rested. Major Cuffaud, a local Catholic gentleman and one of Winchester's most trusted men, assumed responsibility for the southern works overlooking the park. Major Langley oversaw the gardens and the western approach from Basingstoke. Lieutenant Colonel Johnson took care once again of the Grange, the river and the threat from Cowdery's Down, while Colonel Rawdon protected the New House from the village in the east. The artillery was entrusted to Lieutenant Colonel Peake, whose company served as a reserve for 'all places as any need required'. Necessity also demanded that the troopers swap their pistols for muskets. Cuffaud, Langley, Johnson and Peake took their turn as captain of the watch. Sixty-one-year-old Rawdon was excused 'by reason of his years'.

On 24 June, Norton's forces were augmented by two more companies and they edged ever closer to the house. They camped in the village, the park and the west lane, 'shutting us up on three sides'. On the fourth side, where there was river and marshland, the parliamentarian horse camped further afield, upon Cowdery's Down. Thomas Johnson kept his sharp botanist's eye on them. At night, the parliamentarians were busy with pickaxe and spade, digging trenches, batteries and a sconce in the park. 'Three of ours run to them,' the diarist noted that day.

On 28 June, there was good news at last for the garrison as Norton was called out to reinforce Sir William Waller. The Earl of Essex had not stuck with Waller as planned after the battle of Cheriton. Instead, he had marched south-west to raise the siege of Lyme Regis and flush the royalists out of their heartlands. Waller continued to shadow the king in Oxfordshire. Norton took five troops with him, but was too late to prevent Waller's loss to Charles at Cropredy Bridge the following day. They heard the news in Basing House that night when a fearless messenger, Edward Jeffrey, slipped through enemy lines. They celebrated with volleys of shot, but the besiegers replied with a demi-culverin that threw nine-pound balls at the kitchen and great gatehouse.

Over the next few weeks, whispers of a terrible royalist defeat began to filter down from Yorkshire. With hindsight it is clear that Marston Moor on 2 July 1644 was the greatest battle of the first civil war. It won the north for Parliament and Oliver Cromwell his 'Ironside' reputation. In the 'fire, smoke and confusion' of the day, however, there was a great deal of misreporting, and it was not immediately clear which side was winning. The royalist Arthur Trevor encountered runaways from both sides – 'so many, so breathless, so speechless and so full of fears that I should not have taken them for men'. Coasting the county afterwards, he heard 'a shoal of Scots crying out *Weys us, we are all undone* . . . as if their day of doom had overtaken them'. Soon afterwards, he met with 'a ragged troop reduced to four and a cornet; by and by with a little foot officer without hat, band, sword or indeed anything but feet and so much tongue as would serve to enquire the way to the next garrisons'.[13] One such straggler, Tamworth Reresby, would make it down to Basing House.

On 3 July, the siege lines were drawn to within half a musket shot of the house. 'Continual firing,' recorded the diarist, 'pouring lead into the garrison, they spoil us two or three a day, passing within our works, and shoot the marquess himself through his clothes.' The following day the garrison had to dump 'stinking beer' over the walls. A letter sent by a Roundhead to London on the 5th reported that the Cavaliers were in serious trouble. 'Since our throwing up a trench against them, the enemy are very still . . . We hope they cannot long hold out.'[14]

On 8 July, the besiegers tried to lure the garrison out by pretending to leave an artillery piece unguarded. It didn't work. Instead, a captured Cavalier sprinted back into the house 'under the hazard of 100 shot'. The Roundheads were so 'chafed' by his escape that they bombarded the house for the rest of the night.

With reinforcements arriving on 11 July, Norton's deputy, Colonel Morley, sent a message to Winchester:

My Lord,
    To avoid the effusion of Christian blood, I have thought fit to send your lordship this summons to demand Basing House to be delivered to me for the use of king and Parliament. If this be refused, the ensuing inconveniences will rest upon your self. I desire your speedy answer and rest, my Lord,
    Your humble servant,
    Herbert Morley

The marquess, 'upon small deliberation', replied:

Sir,
    It is a crooked demand and shall receive its answer suitable: I keep the house in the right of my sovereign and will do it in despite of your forces. Your letter I will preserve as a testimony of your rebellion.
    Winchester

Over the next few days, 'horrible Herbert Morley' (as he was called by *Aulicus*)[15] took out his anger on the garrison's waterhouse. On 20 July, Norton was back with two mortar pieces. These squat iron toads croaked deadly fireworks – the dreaded granadoes – up into the sky and down onto the house. The exploding iron shells shredded nerves as well as flesh and were terrible for morale.

On 22 July, the parliamentarians completed the construction of their fort in the park and started throwing eighteen-pound culverin balls at the house. The marquess was hurt by one. Two men were killed by another. The following night, 'being dark and stormy', eight prisoners escaped from the garrison. 'At night, more granadoes,' recorded the Siege Diary. On the 26th, six more granadoes. 'One, falling in our granary, spoiled some corn.' That night, 'two soldiers run to them'.

On the last day of the month, which marked a year since Basing House had been garrisoned, the besiegers ran a communications trench from the church to their gun platform near the park. More granadoes were launched, and one set fire to the hay in the barn, but 'our diligence soon quenched it'.

And so it went on throughout the sweltering summer. The besiegers continued to throw up works and batter the house, experimenting with new missiles like crossbars (logs bound with iron hoops) and fireballs (flaming pitch balls that could only be put out with wet animal skins). The besieged – like the royalists in the wider war – continued to shore up crumbling defences and punish lapses of concentration on the lines. It was certainly no picnic for the besiegers, who slept in makeshift huts and lay in trenches during the day. On 25 July, rain forced the men out of their trenches to within range of the garrison, and 'our marksmen spoiled diverse'. One of Colonel Morley's captains was shot dead on 20 July. Three weeks later, Morley himself was 'bored through the shoulder' while viewing the works in the park.[16]

Inside the house, they continued to wonder if they were to be stormed or starved. Their bellies and their children told them the latter. Their ears resounded to the former tune. Every night, thirty-six-pound stone balls hailed down on them. These and the explosive granado shells 'seemed troublesome' for a while, noted the diarist – perhaps with an eye to an Oxford publication – but were soon 'so familiar to the soldier that they were called, as they counted them, baubles'. The London press, on the other hand, suspected that the garrison was on the verge of surrender, or mutiny.

On 4 August, 'perceiving the intention of the rebels rather to starve than storm us', the garrison launched some wild sallies on the enemy lines. Cornet Bryan, Major Cuffaud, his son Lieutenant Cuffaud and Lieutenant John Snow were the mavericks of these lightning raids. They rode 'at rate' at the parliamentarians, spiking their guns, torching their gabion baskets and taking away arms and horses. 'These sallies were so much unto their loss', the Siege Diary gloated, 'and touched so near their honour' that the parliamentarian captain of the guard was court-martialled for neglect, cowardice and suspected communications with the garrison. On 14 August, though, the royalists overreached themselves with an assault upon Cowdery's Down. Ensign Amery was killed and Cornet Bryan was taken. Such was Bryan's value that the Roundheads refused the offer of a lieutenant and a corporal in exchange.

The siege diarist took a moment at the beginning of August to hail the esprit de corps in the garrison. He pointed out that the gentlemen and troopers were now working twenty-four-hour shifts alongside the foot soldiers and putting hand to musket and spade. The London press, on the other hand, stressed the defenders' dwindling morale. Many were 'weary of the fort', The Weekly Account claimed on 3 August. 'There is some division amongst them,' it added three days later. The Parliament Scout painted the rift along religious lines, with the Protestants apparently urging the marquess to accept terms and his Catholic co-religionists insisting on no surrender. On 17 August, some of the royalists taken at Cowdery's Down admitted to their captors that the garrison was under intense pressure from Oxford to hold out. The defenders apparently considered their situation so desperate that even if they were able to escape, 'they knew not how to live, nor where, most of them being broken citizens and notorious papists'.[17]

Alongside this constant tension stalked the grim reapers of smallpox and hunger. Smallpox was a viral disease perfectly incubated in the cramped, insanitary conditions of a wet summer siege. It began with a fever, before telltale pustules appeared all over the body and face. As Honora Winchester had discovered when she had been afflicted as a girl, there were all sorts of quack remedies for the disease, and 'women's medicines for her face', but there was no cure, and about a third of all cases were fatal.[18] The 'reigning of the pox', in the diarist's phrase, tyrannised Basing House and executed more of its residents than flying metal and stone. Those lucky enough to survive it had a long road to recovery. The infected were put in a separate part of the house, but on 20 July, two eighteen-pound culverin balls 'passed through the quarters where our sick men lay'.

Nowhere was safe, as the Marquess of Winchester discovered when a cannonball careered through his private quarters. 'He was so stricken with fear,' alleged *The Weekly Account* on 23 August, 'that he leapt out of his bed and ran into another room without his breeches, crying that he wondered how the devil the Roundheads could find him out for he thought he had been safe in his bed.'[19] Four days later, the Committee of Both Kingdoms in London sent another 400 rounds of culverin shot and 150 demi-cannon balls to the besiegers.[20]

Feeding around 200 combatants and 140 'useless mouths' was an almost impossible task. Staples like flour and corn were scarce. The garrison quickly ran out of salt, an essential preservative in the summer. The meat was rancid and many people reportedly died of food poisoning. The well survived its bombardment, but there was 'only puddly and bad water to drink'.[21] Fresh produce could not come in from outside and the royalists largely survived on peas and oats, 'our stock of wheat being spent'.

The horses were suffering too, their ribcages peeping through parchment hides. The troopers had to sneak up to the river at night and cut grass for them on the meads. They put up an earthwork to protect themselves from the guns on Cowdery's Down, but the firing was 'too hot' and they didn't have the numbers to keep it. By the beginning of September, the Roundheads had brought their line forward and cut off the garrison's only source of fodder. According to the Rawdon family history, the hunger was so pinching that the marquess, 'seeing little hope of relief', seriously considered surrendering. 'My Lord,' Sir Marmaduke replied, 'you have in the house good store of sack [wine], and you have good store of good tobacco. I pray let me have some of it for my soldiers and you may be confident [that], with the grace of God, as long as there is ever a horse in the house, dog, cat or rat, or anything that is eatable, I will never deliver up the garrison.'[22]

Even allowing for two decades' retelling, this anecdote gives a sense of their desperation. The Siege Diary, on the other hand, betrays little emotion. The writer's identity is a mystery, though their military, political and biblical knowledge suggests an officer or chaplain. The dead and the maimed are coolly counted. The breached towers and broken guns are carefully inventoried. Each false alarm is recorded, every desertion listed: 'three of ours run to them' (24 June); 'at night two soldiers run to them' (26 July); 'this night three run to them, and one the night before' (17 August).

On 22 August, arrows were shot into the house with notes attached, 'persuading mutinies and labouring divisions twixt the regiments'. This at last produced a flicker of emotion in the diarist. He fulminated against the 'baseness' of those who resorted to trickery. Some 'faint-hearted knaves' took the bait, he wrote. Three nights later, two more men deserted. The following night, an additional four, 'enforcing us to seasonable justice in executing one who had attempted to have gone with them'. The body on the gibbet kept the soldiers fixed to the garrison for a while afterwards, 'though our necessities grew fast on us'.

But what was it like? What was it like to sweat and shake with fever in this faction-riven garrison? What was it like to have tasteless rations halved and halved again? What was it like for Mary Amery, the vintner's wife, to have a husband in the garrison, a son in a Roundhead prison and another just killed in the sally on Cowdery's Down? What was it like for the children – the hungry, bored, snotty, lice-infested, irritating, heartbreaking children? How did the garrison keep clean? How did they stay sane? Did they hold fast to past certitudes? Did they remain civilised?

These are the hardest questions and we don't know the answers. Most got on with it and never recorded a word. Those who did write about their experiences gave operational details or jolly tales lacquered in a stoic gloss. Fortitude was privileged over trauma. In 1646, though, a strange little book appeared called *Meditations upon a Seige* [sic]. It was written by a London-born clergyman and chaplain of the king called Humfrey Peake. He was dead when the book came out, having 'sacrificed both himself and his family' in the royalist cause. His widow, Mary, spent the rest of her life petitioning the dean of Canterbury Cathedral, where Peake had been a prebendary, for charity.[23] His book was quickly forgotten and is barely remembered today.[24]

Peake had been in hot water before the war for venting his spleen at a dinner party in Kent. His 'base and scandalous' words about the radicals in London had been leaked by his curate and published in a pamphlet. He was denounced as a 'hollow-hearted, evil-thoughted' clergyman, 'engrafted' to the tree of Canterbury.[25] The following year, on 9 November 1642, the Long Parliament labelled him a delinquent and summoned him to London to explain a 'seditious sermon' preached on Bonfire Night. A week later, he was impeached.[26] At some point, he had escaped to Oxford, where other loyalist clergymen congregated. One of them was Matthew Griffith, another royal chaplain, who would take his family on to Basing House. It is possible that Peake did the same. It is very likely that Lieutenant Colonel Robert Peake, the Holborn print-seller, was a kinsman. Humfrey's son Gregory was certainly very close to his 'noble and worthy friend' Robert; he would act as an executor of his will and take possession, after his death, of his watch, escutcheon and sword.[27]

Nowhere in his *Meditations* does Peake name Basing House or any other actual siege. He discusses various aspects of siegecraft and concludes each chapter with a godly lesson. Avoid gluttony in the good times, he says, because it will exacerbate hunger in the bad. He covers various scenarios – sieges of towns, sieges of houses with moats – but some of his passages shadow the circumstances at Basing House so closely that, considering his network and clear personal trauma, there must be a strong possibility that he was there.

Whether specific or general, Peake takes the reader into the bowels of a civil war siege like no other source. It is a very dark place. He thinks a lot about death – the 'sad spectacle' of it, the 'intolerable stench' of it; death in 'a ditch, or a pit or the open field'; death by sickness ('rotting and decaying part by part'), or from the sky by a granado, or by case shot 'that scatters so'; death by 'poisoned bullets' that have been 'chawed with men's teeth' to 'rankle and gangrene' the flesh. He considers the torments of famine and palate-sticking thirst. He dwells on the effects of fireballs, which leave people so horrendously burned that he wonders if it would be perhaps 'better for them to have perished'. Fire is dreadful in peacetime, he writes, 'but war adds so much to the horror'.[28]

Death's soldiers beleaguer him, 'mustered together in such hideous shapes'. They breach his dreams so that when he awakens, 'he knows not whether it be sleep or Death that hovers over him'. Sleep is rare in

any case: 'forc't, catch't now and then by snatches'. Even when he set-
tles, the 'panic terrors' of others disturb him. Their 'shrieks, and cries,
and noise, and tumult' make him toss and turn. The homily here is to
avoid in peacetime a 'slothful bed', for those who are used to rising at
noon with 'the effeminate lord or wanton lady' will find in war that
'this sad unrest will teach them *what they are*'.[29]

The cramped conditions are another horror: 'many are pestered
together in a little room', and the very air they breathe is offensive. It is
hard in such circumstances to keep up with prayers, 'the tranquillity of
mind (from which devotion takes her surest pitch) almost quite lost in
such variety of successive troubles'.[30]

They have no control of time. 'We must wake every night and every
hour of the night' and stand on the lines in the freezing cold. A system
of watches should allow some to sleep, but when the alarm sounds,
'the whole garrison hastens to arms and with all speed and diligence
prepares for a serious defence when perhaps the enemy intended but
to fright them and, having attained his end, goes off laughing to think
that he hath created so much trouble'. This can happen two or three
times a week, sometimes two or three times a night, 'for thus [the
enemy] drives on to his main end, which is to break the defendant with
continued toil and watching until he grows so tame that he may admit
conditions of surrender'.[31]

Non-combatants 'clog' a garrison, Peake observes. They eat up the
food and 'dishearten and discourage the soldier'. And yet they have
'necessary uses', not only in the kitchen, laundry and sick bay, but also
'in the pinch of service', when they can throw stones and melted pitch
onto assailants from the walls. 'For such purposes,' he argues, 'women
and boys are as fit as men and should not be spared at such a time from
any labour.' It is, moreover, 'a good corrective to man's pride (into
which he falls too often and too easily) that he is many times necessitated to admit such helps as of women and children, which otherwise
perhaps he would despise'.[32]

For those on their own in the garrison, it is a torment to be sealed
off from loved ones: 'It grieves us that we cannot hear from them,
and it grieves us that they cannot hear from us, whereby they may
know the truth and apprehend things neither better, nor worse, but
just as indeed they are.' Not knowing suspends them in a kind of
purgatory – 'the dark night of utter ignorance clouds every beam of

light' – and renders them, for the present, 'mutually dead' to one another. 'Let the faithful husband of a good and loving wife, or the tender father of sweet and duteous children judge of this bitterness.'[33]

Peake is a compassionate observer. He despises 'brutish excess' and despairs of the engines of war: 'How unhappily witty men are to invent daily new instruments of mischief to one another!' But he also knows that 'tender pity can have no place' in combat. When it is over, he counsels, when the smoke has cleared, a soldier might be permitted 'to shed a tear over a noble enemy', but in the thick of it, 'the eye must not see their wounds, nor the ear hear their groans, nor the heart pity their distresses'. He must strain every sinew to keep his fort – 'to drown them, to shoot them, to blow them up, to knock them down, mangle and dismember them, any way to force them back or disable them from coming on'. This must be his only concern and he must not care how he does it. 'Such are the sad enforcements of bloody war.'[34]

By September 1644, Basing House had been under siege for three months. The besiegers' trenches ran through the park, linking their platform in the west to the church in the east. They were close enough now to throw in hand grenades.

On Monday 2 September, Norton sent Winchester another summons to surrender. 'I expect your answer by this drum,' he wrote, 'within one hour.' The marquess had been sending increasingly frantic pleas for help and had just received word that a relief force would be with him in forty-eight hours. He returned Norton's drum straight away:

> Sir,
>   Whereas you demand the house and garrison of Basing by a pretended authority of Parliament, I make this answer: that without the king there can be no Parliament. By His Majesty's commission, I keep the place and without his absolute command, shall not deliver it to any pretenders whatsoever. I am
>   Yours to serve you,
>   *Winchester*

It was a risk to test a besieger's patience like this. Everyone had heard of 'Magdeburg justice', the infamous sack in 1631 of the Protestant German city, whose citizens had been raped, burned and slaughtered for holding out for a relief force that never came. Upon receipt of Winchester's discourteous reply, Norton sent in a thunderstorm of great and small shot. It lasted for six hours and was so intense that the cannon overheated and had to be withdrawn. Another tower was toppled, three men were killed and a woman was hurt. But they only had to hold out for two more days.

'The day of promised relief,' began the siege diarist on Wednesday 4 September. 'Our men in readiness.'

13

A Special Operation

'Noon come,' continued the diarist, 'and no appeareance of them.'

The garrison had prepared the horses and said their prayers. Adrenalin pumped through their veins, supercharged by the fury of frustrated hope. The promised help had not arrived, but they sallied out anyway from the garrison gate. Forty troopers with sharpened bills fell on Colonel Onslow's quarters in the west and dragged away his demiculverin. The Roundheads rallied and spewed case shot at the raiders, killing three and injuring another. The great guns were awake now, bellowing from both sides. Then Sir William Waller appeared on the horizon.

He was with two advance guards of cavalry and his wife Anne, who often accompanied him on campaign. Waller was on his way to assist the Earl of Essex, who had been pursued by the king into Cornwall. He was keen to storm Basing House first, but the orders were to go west with all speed. He stayed long enough 'to see the sport'. One of his captains strayed too close and was killed by a royalist roundshot.[1] The garrison withdrew behind its walls and put every man on duty. For the next two days, they watched Waller's forces march past, 'tongues boasting' that they would be back. The weary diarist returned to his journal: 'We again, with our old guests, are left to try it out.'

The marchioness, meanwhile, was in Oxford, having slipped out earlier in the summer. When, in July, Charles had ridden into the south-west to go 'Essex-catching', his council had requested that he drop down first to relieve Winchester's seat. According to Clarendon, he had refused to assist his old chess partner, arguing that such a move would have 'retarded his march' and encouraged Waller to follow sooner. Basing House, it seemed, might be sacrificed. Thus Honora

had made the perilous journey to Oxford. She probably stayed in Christ
Church with her half-sister Frances, whose husband, the Marquess of
Hertford, was chancellor of the university. Over the din of the cattle
penned in the quad, the sisters urged Hertford to 'take this business to
heart'.[2]

Oxford was a pinched place – the faces, the provisions; even William
Dobson in his studio in St John's College would soon be eking out his
paint and skimming his Cavaliers of their impasto swagger. Tempers
were frayed by 'discomposures, jealousies and disgusts'.[3] There were
snakes in the grass and deep fissures within the council of war. Duels
were common, morale was sapped and the beer was small. The plague
too had returned. 'I am a dead woman and not a woman of this world,'
one wife told her husband in a house nearby.[4] But the risk was worth
taking for Honora if it meant saving her husband's seat.

'Very diligently', she begged influential men and women to remember Basing House. According to Clarendon, she made everyone want
to gratify her, 'being a lady of great honour and alliance'. Her charm
had no effect, however, on Oxford's governor. In his long and distinguished military career, Sir Arthur Aston had fought for Russians
against Poles, for Poles against Turks and for Gustavus Adolphus
against the Holy Roman Emperor. He had seen too many doomed
operations to wave this one through. He pointed out, not unreason-
ably, that Basing House was forty miles away inside enemy territory. A
relief force would have to outfox spies at both ends, bypass parliamentarian garrisons at Abingdon, Reading and Newbury, cross not just the
Thames but the Kennet, and the Loddon, and then break through Norton's cordon. The men would have to supply the house with food,
fodder, powder and match, and then return, exhausted, with the
Roundheads hopping mad and patrolling every road and bridge. It was
'full of more difficulties', he believed, 'and liable to greater damages
than any soldier who understood command would expose himself and
the king's service to'.

Honora was determined, however, and continued to press her suit.
She appealed to the Cavalier sense of honour and – to those Catholics
in town – to their shared communion in Christ. The marquess too
managed to get a final, desperate note out, insisting that in ten days'
time he would have no choice but to submit to 'the worst conditions
the rebels were like to grant to his person and to his religion'. Honora

redoubled her efforts. When the council next met, Aston was still unmoved, but his deputy, Henry Gage, offered to lead a relief column of gentleman volunteers. It was a mission 'full of hazard', he admitted, 'especially the return', but he had a plan.

Gage, like Aston, was Catholic, and a veteran of continental warfare, but his flashy faith and bullish confidence were a world apart from Aston's rigid professionalism. His star was shining brightly that summer after his successful recapture of Boarstall House in Buckinghamshire. Aston thought him a silky Jesuit and 'hated him perfectly', but the lords of the council were won over and resolved to do all they could to help.[5]

At 10 p.m. on Monday 9 September 1644, Gage left Oxford with 400 foot, 250 horse and a team of packhorses bearing powder and match. Each man wore an orange-tawny scarf and had an orange-tawny ribbon in his hat. These were Parliament's colours and were intended to dupe the enemy, at least from a distance. They marched all night, stopping only at dawn to rest and rendezvous with Captain Walters of the royalist garrison at Wallingford. He brought in another 50 horse and 50 foot.

Gage sent an express messenger to another local ally, Sir William Ogle, the governor of Winchester Castle, which was still holding out for the king. He asked Ogle to make good his pledge of 100 horse and 300 foot, requesting that they appear in the park south of Basing House between 4 and 5 a.m. the following morning. At the signal, Ogle would distract the besiegers from the south, the garrison would sally out from the centre and Gage would fall on from the north.

After a short rest, Gage proceeded on a quick march through the enemy-patrolled territory between Newbury and Reading. His plan, once over the River Kennet, was to rest again at Aldermaston before the last leg to Basing. Captain Walters and the quartermasters went ahead to secure provisions, but found hostile scouts in the town. Walters forgot that he was supposed to be an orange-scarfed Roundhead and fell on them, taking several prisoners. Word soon spread that there were Cavaliers about.

The tail of Gage's column arrived at Aldermaston at eight on Tuesday night. They rested for three hours before undertaking their second night march. The infantrymen were footsore and faint, but were relieved by shifts on horseback, with some of the troopers sharing their saddles and others taking turns to match. Gage was the first to do this, inspiring the rest to follow. His promises of pillage and money upon the completion of the mission also helped alleviate fatigue.

They arrived at Chineham, two miles north of Basing House, between four and five on Wednesday morning. This was the appointed hour for Ogle to appear in the park with his promised four hundred. All seemed to be going to plan, despite the mishap at Aldermaston, when Gage received devastating news: the enemy was too thick between Winchester and Basing. Ogle was not coming. At a stroke, Gage lost a third of his force. He consulted with his officers and resolved to carry on regardless, in one fell swoop from the north. 'I commanded the men to be ranged into battalions,' he later recalled, 'and, riding up to every squadron, gave them what good words and encouragement I was able.' It was hardly necessary, he added, 'most of them being so well resolved of themselves'. Each man now tied a white handkerchief above the elbow of his right arm. Gage gave them their password: 'St George'.

At Basing House, they lit a fire on the gatehouse roof to serve as a beacon for their hoped-for saviours. 'Through the fog,' the siege diarist noted, 'it hardly could be seen to the next hill.'

Upon the next hill, by the crest of Cowdery's Down, Norton drew up five troops of horse. His scouts had warned him about the royalists in Aldermaston and his musketeers lined the hedgerow on the left. His men were 'fresh and prepared'. The wind was behind them.[6]

Gage, meanwhile, marched on, the foot flanked by the horse. Un-aware of Norton's near presence, he dismounted and led up the foot, his sword cutting through a mist 'so thick as made the day still night'. With a mile to go, he sounded his trumpets and drums to alert the garrison to his approach. The sounds echoed quickly, too quickly. A few paces up, Gage and his men discerned the shapes of Norton's troopers, 'in very good order to receive us'.

A volley of shot cracked out of the hedgerow on their right. This was 'more terrible than damageable', Gage recalled. The shock of it spurred his horse to charge Norton's cavalry, both wings falling on so furiously that the parliamentarian horse broke and fled, the fog 'befriending' them in their retreat.

Norton's foot remained. They stood 'handsomely', but alone. For two hours they contested every hedge. Slowly, though, Gage pushed them back towards the house. At the same time, Lieutenant Colonel Thomas Johnson and his musketeers charged out from the Grange. They beat the besiegers off their line and chased them up to Cowdery's Down. Not wanting to be crushed between the two forces, the Roundheads ran. The path was clear for Gage and his men.

'Our joys are echoed,' wrote the siege diarist, 'whilst the sad prisoners are led in to see the house they lay so long about.' Sixty-four Roundhead soldiers, two sergeants and one lieutenant had been captured. The injured were shown mercy – their wounds were dressed and they were returned to their lines – but two turncoats 'had execution'.

Gage did not linger. He paid his respects to the marquess, deposited the ammunition and a hundred men, then marched on to Basingstoke, where, as he knew, it was market day. After a short skirmish, he took the town and stripped it bare. 'All that day I continued sending to Basing House as much wheat, malt, salt, oats, bacon, cheese and butter as I could get horses and carts to transport.' He also drove in fifty cattle, a hundred sheep and a small supply of muskets and powder kept by the parliamentary committee in town.

While Gage was plundering Basingstoke, the garrison sallied out left and right, attacking the besiegers in their works. They killed forty-five men and took thirty prisoners, including two captains from prominent local families. The rest escaped into the big fort in the park, which was too strong to attempt. The royalists contented themselves with setting fire to the three other enemy camps. With the flames dancing in their eyes, they watched the huts light up 'one by one'.

Gage and his men slept that night at Basing House, having executed a skilful withdrawal from Basingstoke when Norton's troops had started to regroup. Gage feared that the extraordinary discipline that his men had hitherto shown might crack with exhaustion, hunger and the high of victory. He had half a mission, the harder half, still to go.

The following day, Thursday 12 September, he sent his men out to round up more supplies. When they returned to the house in the evening, he told them that they would be marching straight on to Oxford. His scouts had been busy that day, watching the Roundheads file out of Abingdon, Newbury and Reading to take up positions along the River Kennet. Elsewhere on his planned route, the Roundheads destroyed bridges and blocked passes. He also learned that Norton intended to hound him in the rear the moment he left. He decided, therefore, 'without acquainting any man', to get out that night. In order to mislead Norton (and indeed the spy or spies inside Basing House), he issued warrants, which he knew would be intercepted, requiring local towns to bring in corn the following day, by noon, upon pain of fire. He also arranged a prisoner exchange for midday on Friday. Norton thus assumed that Gage would stick around for at least another day.

At eleven o'clock on Thursday night, Gage moved out 'without sound of drum or trumpet'. He followed two of the garrison's best guides and told his men that if they encountered any hostile forces, they must pretend to be Roundheads on their way to intercept the Oxford malignants. They took a different route back, via Burghfield Bridge, but found it broken, so they swam their horses over the river, with the troopers taking the musketeers up on their saddles. In the quickening light, they marched dangerously close to the Roundheads at Reading, forded the Thames at Pangbourne, rested for the night at Wallingford and continued, 'God be praised', to Oxford. Gage claimed to have lost only eleven men in the entire operation. A further forty or fifty were injured, 'but not dangerously'.

It was a tactical masterclass, 'the most soldier-like piece these wars have ever yet afforded', thought one admiring royalist. Gage was hailed as a hero. People lined the streets to cheer his entry into town. As soon as he could, he slipped away from the throng and quietly returned to his lodging, 'as if he had been nothing concerned in these expressions of joy and as if this triumph had had no relation to him'.[7]

14

The Hand of God

The injuries sustained during the fighting on 11 September were nasty. A parliamentarian surgeon recorded his cases: one man shot in the shoulder, another in the back of the head and a third, Sergeant John Simons, 'in his members'. One patient had a powder burn to his face, another had case shot in both thighs. A few days later, a trooper called Nicholas Turner was carried in from a cornfield. They thought he was dead when they found him. He had been slashed five times in the head and face. The laceration above his left ear was five inches long and the gash on his forehead contained a bone fragment. He also had sword wounds in his shoulder, stomach, hip, groin and hand, which was half off.[1] Maggots were crawling all over his wounds, gorging on the dead flesh and gobbling up bacteria. They probably saved his life.*

Maggots could not, however, remove musket balls or bone slivers or the scraps of clothing that bullets often took into the body. Richard Wiseman, who wrote a treatise on gunshot wounds based partly on his experience as a surgeon in Ralph Hopton's army, understood the danger of 'mortification' from foreign matter. It had to be removed quickly, he advised, ideally while the patient was still 'warm with the heat of battle'. Plier-like tools with names like crow's bill, crane's bill and duck's bill were used for extractions, and must have felt to the patient as if a real bird was pecking at his flesh. 'Take great care', warned Wiseman, that 'you lay not hold of some nerve or tendon and so pluck them along with the bullet, for by so doing you may cause intolerable pain'.[2]

---

* So effective is 'maggot therapy' in the removal of necrotic flesh that it has been reintroduced to modern medicine.

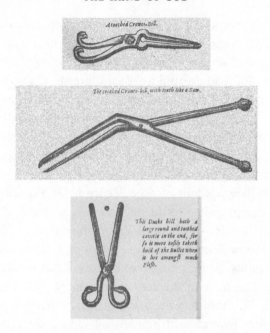

Wiseman was in his early twenties and not even formally out of his apprenticeship when he went to the wars. At the siege of Taunton in 1645, his colonel ordered him to treat a man who had been hit with case shot. The man's eyes, nose, mouth and chin had been blasted off and what was left of his face had been driven inwards. Wiseman could see his brain working through the gaps in his scalp. He was 'somewhat troubled where to begin'. He decided to clear his patient's throat, pour in some milk and dress the wounds as best he could. A week later, when the regiment moved out, the 'deplorable creature' was still alive.

At Melcombe Regis, Wiseman was called to attend a multiple skull fracture caused by a 'grazing' cannonball. The patient's forehead was gone and shards of bone were embedded in his brain. Wiseman pulled them out and applied a cephalic balsam and bandage, 'supposing I should never dress him any more'. But the patient started to recover, and on the fifteenth day he was able to walk along Weymouth pier hand in hand with another soldier. Two days later, however, he fell into spasms and died 'howling like a dog, as most of those do who have been so wounded'.[3]

Wiseman wanted future generations to learn from his discoveries and mistakes. This was a view shared by the apothecary of Snow Hill, Thomas Johnson, who had challenged old precepts not for the sake of it, but because observation and experiment demanded it. Johnson believed that God had created a treasure house of knowledge to be unlocked by man. He wanted to throw open the gates, and he hoped that 'chance or a more curious generation than yet is in being' would continue to break the bounds.[4]

The war thus provided an opportunity, with the sheer volume of casualties, the repetition of treatments, increased anatomical knowledge and the development of an evidence base. The disruption and urgency of campaigning could produce tension and disagreement amongst medical men – William Waller cashiered one of his surgeons for calling a senior doctor an ass and a coxcomb – but it also yielded unexpected results. 'At that time I was a fresh-water soldier,' Ambrose Paré had recalled back in the sixteenth century, 'I had not yet seen wounds made by gunshot at the first dressing.' Other doctors had been cauterising entry wounds with scalding oil and treacle, but Paré lacked the supplies, so he had improvised with a cool mixture of egg yolk, rose oil and turpentine. 'In the night I could not sleep,' he recalled, terrified that he had killed his patients. He got up very early for his rounds and found the wounds healed beyond expectation, with no inflammation and little pain. 'I resolved with myself never so cruelly to burn poor men wounded with gunshot.'[5]

This lesson, conveyed by Thomas Johnson's translation of Paré's works, was taken into the English civil war by young Richard Wiseman in the west and James Cooke for Parliament in the Midlands, as well as other doctors and surgeons elsewhere. They made advances of their own in bone-setting, prosthetics and the management of infection. Delayed primary closure, for example – keeping the wound open till it looked like 'flesh long hanged in the air' – promoted the accumulation of lymph and fortified the immune system. It is still in use today.

Civil war surgeons did not yet have a technical vocabulary, or knowledge of microbiology, or the benefits of anaesthetics, antibiotics and surgical steel. Many patients died. Wiseman's *Severall Chirurgicall Treatises* was popularly known as 'Wiseman's Book of Martyrs'. Thousands, however, did not die. William 'Blowface' Forbes lived to endure his nickname, while Edward Bagshaw of the West Riding of Yorkshire had nine bones taken out of his skull and at one point could only drink through a hole in the side of his head. Yet he too survived.[6]

Johnson's edition of John Gerard's *Herball* was also used in the war. One surviving copy was owned by a royalist family caught up in the siege of Newark in Nottinghamshire. It is covered in manicules – little hands drawn in the margins – pointing to the medicinal virtues of various plants.

> ☞ A   Shepheards purfe ftaieth bleeding in any part of the body, whether the iuice or the decoction thereof be drunke, or whether it be vfed pulteffe wife, or in bath, or any other way elfe.
>   B   In a Clyfter it cureth the bloudy flix: it healeth greene and bleeding wounds: it is maruellous good for inflammations new begun, and for all difeafes which muft be checked backe and cooled.
>   C   The decoction doth ftop the laske, the fpitting and piffing of bloud, and all other fluxes of bloud.

'Shepherd's Purse stayeth bleeding in any part of the body.'

Most of the marked passages relate to general wounds, followed by 'bloody flux' (dysentery), spitting blood, bleeding, ulcers (a manifestation of smallpox), 'laske' (diarrhoea) and 'women's courses', which suggests the book's perusal by a female practitioner and is a reminder of how difficult sieges must have been for menstruating women.[7]

Another copy of the *Herball* is mentioned in the will of a London apothecary called John Thomas. He would take Thomas Johnson's son as an apprentice after the war, and since he also knew Faithorne and Peake, it's possible that he served at Basing House himself. His *Herball* went to his 'loving friend' Stephen Fawcett, one of the king's overworked surgeons in Oxford. When Fawcett was captured by Parliament, two certificates were added to his file pointing out that he had looked after wounded parliamentary prisoners 'with much care and willingness' and at his own charge.[8] At Basing House, the garrison doctors also recognised a basic humanitarian duty of care. Even after three months of starvation, bombardment and dirty tricks by the besiegers, seventeen 'dangerously wounded' parliamentarian prisoners were brought into the house to be dressed after the fighting on 11 September. They were returned safely afterwards for further treatment by their own side.[9]

Thomas Johnson's medical knowledge was a great asset to Basing House, and his advocacy of simple remedies over complex compounds would have made treatment more viable.[10] He was also used to dealing with the many minor complaints that had been aired in his shop over the years. The manuscript that contains his pre-war lectures gives remedies for sore eyes, 'stinking breath' and 'melancholy fits', as well as advice on how 'to keep the smallpox from pitting the face' (almond oil and spermaceti applied with a feather), how 'to take away the smell of stinking armholes' (myrtles, bay leaves and sweet marjoram) and how 'to make hairs grow on the head' (tartar oil). More practical tips, such as how to prevent beer from souring and how to snare pigeons (which involved easily obtained dung-water), would have been particularly useful to the garrison.[11]

Johnson may have had help sourcing supplies from his old friend and collaborator John Goodyer, a Hampshire man and 'second to none in his industry and searching of plants'. Just before the outbreak of war, Johnson had announced their plan to publish a comprehensive British flora together. Goodyer does not seem to have taken part in any fighting, but under his floorboards, striped with damp and still in existence, was a protection order signed by Ralph Hopton (see plates).[12]

It was not as a medical practitioner that Thomas Johnson was called to the burned-out village of Basing on 14 September 1644, but as the lieutenant colonel of Sir Marmaduke Rawdon's foot regiment. This was two days after Gage had left. Norton and the besiegers were still confining themselves to their fort in the park. One hundred musketeers from the garrison had gone to the village to round up more provisions for the house. Still drunk with victory, they soon became drunk indeed. They were 'in no good order' when Norton attacked. After an hour of vicious fighting in the churchyard, the Cavaliers were about to be overwhelmed when Johnson rushed in with his company. He fell on the Roundheads and beat them out of the church and back to the park. A handful of men from both sides were killed. Johnson was shot in the shoulder.[13]

He was rushed back to the house. The musket ball would have been taken out along with any obvious pieces of fabric. Rose oil, egg yolk and turpentine, if available, would have been applied to the entry wound. But Johnson fell into a fever, which suggests that some foreign matter was left inside. It was touch and go for a fortnight. The doctors would have attempted various syrups and balms to draw the heat from the body. He probably wouldn't have been aware of the events around him – of Norton taking back the church and village and recircling the house.

Perhaps, like Falstaff, he babbled of green fields. Perhaps, in his delirium, those old lists streamed through his head: the 'red whortle or hurtle berries in the wild moors of Northumberland', the bent grass 'with which we in London do usually adorn our chimneys in summer time', Canterbury bells, ivy bells, the bells of Basing sounding the alarm, the bells of Old Bailey ferrying the dead, Snow Hill, Mount Snowdon, cloudberry, his picnic in the clouds, the mist when Waller attacked, and when Gage came, the mist 'so thick as made the day still night'.[14]

Thomas Johnson died on 24 September. He is thought to be buried in the orchard. The siege diarist interrupted his commentary to cry 'funeral tears', for the self-effacing, talismanic officer, who was 'no less eminent in the garrison for his valour and conduct as a soldier than famous through the kingdom for his excellency as a herbalist and physician'. According to Fuller, Johnson was mourned by both sides.[15]

By mid October, the garrison was very low. Their new supplies had dwindled and their ragged clothes hung limply from their bones. They failed to retake the church. The besiegers brought in water-levellers to draw off the river and firm up the ground in front of the house. There were skirmishes, and deaths, almost every day.

King Charles, they heard, had set his heart on saving them. He was coming back from Cornwall, having scored a major victory against Lord General Essex at Lostwithiel. Honora's half-brother had escaped to sea in a fishing boat, leaving his entire infantry to surrender. Six thousand soldiers and their camp followers were marched in the rain through the places they had just pillaged. In contravention of the articles of surrender, they were beaten and stripped by vengeful civilians and the royalist rank and file. Some female camp followers were thrown off Lostwithiel Bridge by a group of Cornish women. Other prisoners were forced to drink water 'worse than runs in the channels in London streets'. Thousands died of disease and exposure and it was not forgotten.[16]

When Essex returned to dry land, he gathered the remnants of his mauled force for a rendezvous at Basingstoke with Sir William Waller's army and the Earl of Manchester's formidable Eastern Association. They were determined to block the king's relief effort. The garrison at Basing House spotted Manchester's vanguard from the watchtower on 17 October. Over the next three days, 'rain fell incessantly' as Parliament's southern armies converged. 'You may now look upon the forces as joined,' the commanders reported from Basingstoke on the 20th. 'We hope there will be a battle shortly; to our understandings it cannot be avoided.' They totalled 19,000 men, one of the largest forces gathered in the war. They expected Charles on 21 October and drew up in battle array. The battle of Basing might have been the decisive engagement of the war. Instead, on Tuesday 22 October, upon hearing that Charles had wheeled about towards Newbury, the Roundheads took the Reading road after him.[17]

At the second battle of Newbury, on 27 October, the royalists were outnumbered by almost two to one, but the terrain was tricky and the parliamentarians were hesitant and disjointed. 'In a pace slower than a flight and faster than a retreat', Charles was able to extricate his forces and get back to Oxford. Sir Marmaduke Rawdon's son Thomas, now Colonel Rawdon, was there for the king. He was shot in the belly, but his buff coat 'deaded' the bullet. He didn't even notice until the end of the day, when he took off his clothes and a pistol ball fell out.[18] It encapsulated the fight, and indeed the broader parliamentarian effort. Despite every advantage, the Roundheads had failed to penetrate. There was no trust between Waller and Essex, or between Manchester and his cavalry commander Oliver Cromwell, or between Cromwell and Essex. The Committee of Both Kingdoms in London had even had to remind them all to lay aside their differences before the conjunction of their armies. The recriminations glowed red-hot after the Newbury campaign.

At the heart of the matter was the question of whether the war should be fought to a hard end, with Charles trounced on the field and far-reaching reforms imposed, which was what Cromwell wanted; or whether the king should be manoeuvred towards a negotiated peace, which was what Manchester had come to favour after the carnage at Marston Moor. 'If we beat the king ninety-nine times,' he reputedly told the council of war, 'yet he is king still and so will his posterity be after him, but if the king beat us once, we shall be all hanged and our posterity be made slaves.' Cromwell was appalled. On this logic, he asked, why take up arms at all? 'This is against fighting ever hereafter.'[19]

The night after the armies had moved away from the churned-up fields around Basing, a storm blew down one of the house's battered towers. It landed on five men and killed one of them. The sallies were hand-to-mouth affairs now. Low on bread, low on corn, Lieutenant Colonel Robert Peake brought in sixteen cartloads of sheaf and eight cattle on 1 November. Four days later, on the anniversary of the Gunpowder Plot, the beer ran out and they all had to drink water. The rations were reduced to one tiny meal a day. A soldier ran away, 'telling our wants unto our enemies, now animating them, before disheartened'. On 6 November, Norton detained a royalist messenger heading to Oxford with a desperate plea for help. Three days later, though, during a heroic sally headed by Major Rosewell, two of the garrison managed to slip through Norton's cordon. 'Prince Rupert will speedily relieve Basing House,' a parliamentarian scout wrote on 12 November. 'We had news that all our forces were drawn towards Basing, thereby to prevent the relief of the house,' reported a London newsbook in the third week of the month.[20] There were many orders, many rumours, but no sign, yet, of help for either side.

Besieger and besieged were holding out, but barely holding on. Norton was 'wearied with lying 24 weeks, diseases, with the winter seizing them, his army wasted from 2,000 to 700'. The garrison was 'drawn down by length of siege almost unto the worst of all necessities, provision low, the soldiers spent and naked and the numbers few'.[21]

On Sunday 17 November, the Earl of Manchester left Newbury to reinforce Norton at Basing. His men began to desert and he soon turned back. In London two days later, three suns appeared in the sky. The astrologer William Lilly, noting their conjunction with the king's birthday, thought they portended no good for him. But 19 November was Richard Norton's birthday too. At 8 a.m. the following day, he drew off his wagons and guns. At noon, he fired his huts and pulled his foot from the siege lines. His horse covered the retreat.

The next night, Henry Gage – now Sir Henry – descended on Basing House with a host of a thousand angels. Each trooper carried a bag of provisions and had match cord tied round his waist. They expected a fight, but the place was deserted except for the ragtag garrison and their wretched families. The diarist admitted that they had lost nearly one hundred 'by sickness and the siege'. The survivors were in desperate need of clothes, shoes and stockings. They looked more like 'prisoners of the grave than the keepers of a castle'.[22]

But the blockade was over. The diarist composed his last entry. Seldom, he wrote, had there been a siege 'wherein the preservation of the place more immediately might be imputed to the hand of God'. It was a marvel, he continued, that in such a long siege, 'with all the sufferings incident thereto', there had been no mutiny. The garrison and its civilians had been saved, he wrote, 'as if by miracle'. There had been moments when they had teetered on the brink, but God 'that holdeth all things in His hand, appointing times and seasons', had sustained them. It was vain, therefore, to question the 'valour or discretion' of the enemy, or to praise 'the care and diligence' of the marquess, or 'the skill and valour' of the officers, or 'the courage and obedience' of the soldiers, 'though all these did their parts'. It was God who had kept the place: 'Let no man therefore speak himself an instrument, only in giving thanks that God had made him so, for here was evidently seen He chose the weak to confound the strong. *Non nobis Domine*. Not unto us, not unto us, O Lord, but to thine own name be all glory for ever, AMEN.'

There was another man, though, who was speaking of himself as an instrument and giving God thanks for making him so. After the battle of Marston Moor, Oliver Cromwell had praised the Lord for rendering the royalist cavalry 'as stubble to our swords'.[23] This forty-five-year-old Puritan farmer was as certain as the siege diarist of the righteousness of his cause. His side now controlled 70 per cent of England, 30 per cent more than at the beginning of the year.[24] Parliament had the foundries and the powder mills of the south-east. It had London's trade and money. It had the navy and the harbours closest to the Continent. It had the north. Cromwell had been a fresh-water soldier when the standard was raised, but he had not lost a battle. There was no doubt in his mind that God had put iron in his side. Equally clearly, though, God was withholding victory. The failure of Parliament's mighty composite army to reduce Basing House and salvage something from the wreckage of Newbury was a clear sign of His wrath.

But there was a way. If the corpse was infected with regional sores, the necrotic flesh must be excised, the bad blood let and the wounds sealed with a holy balsam of prayer and abnegation. Something fitter must arise with stronger sinews, improved competencies and greater integrity. There must be better training, better fuel, better pay, a strict regimen, a fusion of command: a new model.

PART FOUR

THE STORM

He that prays and preaches best will fight best.

Oliver Cromwell[1]

15

Figures Set upon Horory Questions

The astrologer walked along the Strand, past the spot where they'd pulled down the maypole and down the lane towards the waterside. His appearance was unremarkable. He had dark shoulder-length hair, a moustache and slightly river-blasted cheeks. He wore a black cloak and a white collar band. In 1645, he was forty-three.

He had learned how to read the stars a decade earlier, mainly, he said, from the books sold in Little Britain up by Smithfield. He'd studied 'twelve, or fifteen, or eighteen hours day and night'. He'd always had to help himself. His Latin was good enough for Cambridge, but his father didn't have the money, so when he was almost eighteen, William Lilly, 'a bean-belly' from Diseworth in Leicestershire, had walked all the way to London 'with an hundred pence in my purse and no more'. He became the servant of the Master of the Salters' Company at the corner house by the old Strand Bridge. He'd shined his master's shoes, weeded his garden, swept his porch, fetched his water and nursed his wife in her last illness. Very soon after his master's death, he had married the second wife, regardless of, or very much regarding, 'the disproportion of years and fortune'. He thought her short, fat, ill-educated and plain, but they lived together 'lovingly', and when she died six years later, he received a fortune.[1]

He published prophetical stories like that of the 'White King' of Britain who had died a thousand years earlier after a bloody siege in a civil war of his own making. He interpreted strange apparitions like the three suns on Charles's birthday in 1644, which portended the 'violent death' of 'some very great man'.[2] That year he also issued his first almanac with monthly horoscopes. It was sold well to an anxious public. At the same time, over in the fen-sucked fogs of East Anglia, fears of a busy devil were translated into witch trials conducted by Matthew Hopkins, that other self-appointed seer of the occult. Styling himself Witch-Finder General, Hopkins rode from village to village asking communities to bring out their maleficents. Over one hundred people, mainly older women, died on the gallows or after interrogation in prison as a result of this man and his moment.[3] In London, though, folk were more likely to take their troubles to the sprawling medical community, or to William Lilly, the English Merlin on the Strand.

After twenty-five years in the corner house, at 11.54 a.m. on Sunday 4 May 1645, Lilly moved a few doors up the row.[4] Precise time mattered to him. His work was based on the position of the stars at any given moment. A client would ask him a question and he would draw up 'a figure of heaven', in the middle of which he would write the day, year and hour at which the consultation began. His study was full of astrological devices and charts to help him interrogate the stars.

Trade was brisk. Lilly could get through a handful of consultations a day. He usually charged half a crown, less for the poor and significantly more for high-ranking clients, of whom he had several. In a few years he would start receiving £100 a year for secret services to Parliament.[5] His querents were young and old, male and female, Roundhead and Cavalier. Some came in person. Others sent letters. Their questions ranged from the whereabouts of a lost handkerchief to 'what death Canterbury should die and when'.* One man asked if

---

* Archbishop Laud was beheaded for treason on 10 January 1645. He was 71 years old. His trial had been a drawn-out affair and the evidence against him was greater in quantity than quality. The illustrated Bibles of 'one Peake, a stationer, now in arms against the Parliament' – i.e. Lieutenant Colonel Robert Peake at Basing House – were cited at the trial as 'irrefragable evidence' that Laud had endeavoured by 'Jesuitical stratagems' to subvert God's true religion (William Prynne, *Canterburies Doome* (1646), 109–10). The prosecutor was William Prynne, the pamphleteer who had lost his ears to Laud's censorious regime. Part of Laud's library went to the Puritan preacher Hugh Peter, who considered gifting it to Harvard College. Laud's pet tortoise, which had come to Lambeth with him in 1633, was allowed to remain in the palace garden. Rawdon might have met it when he searched Lambeth for arms in 1642. It reportedly lived until 1753 and its shell is now on display in the palace Guard Room.

An Essex vicar, Ralph Josselin, recorded Laud's execution in his diary: '10 January 1645. The Archbishop, that grand enemy of the power of godliness, that great stickler for all outward pomp in the service of God, lost his head at Tower Hill, London, by ordinance of Parliament. This week the great snow melted gently, never were houses in many years so filled with snow and paddled when it melted away.' (Ralph Josselin, *Diary*, 31.)

he should support the king or Parliament. Others wanted to know how they could get their jewellery back, or their health, or their boys who had gone to the wars. Mr Whitby was 'full of sorrow' for a son who was determined to enlist; Lilly reassured him that his boy would return home safe and with a sound reputation.[6] Should Mr Fowler travel to the East Indies? Should Mr Banks marry Mrs F? Was Lady Tufton pregnant? Was a gentleman's love real, a spurrier's wife wondered at 9.17 a.m. on Thursday 29 May 1645. A woman in Lincoln's Inn Fields just wanted Lilly to tell her 'the cause of her husband's anger'.[7]

On Monday, 4 August 1645, a 'Mistress P' called at Lilly's new house on the Strand. She asked the astrologer *'de amico in Basing'* (about a friend in Basing). He drew up a chart. Over the next five weeks he fielded enquiries about Mrs Veisey's sick mother, Mrs Pooly's absent brother and Lord Crumpton's trip to France. Mrs Heicock dropped in on the morning of Thursday 11 September looking for a lost cloak.[8] At 2.45 that afternoon, Lilly received a letter containing a question that people had been asking for more than two years: 'if Basing House would be taken'. He turned to a fresh page, noted the time, consulted his ephemeris and began.

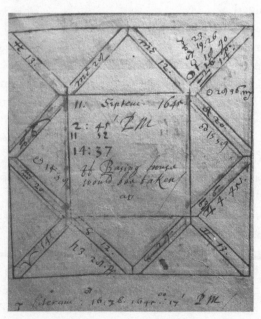

16

Exodus

The Siege Diary of Basing House was published at the beginning of 1645. It was a sham. Even as he lauded the house's blessed unity, the writer knew that it was about to split open. He praised the Marquess of Winchester for his astute leadership, but the military governor, Sir Marmaduke Rawdon, hardly features except as the officer excused from guard duty 'by reason of his years'.[1] When Sir Henry Gage reported to Prince Rupert on the wretched state of the place in November 1644, he had added a passage in cipher. Basing House was on the verge of mutiny, he warned; the officers and soldiers were 'disgusted' and the men 'ill-commanded'. The marquess 'desires much to have the garrison changed'.[2]

The antipathy between Winchester and Rawdon had only grown since the marquess's poaching of Lieutenant Colonel Peake. Rawdon had swaggered into the house bristling with grievance. His men had fought their London battles and paid their dues. His regiment was the first one noted in the royalist ordinance papers to assume the cost of its arms.[3] His home had been raided and his wife plundered of 'all she had'. He was risking his life and those of his men and their families to defend this Catholic aristocrat's seat. Rawdon was 'always a friend to men forward and courageous', insisted his nephew, 'so a foe to the timorous and slothful'.[4]

Lord Winchester was not cut out for combat, despite his colonel's commission and a portrait of himself in shining armour. The furthest he had advanced with his men was part of the way to Odiham the previous spring. After doling out the soldiers' bonuses for their ill-fated raid, he had trotted back to the house. His courage was trumpeted in *Mercurius Aulicus*, which printed dispatches from the Siege Diary, but the London press thought him an indolent coward who battened himself from the world. His reputation never really recovered from the image of him caught by a cannonball with his pants down; thereafter, he was 'the untrussed marquess'. He was 'a gentleman indeed of a most courageous breed', sneered Marchamont Nedham of the Roundhead *Mercurius Britanicus*, 'and at every siege (I hear), though there be no storming, yet there is a tempest ever and anon in his breeches'. Nedham satirised Winchester's 'admirable faculty' for blocking his ears to gunfire and hiding in the cellar: 'You understand, then, the courage and diligence of this dreadful pigwiggin,* this scarecrow of honour.'⁵

When the garrison had been at its most desperate, however, it was reportedly Rawdon's regiment, not Winchester's, that had wanted to discuss terms of surrender.⁶ A few officers had apparently tried to break out with money quilted into their clothes, but the besiegers were tipped off 'by one whom they had formerly taken prisoner'. This report from London's *Parliament Scout* sits uncomfortably with the Rawdon family legend of Sir Marmaduke vowing never to surrender while there were still dogs, cats and rats about. It may be, though, that some of his men were less resolute. There was a question mark over Thomas Langley, who had been so swiftly released after the rout at Odiham. The Roundhead story was that they had taken him wounded, but that he was so shabbily dressed, 'more like a tinker than a gentleman', that they had let him go. Despite his promotion to lieutenant colonel after Thomas Johnson's death, he was never fully trusted by Rawdon. His wife was the niece of Colonel Dalbier, 'a great man then for the Parliament and she at that time in their headquarters'.⁷ If Langley was indeed a spy, and if we remember the betrayal of Winchester's brother, then both regiments had large snakes in the grass. It is hardly surprising that there was a breakdown of trust.

Rations were another sore point, as Rawdon's pointed reference to Winchester's hoard of tobacco and wine during the blockade attested. Related to this was the perennial issue of useless mouths: each regiment accused the other of having too many encumbrances.

Serving under the governors was an array of dominant characters. Winchester's Lieutenant Colonel, Robert Peake, had ruled the roost in his little patch of London at the foot of Snow Hill and had persuaded

---

* Pigwiggin/pigwidgeon: a fairy or dwarf; a small or insignificant person or thing; a stupid or contemptible person. (*OED*)

his apprentices to follow him. The Cuffaud brothers, a major and a lieutenant, had ancient roots in Hampshire and a manor house just north of Basing.[8] They led some of the garrison's boldest sorties. Like other 'papists' in Winchester's regiment, they knew that if captured, they would face sterner penalties than the royalist 'malignants'.[9]

With Rawdon and Langley in 'the London Regiment' was Major William Rosewell, who had survived the noisesome hole at Farnham to return on a prisoner exchange. He was a popular officer and very active on the lines. This trio, it will be remembered, had ventured to the House of Lords in January 1643 to ask for their peace petition to be heard. Rawdon's first captain, and probably his most trusted officer, the vintner Robert Amery, was another man of strong opinion. He had nearly been lynched for defending the king after the botched arrest of the five members of Parliament in January 1642. His profile was such that his wife and two sons – one now dead – had been hounded out of town. Not one of these officers was likely to roll over in a dispute over tactics, or rations, or guard duty, or the many minor squabbles that became exaggerated during a twenty-four-week siege. Rancid meat, puddle water, bombs, disease, desertions, pain, grief, exhaustion and daily cruelties – both inflicted upon them and committed by them – made their 'disgust' as sharp as their bones.

And then there was religion, pitting Rawdon's Protestants against Winchester's Catholics. The press made much of the clash, but perhaps it hadn't been inevitable. Rawdon was a 'high church' Laudian. He saw himself as 'a true son of the Church of England, not adhering', as his chaplain put it, 'either to the right hand or to the left, neither to the superstitions of the Romish Church, nor to the schisms and dissensions of this'.[10] He and his officers considered themselves to be moderates who had traded with people of all faiths. That did not necessarily make them tolerant of Catholics, but nor did they harbour a visceral Puritan fear of the Pope as the Antichrist. They would not have liked the sight of Jesuit priests at Basing House, but they would have appreciated having their own chapel and chaplain there.

In Winchester's camp, Robert Peake, the print-seller, was no fanatic either. If he was a 'papist', as his enemies always claimed, there is no record of it beyond his production of illustrated Bibles for Archbishop Laud and his defection to Winchester's regiment. Like Rawdon and Captains Robert Amery and Isaac Rowlett, he was a member of the

Honourable Artillery Company, which required members to be Protestant.[11] He was never a recusant. Nor was William Faithorne, nor
Inigo Jones, another two around whom Catholicism was whispered
but never demonstrated. The Marquess and Marchioness of Winchester were staunch in their faith, but Basing had not been a sectarian
hothouse before the war.

The prospect of sudden death was a sharpener, though, both of indi-
vidual faith and of the lines between alternative doctrines. If, as the siege
diarist noted, God had made the garrison his instrument, then the question was: which tune should it be playing? If there was only one True
Church, it did rather follow that prayers to the false one were as much an
act of sabotage as a mine under the foundations or a snake in the grass.
The parliamentarian newsbooks savaged the notion of Basing House as
a holy seat. 'Ye have a blessed cause indeed to maintain,' sneered Marchamont Nedham in *Mercurius Britanicus*, 'a cause that was first forged in
Italy, fomented in Spain and now most bloodily prosecuted in England
and Ireland by the scum of antichristianism and atheism.'[12]

Once Colonel Norton had pulled his men from the lines in November (always a sparky month for Protestant–Catholic relations), there
was more time for the garrison to quarrel and less reason to unite.
Bolstered by his fellow Catholic, Sir Henry Gage, Winchester now
resolved to remove Rawdon from his house. He put Robert Peake in
charge and rode to Oxford. There he persuaded Prince Rupert, the
newly appointed commander-in-chief of the royal army, that his
impossible governor had to go.

Rawdon soon realised what the marquess was up to and held a crisis
meeting with his officers, who urged him to hurry up to Oxford himself. Before leaving, he wrote a 'humble declaration', countering
Winchester's charges and fielding his own:

> I am traduced that my officers were mutinous and quarrelsome when
> indeed they received indignities from my lord's officers, as may easily be
> proved.
>
> Whereas it is alleged that I have diverse women belonging to my regi-
> ment, it is known that my lord hath (at least) 3 for one in his regiment.
>
> Upon these two pretences, my lord doth endeavor to remove me
> with my regiment from Basing to my great dishonor, giving me no inti-
> mation of his intention.

My lord, in his absence, hath made Lieutenant Colonel Peake his
deputy governor, who refuseth to give us any account of the arrears of
the contribution, but when and what he pleaseth.[13]

Rawdon saddled up and rode to Oxford, accompanied by Captain
Amery and a small guard. He had allies there too, including the City
grandee Sir George Benyon, who confirmed that Winchester was in
town and had obtained an order to remove Rawdon from his
post. Benyon advised him to take his complaint directly to the king.
Rawdon then sought out his 'old acquaintance and great friend' Endymion Porter, who was a Groom of the King's Bedchamber. Porter
took him straight to Christ Church. Charles was in the garden, surrounded by his noble entourage. He looked older than his forty-four
years. His beard was grey and shorter than before. His eyes were ringed
and his hair had receded, accentuating the contours of his skull. Porter
whispered something in his ear. Charles looked up, strode over to Rawdon and embraced him, thanking him for his good service.

'Sir,' said Rawdon, 'I give God hearty thanks that he hath been
pleased to make me an instrument of doing Your Majesty any service
and I shall endeavour to do it as long as I live, though I am afraid I shall
be ill rewarded.'

Charles looked puzzled and asked Rawdon what he meant.

'I am informed that I am dispossessed of the government Your Majesty was pleased to bestow upon me.'

Charles said that he knew nothing about it and that it was Prince
Rupert's doing. 'If I be King of England,' he vowed, clapping his hand
upon his breast, 'it shall be remedied.'

According to the Rawdon version, 'the king was as good as his
word'. He stopped Winchester's proceedings and insisted that Sir Marmaduke stay on as governor during his pleasure. The rivals returned to
Basing House and stewed it out for the winter.[14]

The new season was relatively quiet for the garrison. The fortifications
were repaired and the stores replenished. Parties rode out to collect the
county contributions and disrupt the traffic between London and
the west. It was necessary but not honourable work. The soldiers were
little better than racketeers and highwaymen, or 'foxes and wolves', as
the Roundheads put it.[15] Many local people had dreaded the raising of

the siege for this reason. They knew that garrison troopers would come for back payments or revenge. 'We are in great fears,' an estate manager had confided to his master the previous autumn. A parliamentary commissioner called Moore Fauntleroy had a royalist brother in the garrison, but that didn't stop them coming to his house and taking 'his beds and all'.[16] On 2 February, garrison troopers interrupted the Sunday service at Tilehurst and threatened to take away the minister and prominent parishioners unless they paid arrears of £300.[17] There were frequent skirmishes with local Roundheads, and occasionally the garrison lent support to Lord Goring, the Cavalier general in the west who was harrying the region with his army of 'roaring boys'. Fed up with the depredations of both sides, local associations began to spring up. They were known as 'Clubmen', and they defended their farms and families against all comers.

All the while, the Marquess of Winchester continued to plot against his objectionable guests. According to the Rawdon family history, he never stopped lobbying his friends, 'and in particular the queen from whom, as he was a Roman Catholic, he had much favour'. Henrietta Maria was in France but abreast of developments at court. Oxford, no less than Basing House, was hobbled by religious factionalism, clashing egos and a weak king.

The new year saw a new petition from the marquess and 'His Majesty's Catholic subjects' at Basing House. They had 'just cause', they claimed, both during and after Norton's blockade, 'to suspect diverse persons' in Rawdon's regiment of compromising their security. 'By reason of their different opinions from us,' they wrote, 'we do generally hold it more safe that this garrison, which hath been very serviceable to His Majesty, may consist of persons (both officers and soldiers) of one religion.' Naturally, as those 'most deeply engaged in the present war', they themselves were 'the fittest defendants and maintainers' of the place.[18]

Winchester and his advisers must have deemed it necessary, but it was a terrible act of self-harm. Loyalty House had become a liability. At the end of February, Charles reneged on his promise to keep Rawdon at Basing and asked him to take over the garrison at Weymouth. Three days later, however, Weymouth was taken by the Roundheads, so Rawdon and his regiment stayed put. On 27 March 1645, Robert Peake was knighted. There seems to have been some last-minute jostling, as it was reported on 25 April that Rawdon had been reinstated at

Basing, but a week later, on May Day, he mounted his chestnut charger and led his men out of the house for the last time.[19] Fifteen hundred dragoons under Lieutenant General Cromwell tried to ambush them in Berkshire, but Rawdon received a tip-off and made it safely to his new post. Faringdon House was a modest manor compared to Basing, but Charles promised Rawdon 'some better place' soon. 'If His Majesty should send him to keep a molehill,' Rawdon replied, 'he would defend it as long as he had life.'[20]

Five days later, in what must have been a sweetener, Sir Marmaduke's eldest son, Thomas, was given the consulship of Portugal. It was a substantial post, worth £1,500 a year, and was granted by letter patent under the king's signet. Soon afterwards, though, it was invalidated by another appointment under the overriding authority of the Great Seal. When Rawdon found out, he went to the king and asked him what Thomas had done to offend him. In an apparent rehash of their previous conversation, Charles looked very earnest and pleaded total ignorance. 'Sir,' he said, 'your son hath done nothing that hath in the least displeased me.' He clapped his hand upon his breast and vowed to reinstate Thomas or give him 'something more considerable'.

Charles had more important things to deal with in the spring of 1645, but he did not keep his word and Thomas Rawdon did not go to Lisbon. 'The good king meant well,' the family decided, twenty-two years later.[21]

17

The Face of God

The New Model Army took the field in April 1645. It had new officers and a new commander-in-chief: Sir Thomas 'Black Tom' Fairfax, the thirty-three-year-old battle-scarred hero of the north. It also had a new staff of chaplains, the most prominent being Hugh Peter, the Puritan preacher of St Sepulchre's, who had been sniffing out sin on Snow Hill and taking the reformation to Massachusetts Bay. He had prayed with Essex's forces on campaign, but it was service in Fairfax's army, he told the new commander, and the sight of God's presence within it, that was 'one of the greatest comforts I have had in this world'.[1]

Essex, Manchester and Waller were out, expelled by the Self-Denying Ordinance, which required all peers and Members of Parliament to resign their military offices. Waller was 'so heartily weary of this war' that he surrendered his commission without demur.[2] He had played the part assigned to him in this tragedy.

Essex and Manchester did not go quietly. They pushed back hard in the House of Lords and very nearly succeeded in blocking Fairfax's officer list in March. When the vote was tied, the remodellers tendered the proxy of Fairfax's grandfather, the Earl of Mulgrave. Essex then pulled out his own proxy, which his half-brother Ulick, Marquess of Clanricarde and Earl of St Albans, had given him in 1641 before heading for Ireland.[3] But Ulick, like his sister Honora, Marchioness of Winchester, was Catholic, and his proxy was rejected. The list went through. Essex and Manchester lost their commands and Fairfax received his commission. It did not bind him, as it had committed his predecessor, to preserve the safety of the king's person.

The targeted strength of the new army was 22,000 men in twelve regiments of foot, eleven of horse and one of dragoons (mounted infantry). It was funded by an £80,000 loan from the City of London

and thereafter by a monthly assessment levied on the seventeen counties under parliamentary control in East Anglia, the Midlands and the
south-east. Most of the cavalry and about half the infantry – 13,800
men – came in voluntarily from the disbanded armies of Essex, Manchester and Waller, but the rest were conscripts, drawn mainly from
the south-east. They received a shilling of 'pressed money' upfront,
eightpence a day, and a uniform: grey breeches and a red coat. Four
thousand deserted in the first two months. 'Most countries press the
scum of all their inhabitants,' observed Colonel John Venn, '. . . men
taken out of prison, tinkers, pedlars and vagrants that have no dwell-
ing, and such of whom no account can be given. It is no marvel if such
run away.'[4]

Fairfax was in charge of shaping these 'off-scourings of the world'
into a powerful military force.[5] He was aided by Philip Skippon, Major
General of Foot, and Thomas Hammond, Lieutenant General of Ordnance. Second-in-command and Lieutenant General of Horse was the
controversial exemption from the Self-Denying Ordinance – the Member of Parliament for Cambridge, Oliver Cromwell.

Hugh Peter was everywhere and everything in this army, advising at
the council table, preaching on the lines, shuttling to and from Westminster with war reports and promoting the godly vision in the shires.
By his reckoning, he converted 3,000 West Country Clubmen in a single day.[6] He was not modest – nor quite truthful in this case – but he
knew how to win a crowd. 'Bear with my rudeness,' he would begin.
He addressed his hearers as 'dear brethren and sisters', and used vivid
imagery to mock the 'curled and pearled' worshippers of church festi-
vals, for example, or the bishops whose vestments hung down to their
codpieces, 'with bells and pomegranates jengling and jangling (like our
morris dancers)'.[7] He loved to shock: 'Dig up a carcass dead of the
plague and go and kiss it. Sin is more horrible.' And he could hold listeners for up to three hours with his 'unministerial levity and pulpit
scurrility'. So expressive were his performances – 'his fingers, eyes and
nostrils helped his tongue' – that it was rumoured he had once been an
actor. One critic called him a 'pulpit buffoon', but his intent was serious
and clear.[8] He wanted God's word spread throughout the world; he
sought justice for all believers and he needed victory in war. He instilled
'undaunted courage and resolution' in his audience and 'put much life
into them'.[9]

The New Model Army was unique in its fervid religiosity. Peter and the other chaplains held 'days of humiliation', when the men would pray and fast together. Bible reading, self-abasement and impromptu prayers were encouraged. There was a sense of Christian equality evident from the start, when Fairfax insisted that every foot regiment take a turn marching up front. Discipline was stiffened on and off the field. Blasphemers had a hot iron bored through their tongue. Drunkards were made to sit on a wooden horse with their head strapped to their heels. Fornicators were whipped out of the army and plunderers were shot. Fairfax realised that putting an end to looting was the key to winning hearts and minds in the countryside. He ensured that the men were paid centrally and regularly, and could afford food and lodging on the move. There were substantial teething problems, but his troops soon had a far better reputation than Lord Goring's 'roaring boys' or the 'foxes and wolves' at Basing House.[10]

The less palatable side of the army's spiritual enthusiasm, at least to modern sensibilities, was its intolerance. This was directed at 'idolatrous' images – Hugh Peter would have had the soldiers destroy 'the monuments of heathenism' at Stonehenge had their schedule permitted it – and against people, 'fraternity', as is so often the case, coming at the expense of others. 'Our God is not as their God,' the preachers insisted. 'Papists' were considered the agents of the Antichrist. The most feared, and therefore the most hated, were the Irish Catholics, who had surged against the Protestant settlers in 1641 and now seemed to be flooding England's shores. Their slaughter was sanctified by God, the soldiers were told, and by parliamentary ordinance. From 24 October 1644, any Irishman or Catholic born in Ireland taken in arms against Parliament was to be put to death 'forthwith'. Any officer who neglected his duty would be punished as 'a favourer of that bloody rebellion of Ireland'.[11]

On 31 May 1645, Prince Rupert stormed and sacked Leicester in the presence of the king. Hundreds of soldiers and civilians were killed, including women and children. According to military convention, if a city held out after it had been summoned to surrender, and if its defences were breached, the besiegers were entitled to refuse quarter and plunder the place. They could even claim the city's bells. Civilians defending their homes and property were rarely distinguished from combatants. Most besieging commanders showed restraint, but Prince

Rupert of the Rhine was notorious for not doing so, and at Leicester, where he lost four hundred men in the assault, there was 'no quarter given in the heat'.[12] The royalists then marched south. The New Model Army marched north. Two weeks later, they faced each other on two long ridges in a field in Northamptonshire just north of the village of Naseby. 'The place where they fought is called Dreadful Down,' noted one London newsbook.[13]

Fairfax fielded 15,000–17,000 men, Charles between 9,500 and 12,500. The king's army desperately needed reinforcements, but Colonel Gerard's troops were in South Wales and Lord Goring's were besieging Taunton in Somerset. Too late, Charles ordered Goring to bring up his army. Goring refused to budge, but would not in any case have made it in time. Prince Rupert wanted to withdraw to safety, but with Fairfax so close, Charles decided to engage. Parliament had the advantage of ground and also the stars, according to the astrologer William Lilly. 'Without doubt the day is ours,' he predicted, 'if God give us but wisdom to husband time well.'[14]

The royalists advanced at around 10 a.m. on Saturday 14 June. Prince Rupert charged and broke the parliamentarian left wing of horse, but was held up by its rearguard and baggage train. The royalist foot had the better start in the centre as well. They broke through Skippon's front line just as his protective flank of horse was taken out by Rupert. Skippon was accidentally shot by one of his own musketeers. The ball blasted through his armour and produced an eight-inch exit wound, but he refused to leave the field and brought up his reserves in time to check the royalist advance.

Cromwell's front line of horse on the parliamentarian right wing, meanwhile, successfully drove off his opposite number. He then threw the rest of his wing against the exposed flank of royalist foot. Fairfax, who lost his helmet in the fighting, divided the cavalry to fix the left wing broken by Rupert. He and Cromwell advanced from both sides. Hugh Peter reportedly rode 'from rank to rank with a bible in one hand and a pistol in the other, exhorting the men to do their duty'.[15] The ragged royalists were overawed by this superior synchronised force. The battle was over in two and a half hours.[16]

The king took flight. He lost 2,000 horses, most of his infantry, all his artillery and the baggage train. This included his private papers, which were filleted and published to expose him as a 'dexterous' dealer not interested in peace – despite his public pronouncements during recent negotiations – but plotting to secure Irish and French aid.[17] Naseby was the decisive battle of the war. 'This is none other but the hand of God,' exulted Cromwell, 'and to Him alone belongs the glory.'[18] The New Model Army had passed its first test with a dazzling display of courage and discipline. Then they saw the women on Farndon Field.

These were the king's camp followers, desperately scurrying northwards away from the battleground. They were overtaken 'in the south part of Farndon Field within the gate-place in the road between Naseby and Farndon'. At least one hundred of them were slaughtered and many more were mutilated with the 'whore's mark' – a slash to the face or nose. The parliamentarian press was not concerned by the sins of its soldiers. The victims, they told their readers, were just 'drabs, Irish women and leaguer bitches'.[19]

It seems that most of the women were not Irish. Some might have been Welsh; others were English (and Protestant). The heat of the battle, the rush of victory, the anticlimax of a short fight, the ease of opportunity – all might have been factors in the savagery. The soldiers were also slaking a deep thirst for revenge after past atrocities suffered by their own side, especially by the women who had been thrown off Lostwithiel Bridge in Cornwall the previous September. The Roundheads had talked of the need for a 'proportionable requital', and Farndon had presented the field.[20]

The road to Farndon Field was also littered with pamphlets and newsbooks denouncing outlandish women, women with weapons, women preaching, women turning the world upside down – transvesting and transgressing, above nature and against nature. There were innuendoes about the women in the king's train: 'the delights and diseases of his camp', committing 'luxuriant sins which deserve a hotter punishment'.[21] There were reported sightings of royalist witches at Newbury and knife-wielding Celtic viragos. And there was talk, going back almost a century now, of the existential papist menace. All the incendiary inches, amplified by the preaching padres, dehumanising the enemy and steeling the soldiers for the battle against the Beast; all this noise, all this prejudice was worked up into a bloody lather on no ordinary afternoon in June. When the soldiers saw the women on Farndon Field, they wouldn't have seen wives, mothers, sisters and daughters.

They saw a monstrous regiment of 'trulls', Irish savages with 'cruel countenances', 'harlots with golden tresses', and the Whore of Babylon.[22] And so they tore her face up and rode on.

Instead of chasing Charles into the Welsh hills, Fairfax went after his other main field force: Lord Goring's army in the west. They found him at Langport in Somerset on 10 July. Goring entrenched himself on a steep hill above a swollen stream. His musketeers lined the hedges all the way up. The New Model Army blasted them with artillery, forded the stream, powered up the hill and utterly defeated them. 'To see this,' asked Cromwell, 'is it not to see the face of God?' Another officer, Major Thomas Harrison, broke out loudly in praise of the Lord 'as if he had been in a rapture'.[23]

Parliament's 'home-bred, new-bred soldiers'[24] were unstoppable, and the royalist garrisons fell like tenpins: Bridgwater on 23 July, Bath on the 29th and Sherborne Castle on 15 August. Writing to the Marquess of Ormond from Cornwall three days later, his agent Arthur Trevor found himself cut off: 'lodged until I pay the *ultima* solution'. If the Roundheads advanced, he wrote, 'we must try the experiment who can swim best'. He was more frightened of the New Model Army than the wild sea. 'I find the question asked, why do the people rage? But I do not remember to have read any answer to it.' The king was heading north, he reported, and planned to send the Prince of Wales to France. 'What will follow hereupon may be foretold without the aid of the wisewoman on the bank ... The war is at an end in the west. Each one looks for a ship and nothing more.'[25]

18

More Sulphur for Basing

It was not over in Ireland, where the Catholic Confederates were fighting their own battles and might yet send more men to help Charles; nor in Wales, where he still had strongholds; nor in Scotland, where the royalist Marquess of Montrose extended his winning streak on 15 August at the battle of Kilsyth. And it was not over in Hampshire, where Winchester and Basing House still stood for the king.

On 19 August, a fast was held in Christ Church, London. This was the parish on Newgate Street where, before the war, an old blind woman had torn the vicar's 'Babylonish' surplice from his back. That was in the Puritan *annus mirabilis* of 1641, when the momentum had been all for the fall of Babylon. Four years later, the Antichrist had not yet been overthrown, but Parliament's praying army was determined to finish the job. As they marched on plague-ridden Bristol, Colonel John Dalbier was sent out to break the 'limb of Babylon' in Hampshire. The fast at Christ Church was to implore God to bless his expedition to Basing House.[1]

He arrived the next day with eight hundred men. Dalbier was a German (some said a Hollander) with two decades' experience of the art and business of war. He had served everyone from Gustavus Adolphus to the Earl of Essex. He was too old guard for the New Model Army, but his regiment was still useful to Parliament.* He was put on a short contract with a small down payment 'and the rest afterwards'. He was promised two thousand men from Hampshire and Sussex, but the county committees had their hands full dealing with Clubmen uprisings and could not muster half the number. Reinforcements eventually

---

* The New Model Army was Parliament's main fighting force, but there were still some regional units in the field, like Colonel Massey's western army and the London trained bands.

arrived from Reading and Southwark, but not enough to cover Basing's mile-and-a-half-long perimeter. The lesson, in any case, from Idle Dick Norton's summer siege was to avoid a costly blockade and adopt a more targeted approach.[2]

Dalbier took over the village and church with a team of expert miners, 'such as used to dig in coal pits'. Orders were placed for picks, mattocks, cannonballs, granado shells and scaling ladders. The ground was hard and rocky, one newsbook noted, but the rain helped. A trench was soon down and a battery up.[3] The news from the field was devastating for the royalists. Prince Rupert surrendered Bristol on 11 September, and two days later, the Marquess of Montrose was routed at Philiphaugh in the Scottish borders. As at Naseby, female camp followers were slaughtered in the aftermath.

On 20 September, Sir Robert Peake's groom deserted to Dalbier's camp and, 'to make himself more welcome', took his master's charger with him. Two days of heavy bombardment on 22 and 23 September brought down one of the main towers of the Old House and blew breaches in the New. Dalbier concentrated his fire on a wall in the New House. The bricks were loosened and a crack appeared. He then aimed high and toppled a turret. The force of the fall brought down the weakened wall. The besiegers saw 'bedding and other goods fall out of the house into the court'. The garrison scrambled to staunch its gaping wound, but Dalbier maintained the breach. All the while, the granadoes did 'good execution'.[4]

The news in London was that the New House had fallen. This was wishful thinking, but Basing House, like Bristol, no longer seemed impregnable. The Marquess of Winchester was severely shaken and swore that Dalbier was a greater trouble to him than any previous assailant.[5] There were more desertions, too, including possibly Lieutenant Colonel Thomas Langley, whom Sir Marmaduke Rawdon had left behind in May 'sick and under some suspicion of corresponding with the enemy'. His wife was Dalbier's niece and he disappears from the record at this point.[6]

Apart from the 'hen-hearted' marquess, *The City-Scout* acknowledged that there were 'notable desperate fellows' in the garrison. This was a backhanded compliment to Peake and his men – desperate to fight, not flee – but many of the rank and file brought in to replace Rawdon's regiment were raw conscripts. Most were not even eighteen,

The Moderate Intelligencer claimed, 'some not 12'.[7] Over a dozen Irish soldiers had also made their way in, hoping perhaps for the protection of the half-Irish marchioness. Since the October ordinance that sanctioned their slaughter, they were acutely vulnerable in the field. There were also 'reformadoes' – officers whose companies had been disbanded over the course of the war. One was Tamworth Reresby, who had served in the north under Colonel Rowland Eyre. After Marston Moor, he had ridden south to Hampshire, where he had family connections, and joined the Marquess of Winchester, whose faith he shared. He was a charming 'healthful, handsome man'.[8]

Another new face, though familiar to London's theatregoers, was the actor William Robbins. He had been the principal comedian of Queen Henrietta's Men, and since 1636, a member of the King's Men. This attached him to the royal household as a Groom of the Chamber. He had played the repulsive Rawbone (a 'thin citizen') in James Shirley's *The Wedding*, and the witty eunuch Carazie in Philip Massinger's *The Renegado*, a role that required him to sing well enough for the audience to stand 'amazed'.

Robbins was probably older than the century, having acted since 1617. His wife Cicely, whose brother and first husband had also been players, was the sister-in-law of Christopher Beeston, London's leading impresario. It is not known if she was at Basing House with William, or still at home in Clerkenwell.[9]

The acting world had been in the eye of the storm during Charles's Personal Rule, when William Prynne had called actresses 'notorious whores' and accused players of being pimps. Prynne had lost his liberty – and his ears – and had then been cheered out of prison at the beginning of the Long Parliament. The theatres were shut down in September 1642, since 'public sports do not well agree with public calamities, nor public stage-plays with the seasons of humiliation'. The actors, like the reformadoes, became players without companies. Robbins swapped his stage sword for the real thing and offered it to his master the king. By the autumn of 1645, he was a major at Basing House and reportedly baiting the Roundheads with clownish sketches from the ramparts.[10]

Estimates of the strength of the garrison at this stage vary from 300 to 500 men. As the newsbooks pointed out, the higher figure made it half as strong as Dalbier's force and therefore able to resist an assault.

Contemporary thinking was that a besieging army should outnumber the garrison by a ratio of at least 7 to 1 before attempting to storm it. 'It may be,' speculated *The Moderate Intelligencer* on 25 September, that 'Lieutenant General Cromwell may come.'[11]

After the fall of Bristol on 11 September, Fairfax took the New Model Army deeper into the south-west, but Cromwell detached a brigade and headed for Wiltshire and Hampshire with an eye to clearing the royalist garrisons that threatened the supply lines from London. Devizes surrendered on 23 September, and Cromwell laid siege to Winchester, twenty miles from Basing, on the 28th.

Dalbier was keen to receive credit – and payment – before the arrival of the russet-coated glory-guzzlers. 'There is a design,' hinted a newsbook, 'to show the enemy there a gallant stratagem of war, but I had rather let them study to find it than let my pen tell tales out of school.'[12]

There was no shortage of 'designs' in the civil war, the impulse to create ever being the running mate of the urge to destroy. A rudimentary 'sow' (effectively a mobile hut) had been used during Norton's summer blockade of Basing House, but there were more ambitious inventions elsewhere, including a prototype tank designed by Edmond Felton to protect infantry from all but the heaviest artillery.[13] Sponsors of Felton's engine included the 'chemical gentleman' Sir Cheney Culpeper, the educational reformer Samuel Hartlib and (probably) the poet John Milton. These men shared a vision of the world where God's light could shine freely. They thrilled to the moment, believing that God had raised their spirits out of 'this mud of custom', as Culpeper put it, for the betterment of society. Culpeper saw things clearly and urgently. Every day for him was a battle between 'Protestancy and liberty on the one side and Popery and tyranny on the other'. Every step towards enlightenment – towards a 'greater shining forth of truth into the heart of all nations' – brought them closer to the fall of Babylon and the heavenly feast described in the Book of Revelation.[14]

Over the autumn of 1643, Culpeper and Hartlib had written to each other about various inventions, including lightweight leather guns and a bulletproof doublet made of 'sinews and silk', which could be found at the sign of the Eagle and Child on Snow Hill.[15] Just after Waller's first failed assaults on Basing House in November, Culpeper had also sent

Hartlib an extract from a sixteenth-century book proposing an early form of chemical warfare. 'First, we must consider the wind,' instructed its author, Giambattista della Porta, 'that it may be on the backs of our men.' Next, fill paper lanterns with powdered euphorbium, pepper, quicklime, vine ashes and arsenic sublimate. Once fired from a cannon, 'the smoke of the powder, if it come at the eyes of the enemies, will so trouble them that, casting away their weapons, they can hardly save their eyes'. Improvements could be made to this design, Culpeper suggested, if the poison was packed inside a granado shell and shot from a mortar. If used on 'so small a circuit as Basing House', he added, 'it would (no question) have smoked them out of the fume' and '(if not already), may, with a small addition, be made deadly to the brains'.[16]

Culpeper's sense of his own moral purity seems to have fastened his soul against any ethical doubts. He believed that he was on the right side of God in an existential war and that the enemy could be destroyed by any means possible. 'War is self-defence that knows no law', as it was put almost three centuries later, after Ypres.[17]

Chemical warfare is as old as poison and is mentioned in contemporary military manuals, but it was not really a feature of the English civil war. Soldiers and civilians were smoked out of buildings, and occasionally slow-burning firebombs and 'wildfire' were used, but the addition of arsenic was a novelty. While Culpeper's idea was shelved in 1643, it re-emerged two years later, when John Dalbier had another fling at Basing.

'He hath a design,' reported *The True Informer* on 24 September 1645, 'to smoke them out, good store of straw being brought in from the county for that purpose.'[18] Two days later, *The Scottish Dove* confirmed that Dalbier 'smokes them with the sulphur of brimstone, an emblem of their future vengeance'.[19] It was a 'strange kind of smoke', reported *Mercurius Veridicus*, 'a compounded stifling smoke' that drove the defenders out of part of the New House.[20] On 29 September, another paper, *Mercurius Britanicus*, returned to its favourite theme, the Marquess of Winchester's alleged cowardice. 'He loves not the smell of gunpowder, and therefore (in commiseration) Colonel Dalbier hath this last week tried to smoke him out with straw, just as they used to serve eels in old walls' – a reference to Catholic missionaries being flushed out of priest-holes. 'If this trick will not take,' *Britanicus* continued, 'there is another nameless stratagem in acting, for [the] gallant colonel is resolved to have his pay.'[21]

In *The Parliaments Post* the following day, arsenic was explicitly mentioned:

> They are all papists in that garrison and if there were ever purgatory on earth, the papists do find it and feel it there, for besides the thick and perpetual darkness, which the wet and smoking straw doth make, the burning of brimstone and arsenic and other dismal ingredients doth infinitely annoy the besieged, which makes them to gnash their teeth for indignation. In the meantime, the cannons do perpetually thunder one against another. On every side, desolation dwells about them, and to subdue the place there are those things [that] are put in execution which the nature of man doth tremble at.[22]

'No smoke now, but fire,' reported another newsbook on 1 October, and that seems to have been the end of the poison gas.[23] 'The defendants have been so used to the strong breath of old priests and Jesuits,' opined *Mercurius Veridicus*, 'that straw and sulphur will not stifle them out of the house, therefore Dalbier daily sends pellets amongst them, and hath beat down part of the house and so terrified some that they have stolen out of the house and got quite away.'[24]

Many others could not get away. At seventy-two years old, Inigo Jones was probably the oldest person in the house. In the past, he too had created a 'horrid scene' of desolation, but it had not been real. For the last masque performed at court in 1640, he had designed a hellscape that looked 'as if darkness, confusion and deformity had possessed the world and driven light to heaven'. But then out of the clouds, Charles and Henrietta Maria had emerged – Jones had used pulleys to draw their thrones twenty feet above the stage – and they had danced the country out of its troubles. The show had climaxed with the royal couple serenaded in the sky:

> All that are harsh, all that are rude,
> Are by your harmony subdued.[25]

It hadn't worked out like that, and now it was Colonel John Dalbier who controlled the clouds.

For the past decade, Jones had been documenting his deteriorating health in the flyleaves of his treasured copy of Andrea Palladio's *I Quattro Libri dell'Archittetura*.* He had consulted several doctors and apothecaries, including Thomas Johnson's old master, William Bell. He noted remedies for kidney stones (the 'gravel'), headaches, insomnia, bloodshot eyes, constipation and gout. He was regularly afflicted by melancholy, against which, he wrote, 'copulation must be utterly eschewed, for that thereby the best blood of a man is wasted and natural strength enfeebled'. He reminded himself 'to comb the head often, to sing, use music'.[26]

He might have been comforted by the sound of Mary Griffith, who could sing and play the lute like an angel, according to her epitaph. She was ten years old in 1645 and must have been one of the youngest people at Basing House. She was there with her three older sisters, the 'handsome daughters' of the Reverend Matthew Griffith and his wife Sarah.[27] Griffith had been the rector of St Mary Magdalen, Old Fish Street, for almost twenty years and a lecturer at St Dunstan-in-the-West, where his patron, the great John Donne, had been the vicar.[28]

In 1633, two years before Mary was born, Griffith published a book called *Bethel*. A five-hundred-page doorstopper, it was essentially a prescription for the perfect patriarchal household. A family was like a house, he wrote, 'in which all sorts of both sexes are so squared and framed by the word of God as they may best serve in their several places for useful pieces in God's building'. The king was 'an earthly god', he insisted, and must be feared and obeyed without question. 'Wives must be in subjection to their husbands' and children to their parents.[29] He sounds severe, but Mary's epitaph suggests a softer side to the man 'who from the cradle cherished her and in her tender girlhood taught her'.

Matthew Griffith was certainly brave. He had first been arrested on 24 October 1642, the day after the battle of Edgehill, for a 'scandalous and seditious' sermon denouncing fanatics and warmongers. He had hoped that peace could be restored and told his audience that what was

---

* This book, written in 1570 by the Padua-born Palladio, has had an extraordinary cultural impact. The third US president, Thomas Jefferson, called it his bible and owned a copy of the 1742 edition, which included Jones's transcribed notes. In 2010, in honour of the quincentenary of Palladio's birth, the United States Congress agreed a concurrent resolution honouring his 'tremendous influence' on American architecture.

happening on the Continent and in Ireland might yet be prevented in England:

> God be thanked, we never yet knew what it is to hear the murdering pieces [cannon] about our ears, or to see our churches and houses flaming over our heads . . . we never yet heard the fearful cracks of their falls, mixed with the confused outcries of men killing . . . and the hideous shrieking of women and children. God be thanked we never saw tender babes snatch'd from the breasts of their mothers . . . and the poor, pure virgin ravished ere she may have leave to die.[30]

For hindering the public defence of the kingdom, Griffith had been imprisoned in Newgate and ejected from his living. He had been released on bail, but much to Lord Mayor Penington's irritation, had become 'more insistent than ever'. Penington advised the Speaker of the House that an example be made of the outspoken cleric. Griffith was 'forced to fly'.[31] The family packed their bags and Mary's tender girlhood came to an end.

She was not alone. Up and down the land, the wives and children of sequestered vicars were being booted out of their well-ordered rectories and thrown upon the charity, and frequently the hostility, of the parish. In Tiverton in Devon, George Pierce's sons remembered being tossed out of their beds, the sheets whipped away from beneath them. In Allerton, Norfolk, John Reeve saw his father's library being carted away. Frances Manby, the daughter of the rector of Cottenham, Cambridgeshire, remembered that no one wanted to play with her any more. When she and her sister tried to join in, their old friends shrank from them. The children were 'so full of hatred', she recalled, 'taking it from their parents'. A boy stabbed her in the forehead with a fork: 'the scars of I have yet'.[32]

There are hundreds of stories like this, provided, it must be noted, in response to a request for the memories of churchmen's families sixty years later and therefore subject to distortion. Some children claimed to have suffered serious violence, but for many it was pain enough to lose their homes and see their parents scorned. A recurring theme in these reflections, as with children in all wars, is an obsession with food – the blandness of barley dumplings, the delight of a juicy blackberry. Roger Trosse's family had been allowed to stay on in an outhouse kitchen when they were kicked out of the parsonage. One day, the story goes, the children were unable to resist the smell of apple pie curling into their nostrils. They opened the oven door and stole a slice. 'You need not be so angry,' one of the lads replied when caught, 'I'm sure the apples were ours.'[33]

Mary Griffith and her siblings fled to Oxford, where Charles made their father a royal chaplain and a doctor of divinity. The parliamentary press reported the news in July 1643, calling Griffith a 'boutefeaux [incendiary] and stirrer up of sedition'. He was still with the court in February 1644, when *The Spie* referred to him as a 'conceited rabbi of royalists'.[34] At some stage he and his family moved to Basing House. He must have thought it would be a place of greater safety.

On Sunday 21 September 1645, the parliamentarian preacher William Beech gave a sermon to the troops before Basing House. It was published in London five days later under the title *More Sulphure for Basing*. It was meant to steel Colonel Dalbier's soldiers for what was to come, but it was also directed at the Hampshire Clubmen in an attempt to turn them towards 'the good old cause'. The frontispiece of the printed text quoted Revelation 14:11: 'And the smoke of their torment shall ascend evermore, and they shall have no rest day nor night which worship the beast and his image.'

Beech began his sermon with the Old Testament story of the Midianites, an idolatrous tribe of desert bandits who had terrorised villages, stolen cattle and sucked the produce from the land. The Israelite chieftain Gideon had attacked them with a small but blessed force and utterly destroyed them. 'Do unto them, as to the Midianites,' ordered Beech.

God's people now faced a more formidable enemy, he continued, 'the bloody papists'. They collaborate with Satan in mines and mazes, 'under board, under deck', contriving armadas, powder plots 'and (as now) civil wars, and all to bring our kingdom and religion to utter devastation and confusion, as they have done (already) upon Germany'. They are growing in power, these 'cannibals', these 'vermin', these 'tigers of Rome'. Their swords are 'touched with the magnetic stone of inhumanity to draw blood'. They must be crushed, Beech insisted, 'like the breaking of a potter's pot'. God's army will prevail, as it is foretold in the Book. Witness Naseby, Taunton, Bristol. 'Tell them of

Babylon (and you may [tell] them of Basing too), it will certainly go ill
with them . . . Let this be terror and astonishment to them, more than
either the roaring of our cannon or the terrible bursting asunder of the
granado. Let their joints loosen for fear and their knees smite together
for horror, for as true as God is in Heaven, they shall perish . . . Their
destruction shall be terrible, it shall be timely, it shall be total.'

Addressing those who had friends and relations inside Basing House,
or who worried about harming Protestants and non-combatants,
Beech insisted that they must not flinch from the task. 'True, indeed,
there are some of our own there, unhappy wretches!' but they are
enchanted, lost, just as the king is currently lost to 'a cruel stepmother'.
The cause was vital: 'Here Religion, and Laws, and Liberties, and the
very being of our English Nation lie at stake.' They must act 'now or
never. Now, if ever.' And so again, he implored his countrymen, for he
too was a son of Hampshire, a child of the chalk and the clay: 'Arise,
arise in the name of God, let cursed neutrality go to hell.' Destroy
'those horrible monsters', he cried:

> God calls,
> man calls,
> mercy calls,
> judgment calls,
> the Church calls,
> the Commonwealth calls,
> the wife calls,
> the child calls;
> this and future ages and generations all call upon you presently to
> set about the work.[35]

MORE

3

SULPHURE

FOR

BASING:

O R,

God will fearfully annoy and make quick riddance of his implacable Enemies, surely, sorely, suddenly.

Shewed in a Sermon at the Siege of
BASING

On the last Lords day, *Sept.* 21. 1645.

Together, with a word of advice, full of love and affection to the Club-men of *Hampshire*.

By *William Beech* Minister of the Army there, elect: Min: of O. in the County of *Suffolke.*

Imprimatur. *Ja. Cranford.* Sept. 26. 1645.

REV. 14. 11.
And the smoke of their torment shall ascend evermore, and they shall have no rest day nor night which worship the beast and his image.

London printed for *Iohn Wright* at the Kings Head in the old Bayley. 1645.

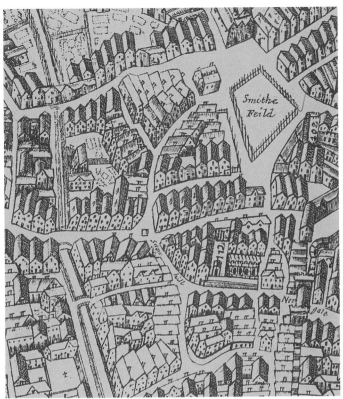

Snow Hill, north-west London. Home to Thomas Johnson the apothecary, Robert Peake the print-seller, Isaac Rowlett the scrivener and William Faithorne, who engraved this map. They all fought at Basing House.

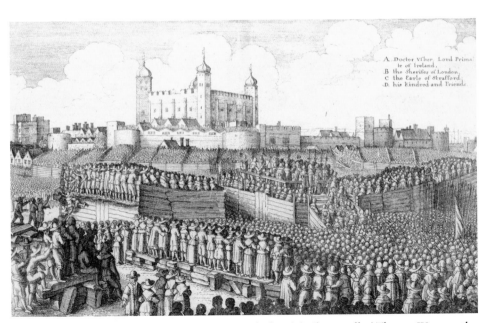

A Doctor Vſher, Lord Prima
   te of Ireland,
B the Sherifes of London
C the Earle of Strafford
D his Kindred and Friends

Tower Hill, south-east London. Here, in May 1641, the king's 'evil counsellor' Thomas Wentworth, Earl of Strafford, was executed before an estimated 100,000 spectators. The nearby streets, including Water Lane where Marmaduke Rawdon lived, would have teemed.

'The Apothecary's Shop opened.'
Engraving by William Faithorne.

Thomas Johnson's
edition of John
Gerard's *Herball*. His
bananas top the
arrangement in the
bottom-left corner.

Inside a seventeenth-century printing house, similar to the one where William Faithorne and
Thomas Rowlett worked for Robert Peake. Note the physicality of the job.

The carved stern of the *Sovereign of the Seas*, Charles I's prestigious ship, built in 1637 and boasting 102 bronze guns. To Marmaduke Rawdon, ships were 'the jewels that adorn the kingdom and the walls of the land'. Others saw them as an excuse for Charles to levy tax.

A panel painted by Rubens in the ceiling of the Banqueting House. Hercules, representing Heroic Virtue, takes a club to Civil Discord.

Charles I by Van Dyck. Those who did not bow to divine majesty as readily as his horse might face ruthless measures.

Alleged Catholic-on-Protestant atrocities during the Irish rebellion of 1641. The king and queen were accused of encouraging the uprising to facilitate the raising of an army against Parliament.

Hugh Peter, Puritan preacher of St Sepulchre's and Salem. The 'cursed and damned' Cavaliers will 'rape your handsome wives and deflower your sweet virgins,' he told Londoners, '(but you that have ugly wives and daughters' you shall escape better).' In William Faithorne's engraving, Peter gathers sacks of money for the parliamentarian war fund.

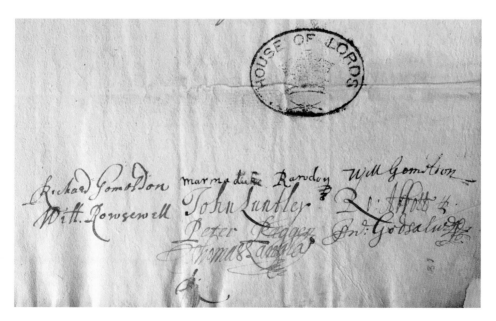

The delegates of a peace petition, which was signed by thousands in December 1642 but rejected in the House of Lords. Three of the signatories – Marmaduke Rawdon, William Rosewell and Thomas Langley – will head 'the London Regiment' at Basing House.

One garrison, two governors:
John Paulet, 5th Marquess of Winchester, Lord of Basing House.
His cornet bears the family motto: *Aimez Loyaute* (Love Loyalty).

Marmaduke Rawdon, garrison governor. His cornet depicts a stoat, an animal that reputedly gave itself up to the hounds before besmirching its ermine fur. The motto translates as: I would rather die than change my course.

Honora, marchioness of Winchester,
chatelaine of Basing House.

Honora's beloved half-brother, Robert Devereux, 3rd Earl
of Essex, Lord General of the parliamentarian army.

19

Babylon is Fallen

Oliver Cromwell arrived on 8 October sparkling with victory. Winchester Castle had been easy enough in the end. A wide breach in the old wall had made the governor submit like a puppy. According to the terms of surrender, the New Model troops were deprived of their blood and plunder. Their chaplain, Hugh Peter, had peeled off to Westminster to report on this latest manifestation of God's favour, and Lieutenant General Cromwell had proceeded to Basing with the big guns. The largest, the cannon royal, weighed 8,000 pounds, fired 63-pound balls and needed at least 40 draught horses to pull it. The earth would have quaked.

Cromwell liaised with Dalbier, who briefed him on some recent royalist desertions and a few brazen sallies launched from the Old House.[1] As the two commanders surveyed the works, a gentleman of the garrison rode out to get a better look at them. One of Cromwell's men, 'not enduring to be stared upon', galloped up and pistolled him in the neck. 'His body was buried,' reported *The Moderate Intelligencer*, 'but not his clothes for they were very good ones.'[2]

The great guns were drawn into the park and the fireworkers soon had the mortars spewing out granado shells. One smashed into the Marchioness of Winchester's lodgings, just missing her but killing her gentlewoman and a waiting maid.[3] There is no mention of Honora's children (and hasn't been since November 1643); they were presumably elsewhere. She now tried to escape, but was caught in Cromwell's cordon. Reports are vague and contradictory, but it seems that after prisoners were exchanged, Honora was allowed to ride away.[4]

On 9 and 10 October, Cromwell raised his batteries towards the south-east side of the New House. He had 6,000–7,000 men with him, including four out of seven of 'the chiefest praying and preaching regiments in the army'. These were Pickering's, Montagu's, Hammond's and Fleetwood's units. Two more – Sir Hardress Waller's foot and Thomas Sheffield's horse – completed the brigade. John Pickering, 'a little man, but of a great courage', had been singled out as a radical evangeliser even before the New Model Army had taken to the field. 'Instead of drinking, swearing, roaring, carding, dicing and drabbing [whoring],' one newsbook noted approvingly, 'he spent that little time he had to spare in the study of scriptures and exercising his regiment.'[5]

Another notable 'preaching officer' was Major Thomas Harrison, the son of a butcher and the commander of Charles Fleetwood's regiment of horse. At twenty-nine, he was the same age as Pickering and also a veteran of Marston Moor and Naseby. After the New Model Army's victory at Langport in July, he had been seen rhapsodising over God's glory. He believed that the kingdom of Christ on earth was imminent and that a biblical judgement should befall that 'man of blood', Charles I.[6]

Since joining the New Model Army, none of these men had tasted defeat. 'Doubtless God is with them,' Hugh Peter had declared after the fall of Bristol. 'He must be a very atheist that doth not acknowledge it,' agreed Cromwell.[7] Their morale was sky-high when they came to Basing House. They had heard the tales of this 'invincible garrison' that had defied a twenty-four-week blockade. They had been told that it was shrouded in fog and protected by 'Antichrist, the Pope, the devil and all'. They knew about the marksmen who could take out a man 'at half-head, as one would kill a sparrow', and about the treasure inside, and the Irish. They would also have been aware of the doubters: 'Some seem to think [it] will not be so suddenly taken,' warned Sir Robert Honeywood. They only had to look up to see a fortress 'as strong and defensible as nature and art could imagine'. But they could also read the words on Colonel Sheffield's battle standard: *Deo duce, nil desperandum* – 'With God as our guide, never despair'.[8]

As for Cromwell himself, the gentleman farmer who would soon rule three kingdoms: he was, at the age of forty-six, outstanding only on the battlefield. He was an instinctive tactician, a wily strategist and a great cavalry commander. 'His figure did no ways promise what he performed,' observed the nephew of the Basing renegado Tamworth

Reresby. 'He was personable, but not handsome, nor did he look great, nor bold. He was plain in his apparel and rather affected a negligence than a gentle garb.' Another royalist, Sir Philip Warwick, recalled the red face, bad suit and blood-flecked collar. Sir William Waller, who had spent the past spring with Cromwell, gave his sightings of 'this eagle in his eyrie'. At this time, he reflected, Cromwell had 'never shown extraordinary parts, nor do I think that he did himself believe that he had them, for although he was blunt, he did not bear himself with pride or disdain'.[9]

Cromwell may not have believed in himself, but after a life of toil, stress and intense soul-searching, he had a gnawing conviction that God did, in fact, believe in him and had sanctified his sword as an instrument of divine wrath. This gave Cromwell a providential glow and a dutiful ruthlessness that was irrepressible. 'He is a prosperous man,' *The Scottish Dove* reported happily upon his arrival at Basing House. 'God hath blessed him and I trust He will still make him victorious.'[10]

On the evening of Saturday 11 October, with his guns emplaced and the house surrounded, Cromwell sent Winchester a summons to surrender. The garrison was 'a nest of Romanists', he said, and if they refused to submit, they could expect no mercy, 'but all the severity that in a just way of arms might be made good'.[11] The marquess refused to parley and kept his black flag flying. His odds were terrible, but his faith was deep. As the siege diarist had noted after their salvation the previous year, God chose the weak to confound the strong. Winchester might have argued that his little garrison was the true tribe of Israel, and that the thousands of Ironsides beyond the wall were the Midianites with blood-sucking swords. The London newsbooks blamed the marquess's Jesuit confessors for whispering martyrdom in his ear, and perhaps they were right, but he was also still hoping for relief, either from Oxford or the heavens. It would soon be winter; it was just possible. *The Scottish Dove* had a theory: 'Such is the devil's power in and with the children of disobedience that when they are nearest destruction he makes them most confident and resolute.'[12]

That evening, a thick mist enveloped the house. Cromwell's youngest colonel, twenty-four-year-old Robert Hammond, left the village to check on the horses with Major Nathaniel King and two soldiers. The sentry at the checkpoint told them that all was well, so they rode on into the mist.

Another party of horse appeared at the checkpoint. The sentry bade them stand.

'Who are you for?' he asked.

'For the Parliament,' they replied.

When they drew closer, he realised that they were not for the Parliament. There was a firefight and the sentry was shot in the back. The Cavaliers wheeled about, overtook Hammond's small group and forced them into the house.[13]

According to the *City-Scout*, the royalists treated their hostages civilly, neither stripping nor plundering them, 'not so much as [taking] their rings from their fingers'. Hammond was a distant kinsman of Honora Winchester, and although one of his uncles was the New Model Army's Lieutenant General of Ordnance, another was a royal chaplain in Oxford. Some even suspected that Hammond had allowed himself to be taken to save the marquess, but Cromwell, who knew 'dear Robin' well and had witnessed his impeccable conduct at the storming of Bristol the previous month, did not doubt him.[14] He sent Winchester a furious message demanding the immediate exchange of his officers. If any wrong or violence was offered these men, he warned, 'the best in the house should not expect quarter'. The garrison released all their prisoners apart from Hammond and King.[15]

Over the next two days, Cromwell and Dalbier subjected Basing House to a ferocious cannonade. A drawbridge was beaten down, fifteen defenders fell to granadoes in an afternoon, and a cannonball killed some women at Mass.[16] A half-hearted rescue effort was mounted from Oxford, 'but upon second thoughts', reported one newsbook, 'they considered the difficulty of the service and went back again'.[17] By Monday evening, 13 October, there were two effective breaches in the walls of the New House. The marquess's flag stayed up. According to convention, Cromwell was within his rights now to refuse quarter in a storm and withhold all mercy. 'The dearer it costs the assailant, the more he is enraged,' wrote Humfrey Peake, 'and the more he is enraged, the more mischief he doth after he enters.'[18] Cromwell told his men to be ready at daybreak, and retired to his chamber.

The guns were silent that night, and we can only imagine what was happening inside the house: the last-minute preparations and rituals; the gun-cleaning and sword-sharpening; confession, communion, Mass. The non-combatants barricaded themselves in their rooms or hid in the vaults. The Marquess of Winchester kept his hostage Hammond close. Robert Peake locked away his jewels and engravings. Robbins the actor was spotted a little before the storm 'mocking and scorning the Parliament'.[19] Each defender took up his position and glowed his match.

Cromwell spent much of the night to the drumbeat of prayer. He 'seldom fights without some texts of scripture to support him', noted Hugh Peter, 'and this time he rested upon that blessed word of God written in the 115 Psalm, and the 8th verse'.[20] The text denounces false worship. The idols of the heathens, writes the psalmist, 'are silver and gold, the work of men's hands'.

> They have mouths, but they speak not: eyes have they,
>   but they see not:
> They have ears, but they hear not: noses have they,
>   but they smell not:
> They have hands, but they handle not: feet have they, but they
>   walk not: neither speak they through their throat.
> *They that make them are like unto them; so is every one that*
>   *trusteth in them.*
> O Israel, trust thou in the Lord: he is their help and their shield.
> O house of Aaron, trust in the Lord: he is their help and their shield.
> Ye that fear the Lord, trust in the Lord: he is their help and their
>   shield . . .

Four great guns severed the silence of a taut autumn morning at six o'clock on Tuesday 14 October 1645. A moment later, Pickering's soldiers poured through the great breach of the New House and into the outer courtyard. The defenders were waiting for them in the upper storeys of the raised inner court, their guns peeping through windows and holes in the walls. As the New Model Army surged in, the defenders picked off the first few and blasted those that followed with hand grenades, but nothing could hold the charge for more than an instant.

Dalbier's forces now broke in from the north. They slipped through the windows and rammed down the doors. They chased the defenders up stairs and along corridors. They hacked and they bludgeoned until the ground was carpeted in bodies. 'The dispute was long and sharp,' reported the first man back at Westminster, but Roundhead waves kept rolling in. The defenders screamed for a parley, 'which our men would not hear', wrote Cromwell afterwards. It was too late for that. 'You must remember *what* they were,' explained the reporter, 'they were most of them papists; therefore our muskets and our swords did show but little compassion.'[21]

Some defenders continued to battle it out, but many ran into 'holes and corners to hide themselves'. Others tried to escape beyond the wall.[22] Majors Cuffaud and Robbins were scrabbling over the outworks when the fanatical Thomas Harrison caught up with them. He killed them 'with his own hands'. Three years later, it was put about by a hostile source that he had butchered the officers in cold blood, roaring as he did so: 'Cursed be he that doth the work of the Lord negligently!' Half a century later still, a royalist historian added that Harrison had shot Robbins in the head after the actor had laid down his arms. The scriptural ejaculation was in keeping with Harrison's character, and he was unlikely to have granted anyone quarter in the heat of combat, let alone the actor who had been baiting them beforehand, but we cannot know exactly what happened. 'The fool slain as he was turning and acting like a player,' reported *Perfect Occurrences* three days after the storm. The paper's readers might have been able to recall Robbins's mannerisms on the stage. 'He was in Drury Lane a comedian,' added another London newsbook, 'but now he acted his own tragedy.'[23]

The New House had fallen. The few remaining defenders fell back to a postern gate in the Old House via a small wooden bridge linking the two buildings. Their comrades threw grenades at the pursuers to hold them off. The fighting here was particularly savage. (A decapitated skull was found in a gully in 1991 with a massive gash across the crown.)[24] Those who made it over the bridge fired it behind them, but the citadel proved to be no sanctuary. Fireballs rained hot and thick from the sky, while Montagu and Waller's foot regiments attacked from the park. Like a colony of army ants, they skittered over bastions and walls, down the thirty-six-foot ditch and up their scaling ladders.

They overwhelmed the ramparts, working in concert and destroying everything in their path. 'I never in all my life saw a thing better ordered, nor more carefully followed with such valour and wisdom,' marvelled one Roundhead. 'I am persuaded that this garrison was a nest of the vilest vermin in all the kingdom,' he added, 'but desperate soldiers in their resolutions.'[25]

'Fall on, fall on, all is our own!' the attackers cried.[26]

'Down with the papists, down with the papists!' they chanted.

The defenders were running out of ground, but continued to resist. They showed 'incredible boldness', wrote one reporter, 'for although they knew that it was impossible for them to subsist, yet they fought it out to the last and disputed every pass and every entry with the edge of the sword'.[27]

It was over in the better part of an hour. 'To give them their due,' admitted *The Scottish Dove*, the royalists 'fought lustily and resolutely, while there was any hope'.[28] One satirical pamphlet had the Marquess of Winchester hiding in an oven with his rosary beads, but most reports placed him in his chamber with his hostage Hammond. When it was time, Winchester relinquished his sword and became Hammond's prisoner. The soldiers wanted to lynch him, but Hammond held them back, reportedly risking his own life to save the marquess. Other royalist officers clawed at Hammond and the other hostage, Major King, begging to be taken under their protection.

'Sir, save me!' cried one.

'Me!' screamed another.

Robert Peake was in mortal danger. He threw his keys at his assailant and promised to lead him to his treasure. Thus he was spared.[29]

'Others minded not booty,' claimed *The Moderate Intelligencer*, 'but fell upon them and killed many.' The Roundheads hunted from room to room, clearing pockets of frightened resistance. 'In this action diverse women were wounded who hung upon the soldiers to keep them from killing their friends.' Six Roman Catholic priests were found and executed on the spot. Four others were plundered of their vestments and 'reserved for the gallows'.[30] When the soldiers came upon the Griffith family, they piled onto the proud patriarch and might have beaten him to death had one of his older daughters not screamed at them to stop and tried to pull them off. A soldier silenced her with his sword, swinging it onto her head and killing her instantly. Her battered father and the 'three handsome daughters' who remained – Sarah, Elizabeth and ten-year-old Mary – were taken into custody.[31]

Inigo Jones was found in another room and stripped. This was an accepted privilege of plunder and it happened to them all, even the marquess and probably also the Griffith girls (though a claim that the slain 'virgin' was 'shamefully left naked' was only made by a royalist historian eighteen years later). Stripping usually meant that the prisoner lost his cloak, shoes and outer garments and had to shiver in his smock. The frail seventy-two-year-old architect was 'carried away in a blanket'.[32]

In another chamber, eight or nine 'gentlewomen of rank' were huddled together. They would have known about the massacre and mutilation of the royalist women at Naseby.[33] When the moment came and the door flew open, they ran at the men as one. They were 'entertained by the common soldiers somewhat coarsely', Hugh Peter told the House of Commons two days later, 'yet not uncivilly; they left them with some clothes upon them'.[34]

Over one hundred royalists, including fifteen 'Irish rebels and papists', were allowed to live in the end. The New Model soldiers clearly displayed restraint in some quarters. Men who were spared included Lieutenant Faithorne the engraver; Captain Cuffaud, who had just lost his father; and Humphrey Vanderblin, a Dutch engineer. Mercy was also shown to Winchester's retinue, including his baker Robert Hodskins, 'a spy' called William Browne and – last on the list – 'Edward Pawlet the hangman'.[35] The reformado captain Tamworth Reresby was severely injured, but survived. Writing 'in high necessities' from prison afterwards, he begged his brother for money to pay the surgeon. He too had lost his clothes, 'an affliction', he explained, 'which constantly waits on prisoners taken by storm, though the plenty of my pocket procured me indifferent quarter'.[36] That was how it was. The young county conscripts who had nothing in their pockets were far more likely to be slain, even if they were far less likely to have ever heard a Catholic Mass.

The news of the fall of Basing House was broken in Westminster before noon. Early rumours that a mine had been exploded and that Winchester and Peake were both dead were corrected in later reports.[37] Hugh Peter the 'news-preacher' compiled a detailed account

for Parliament, which he read in the House on Thursday morning, 16
October, and published two days later.[38] In the aftermath of the storm,
he had spent some time talking to the defeated governor Sir Robert
Peake, whom he had known from the parish of St Sepulchre's before
the war. London's journalists had fun with Peake, mocking him as the
'old ballad-seller of Snow Hill' and 'the governor, now a poor knight,
scarce so rich as when he sold picture-babies for children near Holborn
Conduit'.[39] But Hugh Peter was uncharacteristically placid about his
old neighbour: it could be that some past connection or residual *campanilismo* kept him in check.

The marquess, on the other hand, was 'the Pope's devoted vassal'.
Peter enjoyed taking his colours from him and haranguing him in his
moment of defeat. Winchester was unrepentant: 'If the king had no
more ground in England but Basing House,' he said, 'he would adventure as he did and so maintain it to his uttermost.' His house, he added,
'was called Loyalty', and he hoped 'that the king might have a day
again'.

Basing House was indeed 'a nest of idolatry', Peter informed his
audience. The new building surpassed the old in beauty and stateliness, but both were 'fit to make an emperor's court'. He knew what
made good copy – priestly vestments, 'cabinets of jewels and other rich
treasure', bulging cellars and gross quantities of food ('for some years
rather than months'). One chamber even boasted a richly decorated
bed worth £1,300 – an obscene manifestation of the voluptuary life.
Peter's speeches had always been full-bodied, nostril-flaring, eye-
bulging affairs; this one before Parliament would have been some
spectacle.[40]

Of the corpses on the ground, one was freakishly tall, apparently
measuring nine feet from head to toe. They worked out the officer's
height by comparing him to 'a gentleman of an ordinary size who was
then present' (seventeenth-century feet were smaller than modern
feet, but it's still a stretch).* Peter counted seventy-four bodies in total,
'and only one woman, the daughter of Doctor Griffith, who came

* In 1940, the skeleton of a man over 7ft in height was found in the orchard by a
woman burying her pet rabbit. (Thanks to Alan and Nicola Turton for this
information.)

forth railing against our soldiers for their rough carriages towards her father'. He praised Major Harrison, 'that godly and gallant gentleman', for killing the actor Robbins and the 'notorious papist' Cuffaud.

The plunder was off the scale. One soldier found £300 of gold in a hole. Another pocketed three bags of silver, but made the mistake of crowing about it so that he ended up with just half a crown. The marquess's plate was rated at £5,000 and Sir Robert Peake's at £500. Then there were Peake's jewels, rings and bracelets and another 'box of brass graven plates'. In all, the victors found 1,000 chests and trunks of valuables and 100 'gentlewomen's rich gowns and petticoats', which 'furnished many of our soldiers' wives'. Some very large figures were bandied about: one list of spoils mentioned 200 barrels of beef, 300 flitches of bacon and 40,000 lb of cheese.[41]

Word soon spread that there were rich pickings to be had at Basing House, and an impromptu sale was held in the grounds. There was so much wheat that the local price collapsed. One hundred hackney coaches charged up from London to grab a bargain, and soon the little lane leading to the house was jammed with horses and carts.[42] 'There was not one iron bar left in all the windows,' noted Peter, and barely a gutter of lead.

All this time, as the plunderers hunted for booty and Hugh Peter scrawled his notes, around one hundred royalists were hiding under the house in secret vaults and chambers. Most of them, it seems, were soldiers who had gone to ground in the New House at the start of the storm, but civilians were probably also sheltering there. Peter spoke of 'vaults that are far under ground for their popish priests'.

Some time in the afternoon, they would have smelled the smoke. A fire had broken out, if we believe Hugh Peter, 'by the neglect of the enemy in quenching a fire-ball of ours'. Soon flames were licking thirstily through the debris, and by nightfall, Basing House was ablaze. 'What the soldiers left, the fire took hold on,' reported Peter, *'joy was more than ordinary*, leaving nothing but bare walls and chimneys in less than twenty hours.' It seems that Peter's glee was too much even for the New Model Army, for when an official history was published two years later, the words 'joy was more than ordinary' were changed to 'which made more than ordinary haste'.[43]

Peter could hear 'strange and hideous cries' coming from the ground, 'but our men could neither come to them', he claimed, 'nor they to us'. How many died in total? He couldn't tell. It depended on how many had been in the house in the first place. The Roundheads had taken fewer than 200 prisoners, 'and it may be 100 slain, whose bodies, some being covered with rubbish, came not to our view'. Peake had sworn to Peter that he only had 300 men in the garrison, but Peter reckoned that there might have been 500 in the house in all. *The Scottish Dove* put the figures at 120 prisoners and 140 slain (with no more than 10 parliamentarians lost and about 30 wounded). *Perfect Occurrences* listed 300 slain and burned royalists, and 180 prisoners. The outlier was *Mercurius Civicus*, which claimed that not many more than 40 royalists had been killed and almost as many parliamentarians. With 'no perfect list', another newsbook concluded, the figures were 'very uncertain'.[44]

Hugh Peter raced to Westminster with the marquess's colours. He took the fall and fire of Basing House to be a magnificent display of the 'just and righteous' ways of God. Lieutenant General Oliver Cromwell, meanwhile, rode the much shorter distance to Basingstoke, where he could still see and smell the smoke. 'Sir,' he addressed the Speaker of the House of Commons, 'I thank God I can give you a good account of Basing.'[45] It was a sober, professional report. 'Our men fell on with great resolution and cheerfulness,' Cromwell began. 'We took the two houses without any considerable loss to ourselves.' Colonel Pickering receives the credit for taking the New House, and a special mention goes to Sir Hardress Waller (Sir William Waller's cousin), who was shot in the arm but continued to perform his duty with honour. Colonel Hammond was taken hostage 'by a mistake' and deserved the House's thanks. 'We have taken about ten pieces of ordnance, with much ammunition, and our soldiers a good encouragement,' Cromwell concluded.

He recommended that Basing House be demolished ('utterly slighted'). It was not worth keeping as a garrison as it would take eight hundred men to defend; it was poorly sited – in the 'bowels' of the county rather than the 'frontier' – and 'exceedingly ruined' by great shot and fire.

Like Matthew Griffith before the storm, Cromwell had four

daughters whom he cherished. At sixteen, his Elizabeth was the same age as Matthew Griffith's Elizabeth, and his daughter Mary was two years younger than ten-year-old Mary Griffith. Tomorrow, he informed the Speaker, he would march west. 'God exceedingly abounds in His goodness to us and will not be weary until righteousness and peace meet.'

Epilogue

On Thursday 16 October, as Hugh Peter performed his speech in the House of Commons and the New Model Army went west, a man emerged from the vaults of Basing House. Another followed him, then another, and another, until about one hundred of them were blinking in the light and gulping for air. *The True Informer* reported that after two days underground, the Cavaliers had finally been forced out of their 'skulking holes' by the fire. *Mercurius Britanicus* confirmed that 'about 100' of the garrison, 'seeing so many of their associates dead on the ground, resolved to bury themselves alive and so betook them[selves] into vaults about the house, where they conversed with darkness and despair some few days, till the house, being set all on flame', they 'resolved upon a Resurrection'. The writer of *The Kingdomes Weekly Post*, having lingered on the 'lamentable cries' that Hugh Peter had heard ('as if they were the yellings of despairing and tormented souls in the chambers of death'), seemed somewhat put out that so many had actually survived. Hearing that some of them were Jesuits, he wondered how this fitted with God's providence. He seemed to think that it would have been a neater ending if 'the greatest incendiaries in Europe' had perished 'by the justice of that fire which they denounce and prepare for others'.[1]

The news of the fall of Basing House was received with a cry of anguish in Oxford, 'as if they had lost their gods'.[2] In London, there was joy. The bells rang out and the City churches gave public thanks on the first Sunday after the storm. The following day, 20 October, the Marquess of Winchester was brought to the bar of the House of Lords and committed to the Tower of London. Sir Robert Peake was imprisoned in Winchester House, William Faithorne in Petre House, and the manacled priests and 'Irish rebels' were incarcerated in Newgate within earshot of the execution bell.[3] A fortnight later, on 5 November, when there was a big bonfire at Cheapside to celebrate the foiling of the Gunpowder Plot, the 'popish pictures' from Basing House were paraded down the street and fed to the flames.[4]

Back in Hampshire, after the fire and the resurrection, local residents arrived with pickaxes and spades. Parliament had decreed that 'whosoever will fetch away any stone, brick or other materials of Basing House shall freely have the same for his or their pains'.[5] A wander through the village today shows what good use they made of this ordinance. There were rumours that before the storm, the marquess had melted down a vast quantity of gold and cast it into statues of calves that he had hidden in and around the house. Not one golden calf has been discovered to date. Another story told of a hoard of plate, money and arms buried by a Dutch engineer 'within and near Basing House'. On 14 December 1648, the Committee for the Advance of Money authorised two men to dig for it, but nothing was found.*[6]

'I need not tell you how glad the country people are hereabouts that Basing is reduced to the obedience of the Parliament,' reported a Roundhead from Cromwell's quarters on the day of the storm.[7] He was hardly impartial, but it was true that most locals did not mourn Loyalty House. They grieved for lost lives and property, though. The garrison had devoured their crops, horses, grass and wood. It had denied them their right to privacy and security. It had blighted the community and scorched the earth, and all too often, the forces that had sat down before it had done the same thing. All those within the manor of Basing itself 'are so miserably poor that there is nothing from them to be had or expected', recorded the Hampshire compounding committee.[8]

The royalist war effort staggered on for another half-year and the roads remained treacherous. A budding chemist called Robert Boyle tried to travel through Hampshire in March 1646, but was diverted

---

* In the 1960s, the then-owner of the estate, Christopher Orde-Powlett, applied to the Ministry of Works for permission to dig for a reputed three million pounds' worth of gold. Two years later, he sent four frogmen down the great well of the New House. They found three tunnels at its base and removed nearly four tons of rubble. The gold, if it exists, remains hidden.

from Basingstoke by the news that a party of Cavaliers had taken all the town's 'superfluous moveables'. He rode down to Farnham and found the countryside in 'a shaking ague'. He met trembling travellers at Winchester and crossed a wood bristling with outlaws. He finally made it onto Salisbury Plain, where a party of horse and foot 'came powdering so furiously upon us that they scarce gave us leisure to draw'. The footmen turned out to be conscripts and the horse were guarding them to stop them from running away. 'I saw one poor rogue,' Boyle informed his sister,

> lackeyed by his wife and carrying a child upon his shoulders. A pretty device, methinks, to make those who have no goods to fight for their wives and children. Good God! That reasonable creatures, that call themselves Christians too, should delight in such an unnatural thing as war, where cruelty at least becomes necessity and unprocured poverty becomes a crime; and a man with his whole family must be subject to be unavoidably undone because the violence, perhaps of those very soldiers that press him, had made him poor.[9]

Parliament had a serious problem with deserters and demobbed soldiers towards the end of the conflict. Some went to the cities looking for work. One captain spotted his old groom begging in London with a muffler over his face and speaking inwardly 'as if he had been eaten up with the Foul Disease'. Others roamed the shires in gangs and intimidated local communities. Parliament eventually gave county committees the power to execute deserters. It resorted, in other words, to martial law – one of the issues on which MPs had originally taken a stand against the king.[10]

Charles gave himself up to the Scots in May 1646 and ordered his outstanding garrisons to surrender. The following month, on the same day that Oxford yielded, Sir Marmaduke Rawdon's officers, formerly of Basing House and now of Faringdon House, laid down their arms. Rawdon had died two months earlier, on 28 April, after succumbing to a sharp illness that made him 'crazy' with pain in his back. It was caused, they said, by too much 'lying upon the ground'. He was told to stay inside, but on better days he went out to inspect the fortifications, 'encouraging always the soldiers in their duty in their defence of their garrison and in their loyalty to their king'. Charles sent his best physicians but nothing could be done.

Just before Rawdon died, he summoned his officers to his chamber. 'Gentlemen and fellow soldiers,' he began, 'I am now going to leave you and to pay that debt I owe to nature. I had a great desire to see you before I die and to give you thanks for the great love and trust I have always found in you.' He urged them to stay fast to the king and, unless specially commanded, never to surrender 'whilst you have a drop of blood remaining in your veins'. He bequeathed clothes to his pages, money to his soldiers and a horse to each of his officers. To the next governor he left his best chestnut horse, 'which was the horse he ordinarily charged upon'. He had the comfort of his chaplain John Jones, but not his wife Elizabeth, to whom he had been married for thirty-five years but whom he had not seen for three.

The enemy was close by, but Rawdon's officers took the risk of having his funeral in Faringdon church. His banner was torn up and distributed amongst the soldiers. Each man kept his piece 'as if it had been a relic', and years later, Captain Thomas Fletcher passed his bit on to Rawdon's nephew. In his eulogy, Jones praised Rawdon for 'his loyal resolution, his gallant conduct' and, in what was surely a dig at the Marquess of Winchester, 'his vast and unwearied patience'. Rawdon's first garrison – Jones did not need to name it – had witnessed 'his happy valour', but had 'lost itself by losing him'.

Jones expressed many moving sentiments that day, perhaps none more than his first: 'There is nothing that doth more advance and sour a man's misery than this one thought and apprehension: that he was once happy.'

Moments after the men had filed out of the church, a huge granado shell crashed through the roof and onto Rawdon's fresh grave. Had it landed fifteen minutes earlier, it would have killed them all. Lucky escapes were a sign of God's providence, but so was defeat. For the royalist writer John Ogilby, one thing at least was clear:

> Since Rawdon lies in honoured dust,
> Our cause no human forces trust.
> When such supporters are pulled down,
> God is angry with the Crown.[11]

The Scots handed their king over to the English Parliament at the beginning of 1647. In June, he was effectively kidnapped by the New Model Army, which had broken away from Parliament. Its officers presented him with peace proposals that would have drained him of executive and military power, but allowed him to keep the crown and his Church. There was a question over whether the army had the authority to negotiate with the king, but the Heads of Proposals, as they were called, were Charles's best chance of a settlement. He thought he could do better, though, and one night in November he escaped from Hampton Court towards the south coast, where he was persuaded to sail to the Isle of Wight. And so it happened that the erstwhile hostage of Basing House, Colonel Robert Hammond, who had retired to the island for a quiet life, found himself the king's jailor for a tortuous year of further failed negotiations, foiled escapes,* apocalyptically bad weather and a second short but vicious civil war, which Charles also lost.

On 25 November 1648, Cromwell wrote a letter to 'dear Robin' Hammond asking him to put the army before Parliament and relinquish the prisoner 'against whom the Lord hath witnessed'.[12] The principled Hammond refused. The army took Charles anyway. The officer chosen to escort him to London was Thomas Harrison, the fanatical major whose sword had shone brighter than any other at the storming of Basing House three years earlier. Charles thought that Harrison had come to assassinate him. The major wanted revenge, certainly, but not 'in a corner'.[13]

The king's trial began on Saturday 20 January 1649. It was sanctioned by the remnants ('the Rump') of the Parliament after the army had surrounded Westminster Palace and prevented many MPs from entering the Commons chamber. (Sir William Waller was one of the purged; his cousin Sir Hardress Waller one of the purgers.) Hugh Peter, who had by now taken to wearing a sword, announced from the pulpit that nowhere in the Bible could he find the words 'privilege of Parliament'. In the run-up to the trial, he put pressure on the waverers: 'This is an age to make examples and precedents in.'[14]

The grey-haired, black-clad, unshaven king was charged with

---

* One scheme involved Charles dissolving his iron window bars with acid. His courageous lover, Jane Whorwood, sought the advice of the astrologer William Lilly. He gave her a hacksaw and a bottle of aqua fortis and almost certainly passed the secret straight on to his paymasters in Parliament.

treason and tyranny. 'I would know,' he demanded, 'by what power I am called hither.' It was a valid question, but it became a toothless refrain over the course of the trial and deprived him of a defence. 'Thou hast destroyed thy land and slain thy people,' preached Peter. The axe fell on 30 January 1649 outside the Banqueting House that Inigo Jones had designed for Charles's father. On the scaffold on that freezing day, the king insisted that liberty was guaranteed by the law of the land, not governance by the people: a subject and a sovereign, he insisted, were 'clean different things'.[15]

Hugh Peter was ill in bed that day but was rumoured to have been the masked executioner. It is so easy to dislike him. His reference to the women at Basing House was repellent and, as with his joy over the fire, was edited out of the official history of the New Model Army.* He enjoyed the trappings of his new office as chaplain to the Council of State, and there were persistent rumours about an affair with a Smith-field butcher's wife, which probably weren't true but which fed the notion that he was a stereotypical hypocritical Puritan. As with many of his brethren, though, Hugh Peter's passion for the gospel was linked to a sincere yearning for social justice. Having remodelled the army and won the war, he now wanted to remodel the entire commonwealth. There were some advances in the provision of welfare: for the first time, widows and orphans of (parliamentarian) veterans could petition the state for aid. But Peter wanted to go further. He wanted hospitals for the lame, penal reform and a bankruptcy law. He wanted to fix the roads and dredge the rivers. He advised that London's 'beastly dirty streets' be widened and paved and that each ward have a proper fire service, as in Holland. He urged government to encourage people to be 'as good as they can, not so bad as they would'. In New England, where he had helped set up a law code and Harvard College – and where there was no war – he was remembered more generously.[16]

The killing of the king was so profoundly shocking that the nation appeared to sleepwalk through it. Thomas Fuller fell into a 'dead pensiveness'. Basing's guns had not managed to stultify the historian, but

---

* The italicised words here in Peter's *The Full and Last Relation* (1645) – '8 or 9 gentle-women of rank, running forth together, were entertained by the common soldiers somewhat coarsely, yet not uncivilly, *they left them with some clothes upon them*' – were altered in Joshua Sprigge's *Anglia Rediviva* (1647) to: 'considering the action in hand'.

the regicide floored him. 'For what shall I write of the Worthies of England,' he asked, 'when this horrid act will bring such an infamy upon the whole nation as will ever cloud and darken all its former, and suppress its future, rising glories?'[17]

Over the next decade, as Cromwell and his allies struggled to form a legitimate government, the survivors of Basing House found ways to endure. Tamworth Reresby, the 'healthful handsome' reformado who had needed a surgeon after the storm, seemed to charm his way through the republic. He escaped from Ely House prison after persuading the woman in the building next door to let him break through her wall and sneak out in her clothes. He married a rich widow and later inherited – and then squandered – his mother's estate, continuing 'lusty and well' for many years. He 'lives constantly in London', wrote his admiring nephew in 1679, 'and follows the diversions of a much younger man'.[18]

Robert Amery found it harder to recover. The outspoken vintner had lost his older son at Basing House and his wife at Faringdon. He was wounded there too, and was a prisoner for a long time afterwards. He swung his sword again for Charles in the second civil war in 1648 and 'likewise suffered much'. His other son was killed in Ireland resisting the Cromwellian conquest. Amery was in a 'sad and ruinous condition', but he somehow made it through the 1650s.[19]

Inigo Jones did not. He died in the summer of 1652, just before his seventy-ninth birthday and seven years after he had been swaddled out of Basing House. He had swallowed a £1,000 fine and the two loyalty oaths that were demanded of royalist 'delinquents'. With the Covenant, he renounced the bishops. With the Negative Oath, he repudiated the king. The alternative was prison and the seizure of his estate. One Cavalier tried to get out of it by sending an impersonator. Others, like Major William Rosewell, quibbled over the wording – he was only 'under the notion of a delinquent', he insisted. Most, though, like Jones, crossed their fingers and subscribed without demur. As one balladeer put it:

> Since Goldsmiths' Committee
> Affords us no pity,
> Our sorrows in wine we will steep 'em.
> They force us to take
> Two oaths, but we'll make
> A third that we ne'er meant to keep 'em.[20]

Jones was not a broken man – he never abandoned the drawing board – but he was not quite whole again either. The theatrical arm of his work had been amputated and his buildings eviscerated. The Queen's Chapel at Somerset House had been desecrated and St Paul's Cathedral used as soldiers' billets. His other great pride, the Banqueting House in Whitehall, would forever be associated with the dissolution of divine-right monarchy and not, as he had intended, the apotheosis of the Stuarts. But if Inigo Jones could not, in the end, turn men into gods, he could still inspire them to heavenly acts. There is a statue of him at Chiswick House, a villa that was built long after his death, but greatly under his influence. Jones looks up approvingly, not only at the villa, but also at the other statue flanking it, which is of his hero Andrea Palladio, whose book was his bible and into which he scribbled his thoughts, dreams and tips for insomnia, melancholy and gout.

The Marquess of Winchester almost died after the storming of Basing House. He had no money to pay for his upkeep in the Tower and the winter was so savage that the Thames froze over. On 15 January 1646, the House of Lords urgently requested that he be given an allowance so 'that he may not starve'. As one of Charles's key supporters, he forfeited his estate (part of which went to Cromwell) and was excluded from a pardon in the various peace negotiations that were conducted before the killing of the king. Honora took up lodgings in the Tower and tried to hold everything together. 'Women were never so useful as now,' observed a royalist.[21] She was granted a small maintenance for the children (on the condition that they were raised as Protestants), and in September 1647, she managed to secure a few months' parole for her husband to recover his health at Epsom Waters. He relapsed the following summer and was 'seeming dead for a great while'. After the regicide in January 1649, the Rump Parliament debated whether Winchester should also stand trial for his life, but the king's sacrifice was deemed sufficient, and soon afterwards, he was released.[22]

In 1655, Winchester was implicated in a failed rebellion in the West Country known as Pendruddock's Rising. A servant of the eponymous Penruddock was spotted taking a greyhound to the marquess 'as a token', but there was no real proof and John Penruddock

exonerated Winchester on the scaffold.[23] The marquess was imprisoned again for non-payment of debts in January 1656, but he and
Honora had smart lawyers and good friends and he never went hungry again. Thanks to the tireless efforts of their business agent Daniel
Wycherley (father of the Restoration rake William Wycherley), they
were able to buy back most of the estate on credit and then repay the
debts with leases and mortgages. This was fiendishly complicated,
not least because all the deeds had been destroyed in the fire at Basing House.[24]

They settled at Englefield, an Elizabethan manor house overlooking
a deer park once enjoyed by Honora's mother. The marquess steadied
his mind with translations of Jesuit devotional texts and, in 1652, a book
called *La Gallerie des Femmes Fortes* (*The Gallery of Heroic Women*). It was
a celebration of female worthies from the Jewish prophet Deborah to
Mary, Queen of Scots, whose execution is lamented as 'not only inhumane, but monstrous'. The frontispiece depicts several women
standing in the niches of an ancient temple, reading, writing and making speeches. In his dedication to the ladies of England, Winchester
praises their 'virtuous carriages and improved actions in this land of
trial'. His translation was a 'little tribute of respect', for them and,
surely, for one heroic woman in particular.[25]

Honora Winchester had earned her garlands, whether it was by
stripping lead from the roof of Basing House to make musket balls, or
by persuading Colonel Gage to come and save them, or by raising the
children and their father from the ashes. She referred to this period as
a 'smothered' time. She didn't dare write to her friend the Marquess
of Ormond, who was in exile with Charles Stuart, 'all letters carrying
so much the face of danger'. She longed for fresher air and hoped,
as her husband had said to Hugh Peter, 'that the king might have a
day again'.[26]

The day came on 29 May 1660, Charles Stuart's thirtieth birthday
and henceforth 'Oak Apple Day', when London's loud, lusty bells rang
him into the capital as Charles II. Oliver Cromwell had died twenty
months earlier, having conducted bold experiments on England's first,
and only, republic. There had been a Nominated Assembly of 'saints'
based on the ancient Jewish Sanhedrin. (This was Major Harrison's
idea and was supposed to usher in Christ's rule on earth; it lasted less
than six months.) There was a Protectorate with His Highness Oliver P

as a surrogate rex. (Cromwell's bed at Whitehall 'after the Indian fashion' raised almost as many eyebrows as Winchester's had done.)[27] There was also, infamously, the brief but devastating Rule of the Major Generals, which saw the country divided into military zones and subjected to a clampdown on sin. Large outdoor gatherings were prohibited, indoor meetings were restricted and the pubs were shut. The experiment failed, ultimately, because it was founded on the sword, not the law, nor even the privileges of Parliament. Cromwell's abiding concern was freedom of conscience, but he found it much harder to hear God's voice in the council chamber and counting house than in the hubbub of battle. Yet even as it unravelled, the Republic created a maelstrom of ideas, beliefs and opinions that the next regime could not contain. Even in failure, it was thrilling. John Milton's *Paradise Lost* is the longest and most sublime scream in the English language.

'Now we begin to breathe in a more calm and fresher air,' rejoiced Honora to Ormond on 10 May 1660. She was delighted that 'after many hopes and fears' she could finally congratulate Charles II on his restoration. 'In this time of general joy,' she continued, 'it were too sad a story to entertain you with the relation of the condition of my lord (who is your faithful servant), myself and all mine.' She would save it, she wrote, 'until I have the honour to see you'.[28]

The following month, her eldest son John died. On Christmas Day, her daughter Honor died. They lie together under black marble stones in Englefield church, a few paces from the house. Their ages are recorded with loving precision: Lord John saw 22 years, 4 months and 1 day; Lady Honor 21 years, 5 months and 6 days. Three months later, on 14 March 1661, Honora followed her children to the grave. She was fifty-one. Her epitaph hails a 'heroina'.[29]

Winchester lived for another fourteen years. He married again and stayed on at Englefield. The estates were restored to him, but only after ugly battles with sequestrators and his son from his first marriage. The House of Commons proposed compensation for his losses, but it was rejected in the Lords as it went against the Act of Indemnity. A direct appeal to the king was suggested, but nothing came of it. Winchester died on 5 March 1675. 'Few subjects could a king like thine deserve,' John Dryden wrote in a pointed elegy.[30] Winchester's epitaph hails his 'exemplary piety', his 'inviolable fidelity' and the defence of his home 'to the last extremity'. There is no evidence to suggest that he or Honora ever went back to Basing House.[31]

His son Charles, 6th marquess of Winchester, also known as 'the mad marquess' and, later, the 1st duke of Bolton, lived a topsy-turvy life, boozing at night and sleeping during the day. He built a lodge for his torchlit hunts next to the barn overlooking the ruins of Loyalty House.[32] Over the centuries, the bone-riddled ground has hosted a vineyard, a bowling green, a canal, anti-aircraft guns and the Home Guard.

With the return of the king in 1660, the republic was redacted. Charles II's reign was dated to the day of his father's death and an Act of Free and General Pardon, Indemnity and Oblivion was passed, protecting parliamentarians from prosecution. Anyone using abusive labels or words 'any way tending to revive the memory' of the troubles was to be fined.[33]

First, though, there had to be a reckoning. On the anniversary of the regicide, Charles II had Oliver Cromwell's mouldering corpse exhumed from Westminster Abbey and strung up at Tyburn. The head was cut off and showcased on a pole at Westminster Hall. Ten surviving regicides were executed for treason. The first was Major Thomas Harrison, who was hanged, drawn and quartered at Charing Cross on 13 October 1660. His millenarianism had only intensified after the storming of Basing House and he faced the scaffold without fear. 'By God I have leaped over a wall,' he declared, 'by God I have run through a troop, and by my God I will go through this death and He will make it easy to me.'

'Where is your Good Old Cause now?' shouted a heckler.

'Here it is,' Harrison replied, hand on breast, 'and I go to seal it with my blood.'

He died bravely before an exultant crowd. Legend had it that he even managed to land a punch on the hangman as his body was being butchered. Samuel Pepys, who was in the crowd, thought that Harrison looked 'as cheerful as any man could do in that condition'.[34]

Hugh Peter was executed three days later, just after his friend John Cook, the chief prosecutor at Charles I's trial (Harrison's head was fixed to Cook's hurdle so that it faced him when he was dragged from Newgate). One account has Peter trembling at the gibbet as he awaited his turn. Another relates that the executioner, turning from the law-yer's carcass, clapped his goried hands and snarled:

'Come, how do you like this, Mr Peter, how do you like this work?'

'I am not,' said Peter, 'I thank God, terrified at it, you may do your worst.'

And he did. 'There never was [a] person suffered death so unpitied,' reported one newsbook. The crowd jeered him up the ladder and cheered when the noose was put round his neck. When his head was presented on the end of a spear, there was a roar 'as if the people of England had acquired a victory'.*[35]

Matthew Griffith was in no mood to celebrate. He could not embrace what the new Lord Chancellor called 'this excellent art of forgetful-ness'.[36] Nor was he able to forgive the killing of his daughter at Basing House. He had spent the intervening years in and out of prison, preach-ing to clandestine congregations and suffering several violent assaults.[37] In the spring of 1660, he published a royalist tract that landed him in prison once again. It was a dyspeptic piece of writing that picked at old scabs and claimed that the Roundheads had always meant to murder the king. It enraged all those who were trying to smooth the path towards a peaceful restoration. He remained out of temper with the times even after his release and the return of his old church livings. The war never really ended for him. He was, he said, 'too old to fear and too great a sufferer to flatter'.[38] He moved to north Oxfordshire, near his daughter Elizabeth, and died after bursting a blood vessel preaching in Bladon church. He is buried in the chancel. The date of his death was 14 October 1665, the twentieth anniversary of the fall of Basing House.†

Two and a half years later, Griffith's daughter Mary, the youngest known child of the storm, lost her husband and infant son to illness. She married again and settled at Dudmaston Hall in Shropshire, where she had two more boys and continued to play the music that her father had taught her. According to her adoring husband, 'her meek and gentle ways concealed true strength of character'. She died in childbirth in

* Five days later, Samuel Pepys climbed the turret of a friend's house to get a good look at the heads on the spikes of Westminster Hall. 'Here I could see them plainly,' he wrote, 'as also a very fair prospect about London.' (Pepys, *Diary*, 21 Oct. 1660.)

† Three hundred years later, Winston Churchill was buried in Bladon churchyard.

1678 and reclines in effigy in the church of St Andrew, Quatt. There is a lute in her hand.[39]

Sir Marmaduke Rawdon lies under a simple stone in All Saints Church, Faringdon. He had sponsored grand windows at All Hallows, Barking, and St Giles-in-the-Fields in Holborn, and his motto was carved on the wall of Hoddesdon Chapel in Hertfordshire, but it was his lot to be buried in a church that did not know him. His nephew Duke went to Faringdon in 1665 to pay his respects. He spoke to the old woman who had nursed his uncle on his deathbed, and then rode across to Abingdon to dine with Rawdon's old French servant John Provest. He also tracked down some of Sir Marmaduke's former officers, including Major William Rosewell, who was still troubled by a wound in his thigh.[40] Bit by bit, he pieced together his uncle's story for the family record. It is a proud memorial, but there is also an edge to it, since the Rawdons, like many old Cavaliers, felt underappreciated by the politique new king.

Sir Marmaduke's son Thomas, who had fought at Cheriton and Newbury, never received the Portuguese consulship he was promised. He returned from exile after the Restoration and spent almost two years, 'and no small expense', chasing Charles II for favours. He received many fair promises, 'but all proved but aery hopes'. He caught a fever in the summer of 1666 and died at Hoddesdon. 'He had very high thoughts,' observed his cousin, but little success, 'which did make him inclining to melancholy before his death'.[41]

The Rawdons did just fine in the end, though, because they had their estate in Barbados. The tiny 'tobacco island' of the 1620s had undergone the sugar revolution of the mid century to emerge as England's most profitable colony. In the 1650s, tens of thousands of Africans were seized and sold as chattels (a word that has the same root as cattle) to provide forced labour on the plantations. The model was soon replicated throughout the colonies, so that by 1807, when the British slave trade was abolished, more than three million Africans had been shipped across the Atlantic against their will.[42]

One of the first men to cultivate sugar in Barbados was James Holdip, who in 1609 had been apprenticed to Marmaduke Rawdon in the Clothworkers' Company. He had worked as Rawdon's factor in Bordeaux and then as his agent in Barbados. While Rawdon was distracted at Basing House, Holdip 'unworthily deceived his trust' and embezzled his estate.[43] Thomas Rawdon sailed out in 1654 and clawed back half of it. He stayed on for a few years and 'prospered very well, making every year good quantity of sugars'. His wife Magdalene is credited with helping him manage the business. There is no word in the family history about those who actually produced the sugar.[44]

The first English ship to take a cargo of enslaved Africans from the Gold Coast to Barbados in 1641 was called *The Star*; 299 people embarked; 239 disembarked.[45] It was co-owned by Sir Nicholas Crisp, Sir Marmaduke's old London ally and Thomas Rawdon's commanding officer in the civil war. Crisp was influential in the Guinea Company and built the first English trading post on the Gold Coast, Fort Cormentine,* which was taken by the Dutch in 1665. He died the following year, lamenting his losses. He had no doubt, he wrote, that 'my nation (when I am dead) will make compensation or amends to my family for so great a service done to my country at my so great loss, which will be better understood in the future'.[46]

In March 1659, there was a debate in Parliament about 'Barbadosing', the Cromwellian policy of selling prisoners of war to plantation owners for indentured servitude. The debate was sparked by a petition submitted by seventy royalists who had been shipped to Barbados after Penruddock's Rising. They claimed that they had been transported like cattle, sold as chattels, worked like dogs and fed only potato roots. They slept like pigs and were 'whipped at the whipping-posts (as rogues) for their masters' pleasure'.

The honourable Members of Parliament were horrified. This concerned 'the liberty of the free-born people of England', declared Sir Henry Vane.

'I could hardly hold weeping when I heard the petition,' lamented Sir Arthur Hesilrige.

'I hope it is not the effect of our war to make merchandise of men,' swelled Sir John Lenthall. 'If my zeal carry me beyond its bounds, it is to plead for the liberty of an Englishman, which I cannot hear mentioned but I must defend it.'[47]

On the liberty of the Igbo people, or the Ibibio, or the Ewe or Fon

---

* Known today as Fort Amsterdam, in the Central Region of Ghana.

or those of Akan ethnicity, whom the English called 'Coromantee' after Crisp's fort, these righteous men were silent.

It seems that we have come a long way from the bells of Old Bailey and the pre-war rhythms of Snow Hill, though not, perhaps, so very far. The apothecary shops continued to put on a show, whether it was stuffed snakes or 'outlandish fruit' from Bermuda. Thomas Johnson's friend John Tradescant had an 'Ark' of curiosities that included the head of an elephant, the robe of Powhatan 'King of Virginia', and a dodo. It would form the nucleus of the Ashmolean Museum in Oxford. Curiosity could lead to astonishing discoveries and outstanding advances – or 'improvement', to use the word of the day – but curiosity could also be harmful. On the trade winds, it could lead to covetousness. 'Too much curiosity lost Paradise,' quipped the playwright Aphra Behn.[48]

The apothecary of Snow Hill encapsulates the ambivalence of his age. Thomas Johnson had been in a hurry to add to the stock of human knowledge, but he had also wanted to tread lightly. 'I verily believe,' he wrote, 'that the divine Providence had a care in bestowing plants in each part of the earth fitting and convenient to the foreknown necessities of the future inhabitants, and if we thoroughly knew the virtues of these, we needed no Indian nor American drugs.'[49] His British flora, unfinished at the time of his death at Basing House, was his own treasure hunt. The shop on Snow Hill was taken over by his kinsman and former apprentice, George Johnson, and received a visit from Thomas Fuller when he was fact-checking his *Worthies*.[50]

William Rosewell, the other apothecary at Basing House, survived the war despite his hellish experience in the hole at Farnham Castle and the thigh wound noticed by Rawdon's nephew. He swallowed Parliament's oaths and continued in his buff coat with the trained bands. He lived with his wife Philippa and two sons in Bloomsbury.[51] At the Restoration, he was appointed 'Apothecary to the Queen',* and, at the new king's direct request, he was elected Master of the Society of Apothecaries. He picked up the sword of his fallen comrade Johnson

---

* As well as supplying Catherine of Braganza with medicinal remedies, Rosewell was also responsible for 'all perfumes for her chapel'. (*CSPD, 1664–5*, 98.) He might have worked with Bridget Rumney, a 'herb woman' whose mother had been massacred after Naseby.

and fought a series of battles with the College of Physicians for the apothecaries' right to practise medicine.[52]

William Faithorne, the boy from Whitechapel apprenticed to Robert Peake, had the most interesting afterlife. He was, it turned out, England's first great portrait engraver. Following prison and some time in Paris, where he had spent a fruitful exile at the feet of the French engraving masters, he returned to London in the early 1650s and set up shop at the sign of the drake against the Palsgrave's Head tavern. This was just outside Temple Bar, where his comrade, Thomas Rowlett, also ran a print business. Faithorne sold his own prints and also those of his friend, the Bohemian etcher Wenceslaus Hollar, who worked on his plates in the shop.[53] Faithorne was thirty-two when he married Judith Graunt, and not yet forty when, on 12 October 1660, he was appointed Charles II's 'Engraver in Copper'.*[54]

This was a busy time for the artist. He engraved Roundheads and Cavaliers, bishops and preachers, doctors and an Irish healer called Valentine Greatrakes, who was known as 'the stroker' and was championed, amongst others, by the chemist Robert Boyle and Faithorne himself, whose paralysed apprentice he treated.[55] Faithorne also carved a satirical portrait of a dwarfish-looking Hugh Peter with a massively receding hairline (see plates). We can't read his politics into his work, but he must surely have enjoyed digging his burin into that one.) His best-known portrait was of Charles II's mistress, Lady Castlemaine. Samuel Pepys saw the preliminary chalk sketch in Faithorne's shop and declared it 'the finest thing I ever saw in my life'. He wanted to buy it there and then (he was enraptured by all things Castlemaine and stirred by the sight of her petticoats on the washing line). Faithorne wouldn't let him have it until he had finished his plate. A month later, he was done, and Pepys bought three prints.[56]

Every writer wanted a Faithorne in their book, either as an elaborate title page or an engraved portrait, the author photo of its day. As a friend put it, 'a *Faithorne sculpsit* is a charm can save / from dull oblivion and a gaping grave'.[57] His work reflects the achievements and

---

* Faithorne joined an eclectic royal household that included, alongside the queen's apothecary Rosewell, a periwig maker, a cormorant keeper, a rat killer, a keeper of the gates in the bowling green, a distiller of strong waters, a writer, flourisher and embellisher, an interpreter for Russian affairs and a 'Choccoelate Maker'.

ambitions of the age. He drew nine Fellows of the Royal Society 'from life' and provided technical illustrations for their papers and books. He engraved Robert Boyle's celebrated air pump and the seventy-four plates of Samuel Collins's *Systeme of Anatomy*.[58] He also translated – and beautifully illustrated – a French treatise on engraving and etching, which set the benchmark for standards of accuracy in the visual communication of knowledge. His work helped scientists like Robert Hooke see the microscopic world with a miniaturist's eye and discover the 'true form' of their objects of study.[59] Faithorne himself was not a Fellow of the Royal Society, but as at Basing House, he was the ensign, the standard-bearer.

He looks mournful in his self-portrait (see plates). He suffered from an *iliaca passio* (twisted guts), but, according to his friend John Bagford, was otherwise strong and robust.[60] He eventually retired to Printing House Yard in Blackfriars and worked mainly in crayons. He buried Judith on Boxing Day 1690 and followed her five months later.

He mentioned Basing House on record just once, in 1662, in the dedication of his *Art of Graveing and Etching* to his master and commander 'the Right Worshipfull Sir Robert Peake':

Sir,

The honour of having served his late Majesty (under your conduct) in the garrison of Basing hath given me some reputation in the world, and the happiness of having served yourself before the wars hath given me a condition of living in it . . . You changed the steel of my tools into weapons and the exercise of my arts into arms. When the service of the king challenged the duty of his subjects, you then prompted me unto loyalty. That service unhappily ending, you re-advised a return to my employment. The whole course of my life having thus, in some measure, been an observancy of your directions, to whom should I dedicate the issues of my labours in it but to you? And having now to present my country with something of use, profit, and delight, take occasion by these to speak my gratitude and preserve to myself the honour of continuing what I have been, Sir,

Your humble and devoted servant,

William Faithorne[61]

Sir Robert Peake made his will four years later, just before the long hot summer of 1666. We know frustratingly little about him: he shared the same time and space as Samuel Pepys, but in terms of self-revelation, the two men were a world apart.[62] He resembles instead another contemporary, an old churchman from Devon whose son-in-law despaired of his reticence: 'He is about 80 years old and of perfect memory and could discover [reveal] many useful truths would he speak his whole mind, but he hath the same humours with the men of that generation.'[63]

Peake could have revealed many useful truths, or alternative truths. He had been there from the beginning – on the drill ground of the Honourable Artillery Company and at the foot of Snow Hill, where he sold his 'popish Bibles'. He had endured the entire cruel experiment of the siege, withstanding every attack and change of circumstance, and holding the garrison to its last stand. He was a survivor. He was still a prisoner six months after the storm, but he seems to have been released soon afterwards on a prisoner exchange. He took the National Covenant on 22 August 1646 and the Negative Oath on 9 March 1647, and paid a fine of £222, which was ten per cent of his disclosed wealth. He remained on good terms with the Marquess of Winchester and stood trustee for him in various settlements.[64]

At the Restoration, he became lieutenant colonel of the Yellow trained band and captain-leader of the Honourable Artillery Company – the post that Marmaduke Rawdon had coveted before the war. A panegyric written by a comrade in the company celebrates an inspirational leader apparently 'beloved' even by 'those whose fate it was to be his greatest foes'. There was a hint of trouble, though: 'no detraction from th'impurer sort / shall ere control or silence this report'.[65]

He had a splendid send-off, paid for by himself, at St Sepulchre's on 1 August 1667. Three hundred black-clad members of the Artillery Company escorted his corpse through the streets of London. There were nine extra drums and five volleys of shot. The chief mourners were men of the parish and the Artillery Company, including former Roundheads like Sir Richard Browne, who had commanded London's trained bands at Cheriton.[66]

Peake's will is illuminating. He had a huge network of friends and family – in Virginia as well as England – and a 'valentine' called Mary Saintloe, whose family had moved in royalist resistance circles.[67]

Interestingly, his is the only will amongst those of the garrison survivors that looks back at the siege of Basing House; it stipulates that the poor of the parish of Basing were to receive £10. It wasn't much for a man of his wealth – the valentine got £1,000 – but it was perhaps an acknowledgement of the damage inflicted on the local community.

He stayed faithful to his bell tower, as his father and grandfather had been before him. He set up a trust for two local boys that 'dwell and trade and were born' in the parish of St Sepulchre to be maintained for a term of three years. He put £100 into the trust and hoped that it would continue afterwards 'to others successively forever'. He gave £50 to the poor of his parish* and another £50 to St Bartholomew's Hospital, Smithfield.

Four months later, on 27 September 1666, Peake added a codicil. He reduced his funeral expenditure, gave £50 to the church of St Sepulchre for repairs, and altered some bequests, 'it having pleased God to consume my house and tenements'.

The fire had started in the early hours of 2 September in a baker's house in Pudding Lane. It had been a rainless summer and the wind was strong. The flames spread down Fish Street towards the waterside. Samuel Pepys watched from a boat and noticed how people stayed in their homes 'till the very fire touched them'. The pigeons were also reluctant to leave their roosts. Their wings were singed and they fell.

Marmaduke Rawdon's old world was the first to go up – his house in Water Lane, the warehouses on Thames Street, the Custom House and, finally, Clothworkers' Hall itself, 'in one body of flame', over three days and nights. Cheapside was ablaze, the flames 'leaping from house to house and street to street'. The Guildhall was incinerated. Goldsmiths' Hall was gutted. The Blackfriars precinct was entirely lost – Apothecaries' Hall, the theatre, Printing House Yard. The noise was immense. John Evelyn, the other great diarist on the scene, described 'crackling and

---

* St Sepulchre's post-war accounts reveal the necessity of such bequests. Regular payments had to be made to the widowed mother of a 'distracted daughter', for example, and 8 shillings were needed for Goodwife Cakebread's 'pair of wooden stilts'. There are also sad references to abandoned infants. One was found 'in Mr Walker's dunghill' in 1651. Another was picked up in Chick Lane with the words *Betty Bassett* on her breast. (LMA P69/SEP/B/019/MS03146/001, 11r, 35r (Cakebread), 37v (dunghill), 44v (BB), 53r, 78v; LMA P69/SEP/B/001/MS03149/001, 236, 263.)

thunder', shrieking women and children, the rush of people and collapsing buildings 'like a hideous storm'.

The fire found St Paul's Cathedral on 4 September. It split open Inigo Jones's grand portico and sucked out his wooden scaffolding. 'The stones of Paul's flew like granadoes,' wrote Evelyn, 'the lead melting down the streets in a stream, and the very pavements of them glowing with fiery redness, so as no horse nor man was able to tread on them.' The fire careered along Newgate Street, taking in Christ Church, the prison and the Old Bailey. It charged down Snow Hill and fell on the apothecary shop, making dried seeds pop and drug jars blister.[68] It consumed The George and Peake's old print shop at the Conduit. It finally reached its limit at Smithfield. More than four hundred streets had been devastated. 'London was, but is no more,' wrote Evelyn.[69]

And yet even with the City razed and reeking, there were bright citizens rising to the challenge. 'On the 13th,' wrote Evelyn, 'I presented His Majesty with a survey of the ruins and a plot [plan] for a new city.' St Sepulchre's had lost its roof and interior, so the vestrymen held their meetings at St Bartholomew's, Smithfield. They set up a committee to deal with the most vulnerable pensioners. They had the streets cleared and illuminated with lanterns. They set up a pair of stocks and fixed the fire engines. They salvaged what they could of the molten bell-metal and had it cast anew into three 'sound and tuneable bells'.[70] They knew that there had to be ringing again. And so there was. And so there is.

A. THE OLDE HOVSE . B. THE NEW . C. THE TOWER THAT IS HALFE BATTERED DOWNE . D. THE KINGES BREAST WORKS . E. THE PARLIAMENTS BREAST WORKS .

'The greatest of any subject's house in England.' This engraving of Basing House shows the use of low, thick, earthen breastworks by both sides.

Artillery damage to the barn, which saw particularly hot action during Waller's assault.

William 'the Conqueror' Waller, who launched the first major assault on Basing House.

The postures of the musket. Eight out of thirty-two frames from a contemporary drill manual.

Caricature of a plundering soldier, who would 'rather eat than fight'. His helmet is a cauldron, his shield a dripping pan, his bandoliers wine flagons.

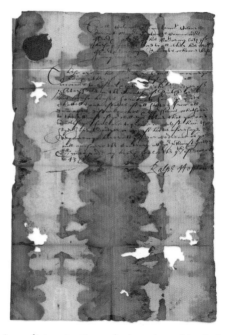

A royalist protection order issued to a friend of Thomas Johnson in Hampshire. The damp stains suggest it was kept under the floorboards.

'You changed the steel of my tools into weapons and the exercise of my arts into arms': engraver William Faithorne (*above left*) to his master and commander Robert Peake (*above right*).

Left: Inigo Jones, one of the greatest talents of the Stuart Age.
Below: Hands by Faithorne.

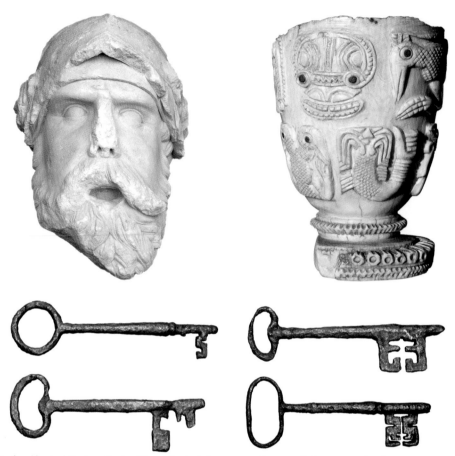

Archaeological finds at Basing House include keys, stone busts and (from a nearby field) a Yoruba ivory cup.

This daybed, owned by a descendant of the Marquess of Winchester, is thought to be the only piece of furniture saved from the house.

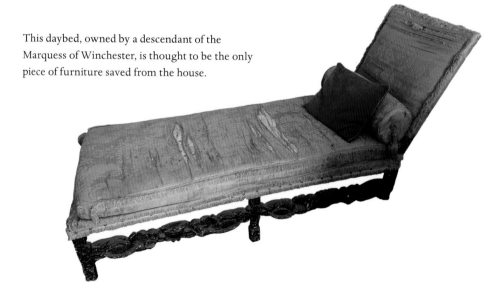

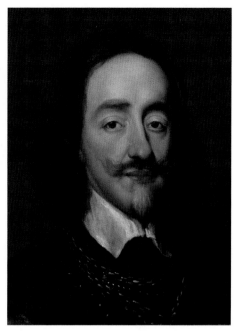

Henry Gage, who was persuaded by the Marchioness of Winchester to lead a daring mission to relieve Basing House. At this point the garrison was on the verge of starvation and mutiny.

Charles I in Oxford: a weak man in thin paint.

Mary Griffith in effigy in St Andrew's Church, Quatt, Shropshire. One of the 'handsome daughters' of the royal chaplain Matthew Griffith, she was a child during the siege. Here she holds a lute, which, according to her epitaph, she could play beautifully.

Oliver Cromwell (*below*) rolls in the heavy guns. 'He is a prosperous man,'
reported one parliamentarian newsbook. 'God hath blessed him
and I trust He will still make him victorious.'

By all accounts the fighting
in the final storm was savage:
a decapitated skull found
during excavations on the
Old House Postern Gate.
Note the sword cut.

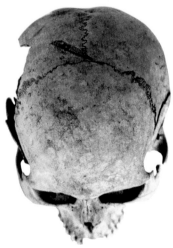

Mural depicting the storm of Basing House by Charles West Cope
in the Peers' Corridor of the House of Lords (1862).

In this imagined scene painted by Charles Landseer (*above*) Hugh Peter downs a goblet of wine
while the Marquess of Winchester, looking much older than his forty-seven years,
is slumped in despair. In the adjoining room, a boy is bound and questioned.

Basing House from the air and (*below left*) hosting the Sealed Knot re-enactment society in 2019. The barn is the only building that remains substantially intact.

Old stone to new building:
Above: a house in the village today.
Right: the west window of Winchester Cathedral, made up of shards of glass broken during the war.

Notes

These notes effectively constitute a running bibliography, with full details given at the start of each chapter or in the abbreviations below. The place of publication is London unless otherwise stated.

Archer   Elias Archer, *A True Relation of the Marchings of the Red Trained Bonds* [sic] *of Westminster, the Green Auxiliaries of London, and the Yellow Auxiliaries of the Tower Hamlets, under the command of Sir William Waller, from Munday the 16. of Octob. to Wednesday the 20. of Decemb. 1643* (1643)

AVB   *The Ancient Vellum Book of the Honourable Artillery Company,* ed. G. A. Raikes (1890)

BL   British Library

Bod   Bodleian Library

Clarendon   Edward Hyde, Earl of Clarendon, *The History of the Rebellion and the Civil Wars in England begun in the year 1641*, ed. W. Dunn Macray, 6 vols. (Oxford, 1888)

CRR   *The Cardew-Rendle Roll: A Biographical Directory of Members of the Honourable Artillery Company from c. 1537–1908*, ed. K. Bennett, 2 vols. (2013)

CSPD   *Calendar of State Papers, Domestic*

CSPV   *Calendar of State Papers, Venetian*

E   British Library Thomason Tracts. The reference denotes the reel position within the collection and can be accessed via *Early English Books Online*

Godwin   G. N. Godwin, *The Civil War in Hampshire (1642–45) and the Story of Basing House* (rev. edn, 1904)

HALS   Hertfordshire Archives and Local Studies

Herball   Thomas Johnson, *The Herball or Generall Historie of Plantes. Gathered by John Gerarde of London Master in Chirurgerie very much enlarged and amended by Thomas Johnson citizen and*

                   apothecary of London (1633, rev. 1636). Unless otherwise stated,
                   I quote from the 1636 edition

HMC   Historical Manuscripts Commission

HRO   Hampshire Record Office

CJ   *Journals of the House of Commons*

LJ   *Journals of the House of Lords*

LMA   London Metropolitan Archives

ODNB   *Oxford Dictionary of National Biography*, ed. H. C. G. Matthew
                   and B. Harrison, 60 vols. (Oxford, 2004)

TNA   The National Archives, Kew

PA   Parliamentary Archives, Palace of Westminster, London

ROLLCO   The Records of London's Livery Companies Online

Siege Diary   [Anon], *A Description of the Seige of Basing Castle; kept by the
                   Lord Marquisse of Winchester, for the service of His Maiesty:
                   against, the forces of the rebells, under the command of Colonell
                   Norton, AD. 1644* (printed by Leonard Lichfield, printer to the
                   University, Feb. 1644/5) (E 27/5)

Souldiers Report   *The Souldiers Report concerning Sir Wiliam Wallers fight against
                   Basing-house on Sunday last November the 12 1643* ([17 Nov.] 1643)
                   (E 76/5)

Waller Report   Sir William Waller to Speaker Lenthall, Farnham, 16 Nov.
                   1643, read in the House of Commons, 18 Nov. (*CJ*, III, 314)
                   and printed in HMC 13th Report, Portland MSS, I (1891)

Author's Note

1   *The Court of Chivalry 1634–1640*, ed. Richard Cust and Andrew Hopper,
      British History Online (http://www.british-history.ac.uk/no-series/
      court-of-chivalry), '703: Wheeler v Sheffield'.

Introduction

1   *The Works of John Adams*, ed. Charles Francis Adams III (Boston, 1851), 394.

2   Geoffrey Parker, *Global Crisis: War, Climate Change & Catastrophe in the
      Seventeenth Century* (pb, 2014), xxv–xxvi.

3   Matthew Griffith, *A Patheticall Perswasion to Pray for Publick Peace* (2 Oct.
      1642) (E 122/17), 29–30.

4   Between 1640 and 1652, around 100,000 men died in combat in England
      and Scotland and 140,000 more to war-related disease and starvation. In
      Ireland, the total figure was at least 300,000, or 15–20 per cent of the
      population. England lost 3 per cent of its population; Scotland 6 per
      cent. In the First World War, by comparison, mortality was 1.6 per cent

of the British population. See Ian Gentles, *The English Revolution and the Wars in the Three Kingdoms, 1638–1652* (Harlow, 2007), 436–7; Tim Harris, *Rebellion: Britain's First Stuart Kings, 1567–1642* (Oxford, 2014), 7.

5   12 Charles II c. 11.

6   Civil War Petitions Website (www.civilwarpetitions.ac.uk): Essex Record Office, Q/SB a2/78: second petition of Jeremiah Maye of Ashdon, Essex, 1652; Berkshire Record Office, R/AZ3/9/23: petition of Elizabeth Kenton, widow (her husband Christopher served in the garrison at Basing House); TNA SP 19/21/83.

7   *The Royalist Ordnance Papers, 1642–1646*, ed. Ian Roy (Oxfordshire RS, 1964, 1975), I, 58; HRO 76M99/1; West Yorkshire Archive Service WYL 156/MX/473. For photographs and a transcription of the notebook, see Jan Woudstra and Sally O'Halloran, '"The Exactness and Nicety of Those Things": Sir John Reresby's Garden Notebook and Garden (1633–44) at Thrybergh, Yorkshire', *Garden History* 36/1 (2008).

8   William Beech, *More Sulphure for Basing: Or, God will fearfully annoy and make quick riddance of his implacable Enemies, surely, sorely, suddenly. Shewed in a Sermon at the Siege of Basing on the last Lords day, Sept. 21. 1645* (26 Sept. 1645) (E 304/3), 21, 23; *Perfect Passages*, 8–15 Oct. 1645 (E 266/2), 408.

9   *The Parliaments Post*, 23–30 Sept. 1645 (E 303/23), 4; *A Diary, Or, An Exact Journall*, 9–16 Oct. 1645 (E 305/7), 7.

10 G. M. Trevelyan, *An Autobiography and Other Essays* (1949), 13.

PART ONE

1 *Snow Hill*

1   There are myriad references to the bells in the vestry and churchwarden accounts of St Sepulchre's in the London Metropolitan Archives. e.g. LMA P69/SEP/B/019/MS03146/001, ff. 67r, 97v, 105. For people sitting on the churchyard wall during executions (as well as the 'clamorous noise and other unruly carriage of youth'), see P69/SEP/B/001/MS03149/002, 27. For the execution bells, see John Stow, *Annales* (1615), 862. For John Donne, who was Dean of St Paul's as well as vicar of St Dunstan's, see his *Devotions upon Emergent Occasions* (1624), Meditation XVII.

2   TNA E 179/252/10, f. 14r (printed in T. C. Dale, *The Poll Tax for London in 1641* (1934–5), 21). The apothecary Thomas Johnson was writing 'from my house on Snow-hill' in October 1633 (Epistle to the Reader in his first edition of Gerard's *Herball*) and was placed 'at his house on Snow Hill' in 1637 (TNA SP 16/363, 27r). It is possible to site it near the bottom of Snow Hill thanks to the 1641 poll tax list, which places him in Holborn

Cross precinct. Two dwellings down from him was the vintner Richard Robinson, who lived 'near the conduit on Snow Hill': *The Court of Chivalry 1634–1640*, ed. Richard Cust and Andrew Hopper, *British History Online*, '560: Rivers v Burley'. For the grocer Roger Reeve, see TNA PROB 4/6513, 5–6; LMA P69/SEP/D/028/MS031184.

3   TNA PROB 11/199/625.

4   Charles Dickens, *The Life and Adventures of Nicholas Nickleby* (1839), IV, 23.

5   Jonathan Swift, *A Description of a City Shower* (1710), in *The Poems of Jonathan Swift*, ed. Harold Williams (Oxford, 1958), I, 59–63.

6   *Bartholomew Fair*, ed. John Creaser, in *The Cambridge Edition of the Works of Ben Jonson*, ed. David Bevington, Martin Butler and Ian Donaldson (Cambridge, 2012), IV. Quotations at 1.3, ll. 108, 114–15; 3.6, ll. 23, 26, 35, 44. See p.268 for the play's textual history. *Bartholomew Fair* was printed in 1631 and a few presentation copies were circulated, but it was not published until 1640, after Jonson's death, probably due to the hundreds of errors entered by Jonson's 'lewd printer'.

7   Anon, *Bartholomew Faire Or Variety of fancies . . . Printed for Richard Harper at the Bible and Harpe in Smithfield, 1641*, reprinted in *The Old Book Collector's Miscellany*, ed. C. Hindley, III (1873), 2–3.

8   *An Order from the High Court of Parliament* (1641) (E 181/1).

9   John Walter, ' "Abolishing Superstition with Sedition"? The Politics of Popular Iconoclasm in England 1640–1642', *Past & Present* 183 (2004), 79–80, 89–92.

10   This is lucidly explained in Diarmaid MacCulloch, *Thomas Cromwell: A Life* (2018), 413–14.

11   John Craig, 'Sermon Reception', in *The Oxford Handbook of the Early Modern Sermon*, ed. Peter McCullough, Hugh Adlington and Emma Rhatigan (Oxford, 2011), 191.

12   Percival Wiburn, *A checke or reproofe of M. Howlets untimely shreeching in her Maiesties eares* (1581), 15v; Patrick Collinson, *The Elizabethan Puritan Movement* (1967), 26–8.

13   Paul S. Seaver, *Wallington's World: A Puritan Artisan in Seventeenth-Century London* (Stanford, 1985), 11.

14   David Booy, *The Notebooks of Nehemiah Wallington, 1618–1654: A Selection* (Aldershot, 2007), 23; *The Diary of Ralph Josselin, 1616–1683*, ed. Alan Macfarlane (1976), 113–14; J. Sears McGee, *An Industrious Mind: The Worlds of Sir Simonds D'Ewes* (Stanford, 2015), 20; John Calvin to Archbishop Cranmer, *c.* April 1552, in *Original Letters relative to the English Reformation*, ed. Hastings Robinson, I (Cambridge, 1847), 712.

15   McGee, *Industrious Mind*, 305.

16   Stow, *Annales* (1615), 892; Stow, *Survey of London . . . inlarged* (1633), 830, 886; Kenneth Fincham and Nicholas Tyacke, *Altars Restored: The*

Changing Face of English Religious Worship, 1547–c.1700 (Oxford, 2007), 92–9;
J. F. Merritt, 'Puritans, Laudians, and the Phenomenon of Church-
Building in Jacobean London', *Historical Journal* 41/4 (1998); *A Series of
Precedents and Proceedings . . . from Act-Books of Ecclesiastical Courts*, ed.
W. H. Hale (1847), 252–3, 258. The man who pissed in the hat was John
Kibbitt of Leigh in 1627. The published transcription redacts the offend-
ing verb, but it is confirmed by the Act Book of the Archdeaconry
of Essex in the Essex Record Office: D/AEA 36, 208v. For the beauty of
holiness, see Peter Lake, 'The Laudian Style: Order, Uniformity and the
Pursuit of the Beauty of Holiness in the 1630s', in *The Early Stuart Church,
1603–1642*, ed. Kenneth Fincham (1993), ch. 7, and Anthony Milton, ' "That
Sacred Oratory": Religion and the Chapel Royal during the Personal
Rule of Charles I', in *William Lawes (1602–45): Essays on his Life, Times and
Work*, ed. Andrew Ashbee (Aldershot, 1998), 70–2.

17 Lancelot Andrew[e]s, *The Patterne of Catechistical Doctrine at large*
(1650), 299.

18 *Complete Prose Works of John Milton*, I: 1624–42, ed. Don M. Wolfe (1953),
557; Graham Parry, *The Arts of the Anglican Counter-Reformation: Glory,
Laud and Honour* (Woodbridge, 2006), 1. For the phrase 'breaden God',
which mocked the Catholic adoration of the consecrated bread and
wine as the body and blood of Christ, see, for e.g., William Beech in
More Sulphure for Basing (1645), 13.

19 William Prynne, *Histrio-mastix* (1633), 214–15, 390, 852–6, and index:
'Women-Actors, notorious whores'; William Lamont, 'Prynne, William
(1600–1669)', *ODNB* ; Mark Kishlansky, 'A Whipper Whipped: The Sedition of William Prynne', *Historical Journal* 56/3 (2013), 603–27.

20 TNA SP 16/525, 67r; Carla Gardina Pestana, 'Peter, Hugh', *ODNB* ;
Raymond Phineas Stearns, *The Strenuous Puritan: Hugh Peter, 1598–1660*
(Urbana, Illinois, 1954), *passim*, but esp. 35–7 (for Peter at St Sepulchre's)
and 140–3 (for his role in the foundation of Harvard College). He spent
some years in the Netherlands, where he was pastor of the church at
Rotterdam, before moving on to New England in 1635. For the sexual
rumours, see *The Tales and Jests of Mr. Hugh Peters* (1660), 26; William
Yonge, *England's Shame, or, The unmasking of a politick atheist* (1663), 19–
20, 27–8; Alexandra Walsham, 'Phanaticus: Hugh Peter, Antipuritanism
and the Afterlife of the English Revolution', *Parergon* 32/3 (2015), 74–5, 85.

21 James Loxley, *Royalism and Poetry in the English Civil Wars: The Drawn
Sword* (1997), 175–6.

22 Maija Jansson (ed.), *Proceedings in the Opening Session of the Long Parliament*, 7 vols. (Rochester, New York and Suffolk, 2000–7), IV, 472. See too
Maija Jansson, 'The impeachment of Inigo Jones and the pulling down
of St Gregory's by St Paul's', *Renaissance Studies* 17/4 (2003), 716–46.

23   Tim Harris, *Rebellion: Britain's First Stuart Kings, 1567–1642* (Oxford, 2014), 367–9, 497.

24   *Persecutio Undecima* (1648) (E 470/7), 56; John Adamson, *The Noble Revolt: The Overthrow of Charles I* (2007), 82. Encouraged by the Earl of Strafford and Archbishop Laud, Charles had been prepared to use Spanish gold to defeat the Scots, and had it not been for a revolt in Catalonia in June 1640, he might have succeeded (*Noble Revolt*, 40–2).

25   BL Add MS 6521, 8v–9r; Bod MS Rawl C 956, 77r; *The Journal of Sir Simonds D'Ewes*, ed. W. Notestein (New Haven, 1923), 541.

26   *Mr Grymstons speech in Parliament upon the accusation and impeachment of William Laud Arch-bishop of Canterbury, upon high treason* (1641) (E 196/22), 5.

27   HMC, *Report on Manuscripts in Various Collections*, II (1903), 259.

28   Revelation 14:8. See David Cressy, *England on Edge: Crisis and Revolution 1640–1642* (Oxford, 2006), 174–5.

29   Adamson, *Noble Revolt*, 298.

30   By John Walter, in 'Crowds and Popular Politics in the English Revolution', in *The Oxford Handbook of the English Revolution*, ed. Michael J. Braddick (Oxford, 2015), 339.

31   Cressy, *England on Edge*, 175–6.

32   Geoffrey Parker, *Global Crisis: War, Climate Change & Catastrophe in the Seventeenth Century* (pb, 2014), xx.

33   *CJ*, II, 287.

34   Adamson, *Noble Revolt*, 392–4.

35   Parker, *Global Crisis*, 349–52, 564, citing Richard Plunkett's conversation with Rev. George Creighton of Lurgan, Co. Cavan.

36   *The Lismore Papers (Second Series)*, ed. A. B. Grosart, IV (1888), 259.

37   Parker, *Global Crisis*, 352.

38   Keith J. Lindley, 'The Impact of the 1641 Rebellion upon England and Wales, 1641–5', *Irish Historical Studies*, 18/70 (1972), 151–2.

39   Philip Lee Ralph, *Sir Humphrey Mildmay: Royalist Gentleman: Glimpses of the English Scene, 1633–1652* (New Jersey, 1947), 39.

40   *A Letter from Mercurius Civicus to Mercurius Rusticus* (1643) (E 65/32), 11–12; *Persecutio Undecima* (1648) (E 470/7), 67; Lindley, 'The Impact of the 1641 Rebellion', 151–2.

41   *CJ*, II, 263; *LJ*, IV, 421; *The Journal of Sir Simonds D'Ewes from the First Recess of the Long Parliament to the Withdrawal of King Charles from London*, ed. W. H. Coates (New Haven, 1942), 68, 102.

42   *A Damnable Treason, by a Contagious Plaster of a Plague-sore* (E 173/23); D'Ewes, *Journal*, ed. Coates, 37.

43   For 'Mr Pimp', see Ralph, *Sir Humphrey Mildmay*, 156. For 'King Pym', see Adamson, *Noble Revolt*, 387, 681 n81. Also Adamson, 433, for the nineteenth-century origin of the term 'Grand Remonstrance'.

44 John Rushworth, *Historical Collections*, III / 1 (1692), 438–51.

45 Clarendon, I, 420.

46 *A Letter from Mercurius Civicus to Mercurius Rusticus* (1643) (E 65/32), 13; Adamson, *Noble Revolt*, 433–6, 467–70 (quotations at 434–5).

47 TNA SP 16/486, 121v–122r, 125r; Coates, 279 n17; *Diurnall Occurrences*, 13–20 Dec. 1641 (E 201/3); *A Coppy of the Prisoners Judgment Condemned Tody from Nugate* (E 180/5).

48 *An Order from the High Court of Parliament* (1641) (E 181/1). The preacher's text was Revelation 2:14. See too Keith Lindley, *Popular Politics and Religion in Civil War London* (Aldershot, 1997), 89.

49 Adamson, *Noble Revolt*, 460–8.

50 TNA SP 16/486, 127r, 26; Lindley, *Popular Politics and Religion*, 105–17; Cressy, *England on Edge*, 384–92.

51 *A Letter from Mercurius Civicus to Mercurius Rusticus* (E 65/32), 15–16. The significance of the Common Council elections is demonstrated by Valerie Pearl in *London and the Outbreak of the Puritan Revolution: City Government and National Politics, 1625–43* (Oxford, 1961), esp. 132–45, and confirmed, with further analysis, by Keith Lindley, in *Popular Politics and Religion*, 180–97.

52 Mark Stoyle, 'The Cannibal Cavalier: Sir Thomas Lunsford and the Fashioning of the Royalist Archetype', *Historical Journal* 59/2 (2016), 4–8, 20–5.

53 *A Bloody Masacre Plotted by the Papists* (1641) (E 181/9).

54 Rushworth, *Historical Collections*, III / 1, 463. See too Cressy, *England on Edge*, 107–9; Stoyle, 'The Cannibal Cavalier', 15–16; Ian Roy, 'Royalist Reputations: The Cavalier Ideal and the Reality', in *Royalists and Royalism during the English Civil Wars*, ed. Jason McElligott and David L. Smith (Cambridge, 2007), 90–1.

55 *The Autobiography of Sir John Bramston*, ed. P. Braybrooke, Camden Society (1845), 82.

56 Lindley, *Popular Politics and Religion*, 111–12; Cressy, *England on Edge*, 391.

57 *A True Relation of the Most Wise and Worthy Speech made by Captain Ven . . . December the 29, 1641* (E 181/21). Also, Cressy, *England on Edge*, 391.

58 TNA SP 16/486, 227.

2 The Apothecary

1 Thomas Johnson, *Iter Plantarum* (1629), in *Thomas Johnson: Botanical Journeys in Kent & Hampstead: A facsimile reprint of his Iter Plantarum 1629, Descriptio Itineris Plantarum 1632*, ed. J. S. L. Gilmour (1972), 101. Original Latin on p.74: '*ignavos illos Pharmacopaeos*'.

2   *Herball*, 459, 589.

3   Thomas Johnson, *Mercurius Botanicus, sive plantarum gratia suscepti itineris, anno 1634 descriptio* (1634), 59.

4   Thomas Johnson, *Descriptio Itineris Plantarum* (1632), in Gilmour, *Botanical Journeys*, 116; *Mercurius Botanicus* (1634), 19, 23, 26, 27, 28, 52; *Herball* (1636), 6, 1582–3, 1604; *Mercurii Botanici Pars Altera* (1641), 17, 18, 22, 25, 26, 28, 35.

5   Society of Apothecaries, Court Minute Book 1617–51, 47, 196. For Johnson's birthplace and the hazards of his name, see *Herball*, 450; H. Wallis Kew and H. E. Powell, *Thomas Johnson: Botanist and Royalist* (1932), v, 13–15.

6   Harold J. Cook, *The Decline of the Old Medical Regime in Stuart London* (1986), 46–7; Harold J. Cook, *Matters of Exchange: Commerce, Medicine, and Science in the Dutch Golden Age* (2007), 28–31.

7   William Shakespeare, *Romeo and Juliet*, 5.1. 43–9 (Wells and Taylor, *Complete Works*, Oxford, 1986).

8   Johnson, *Herball* (1633), 1515.

9   Joe Moshenska, *A Stain in the Blood: The Remarkable Voyage of Sir Kenelm Digby* (2016), 188, 472–3.

10   *Volpone, or The Fox* (1606), ed. Richard Dutton, in vol. 3 of *The Cambridge Edition of the Works of Ben Jonson*, ed. David Bevington, Martin Butler and Ian Donaldson (Cambridge, 2012), 2.2, 54. For the medical marketplace of London, see Cook, *Decline*, ch. 1.

11   Margaret Pelling and Frances White, 'Buggs, John', in *Physicians and Irregular Medical Practitioners in London 1550–1640 Database* (2004), *British History Online*; Cook, *Decline*, 87–90.

12   Johnson, *Iter Plantarum* (1629). I mainly follow Raven and Latham's translation in Gilmour.

13   *Herball*, To the Reader.

14   Johnson, *Descriptio*, 101; *Herball*, 1060.

15   Folger Shakespeare Library, Washington DC, MS E.a.5, ff. 80r–98r (quotations at 81v, 92r, 94v). The manuscript also contains associated lectures by Johnson's herborising friends, John Buggs, William Broad and James Clarke. They were discovered by Dmitri Levitin. See his article ' "Made Up from Many Experimentall Notions": The Society of Apothecaries, Medical Humanism, and the Rhetoric of Experience in 1630s London', *Journal of the History of Medicine and Allied Sciences* 70/4 (2015), 549–87. I am very grateful to Dr Levitin for kindly sending me his article.

16   Johnson, *Descriptio* (1632), 115. Johnson thought it might have been a sea serpent hunting for rabbits in the sandhills, but it was more likely a very

large grass snake, stretched by the process of stuffing (ibid., 145: 'Mr Duck's Sea Serpent', by Maurice Burton).

17 Johnson, *Mercurii Botanici* (1641), Dedicatory Epistle, 7–9, 19, 26, 28, 36. For a translation, see W. Jenkyn-Thomas, *The Itinerary of a Botanist through North Wales in the year 1639 A.D.* (Bangor, 1908).

18 *Herball*, To the Reader, 1572, 1134, 1591, 1625. For Goodyer's contribution, see 'To the Reader', 65, 228, 275, 1625, etc., and John Edgington, 'A Plant List of 1633: Annotations in a Copy of Thomas Johnson's *Iter plantarum*', *Archives of Natural History* 34/2 (2007).

19 TNA SP 16/363, 26r–27r; A. J. Loomie, 'Wotton, Sir Henry (1568–1639)', *ODNB*.

20 *Herball*, To the Reader and 1515; For a scurrilous poem describing Dr Argent as 'too fat to have any skill', see Deborah E. Harkness, *The Jewel House: Elizabethan London and the Scientific Revolution* (2007), 72.

21 *Herball*, An Advertisement to the Readers; Johnson, *Mercurii Botanici* (1641), 1–2; Kew and Powell, *Thomas Johnson*, 135–40; Christopher Merrett, *Pinax Rerum Naturalium Britannicarum* (1666), A2r; D. E. Allen, 'Merret [Merrett], Christopher (1614–1695)', *ODNB*. In his *Mercurii Botanici* of 1641 (p.2), Johnson announced his intention to collaborate with John Goodyer (*'viro amiciss'*) 'in a joint work' (*'juncto opere'*) of botany.

22 Society of Apothecaries, Court Minute Book 1617–51, 385v; TNA E 179/252/10, f. 14r (printed in T. C. Dale, *The Poll Tax for London in 1641* (1934–5), 21). For the apprentices, see Society of Apothecaries, Court Minute Book 1617–51, 366r (Matthew Stephenson, bound for 8 years from 5 Dec. 1637) and 390v (David Bromhall, bound 16 Feb. 1641). References to Johnson's garden are in his *Herball*, e.g. 30, 96, 219.

23 TNA PROB 4/6513. For a copy of Reeve's will: LMA P69/SEP/D/028/MS03184. He is referred to as 'oyleman' in Richard Smyth's *A Catalogue of all Such Persons Deceased whom I knew in their Life Time* (1849), 97.

24 Dagmar Freist, *Governed by Opinion: Politics, Religion and the Dynamics of Communication in Stuart London, 1637–1645* (1997), 118.

25 LMA, Surrey Marriage Bonds and Allegations (via Ancestry.com) MS 10091/12. Cf. Johnson's signature here with his hand in 1642 (Society of Apothecaries, Wardens' Account Book (1626–68), 196), and in 1643 (TNA WO 55/459, pt 2, 363). The marriage took place at St Martin-in-the-Fields, Westminster, on 27 July 1629. An older apothecary, also called Thomas Johnson, lived on Friday Street, but he was married (to Anne) before 1629.

26 TNA PROB 10/673. The two other overseers were William Rivers, a grocer, and Thomas Greene, a salter (Dale, *Poll Tax*, 21, 28), both of St Sepulchre's. It is just possible that another Thomas Johnson is being referred to in Ball's will. Her executor, Morgan Johnson, had a 'kinsman

and servant' called Thomas Johnson, who lived with him in the church precinct of St Sepulchre (Dale, 32; TNA PROB 11/200/200), but he was probably not senior enough to be an overseer to a widow reputedly worth over £1,000 (TNA C 3/433/71). The other overseers were all heads of their households. There were other Thomas Johnsons of St Sepulchre's parish – a brownbaker in Smithfield (Dale, 8), for example – but George Johnson's signature (cf. LMA MA/D/G/41) on Ball's codicil points to the apothecary next door. For George, see Society of Apothecaries, Court Minute Book 1617–51, 204; Thomas Fuller, *The History of the Worthies of England* (1662), Yorkshire, 204; BL Add MS 5063, f. 29; Kew and Powell, *Thomas Johnson*, 28–9.

3 *Waves of the Sea*

1   *A Letter from Mercurius Civicus to Mercurius Rusticus* (1643) (E 65/32), 16–18; Keith Lindley, *Popular Politics and Religion in Civil War London* (Aldershot, 1997), 117–24. For Walker, see Joad Raymond, 'Waker, Henry (fl. 1638–1660)', *ODNB*.

2   *A Letter from Mercurius Civicus to Mercurius Rusticus*, 13–14; Lawson Chase Nagel, 'The Militia of London, 1641–1649' (PhD thesis, King's College, University of London, 1982), 38–9.

3   BL Add MS 26785, f. 59v: Sir Edward Dering to 'my truly dear soul' Lady Dering, Jan. 1642.

4   Clothworkers' Company, Court Orders H (1639–49), CL/B/1/8, 48r–49r; Lawrence Price, *Great Britaines Time of Triumph* (1641) (E 177/17); John Adamson, *The Noble Revolt* (2007), 438–45.

5   *AVB*, 19–20.

6   Ismini Pells, 'Revival, Division & Restoration: The Artillery Company of London, 1611–1660', *Transactions of the London and Middlesex Archaeological Society* 62 (2011), 243–9; *CRR*, I, 3–39. The company went by various names in its first century before settling on the Honourable Artillery Company (confirmed by grant in 1860), which, for ease of reference, is used throughout.

7   William Barriffe, *Mars, his Triumph. Or, the description of an exercise performed the XVIII. of October, 1638, in Merchant-Taylors Hall by certain gentlemen of the Artillery Garden London* (1639), 1–2, 6–7. See too Phil Withington, 'Citizens and Soldiers: The Renaissance Context', *Journal of Early Modern History* 15 (2011), esp. 24–5 for the contemporary sense of 'modern' as a humanist re-engagement with ancient precepts, particularly in terms of military discipline and virtue.

8   *CRR*, I, 52; see too G. Goold Walker, *The Honourable Artillery Company*

1537–1987 (1986), 32. For the sermons, see George Ross Tanton, 'The Shaping of Military Culture in England before the Civil Wars: A Study of Preaching to the Artillery Companies, 1600–1643', MA Thesis, Canterbury Christ Church University (2016), esp. 13–15 and ch. 1.

9   Rawdon was baptised at All Saints, Brandsby on 20 March 1582/3, and married at All Hallows, Barking on 16 March 1610/11; HALS 79959X, 23v, 42ff. For Martha Moulsworth, see Beinecke Rare Book & Manuscript Library, Yale, Osborn MS fb150; Robert C. Evans, 'A Silent Woman Speaks: "The Memorandum of Martha Moulsworth, Widowe"', *Yale University Library Gazette* 69, nos. 3/4 (1995).

10 *CSPD 1628–9*, 290, 292–3; TNA SP 16/497, 201r. Marmaduke's brother Robert, a Bermondsey fishmonger, also had a share in the *Marmaduke* (TNA PROB 11/202/33). Shipowning was a risky business and Rawdon invested as part of a syndicate. See TNA HCA 13/49, 630r–631r for the loss of the *William* by Rawdon's Caribbean syndicate in 1632.

11 HALS 79959X, 43r, 50v; *The Complete Works of Captain John Smith*, ed. Philip L. Barbour (1986), I, 323–4, 425–6.

12 Bod MS Rawl C 94, 2v–3r, 30r; Richard B. Sheridan, *Sugar and Slavery: An Economic History of the British West Indies, 1623–1775* (Baltimore, MD, 1973), 82–4; Larry Gragg, *Englishmen Transplanted: The English Colonization of Barbados, 1627–1660* (Oxford, 2003), 32–6, 58–9. Rawdon was also involved in the settlement of St Kitts in 1623 (Bod MS Rawl C 94, 7).

13 HALS 79959X, 43; John P. Ferris, 'Rawdon, Marmaduke', in *The History of Parliament: the House of Commons 1604–1629*, ed. Andrew Thrush and John P. Ferris (2010).

14 HALS 79959X, 42v–43r. This statement is partially confirmed in the public record: *Acts of the Privy Council* 38, no. 641; 42, II, no. 196; TNA SP 16/77, 30r; *CSPD 1631–3*, 332; *CSPD 1635*, 279.

15 Kenneth R. Andrews, *Ships, Money, and Politics: Seafaring and Naval Enterprise in the Reign of Charles I* (Cambridge, 1991), 1.

16 J. Sears McGee, *An Industrious Mind: The Worlds of Sir Simonds D'Ewes* (Stanford, 2015), 282, 285.

17 TNA SP 16/77, 30r; *CSPD 1628–9*, 290, 292–3: Warrants for issuing Letters of Marque or Commissions to take Pirates.

18 HALS 79959X, 42r, 51v; *The Parish Register and Tithing Book of Thomas Hassall of Amwell*, ed. Stephen G. Doree (Hertford, 1989), 224; *The Life of Marmaduke Rawdon of York*, ed. Robert Davies, Camden Society, OS 85 (1863), 25.

19 HALS 79959X, 37, 56, 71v–72r. The Red Lion Tavern at Billingsgate is mentioned in the City Lands Grant Book, 1616–52: LMA CLA/008/EM/02/01/002, f. 110r.

20   HALS 79959X, 51v, 68; H. F. Hallyar, *The Chronicles of Hoddesdon* (Hoddesdon, 1948), 132–5.

21   HALS 79959X, 42v, 51v. For Rawdon's estate, see TNA SP 23/16, 187, 536, 652; SP 23/18, 807v; SP 23/30, 258; SP 23/62, 235; SP 23/63, 927; SP 23/71, 398; SP 23/182, 749; TNA C 10/66/158. For the vaults, see The Clothworkers' Company, Court Orders H (1639–49), CL/B/1/8, 64v, 73r. See too T. C. Dale, *The Inhabitants of London in 1638* (1931), 3, 5.

22   LMA CLA/008/EM/02/01/002, 77r, 86r–87r.

23   There is rich scholarship on the build-up to war in London: Valerie Pearl's *London and the Outbreak of the Puritan Revolution: City Government and National Politics, 1625–43* (Oxford, 1961) demonstrates the significance of municipal politics, particularly the Common Council elections of December 1641. Robert Brenner's *Merchants and Revolution: Commercial Change, Political Conflict, and London's Overseas Traders, 1550–1653* (Cambridge, 1993) examines the commercial and political alignments of the mercantile networks, coining the term 'new merchants', while Keith Lindley's *Popular Politics and Religion in Civil War London* (Aldershot, 1997) stresses the importance of religion and adds prosopographical depth and nuance. More recently, Robert Brown's *Empire and Enterprise: Money, Power and the Adventurers for Irish Land during the British Civil Wars* (Manchester, 2020) examines the vital role of the Irish Adventurers as facilitators and financiers of the parliamentarian war effort.

24   John Preston, quoted by Pearl, *Outbreak*, 6.

25   TNA SP 16/203, 56: Endymion Porter to 'Captain Royden', 14 Nov. 1631 (for the 'royal regiment'); SP 16/408, 332–3: Advice respecting measures to be taken for restoring the Artillery Company to its former efficiency; Beinecke Library, Yale, Osborn MS fb150: 'The true coppie of all the gentlemen bearing arms in the Artillarie Garden', 3 Dec. 1631; CRR, I, 39–40, 251, App. V; II, 1236–7 (Rawdon), 1467–8 (Venn); *Charter, Royal Warrants, and Orders in Council, 1637–1889*, ed. G. A. Raikes (1889), 21, 62–6; David R. Lawrence, 'The Honourable Artillery Company Quarterage Book, 1628–1643: New Evidence of the Company's Pre-Civil War History', *Journal of the Society for Army Historical Research*, 97 (2019), 235–41.

26   Ismini Pells, *Philip Skippon and the British Civil Wars: The 'Christian Centurion'* (2020), 45, 72; Nagel, 'The Militia of London', 21.

27   *A Letter from Mercurius Civicus to Mercurius Rusticus* (1643), 4.

28   [Robert Chestlin], *Persecutio Undecima* (1648) (E 470/7), 56.

29   Calybute Downing, *A Sermon Preached to the Renowned Company of the Artillery, 1 September, 1640* (1641) (E 157/4), 21, 24, 35; Adamson, *Noble Revolt*, 53, 68–9; Barbara Donagan, 'Downing, Calybute (1606–1644)', *ODNB*; Pells, *Philip Skippon*, 13, 81.

30   LMA P69/ALH1/H/05/001 (All Hallows, Barking, Churchwarden's

Accounts, 1628–1666), 58–63; LMA P69/ALH1/G/01/001 (All Hallows, Barking, Vestry Minutes, 1629–1669), 10v, 25–6; *CJ*, II, 35; TNA SP 16/503/111, ff. 135–6. The dispute is covered in detail in Kenneth Fincham and Nicholas Tyacke, *Altars Restored: The Changing Face of English Religious Worship, 1547–c.1700* (Oxford, 2007), 265–73.

31   PA HL/PO/JO/10/1/67. Marmaduke's brother Robert also signed this petition; Pearl, *Outbreak*, 119–21.

32   Pearl, *Outbreak*, 187–9. Keith Lindley, 'Venn, John (1586–1650)', *ODNB* ; Lindley, *Popular Politics and Religion*, esp. 30–5, 93–5, 97, 150–2, 157, 412; Adamson, *Noble Revolt*, 66, 79, 253fn, 284fn, 455–6, 471; *Persecutio Undecima* (1648) (E 470/7), 34–5, 64; *A Letter from Mercurius Civicus to Mercurius Rusticus*, 4, 9, 14, 20–24.

33   BL Add MS 29974.2, 346r: William Catherens to Edward Pitt, 21 Jan. 1642.

34   *CJ*, II, 376, 426, 428; Nagel, 'The Militia of London', 42–7.

35   PA HL/PO/JO/10/1/116; *LJ*, IV, 609; *A Letter from Mercurius Civicus to Mercurius Rusticus*, 24–5; Lindley, *Popular Politics and Religion*, 201–6.

36   TNA SP 16/490, 136r (*CSPD 1641–3*, 323).

37   *LJ*, V, 50; HALS 79959X, unnumbered section; Ian Atherton, 'Coke, George (1570–1646)', *ODNB*. Hereford was the younger brother of the former Secretary of State, Sir John Coke. For the connection between Jane Coke née Heigham and Elizabeth[?] Thorowgood née Heigham, see TNA PROB 11/89/196 (will of Francis Heigham) and PROB 11/126/463 (will of Thomas Thorowgood).

38   PA HL/PO/JO/10/1/129, 166. Robert Swinarton and Edmund Forster were also visitors.

39   The Clothworkers' Company, Court Orders H (1639–49), CL/B/1/8, f. 67.

40   Lindley, *Popular Politics and Religion*, 218.

41   The Clothworkers' Company, Court Orders H (1639–49), CL/B/1/8, f. 68v. They paid up the following year; *CJ*, II, 700, 702–3; Lindley, *Popular Politics and Religion*, 166–7.

42   *The Works of the Most Reverend Father in God, William Laud, D.D.*, ed. James Bliss (Oxford, 1854), 9–10.

43   Bulstrode Whitelocke, *Memorials of the English Affairs*, 4 vols. (Oxford, 1853), I, 176.

44   *A Letter from Mercurius Civicus to Mercurius Rusticus* (1643) (E 65/32), 32.

4 Blessed Are the Peacemakers

1   *The Private Journals of the Long Parliament 2 June to 17 September 1642*, ed. Vernon F. Snow and Anne Steele Young (1992), 343–4; *A Perfect Diurnall, 5–12 Sept. 1642* (E 239/20), 7–8.

2   Rudyard Kipling, *Edgehill Fight*, in C. R. L. Fletcher and Rudyard Kipling, *A History of England* (1911), 156; Charles Carlton, *Going to the Wars: The Experience of the British Civil Wars, 1638–1651* (pb, 1994), 117–18, 146–7; Michael Braddick, *God's Fury, England's Fire: A New History of the English Civil Wars* (2008), 244–7; Leanda de Lisle, *White King: Charles I – Traitor, Murderer, Martyr* (2018), 166–71.

3   Matthew Griffith, *A Patheticall Perswasion to Pray for Publick Peace* (E122/17), 25, 30.

4   Ibid., 28, 28, 31, 46, 41, 33, 45; *A Collection of speciall passages and certaine informations . . . Octob. 17 till Tuesday Novemb. 1, 1642* (E 242/2).

5   *A Catalogue of Sundrie Knights, Aldermen, Doctors: Ministers and Citizens* (7 Nov. 1642) (E 669.f.6[86]). For connections to Rawdon, see LMA CLA/008/EM/02/01/002 (City Lands Grant Book, 77: Garway); TNA C10/66/158 (Rawdon borrowed £500 from Sir John Cordwell on 1 July 1642 and the same sum 'for the use of Sir Thomas Whitmore', Sir George's nephew, on 22 Nov. 1642). Rawdon and Sir John Jacob went back at least six years (TNA SP 23/93, 443, 448, 452). For Gurney's visitors in the Tower, see PA HL/PO/JO/10/1/129. See too *CJ*, II, 900, where 'Captain Royden' is summoned to the Commons on 23 Dec. 1642 alongside Cordell, Whitmore and other customs officers, and David Lloyd, *Memoires of the Lives, Actions, Sufferings & Deaths of those Noble, Reverend, and Excellent Personages, that Suffered by Death, Sequestration, Decimation, Or otherwise, for the Protestant Religion, And the great Principle thereof, Allegiance to their Soveraigne, in our late Intestine Wars* (1668), *passim*.

6   Keith Lindley, *Popular Politics and Religion in Civil War London* (Aldershot, 1997), 245; *A Perfect Diurnall, 8–15 August 1642* (E239/8); PA HL/PO/JO/10/1/129, 166r.

7   *CSPV 1642–3*, 181, 188.

8   *CSPV 1642–3*, 192.

9   Anon, *The Wicked Resolution of the Cavaliers* (1642) (E 127/142), 2–4; Stephen Porter and Simon Marsh, *The Battle for London* (Stroud, 2010), 49.

10   Porter and Marsh, *The Battle for London*, 85.

11   Bulstrode Whitelocke, *Memorials of the English Affairs*, 4 vols. (Oxford, 1853), I, 190–1.

12   Porter and Marsh, *The Battle for London*, 93–100; Clarendon, II, 396; *A Continuation of Certaine Speciall and Remarkable Passages, 12–17 Nov. 1642* (E 242/14), 2.

13   TNA C 10/66/158 (which states that Rawdon was 'a very rich man & seized of a great real estate & also possessed of a great personal estate', with plantations worth 'twenty thousand pounds & upwards'.); HALS DE/D/1072. The 14 Oct. 1642 deed was witnessed by Rawdon's

accountant Basil Forster (brother of Edmund). The scrivener was Thomas Wannerton, Master of the Scriveners' Company.

14   *England's Memorable Accidents*, 17–24 Oct. 1642 (E 240/45). The captains are not individually named, but it seems likely that if Rawdon had not been there, his absence would have been noted.

15   *September 29. 1642. The persons to whom the militia of the Citie of London is committed* (E 669.f.6/79); LMA COL/AD/01/041, f. 48r; *CSPV 1642–3*, 182; Porter and Marsh, *The Battle for London*, 46, 89. I am grateful to Simon Marsh for his further advice on this point. See too Andrew Robertshaw, 'Cavaliers on the Field of Mars: The Honourable Artillery Company and London Trained Bands as the training ground for the officers of the "London Regiment"', in *A New Way of Fighting: Professionalism in the English Civil War*, ed. Serena Jones (Solihull, 2017), 34–5. Robertshaw makes the important point that Rawdon should be considered at this stage 'a Londoner first and a potential Royalist second'.

16   Clarendon, II, 396. But see Ronald Hutton, 'Clarendon's *History of the Rebellion*', *English Historical Review* 97/382 (1982), for the need for caution when consulting Clarendon.

17   HALS 79959X, 43v.

18   Paul H. Hardacre, *The Royalists during the Puritan Revolution* (The Hague, 1956), 2. For the tax, see Braddick, *God's Fury, England's Fire*, 253.

19   *The Letters of John Paige, London Merchant, 1648–58*, ed. G. F. Steckley (1984), xii.

20   PA HL/PO/JO/10/1/141, no. 69: Petition of divers citizens and inhabitants of the city of London, 6 Jan. 1643; *The petition of the most substantiall inhabitants of the Citie of London, and the Liberties thereof* . . . (1642) (E 244/39), 4.

21   *The Lord Whartons speech, to the petitioners for peace: on the eighth of December, at Habberdashers-Hall* (12 Dec. 1642) (E129/33), A3. I also draw on Keith Lindley's excellent account in *Popular Politics and Religion in Civil War London* (Aldershot, 1997), 337–40.

22   BL Harl MS 164, 245v; *The Image of the Malignants Peace* [17 Dec. 1642] (E 244/12), A2v, A3v.

23   *A Continuation of Certain Special and Remarkable Passages, 12–15 Dec. 1642* (E 244/11), 4; *The Image of the Malignants Peace* [17 Dec. 1642] (E 244/12), A2r, A4; *An Exact and True Relation of that tumultuous behaviour of divers citizens and others at Guild-Hall, December the 12. 1642* [13 Dec. 1642] (E 130/15), 4–5.

24   *The Humble Petition and Remonstrance of divers citizens, and other inhabitants of the City of London, and Borrough of Southwarke . . . As also The humble Remonstrance of the said petitioners, of the great abuses and outrages committed upon divers of those persons who peaceably endeavoured to promote*

the said petition ([26 Dec.] 1642) (E 83/22), 5–7. For Osboldston, see *The Court of Chivalry 1634–1640*, ed. Richard Cust and Andrew Hopper, *British History Online*, '494: Osboldston v Mungre'.

25   Estimates range from 1,000 to 5,000 petitioners. Cf. Lindley, 340 n178. The Venetian Secretary in London reported 3,000 (*CSPV 1642–3*, 218).

26   *CJ*, II, 894; *LJ*, V, 490, 493, 499–501.

27   PA HL/PO/JO/10/1/141: Petition of Divers Citizens and Inhabitants of the City of London, 6 Jan. 1643; HL/PO/JO/10/1/138: Petition of Citizens and Inhabitants of London, etc. praying for measures for the restoration of peace. I am grateful to David Prior, Head of Public Services and Outreach at the Parliamentary Archives, for his consultation with the Collection Care and Heritage Imaging teams and advice on the water damage and irrecoverability of the petition's signatures (email to author, 10 Feb. 2020). I suspect that, had the signatures survived, we would have found a good few more members of the royalist garrison at Basing House. Rawdon, Rosewell and Langley were obviously key players. The vintner Robert Amery also claimed to have acted 'as chief agent to deliver the petition for peace' at the Guildhall (TNA SP 29/25, f. 40r). A fifth man at Basing House, Cornet William Atterbury, was the brother-in-law of the Gomeldon brothers, who were in the nine-man delegation of 6 January (HALS 79959X, 44r, 49v).

28   *LJ*, V, 500.

29   HALS 79959X, 48r.

30   Lindley, 177–9; *CJ*, II, 927; *Speciall Passages*, 10–17 Jan. 1643 (E 85/7), 190; *Two Speeches Spoken by the Earle of Manchester, and John Pym* (E 85/7), 22. For 'that shuttle-head', see Alexander Brome, *Rump* (1662), I, 7.

31   Braddick, *God's Fury, England's Fire*, 255–6; *A Great Wonder in Heaven* (1643) (E 85/41), 5; *The New Yeares Wonder* (1643) (E 86/23), 6–8.

5 *The Bell Tolls*

1   William Lithgow, *The Present Surveigh of London and Englands State* (1643); Valerie Pearl, *London and the Outbreak of the Puritan Revolution* (Oxford, 1961), 262–5; Simon Marsh, 'The Construction and Arming of London's Defences 1642–1645', *Journal of the Society for Army Historical Research*, 91/368 (2013), 275–99. For the latest archaeological research, see Peter Mills, 'The Civil War Defences of East London Reviewed: preliminary results', *London Archaeologist* 16/3 (Winter 2021), 73–81. Thanks to David Flintham for advice on this subject.

2   LMA CLC/L/VA/B/001/MS15201/003 (Vintners' Company Court Minute Book, 1629–38), 23 (the cost of Amery's admission into the

Vintners was £10 'and a good fat buck'); *AVB*, 31. For his wife Mary (née Mort), see *Part of the Visitation of London . . . 1634*, ed. Sir T. Phillipps (1840), 2; TNA SP 29/25, 40r: The humble petition of Captain Robert Amery, Dec. 1660. Amery mentions here that he was forced to leave London in 1642, which, according to the Old Style Julian Calendar, meant before 25 March 1643.

3 TNA E 179/252/10, 16v (printed in T. C. Dale, *The Poll Tax for London in 1641* (1934–5), 23); TNA C 7/414/25: Valance v Rowlett; TNA SP 24/73, pt 3, 28r; SP 23/191, 435–9; TNA PROB 11/160/576: Will of Thomas Rowlett, Rector and Parson of the Church of Uppingham, Rutland; *AVB*, 56; *Scriveners' Company Common Paper*, 116. There are many wills witnessed by Isaac Rowlett in the LMA, including one (MS 9172/41, no. 102) that mentions Robert Peake, his brothers John and Adam, and his maid Elizabeth Gantlett. See too Mary Edmond, 'New Light on Jacobean Painters', *The Burlington Magazine* 118/875 (1976), 81.

4 TNA E 179/252/10, 16v (printed in Dale, *Poll Tax*, p.23); Goldsmiths Apprenticeships (via ROLLCO): Thomas Rowlett, 6 May 1636. This confirms that he was the son of Thomas Rowlett, 'clerk' of Uppingham, and therefore Isaac Rowlett's brother.

5 John Stow, *Annales* (1615), 862.

6 John Vicars, *Behold Romes Monster on his Monstrous Beast* (1643); Antony Griffiths, 'Peake, Sir Robert (*c.* 1605–1667)', *ODNB*.

7 William Prynne, *Canterburies Doome* (1646), 109–10; Michael Sparke, *A Second Beacon Fired by Scintilla* (1652) (E 675/29), 6; George Henderson, 'Bible Illustration in the Age of Laud', *Transactions of the Cambridge Bibliographical Society* 8/2 (1982), 174.

8 Hugh Peter, *A True Relation of the Passages of Gods Providence in a Voyage for Ireland* (1642) (E 242/15), unnumbered. For Peake and Peter as neighbours, see Hugh Peter, *The Full and Last Relation, of all things concerning Basing-House* (1645) (E 305/8).

9 Hugh Peter sermon, Christ Church, London, 7 April 1643: an uncatalogued acquisition now at the Harry Ransom Center, the University of Texas at Austin. The manuscript sermon was in a private collection until acquired by Dean Cooke, in whose catalogue I noticed it (*First Words: A catalogue of manuscripts & rare books to be exhibited by Dean Cooke Rare Books Ltd at the firsts fair Saatchi Gallery, London, 21–4 Oct. 2021*, no. 8). I'm enormously grateful to both Dean Cooke and Aaron T. Pratt, Carl and Lily Pforzheimer Curator of Early Books and Manuscripts at the Harry Ransom Center, for generously sharing the manuscript and allowing me to quote from it while in transit.

10 *September 29. 1642. The Persons to whom the Militia of the Citie of London is committed* (E 669.f.6/79); *CRR*, I, 497; II, 1176, 1192; *A Paire of Spectacles for*

the Citie (E 419/9), 8. Camfield's house on Snow Hill can be traced via his apprentice Daniel Axtell's donation of a horse to Parliament on 24 July 1642 (TNA SP 28/131/3, part 3, f. 24v). See too Dale, *Poll Tax*, 24, 32; Drapers Apprenticeships (via ROLLCO): Daniel Axtell, 26 Nov. 1634. This was not Axtell the future regicide (Alan Thomson, 'Axtell, Daniel (bapt.1622, d.1660)', *ODNB*), but probably a Hertfordshire relation.

11 TNA SP 23/203, 605, 617, 618; SP 19/49, 41v–42r (Miles 'Petty' is named as an assessor for Farringdon Without Newgate in the front matter of this MS). For the February offensive on non-contributors, see Keith Lindley, *Popular Politics and Religion in Civil War London* (Aldershot, 1997), 324–7. The vicar was Thomas Gouge. For the traditionalists, see *Sober Sadnes* ([3 April] 1643) (E 94/28), 32.

12 LMA P93/MRY1/001 (baptism, St Mary Whitechapel, Tower Hamlets, 29 Sept. 1621: 'Wm sonne of Daniel Feithorne & Sarah ux', and burial: 'Daniell Ffeathorne', 7 Sept. 1625); Goldsmiths Apprenticeships (via ROLLCO): William Faithorne, 23 Oct. 1635; BL Harl MS 5910, iv, 135–6: 'The Life of Mr William Ffathorne' by John Bagford (partially printed in Sidney Colvin, *Early Engraving and Engravers in England, 1545–1695* (1905), 132–3. See too plates XXXIII and XXXIV in Colvin for early Faithorne engravings of Charles I and Prince Rupert); Antony Griffiths, 'Rowlett, Thomas', 'Faithorne, William' and 'Payne, John', *ODNB*.

13 John Evelyn to Samuel Pepys, 26 Sept. 1690, in *Particular Friends: The Correspondence of Samuel Pepys and John Evelyn*, ed. Guy de la Bédoyère (Woodbridge, 1997), 224.

14 Thomas Johnson, *Descriptio Itineris Plantarum* (1632), in *Thomas Johnson: Botanical Journeys in Kent & Hampstead*, ed. J. S. L. Gilmour (1972), 122. Rawdon: HALS 79959X (1667), 56v; William Faithorne, *The Art of Graveing and Etching* (1662), sig. A. For an excellent collection of articles on royalism in all its variegations, see *Royalists and Royalism during the English Civil Wars*, ed. Jason McElligott and David L. Smith (Cambridge, 2007), and for the recovery of some ordinary voices, see Dagmar Freist, *Governed by Opinion: Politics, Religion and the Dynamics of Communication in Stuart London, 1637–1645* (1997).

15 There is some uncertainty over which one of Isaac's brothers served alongside him. 'Lieutenant Rowlett' is never named, but considering Thomas was Robert Peake's apprentice, he seems the most likely candidate. Antony Griffiths (in 'Rowlett, Thomas', 1621–52, *ODNB*) points to the marriage of a Thomas Rowlett, 'gent.' and Mary Haines at St Dunstan-in-the-West on 27 April 1643 as evidence that Rowlett stayed in London during the war, but he was only freed from his apprenticeship – and therefore eligible to marry – in 1647. It would be strange, too, for Thomas to be described later as a 'bachelor', as he was upon his death in

1652 (TNA PROB 6/27, 53r), if he was a widower by then. His print business near Temple Bar was set up after the siege of Basing House when Rowlett seems to have been able to buy back both his freedom and his master's confiscated box of copper plates. In June 1644, Lieutenant Rowlett was captured alongside his brother Captain Isaac Rowlett, during a failed raid on Odiham. A London news-sheet described him then as Isaac's 'brother against Holborn Conduit in London'. Only Thomas Rowlett fits the bill. See *A Great Victory obtained by Colonel Norton and his Horse, and Colonell Jones and his Foote, against Colonel Rayden, from Basing House, neere Walneborough Mill, within halfe a mile of Odium* ([5 June], 1644) (E 50/13).

16 Society of Apothecaries, Court Minute Book 1617–51, 41or. One Thomas Johnson of St Sepulchre's is named in the Commons' Journal (*CJ*, II, 972) on 20 Feb. 1643 as an assessment collector who has neglected his duty and must thenceforth be regarded as a 'delinquent'. There were other Thomas Johnsons in the parish, so it is impossible to identify him as our apothecary. Another Thomas Johnson served in the Green Regiment of the London trained bands and is sometimes identified as the apothecary (Keith Roberts, *London and Liberty: Ensigns of the London Trained Bands* (Eastwood, 1987), App. II, 71; Andrew Robertshaw, 'Cavaliers on the Field of Mars', in *A New Way of Fighting: Professionalism in the English Civil War*, ed. Serena Jones (Solihull, 2017), 38). But no linking evidence is provided beyond a reference (T. C. Dale, *The Inhabitants of London in 1638* (1931), MS 345) to a Thomas Johnson living in the parish of St Botolph without Aldersgate in 1638. No reason is given as to why this Thomas Johnson, out of so many in London, should be our apothecary. The 1638 list does not include the parish of St Sepulchre. Johnson's letter 'To the Reader' in his edition of Gerard's *Herball* suggests that he was living, as well as working, on Snow Hill by 22 October 1633. Sir Henry Wooton's letter to Johnson of 2 July 1637 (TNA SP 16/363, 27r) confirms Johnson's place of residence, as does the 1641 poll tax assessment for the parish of St Sepulchre (TNA E 179/252/10, f. 14r). Had Johnson served in the trained bands, he would more likely have been in the Orange Regiment, which covered the ward of Faringdon Without Newgate. P. R. Newman's assertion that Johnson was 'the second son of Alderman Thomas Johnson by Mary Abraham of Buckinghamshire, and married to Frances the daughter of Alderman John Muscott of London' (*Royalist Officers in England and Wales* (1981), 812), is unconvincing. He cites the compounding papers of one Thomas Johnson of New Windsor in Berkshire, who compounded in 1651, by which time the apothecary was dead (TNA SP 23/221, 389, 392–3).

17 TNA E 179/252/10, 38r (printed in Dale, *Poll Tax*, 38); Society of

Apothecaries, Court Minute Book 1617–51, 29, 47, 156, 185, 196; TNA SP 16/408, 61r; SP 16/430, 53r; SP 19/49, 41v–42r; F. G. Parsons, *The History of St Thomas's Hospital*, II (1934), 59–60; PA HL/PO/JO/10/1/141.

18   PA HL/PO/JO/1/138.

19   John Strype, *A Survey of the Cities of London and Westminster* (1720), Bk 3, Ch. XII, 283; John Taylor, *The Carriers Cosmographie* (1637), A4v; TNA PROB 11/263/162: Will of Augustine Bryan, Innholder of London.

20   *Mercurius Veridicus*, 11–18 Oct. 1645 (E 305/10), 180. For examples of royalist tricks, see *Wednesday's Mercury* (1643) (E 61/15, 12–13 and E 63/4, 28).

21   The Clothworkers' Company, Court Orders H (1639–49), CL/B/1/8, 76v; TNA SP 19/37, 16v; 19/49, 59v–60r; HALS 79959X, 43v.

22   These were all forts from the first phase of works. See Marsh, 'The Construction and Arming of London's Defences', esp. 275–83. For the committee to secure London, see LMA COL/AD/01/041, 48r. Rawdon and the team were ordered to 'inform themselves of all and every the passages, inlets and ways through this city walls and other places about the city and liberties and from the river of Thames into the city and by whom they have been made and consider how inconvenient and dangerous the said passages may be unto this city and which of them may be stopped up. And how the rest may be made defensive by making gates thereunto or chaining the same up. And likewise consider what watch houses are necessary and needful to be made.'

23   Staffordshire Record Office D641/2/C/7/3R provides instructions on travelling from London to Hoddesdon to officials looking for Marmaduke Rawdon's daughter, Elizabeth Forster, after the war.

24   *Memoirs of Lady Fanshawe*, ed. B. Marshall (1905), 56.

25   HALS 79959X, 43v, 75v, 99r, 115r; TNA PROB 11/197/598; C 8/73/184; C 10/66/158; J. A. Tregelles, *A History of Hoddesdon in the County of Hertfordshire* (Hertford, 1908), 383.

26   HALS 79959X, 56: 'When he had leisure time from public affairs, which was but seldom, his recreation was the Artillery Garden, a bowling green and a game at tables.'

27   HALS 79959X, 43v–44r; Robertshaw, 'Cavaliers on the Field of Mars', 35.

28   Robert Ashton, 'Crisp, Sir Nicholas (c.1599–1666), *ODNB*; *CRR*, I, 592; *CJ*, II, 933, 936, 940, 978; PA HL/PO/JO/10/1/129, 166v (for Crisp visiting Gurney in the Tower) and PA HL/PO/JO/10/1/141 (for Robert Abbot and the peace petition). For Crisp's disguise, see David Lloyd, *Memoires of the Lives, Actions, Sufferings & Deaths of those Noble, Reverend, and Excellent Personages, that Suffered by Death . . . in our late Intestine Wars* (1668), 627.

29   *A Brief Narrative of the Late Treacherous and Horrid Designe . . . 15 June 1643*

(E 106/10); *A Discovery of the Great Plot for the utter ruine of the City of London and the Parliament* ([9 June] 1643) (E 105/21); Clarendon, III, 38–52 ('kneaded' on p.45); *Cobbett's Complete Collection of State Trials*, IV (1809), no. 172; Ian Roy, '"This Proud Unthankefull City": A Cavalier View of London in the Civil War', in *London and the Civil War*, ed. Stephen Porter (Basingstoke, 1996), 160–2; Geoffrey Smith, *Royalist Agents, Conspirators and Spies: Their Role in the British Civil Wars, 1640–1660* (Farnham, 2011), 47–55; Lindley, *Popular Politics and Religion*, 246–7, 348–51; Nadine Akkerman, *Invisible Agents: Women and Espionage in Seventeenth-Century Britain* (Oxford, 2018), 54–5, 28–30; Warren Chernaik, 'Waller, Edmund (1606–1687), *ODNB*.

30 Lawson Chase Nagel, 'The Militia of London, 1641–1649' (PhD thesis, King's College, University of London, 1982), 110–12; Lindley, *Popular Politics and Religion*, 309–10, 351–3; Sara Read, 'A Women's Revolt', *History Today* 65/8 (2015), 6; *Mercurius Civicus*, 3–11 August 1643 (E 65/4), 87–8; *CSPV 1643–7*, 8.

31 *Docquets of Letters Patent and Other Instruments passed under the Great Seal of King Charles I at Oxford*, ed. W. H. Black (1837), 20

32 TNA PROB 11/183/548: Will of Dr John Buggs, witnessed by Edmund and Basil Forster on 23 May 1640.

33 Clothworkers Apprenticeships (via ROLLCO), 24 Oct. 1626, 30 May 1648, 7 Feb. 1654/5: in the latter two entries, Thomas Langley is described as a 'mercer' of Paternoster Row.

34 Anthony Wood, *Fasti Oxonienses*, II (1820), 67–8.

35 HALS 79959X, 44r; TNA SP 29/25, f. 40r: Petition of Captain Robert Amery, 1660; SP 29/25, f. 98: Petition of Thomas Langley, Lieutenant-Colonel to Sir Marmaduke Rawdon, 1660.

36 TNA SP 16/497, f. 204.

37 Robertshaw, 'Cavaliers on the Field of Mars', 41.

38 Ian Gentles, 'The Iconography of Revolution: England 1642–1649', in *Soldiers, Writers and Statesmen of the English Revolution*, ed. Ian Gentles, John Morrill and Blair Worden (Cambridge, 1998), esp. 93–5, 100–2, 106, 110, 113.

39 *The Royalist Ordnance Papers, 1642–1646*, ed. Ian Roy, 2 parts (Oxfordshire RS, 1964, 1975), I, 217–18, II, 277.

40 Figures from Chris Scott, *The Most Heavy Stroke: The Battle of Roundway Down 1643* (Warwick, 2018), 144, though as Scott points out, mass production was beginning to produce lighter models (around 9 pounds), especially for the parliamentarians.

41 *Memoirs of Lady Fanshawe*, ed. B. Marshall (1905), 56.

42 TNA SP 29/25, f. 40r: Petition of Captain Robert Amery, 1660. See too

Jerome De Groot, 'Space, Patronage, Procedure: The Court at Oxford, 1642–46', *English Historical Review* 117/474 (2002), 1207–9, and Eric Gruber von Arni, '"Dead Hogges, Dogges, Cats and well flayed Carryon Horses": royalist hospital provision during the First Civil War', in *Battle-scarred: Mortality, Medical Care and Military Welfare in the British Civil Wars*, ed. David J. Appleby and Andrew Hopper (Manchester, 2018), esp. 96–7, 99, 104, 108.

43   John Taylor, *Mad Verse, Sad Verse, Glad Verse and Bad Verse* (1644) (E 46/13), 8.

44   [George Wither], *Mercurius Rusticus, or, A Countrey Messenger* [1643] (E 73/2), 1–2.

45   Julie Spraggon, *Puritan Iconoclasm during the English Civil War* (Woodbridge, 2003), 83–6, 258. See too *The Chimney-sweepers Sad Complaint, and Humble Petition to the City of London* (1663), 6.

46   [Bruno Ryves], *Mercurius Rusticus, or, The Countries Complaint of the Murthers, Robberies, Plunderings, and other Outrages committed by the rebells on His Majesties faithfull subjects* (27 May 1643) (E 105/7), 12.

47   *Mercurius Rusticus* (10 June 1643) (E 106/12), 27–8.

48   TNA SP 24/73, pt. 3, 28r; C 7/414/25, pt. 4; SP 29/25, 40r, 41r.

49   *CJ*, III, 76; TNA C 10/66/158; SP 16/497, 201–3r; TNA SP 19/1, 125; SP 20/1, 40v; SP 23/182, 749.

50   HALS 79959X, 99.

51   *Mercurius Aulicus*, 30 April–6 May 1643 (E 102/1), 134; *Wednesday's Mercury*, 25–28 July 1643 (E 62/8), 21.

52   TNA WO 55/459, pt 2, 363.

53   Richard Atkyns, *The Vindication of Richard Atkyns* (1669), 33.

54   Ibid., 35 (bell-ropes), 37 (Armada); John Cleveland, *The character of a London diurnall* (1644), 4 (crabs); Thomas Fuller, *The History of the Worthies of England* (1662), Wiltshire, 165 (bed-cords); Scott, *The Most Heavy Stroke*, 139.

55   Prideaux-Brune MS, reproduced in Mary Coate, *Cornwall in the Great Civil War and Interregnum, 1642–1660* (Oxford, 1933), 77. See too John Adair, *Roundhead General: A Military Biography of Sir William Waller* (1969), 73–6, 231 n16.

56   Max Hastings, *The Oxford Book of Military Anecdotes* (Oxford, 1985), 121.

57   TNA WO 55/459, pt 2, 306; Robertshaw, 'Cavaliers on the Field of Mars', 42.

58   *The Memoirs and Letters of Ulick, Marquiss of Clanricarde, and Earl of Saint Albans*, ed. John Smyth Bourke (1757), 340.

59   Hampshire RO 48/M80/F1; Siege Diary, 1.

60   Fuller, *Worthies*, Hant-shire, 3; *The Souldiers Report* (E 76/5).

PART TWO

6 *Stone Fidelity*

1   Siege Diary, 2; *Mercurius Aulicus*, 30 July–5 August 1643 (E 65/13), 416.

2   Siege Diary, 1. For the following description, I have also drawn on HALS, 79959X, 45r (for the number of buildings in the Grange), *The Weekly Account*, 21–7 August 1644 (E 7/13), 261 (on the marquess's private chambers); *The Souldiers Report* (1643) (E 76/5); Hugh Peter, *The Full and Last Relation, of all things concerning Basing-House* (1645) (E 305/8), 2, and *Mercurius Veridicus*, 11–18 Oct. 1645 (E 305/10), 180. See too Godwin, ch. x; Wilf Emberton, *Love Loyalty: The Close and Perilous Siege of Basing House 1643–1645* (Basingstoke, 1972), ch. 2; Mavis Batey, 'Basing House Tudor Garden', *Garden History* 15/2 (1987); David Allen and Sue Anderson, *Basing House Hampshire: Excavations 1978–1991*, Hampshire Field Club & Archaeological Society (1999), ch. 1; David Allen and Alan Turton, *Basing House: A Tudor mansion destroyed in the English Civil War* (Andover, 2010) and, most recently, Alan Turton, 'A House called Loyalty – The Archaeology of a Civil War Siege', in *Home and Away: The British Experience of War 1618–1721*, ed. Serena Jones (Warwick, 2018), 117–49.

3   *Letters and Papers, Henry VIII*, ed. J. S. Brewer et al. V, 37.

4   Lambeth Palace Library MS 3196, 109: Francis Alen to the Earl of Shrewsbury, 3 Sept. 1560.

5   Edmund Lodge, *Portraits of Illustrious Personages of Great Britain*, III (1828): William Powlett, First Marquis of Winchester, 2; Thomas Fuller, *The History of the Worthies of England* (1662), Hant-shire, 8–9.

6   Bod Ashmole MS 836, f. 212.

7   *Camden's Britannia*, trans. Gibson (1695), 123.

8   *Complete Peerage*, ed. G. H. White (1959) 12/2, 765–6. Also: *Mercurius Britanicus*, 10–17 Feb. 1645 (E 269/25), 554; *The Weekly Account*, 21–7 August 1644 (E 7/13), 261; *The Hartlib Papers* (published by The Digital Humanities Institute, University of Sheffield: https://www.dhi.ac.uk/hartlib), ed. M. Greengrass, M. Leslie and M. Hannon (2013), Ephemerides 1653, Pt 1: 28/2/47B.

9   Bod Tanner MS 115, f. 21r.

10   *The Travels of Peter Mundy in Europe and Asia, 1608–1667*, ed. R. C. Temple, III (1919), 12.

11   Peter, *Full and Last Relation*, 2.

12   *CJ*, I, 549; Paul Hunneyball, 'Paulet, Lord John (*c.*1598–1675)', in *The History of Parliament: the House of Commons 1604–1629*, ed. Andrew Thrush and John P. Ferris (2010).

13   TNA SP 16/413, 50r; *The Lismore Papers*, 2nd ser., ed. A. B. Grosart, IV (1888), 146. (Viscount Kynalmeaky to his father, the Earl of Cork, 9 Oct. 1640).

14   Turton, 'A House Called Loyalty', 119; Peter Leadbetter, 'Private Armouries of the Nobility and Gentry', *Arquebusier: The Journal of the Pike and Shot Society* 26/5 (2019), 46–8. With many thanks to Alan Turton for drawing my attention to the inventory, Stephen Ede-Borrett for sending me the article, and to Peter Leadbetter, who found the unindexed inventory in the British Library (Add MS 69907B, 39r) and kindly provided the reference and transcript.

15   Siege Diary, 1; *CJ*, III, 4; *Journal of Sir Samuel Luke*, ed. I. G. Philip, Oxfordshire RS (1950–3), 18–19, 38, 50; Ronald Hutton, 'Paulet, John, fifth marquess of Winchester (1598?–1675)', *ODNB*.

16   John Milton, 'An Epitaph on the Marchioness of Winchester', in *Complete Shorter Poems*, ed. John Carey (2nd edn, 1997), 130–4; James Howell, 'To the Lady Jane Savage, Marchioness of Winchester', in *Epistolae* (1650).

17   BL Add MS 46188, 120r, 122r, 124r, 126r, 146r, 148r, 166r; Bernadette Cunningham, 'Clanricard Letters', *Journal of the Galway Archaeological and Historical Society* 48 (1996), 193; Jane Ohlmeyer, 'MacDonnell, Randal, marquess of Antrim (1609–1683)', *ODNB*; Longleat MSS, Devereux Papers, I, no. 108, 363v; Wiltshire and Swindon Archives 4186/1A/64 (which mentions Honora's £10,000 dowry).

18   Ioanna Tsakiropoulou, 'Devereux, Frances [née Walsingham], countess of Essex and of Clanricarde (c.1568–1632)', *ODNB*; John Cooper, *The Queen's Agent: Francis Walsingham at the Court of Elizabeth I* (pb, 2012), 79, 321–2; John Morrill, 'Devereux, Robert, third earl of Essex (1591–1646)', *ODNB*; John Gerard, *The Autobiography of an Elizabethan*, trans., P. Caraman (1951), 176–8.

19   BL Add MS 46188, 130r, 138r.

20   *The Memoirs and Letters of Ulick, Marquiss of Clanricarde, and Earl of Saint Albans*, ed. J. S. Bourke (1757), 49; *Letter-Book of the Earl of Clanricarde 1643–47*, ed. J. Lowe (Dublin, 1983), 35, 118 (for the claret).

21   BL Add MS 46188, 128r, 156r, 166r.

22   *Memoirs and Letters of Ulick, Marquiss of Clanricarde*, 15, 84; *Letter-Book of the Earl of Clanricarde*, 40–1, 388; Jane Ohlmeyer, 'Burke, Ulicke, marquess of Clanricarde (1604–1658)', *ODNB*.

23   *Letter-Book of the Earl of Clanricarde*, 354; *Memoirs and Letters of Ulick, Marquiss of Clanricarde*, 49; John Adamson, *The Noble Revolt: The Overthrow of Charles I* (2007), xii.

24   *Letter-Book of the Earl of Clanricarde*, 35, 39. Patrick Little, in ' "Blood and Friendship": The Earl of Essex's Protection of the Earl of Clanricarde's

Interests, 1641–6', *English Historical Review* 112/448 (1997), outlines Essex's considerable efforts to protect Ulick's interests and demonstrates that their ties, 'though strained, were never severed' (939). See too *Journal of Sir Samuel Luke*, 126, where a parliamentarian scout reports that the Winchesters 'had the Lord General's protection'.

25   *A Royalist's Notebook: The Commonplace Book of Sir John Oglander of Nunwell*, ed. Francis Bamford (1936), 103.

26   *Letter-Book of the Earl of Clanricarde*, 35. The only recorded instance of a brother killing a brother during the war is the shooting of Private Hillsdeane, a parliamentarian, by his royalist brother at Wardour Castle. See Charles Carlton, *Going to the Wars: The Experience of the British Civil Wars, 1638–1651* (pb, 1994), 305.

27   HRO 40M93/1.

28   HRO 11M49/F/02; TNA WO 55/459, pt 3, 410.

29   HALS 79959X, 46r, 58v.

30   Eliot Warburton, *Memoirs of Prince Rupert and the Cavaliers*, 3 vols. (1849), II, 325; HRO 40M93/1.

31   TNA SP 29/25, 40r, 41r.

32   HRO 40M93/1.

33   *Journal of Sir Samuel Luke*, 130.

34   *The Souldiers Report* (1643) (E 76/5).

35   TNA SP 23/253, 51; *Journal of Sir Samuel Luke*, 133, 159; HRO 44M69/F5/4/3 (Bundle 1: An estimate of Sir Thomas Jervoise losses, 1660).

36   *CJ*, III, 280; *LJ*, VI, 295.

37   BL Add MS 29974.2, f. 364a, 366r, 368a; Barbara Donagan, 'Family and Misfortune in the English Civil War: The Sad Case of Edward Pitt', *Huntington Library Quarterly*, 61/2 (1998), 223–40.

38   BL Add MS 29974.2, f. 322 (verso: 'Lo: Marquis not sent').

39   BL Add MS 29974.2, f. 364a, 368a; Donagan, 235.

40   BL Add MS 29974.2, f. 375r, 388r, 391v, 401r; Donagan, 230–1, 237.

41   BL Add MS 29974.2, ff. 352–3, 395v.

42   HALS 79959X, 102v.

43   Henry Foster, *A True and Exact Relation of the marchings of the two regiments of the trained-bands of the City of London* (E 69/15); John Gwynne, *Military Memoirs of the Great Civil War* (Edinburgh, 1822), 47; for Atkins, see *The Honest Citizen, or, faithful counsellor to the City of London* (1648) (E 438/5), 4.

44   Bod MS Carte 7, f. 341r (Endymion Porter to the Marquess of Ormond, 3 Nov. 1643). For Porter's friendship with Rawdon, see HALS 79959X, 46v and TNA SP 16/203, 56.

45   Bod MS Rawlinson D 395, 147r: Winchester to Percy, 2 Nov. 1643. See too Charles I's warrant to Percy of 12 Oct. (Bod MS Rawl. D 395, f. 52r); *The*

Papers of Captain Henry Stevens Waggon-Master-General to King Charles I, ed. Margaret Toynbee, Oxfordshire RS, 42 (1961), 23; *The Royalist Ordnance Papers, 1642–1646*, ed. Ian Roy, 2 parts (Oxfordshire RS, 1964, 1975), II, 295, 369, 492 n234.

46 Thomas Johnson, *Descriptio Itineris Plantarum* (1632), in *Thomas Johnson: Botanical Journeys in Kent & Hampstead*, ed. J. S. L. Gilmour (1972), 122; Siege Diary, 2.

47 *Royalist Ordnance Papers*, II, 277. For the geology, see David Allen and Sue Anderson, *Basing House Hampshire: Excavations 1978–1991*, Hampshire Field Club & Archaeological Society (1999), 1.

48 Stephen Bull, 'The Furie of the Ordnance': Artillery in the English Civil Wars (Woodbridge, 2008), 87.

49 Ian Gentles, 'The Civil Wars in England', in *The Civil Wars: A Military History of England, Scotland, and Ireland 1638–1660*, ed. John Kenyon and Jane Ohlmeyer (Oxford, 1998), 112.

50 *Royalist Ordnance Papers*, I, 102, 105.

51 William Barriffe, *Military Discipline: or, the yong artillery man* (2nd edn, 1639), dedicatory epistle 'to all the worthy captains of the City, especially unto those that continue members of the Artillery Garden', 1, 4–5. Barriffe's drill in *Military Discipline* is still practised by the HAC's modern-day Company of Pikemen & Musketeers (*CRR*, I, 228–9).

52 Archer, 3.

53 Waller Report, 154.

7 A Slight Piece

1 *Mercurius Aulicus*, 24–30 Dec. 1643 (E 81/19), 744–5 (mispaginated).

2 Lawson Chase Nagel, 'The Militia of London, 1641–1649' (PhD thesis, King's College, University of London, 1982), 77–84, 89, 108–9, 135–40; Keith Roberts, *London and Liberty: Ensigns of the London Trained Bands* (Eastwood, 1987), 42, 49–50, 62–3. The Westminster trained band was also sometimes known as the Westminster Red Regiment, but I have avoided the colour in order to avoid confusion with Marmaduke Rawdon's former regiment.

3 Patrick Little, 'Writing and Sources XIV: Susan Rodway to Robert Rodway, c. November 1643', *Cromwelliana: The Journal of the Cromwell Association* (2011), 64–6. The parish registers of St Dunstan in the West confirm Dr Little's identification and provide further information on the Rodway family. For Willie (bapt. 18 Nov. 1641) and Hester (bapt. 30 April 1643), see LMA P69/DUN2/A/003/MS010344 and P69/DUN2/A/004/MS010345. For Robert Rodway (bapt. 19 Feb. 1614/15),

see Gloucestershire Archives P31/IN/1/1. Also see Laurence Spring, ' "For God's Sake Come Home!" – Soldiers' Wives, 1620–1660', in *Home and Away: The British Experience of War 1618–1721*, ed. Serena Jones (Warwick, 2018), 107–8.

4   Archer, 2.

5   Roberts, *London and Liberty*, 47, 52–3, 63; Ian Gentles, 'The Iconography of Revolution: England 1642–1649', in *Soldiers, Writers and Statesmen of the English Revolution*, ed. Ian Gentles, John Morrill and Blair Worden (Cambridge, 1998), 112; Barbara Donagan, 'Waller, Sir William', *ODNB*.

6   Waller Report, 154. According to Lieut. Elias Archer of the Tower Hamlets Yellow Auxiliaries, the forlorn hope comprised 500 men; according to the royalist newsletter *Mercurius Aulicus*, just 100 men. The parliamentarian and royalist accounts frequently diverge on the details and each imputes bad faith to the other (for e.g. over the accidental firing of the cannon and the misdirected trumpeter), but they tend to agree on the basic narrative. For the account below, I have chiefly drawn on: Waller Report and Archer's *True Relation* for the parliamentary version, and *Mercurius Aulicus* (5–11 Nov. 1643: E 75/28 and 12–19 Nov: E 77/18) and Rawdon's nephew's account (HALS 79959X, 44r–46r) for the royalist viewpoint. See too: *A Perfect Diurnall*, 6–13 Nov. 1643 (E 252/7), 134, 136; *The Compleate Intelligencer*, 14 Nov. 1643 (E 75/32), 37–8; *Mercurius Civicus*, 9–16 Nov. 1643 (E 76/1), 195; *The Scottish Dove*, 10–17 Nov. 1643 (E 76/7), 39–40; *Journal of Sir Samuel Luke*, ed. I. G. Philip, Oxfordshire RS (1950–3), 190–1.

7   William Lithgow on the siege of Newcastle (1644), quoted in Stephen Bull, *'The Furie of the Ordnance': Artillery in the English Civil Wars* (Woodbridge, 2008), 100.

8   'The Court Martial Papers of Sir William Waller's Army', in John Adair, *Cheriton 1644: The Campaign and the Battle* (Kineton, 1973), 198–221.

9   *The Workes of that famous Chirurgion Ambrose Parey*, translated out of Latin and compared with the French by Th. Johnson (1634), Lib. 29: *An Apologie or Treatise*, 1142. This section of Paré's works was translated from French to English by George Baker.

10   *The Scottish Dove*, 10–17 Nov. 1643 (E 76/7), 39–40. For the rest, see note 6 above.

11   *Mercurius Aulicus*, 5–11 Nov. 1643 (E 75/28), 641–2; Eliot Warburton, *Memoirs of Prince Rupert and the Cavaliers*, 3 vols. (1849), II, 325; *The Papers of Captain Henry Stevens Waggon-Master-General to King Charles I*, ed. Margaret Toynbee, Oxfordshire RS, 42 (1961), 23.

12   Bod MS Carte 7, f. 405: Sir Edward Nicholas to Ormond, Oxford, 10 Nov. 1643.

13   Waller Report, 154; *Mercurius Aulicus*, 24–30 Dec. 1643 (E 81/19), 737.

14 Henry Foster, *A True and Exact Relation of the marchings of the two regiments of the trained-bands* (E 69/15); Humfrey Peake, *Meditations upon a Seige* (1646), 26–8; see too Bull, 'The Furie of the Ordnance', 12–15, 106–8.

15 Waller Report, 154; *A Perfect Diurnall*, 6–13 Nov. 1643 (E 252/7), 136; *Mercurius Aulicus*, 12–19 Nov. 1643 (E 77/18), 660–1; *The Kingdomes Weekly Post*, 9–15 Nov. 1643 (E 75/35), 16. The newsbooks assumed that the Commons motion was made with Basing House in mind, though neither the *Commons Journal* entry of 10 Nov. (III, 306) nor the Ordinance of 20 Nov. (*Acts and Ordinances of the Interregnum*, ed. C. H. Firth and R. S. Rait, I, 343–5) explicitly mentions it.

8 *Another Fling*

1 For the following account, see the sources listed in note 6 above. The 'singing of psalms' is noted in HALS 79959X, 45r. The other major source for the 12 Nov. assault is the anonymous *Souldiers Report* (E 76/5). See too: *CSPV 1643–7*, 41, 44, 46, 48; *Certaine Informations*, 13–20 Nov. 1643 (E 76/15), 342, 344; *The Compleate Intelligencer*, 21 Nov. 1643 (E 76/19), 50; *Mercurius Aquaticus* ([18 Jan.] 1643/4) (E 29/11), sig. C2v; *Mercurius Cambro-Britannus*, 20–7 Nov. 1643 (E 77/7), 4; *The Parliament Scout*, 10–17 Nov. 1643 (E 76/8), 180–5; *A Perfect Diurnall*, 13–20 Nov. 1643 (E 252/8), 141; *Remarkable Passages*, 19–25 Nov. 1643 (E 77/3), 17, 23–4; *The Scottish Dove*, 17–24 Nov. 1643 (E 76/26), 45–6; *The True Informer*, 11–18 Nov. 1643 (E 76/10), 66–7.

9 *The Strongest Place in England*

1 William Waller, 'Recollections', in *The Poetry of Anna Matilda* (1788), with manuscript notes (in the BL copy: C.45.a.6), transcribed from Waller's 'Experiences' in Wadham College, *passim*; Waller Report, 163; Mary Coate, *Cornwall in the Great Civil War and Interregnum, 1642–1660* (Oxford, 1933), 77.

2 *Mercurius Aulicus*, 12–19 Nov. 1643 (E 77/18), 657; Archer, 5.

3 *Souldiers Report*.

4 Waller Report, 155–6; *CJ*, III, 314.

5 *The True Informer*, 11–18 Nov. (E 76/10), 67; *The Parliament Scout*, 10–17 Nov. (E 76/8), 184; *The Scottish Dove*, 17–24 Nov. (E 76/26), 45–6; Lawson Chase Nagel, 'The Militia of London, 1641–1649' (PhD thesis, King's College, University of London, 1982), 102–3, 142–5.

6 HALS 79959X, 45v; *Mercurius Aulicus*, 12–19 Nov. (E 77/18), 660.

7 George Warren had joined the Honourable Artillery Company in 1627. Later members included William Shambrooke and John Levett of the Tower Hamlets Yellow Auxiliaries (*CRR*, II, 1001, 1319, 1492.) They were recruited close to Rawdon's stomping ground (as well as the engraver William Faithorne's place of birth). The Westminster men were drawn from parts of St Sepulchre's, the admittedly teeming parish that encompassed Holborn Conduit and Snow Hill, so there may have been other now-lost links with neighbours in Basing's 'London Regiment'. The Westminster Trained Band was sometimes referred to as the 'Westminster Red Regiment', but it was a completely different unit from Rawdon's old London regiment.

8 *The Souldiers Report*; *The Compleate Intelligencer*, 21 Nov. 1643 (E 76/19), 50.

9 Bod MS Carte 7, f. 638v; *Mercurius Aulicus*, 12–19 Nov. (E 77/18), 659, 660, 662.

10 *Letter-Book of the Earl of Clanricarde 1643–47*, ed. J. Lowe (Dublin, 1983), 487.

11 Siege Diary, 2; HALS 79959X, 45v–46r; *Journal of Sir Samuel Luke*, ed. I. G. Philip, Oxfordshire RS (1950–3), 194.

12 Ralph Hopton, *Bellum Civile: Hopton's Narrative of his Campaign in the West (1642–1644) and other papers*, ed. C. E. H. Chadwyck Healey, Somerset RS 18 (1902), 65–6.

13 *Certaine Informations*, 13–20 Nov. 1643 (E 76/15), 344 (mispaginated); *The Parliament Scout*, 10–17 Nov. 1643 (E 76/8), 185; *The True Informer*, 11–18 Nov. 1643 (E 76/10), 67.

14 Richard Ward, *The Anatomy of Warre* (1642) (E 128/15), 19.

15 Siege Diary, 2.

16 *A Perfect Diurnall*, 20–7 Nov. 1643 (E 252/9), 147; *The Compleate Intelligencer*, 28 Nov. 1643 (E 77/8), 59. For Hopton's 'handsome little army', see *Bellum Civile*, 66.

17 Waller, 'Recollections', 111–12; Bod MS Rawlinson D 395, 193r.

18 John Adair, *Cheriton 1644: The Campaign and the Battle* (Kineton, 1973), 64–70.

19 John Parton, *Some Account of the Hospital and Parish of St Giles in the Fields, Middlesex* (1822), 359; *Mercurius Civicus*, 14–21 Dec. 1643 (E 79/3), 339 and 28 Dec.–4 Jan. 1643/4 (E 80/10), 354–5; *Mercurius Aulicus*, 31 Dec.–6 Jan. 1643/4 (E 29/9), 759.

20 *Mercurius Aulicus*, 24–30 Dec. 1643 (E 81/19), 744–5 (mispaginated). The letter is printed in full at the beginning of ch. 7 above. For Berkenhead and the argument that he was more reliable than people thought, at least in 1643, see P. W. Thomas, *Sir John Berkenhead 1617–1679: A Royalist Career in Politics and Polemics* (Oxford, 1969). On newsbooks, print culture and public engagement, see Joad Raymond, *The Invention of the*

Newspaper: English Newsbooks 1641–1649 (Oxford, 1996), and Jason Peacey, *Print and Public Politics in the English Revolution* (Cambridge, 2013).

21 LMA P69/DUN2/A/004/MS010345 (William Rodway, bur. 19 Oct. 1646); LMA P69/DUN2/A/007/MS010357 (Hester Rodway, bur. 17 June 1644 'rising lights'). The Rodways had more children, including another daughter (also 'Hester') who was born five months after the first Hester's death (bapt. 20 Nov. 1644: LMA P69/DUN2/A/003/MS010344). See too ch. 7, n3 above.

22 Christopher Durston, 'Lords of Misrule: The Puritan War on Christmas, 1642–1660', *History Today* 35/12 (1985).

23 Edward Vallance, 'Preaching to the Converted: Religious Justifications for the English Civil War', *Huntington Library Quarterly* 65, no. 3/4 (2002), 406–7.

24 *Mercurius Cambro-Britannus*, 20–7 Nov. 1643 (E 77/7), 6.

25 Mark Stoyle, *Soldiers and Strangers: An Ethnic History of the English Civil War* (2005), 56–61, 209–10.

26 *The Sharpnesse of the Sword: or, Abners plea for accommodation. A sermon lately preached by John Pigot, curate of St Sepulchres, London* (1643) (E 83/48 and 49), To the Reader.

27 Vallance, 'Preaching to the Converted', 405–7.

28 TNA WO 55/459, pt 4, 775–6; *The Royalist Ordnance Papers, 1642–1646*, ed. Ian Roy, 2 parts (Oxfordshire RS, 1964, 1975), II, 320–1, 498n; *The Papers of Captain Henry Stevens Waggon-Master-General to King Charles I*, ed. Margaret Toynbee, Oxfordshire RS, 42 (1961), 21, 24, 39n; *Journal of Sir Samuel Luke*, 231.

29 HALS 79959X, 46r; William A. Shaw, *The Knights of England*, 2 vols. (1906), II, 217.

30 York Minster Library MS Add 122, 2r.

31 The painting is in a private collection. A backing has been added to the canvas, which unfortunately covers any potential markings that might have provided more information. I am very grateful to the owner's son for this information.

32 *The Life of Marmaduke Rawdon of York*, ed. R. Davies, Camden Society, OS 85 (1863), 32–3; HALS 79959X, 75v–6r and see especially the unnumbered section on 'Marmaduke Rawdon the 3rd'.

33 *Mercurius Cambro-Britannus*, 20–7 Nov. 1643 (E 77/7), 4; *A Looking-Glasse for the Popish Garrisons* (1645) (E 307/2), 2.

34 *The Clarke Papers*, ed. C. H. Firth, 4 vols. (1891–1901), I, 396n.

35 *Journal of Sir Samuel Luke*, 208–10; Godwin, 129, 130, 137; PA HL/PO/JO/10/1/161; William Sanderson, *A Compleat History of the Life and Raigne of King Charles from his Cradle to his Grave* (1658), 835.

36 *The True Informer*, 11–18 Nov. 1643 (E 76/10), 67.

37 *Remarkable Passages*, 19–25 Nov. 1643 (E 77/3), 23.

PART THREE

10 *Paulet the Hangman*

1   Barbara Donagan, 'Family and Misfortune in the English Civil War: The Sad Case of Edward Pitt', *Huntington Library Quarterly*, 61/ 2 (1998), 238.

2   HALS 79959X, 51v, 61, 77r; National Library of Scotland Adv. MS 33.7.16, 2r; Constance Smith, 'A Seventeenth-Century Manuscript of "A Vision" attributed to Thomas More', *Moreana* 37 (1973); Vivian Salmon, 'Hawkins, John (*c.*1587–*c.*1641)', *ODNB*.

3   HALS 79959X, 46r.

4   TNA PROB 10/642/57. The witness was Randal Hankinson, ensign to the Marquess of Winchester. See *A List of Officers Claiming to the Sixty Thousand Pounds* (1663), 143. Seven years after her husband's death, with the annuity no longer coming in, Elizabeth was forced to petition the state for aid. She had 'grown very poor', she wrote, 'and having two children to maintain, must of necessity perish without speedy relief' (TNA SP 23/114/790).

5   *CSPD, 1644,* 2–3.

6   *The Manuscripts of the Earl of Westmorland, Captain Stewart, Lord Stafford, Lord Muncaster, and others,* HMC 10th Report (1906), App. IV, 511.

7   HRO 44M69/F4/15/3.

8   Godwin, 170–1.

9   John Vicars, *Gods Arke Overtopping the Worlds Waves* (1646), 214.

10 *A Collection of Original Letters and Papers, concerning the affairs of England, from the year 1641 to 1660. Found amongst the Duke of Ormonde's papers,* 2 vols. (1739), I, 21: Sir Robert Poyntz to the Marquess of Ormond, 1 June 1643.

11 Godwin, 160; John Adair, *Cheriton 1644: The Campaign and the Battle* (Kineton, 1973), 201–2, 205.

12 *Mercurius Civicus*, 13–20 Feb. 1644/5 (E 270/9), 823–5; *Perfect Passages*, 12–19 Feb. 1644/5 (E 270/5), 125.

13 *Mercurius Civicus*, 28 March–4 April 1644 (E 40/20), 458 (walking stick); John Barratt, *Sieges of the English Civil Wars* (Barnsley, 2009), 93–4 (spy dog), 143 (woman and 'ragged man'); for the strategic significance of intelligence operations during the war and the vitality of garrisons in particular for that work, see John Ellis, *To Walk in the Dark: Military Intelligence during the English Civil War, 1642–1646* (Stroud, 2011), *passim*, but esp. 27–8 and ch. 3.

14 TNA SP 29/113, 173. For Lady Mordaunt, see Nadine Akkerman, *Invisible Agents: Women and Espionage in Seventeenth-Century Britain* (Oxford, 2018), ch. 5 (quotation at p. 174).

15   Stewart Beale, 'Katherine de Luke: Widow, Petitioner, and Royalist Agent' (2019), in Civil War Petitions Online.

16   *Journal of Sir Samuel Luke*, ed. I. G. Philip, Oxfordshire RS (1950–3), vi–vii, 193, 242, 256. For the three cartloads into Basing House in February, see Bod MS Rawlinson D 395, f. 21r; *The Papers of Captain Henry Stevens Waggon-Master-General to King Charles I*, ed. Margaret Toynbee, Oxfordshire RS, 42 (1961), 24, 47n.

17   William Lilly, *History of His Life and Times* (1715, repr. 1823), 184–5; *Journal of Sir Samuel Luke*, vi.

18   *Journal of Sir Samuel Luke*, 256.

19   Thomas Carte, *An History of the Life of James Duke of Ormonde*, III (1735), 253.

20   John Rushworth, *Historical Collections*, III / 2 (1692), 384; *CSPV 1643–7*, 84, 86; *Mercurius Civicus*, 29 Feb–7 March 1644 (E 36/2), 423; *The Spie*, 5–13 March 1644 (E 37/10), 52, 54; Andrew Hopper, 'The Self-Fashioning of Gentry Turncoats during the English Civil Wars', *Journal of British Studies* 49/2 (2010), 246–8; Ian Roy, 'Grenville, Sir Richard (bapt. 1600, d. 1659)', *ODNB* ; Paul Hunneyball, 'Grenville, Sir Richard (1600–1659)', in *The History of Parliament: the House of Commons 1604–1629*, ed. Andrew Thrush and John P. Ferris (2010).

21   Arthur Trevor to Prince Rupert, 8 March 1644, printed in Mary Coate, *Cornwall in the Great Civil War and Interregnum* (Oxford, 1933), 132.

22   BL Add MS 29974.2, 352r–353r.

23   *CSPV 1643–7*, 84–6: Gerolamo Agostini to the Doge and Senate, 25 March and 1 April 1644.

24   Clarendon, III, 422.

25   *Journal of Sir Samuel Luke*, 267–9; *The Letter Books of Sir Samuel Luke*, ed. H. G. Tibbutt, Bedfordshire Historical RS 42 (1963), 633.

26   TNA SP 16/501, 162, 165, 169: Sir Edward Nicholas to Lord Forth, 2, 5 and 7 May, 1644.

27   Godwin, 207. Godwin's chronology is confused. The plot was hatched before the battle of Cheriton, not afterwards.

28   TNA ASSI 42/1, 41; J. A. Sharpe, *Crime in Early Modern England 1550–1750* (Harlow, 1984), 68.

29   Here, as elsewhere, Godwin does not cite his source, but it is *Perfect Passages*, 15–22 Oct. 1645 (E 266/6), 416.

II *Worthies*

1   Anon, *A Paire of Spectacles for the Citie* ([4 Dec. 1647]) (E 419/9), 9. In fairness to Captain William Manby, this is a very hostile source written over three years after the event.

2   Clarendon, III, 335. Unless otherwise stated, my source for the account below is John Adair's *Cheriton 1644: The Campaign and the Battle* (Kineton, 1973), which provides extensive quotation from primary material, though a now-disputed siting of the battlefield.

3   Godwin, 170; *Mercurius Civicus*, 7–14 March (1643/4) (E 37/16), 432.

4   Stuart Reid, 'Ruthven, Patrick, earl of Forth and earl of Brentford (d. 1651)', *ODNB*.

5   HALS 79959X, 98v, 101r.

6   Laurence Lockhart, 'The Diplomatic Missions of Henry Bard, Viscount Bellomont, to Persia and India', *Iran* 4 (1966), 97.

7   Charles Carlton, *Going to the Wars: The Experience of the British Civil Wars, 1638–1651* (pb, 1994), 129.

8   Edward Walsingham, *Britannicae Virtutis Imago* (1644) (E 53/10), 18, 23–4, 28.

9   HALS 79959X, 102r.

10   Adair, *Cheriton*, 137; *Mercurius Civicus*, 28 March–4 April 1644 (E 40/20), 455.

11   HALS 79959X, 103v–107r.

12   Richard Coe, *An Exact Diarie. Or A breife relation of the progresse of Sir William Wallers army* (1644) (E 2/20), 1–2.

13   Clarendon, III, 338.

14   Godwin, 208.

15   A trawl of local parish registers, many of which were interrupted or destroyed by the war, has drawn a blank. The sole source for the wedding is the Rawdon family manuscript written by Sir Marmaduke's nephew in 1667 and probably informed by one of the officers he later interviewed: HALS 79959X, 44v–45r. For the nephew's subsequent contact with some of Rawdon's officers, see ff. 47v (George Mason), 50 (William Rosewell), 59r (Thomas Fletcher).

16   Samuel Pepys, *Diary*, 5 January 1661, 22 January 1661; John Aubrey, *Brief Lives*, ed. Kate Bennett (Oxford, 2016), I, 555–6; Anon, *The Life of that Reverend Divine, and Learned Historian, Dr. Thomas Fuller* (1661), 69, 75–6. See too the excellent recent biography, W. B. Patterson, *Thomas Fuller: Discovering England's Religious Past* (Oxford, 2018), *passim*, but especially ch. 3 for Fuller's movements at this time.

17   *Life of . . . Thomas Fuller*, 67; Dean B. Lyman, *The Great Tom Fuller* (1935), 137; Thomas Fuller, *The Holy State* (1642), 14.

18   Fuller, *The Holy State* (1642), 205–6; Thomas Fuller, *A Fast Sermon Preached on Innocents Day* (1642) (E 86/16), 1–2 (for Christmas), 10.

19   Patterson, *Thomas Fuller*, 103–7.

20   Thomas Fuller, *The Church-History of Britain* (1655), XI, 217; Patterson, *Thomas Fuller*, 252–5.

21   Patterson, *Thomas Fuller*, 262.

22   Fuller, *Church-History*, IV, 168.

23   Siege Diary, 2.

24   *The Life of . . . Thomas Fuller*, 26–30.

25   Thomas Fuller, *The History of the Worthies of England* (1662), Hant-shire, 15.

26   Ibid., Bark-shire, 85; York-shire, 189.

27   Ibid., Hant-shire, 1–3.

28   *The Life of . . . Thomas Fuller*, 31.

29   Fuller, *Worthies*, 40. See too Patterson, *Thomas Fuller*, ch. 9, and Hugh Trevor-Roper, 'Fuller's "Worthies" and the Age of English Charity', in his *Historical Essays* (1957), ch. 19.

30   Fuller, *Worthies*, Yorkshire, 204. Also: Lincolne-shire, 169; Cornwall, 206; Hant-shire, 12–13; Exeter, 276.

31   For Jones's prickly relationship with Jonson, see Martin Butler, 'The Court Masque', in *The Cambridge Edition of the Works of Ben Jonson*, ed. David Bevington, Martin Butler and Ian Donaldson (Cambridge, 2012), I, cxl–cxli, and Jonson's 'An Expostulation with Inigo Jones' and 'To Inigo, Marquis Would-Be: A Corollary', ed. Colin Burrow in volume VI of *The Works*, 375–81.

32   J. Newman, 'Inigo Jones and the Politics of Architecture', in *Culture and Politics in Early Stuart England*, ed. Kevin Sharpe and Peter Lake (Basingstoke, 1994), 229–55.

33   Albert J. Loomie, 'The Destruction of Rubens's "Crucifixion" in the Queen's Chapel, Somerset House', *The Burlington Magazine* 140/1147 (1997) 680–2.

34   *Mercurius Britanicus*, 13–20 Oct. 1645 (E 305/12), 903; *The Moderate Intelligencer*, 9–16 Oct. 1645 (E 305/3), 164.

35   TNA SP 23/177, 777.

36   *The City-Scout*, 14–21 Oct 1645 (E 305/16), 2; William Sanderson, *A Compleat History of the Life and Raigne of King Charles* (1658), 835; David Flintham, *Civil War London: A Military History of London under Charles I and Oliver Cromwell* (Solihull, 2017), 87.

37   David Flintham, '"His Majestie's Scenographer": the Military Art of Wenceslaus Hollar', in *Home and Away: The British Experience of War 1618–1721*, ed. Serena Jones (Warwick, 2018), 150–88.

38   TNA SP 23/177, 781; Michael Leapman, *Inigo: The Troubled Life of Inigo Jones, Architect of the English Renaissance* (2003), 6.

39   Catherine Fletcher, *The Beauty and the Terror: An Alternative History of the Italian Renaissance* (2020), 40, 259–60.

40   Balthazar Gerbier, *The First Publique Lecture, read at Sr. Balthazar Gerbier his Accademy, concerning Military Architecture, or Fortifications* (1649), 1.

41   Ibid., 9; Siege Diary, 2. For an excellent recent account of Basing House's fortifications, see Alan Turton, 'A House called Loyalty – The Archaeology of a Civil War Siege', in Jones, *Home and Away*, 117–49.

42   Most of Jones's drawings are divided between the collections of the Duke of Devonshire at Chatsworth and Worcester College, Oxford. See Jeremy Wood, 'Inigo Jones, Italian Art and the Practice of Drawing', *The Art Bulletin* 74/2 (1992), 247–70. For 'the great ingeneere', see *The Correspondence of Elizabeth Stuart, Queen of Bohemia*, ed. Nadine Akkerman, II (Oxford, 2015), 664, and 665 n10 for the discovery of Jones as 'both poet and painter'.

43   Wood, 'Inigo Jones, Italian Art and the Practice of Drawing', 247; R. Malcolm Smuts, *Court Culture and the Origins of a Royalist Tradition in Early Stuart England* (1987), 122.

44   [B. Buckeridge], 'An Essay Towards an English School of Painters', in R. de Piles, *The Art of Painting*, 2nd edn (1744), 407.

45   *Mercurius Veridicus*, 11–18 Oct. 1645 (E 305/10), 180.

46   The legend that Hollar was in the garrison at Basing House derives from a short biography of Faithorne written by John Bagford at the turn of the seventeenth century. Bagford, who knew Faithorne, should not be dismissed out of hand, but his text was ill-served by George Vertue, who claimed that Hollar was also at the storming of Basing House when he was, by then, certainly in Antwerp. Unless a contemporary source validates Bagford's claim, it seems sensible to keep Hollar out of the story of Basing House. See also Epilogue n53 below. I am grateful to Gillian Tindall and David Flintham for discussions on this subject.

47   C. R. Peers, 'On the Excavation of the Site of Basing House', *Archaeologia* 61/2 (1909), 557; David Allen and Sue Anderson, *Basing House Hampshire: Excavations 1978–1991*, Hampshire Field Club & Archaeological Society (1999), 26.

48   Stephen Moorhouse, 'Finds from Basing House (*c.*1540–1645)', pts I and II, *Post-Medieval Archaeology* 4 and 5 (1970–1), I, 83 (no. 295). The translation is a lovely, loose one posted online in 2009 (at https://allpoetry.com/Battle-of-Red-Cliff) and reproduced in *The Impact and Transformation of Education Policy in China*, ed., Tiedan Huang and Alexander W. Wiseman (Bingley, 2011), 91–2. The name of the translator is not given and I have

been unable to trace them. Su Shi is also known as Su Dongpo and Su Tung-p'o.

49   Fuller, *Worthies*, Wiltshire, 144; Allen and Anderson, *Basing House Hampshire: Excavations*, 80 (no. 53). Fuller includes a story about a trade dispute in which an interloper started putting the distinctive gauntlet mark on his own, inferior pipes. The original gauntlet pipe-maker sued for brand infringement, but the interloper got away with it by arguing that 'the thumb of his gauntlet stands one way, mine another, and the same hand given *dexter* or *sinister* in heraldry is a sufficient difference'.

50   Moorhouse, 'Finds from Basing House'; Allen and Anderson, *Basing House Hampshire: Excavations*, *passim*, but esp. 99–102 for analysis on the skull. Some of the best finds are on display in the Basing House Museum in the grounds.

51   Fuller, *The Holy State*, 201.

52   Gillian Tindall, *The Man Who Drew London: Wenceslaus Hollar in Reality and Imagination* (2002), 76.

53   Stanford E. Lehmberg, *Cathedrals under Siege: Cathedrals in English Society, 1600–1700* (Exeter, 1996), 17–19, 28.

54   HRO DC/F6/1/1: Winchester Cathedral, Book of John Chase (1623–50), 84r.

55   Ibid., 104r. For the statues of James and Charles, see *The Journal of William Schellinks' Travels in England 1661–1663*, trans. and ed. Maurice Exwood and H. L. Lehmann, Camden 5th ser., vol. 1 (1993), 135–6, 140; Emily Sharpe, 'Tate finds 370-year-old bullet hole in Charles I statue', *The Art Newspaper*, 1 Nov. 2013.

56   Fuller, *Worthies*, Hant-shire, 3.

12 *Dog, Cat or Rat*

1   *A Great Victory obtained by Colonel Norton and his Horse, and Colonell Jones and his Foote, against Colonel Rayden, from Basing House, neere Walneborough Mill, within halfe a mile of Odium* ([5 June], 1644) (E 50/13). See too *The Weekly Account*, 30 May–5 June 1644 (E 50/15). For Odiham: John Taylor, *The Honorable, and Memorable Foundations, Erections, Raisings, and Ruines, of divers cities, townes, castles, and other pieces of antiquitie, within ten shires and counties of this kingdome* (1636), unnumbered.

2   *Mercurius Aulicus*, 30 June–6 July 1644 (E 2/30), 1065. Also 7–13 July 1644 (E 3/19), 1076. For Rosewell's popularity, see HALS 79959X, 51r.

3   Richard Ward, *The Anatomy of Warre* (1642) (E 128/15), 8.

4   *A Great Victory* (E 50/13). For Bolton, see Michael Braddick, *God's Fury,*

England's Fire: A New History of the English Civil Wars (2008), 318, and John Barratt, *Sieges of the English Civil Wars* (Barnsley, 2009), 146.

5   HALS 79959X, 44. The anecdote is undated, 'the colonel, being upon a time encountering the enemy', so this is a speculative, though not unreasonable, placement. For Henn, see *The Court of Chivalry 1634–1640*, ed. Richard Cust and Andrew Hopper, *British History Online*, '293 Henn v Chamberlaine'. Also: PA HL/PO/JO/10/1/129, 166r (for Henn visiting Lord Mayor Gurney in the Tower, 19 July 1642).

6   TNA PROB 11/312/404; TNA E 179/252/10, 34r.

7   J. T. Peacey, 'Norton, Richard (1615–1691)', *ODNB* ; Derek Hall and Norman Barber, 'Norton's Horse: The History of a Hampshire Regiment during the First Civil War 1642–1646', *Proc. Hampshire Field Club Archaeological Society* 41 (1985), esp. 225–30, 233, 239; John Adair, *Cheriton 1644* (Kineton, 1973), 160, 179; Patrick Little, 'The Laughing Roundhead?', *History Today* 66/8 (2016), 50. For 'the zealous Lady Norton', see *The Vindication of Richard Atkyns* (1669), 63; Godwin, 156–7.

8   *The Weekly Account*, 4–11 July 1644 (E 54/24).

9   Ibid., 18–25 June 1644 (E 52/15).

10 Ibid., 12–19 June 1644 (E 51/14).

11 *Mercurius Aulicus*, 7–13 July 1644 (E 3/19), 1076; 8–14 Sept. 1644 (E 12/18), 1166; *Mercurius Britanicus*, 20–27 Jan. 1645 (E26/6), 529–30.

12 Siege Diary, 4. Unless otherwise stated, this is the source for the rest of chapter. It was printed by Leonard Lichfield, printer to the university, at the beginning of 1645.

13 Thomas Carte (ed.), *A Collection of Original Letters and Papers, concerning the affairs of England, from the year 1641 to 1660. Found amongst the Duke of Ormonde's papers*, 2 vols. (1739), I, 56.

14 *The Weekly Account*, 4–11 July 1644 (E 54/24); Godwin, 227.

15 *Mercurius Aulicus*, 1–7 Sept. 1644 (E 10/20), 1148; 8–14 Sept. 1644 (E 12/18), 1165–6.

16 Ibid., 11–17 August 1644 (E 8/20), 1124; 8–14 Sept. 1644 (E 12/18), 1165–6.

17 *The Weekly Account*, 31 July–7 August 1644 (E 4/23), 238, 240; 14–21 August 1644 (E 6/32), 253; *The Parliament Scout*, 1–8 August 1644 (E 4/29), 476.

18 BL Add MS 46188, 138r.

19 *The Weekly Account*, 21–27 August 1644 (E 7/13), 261.

20 TNA WO 47/1, 92.

21 *The Court Mercurie*, 10–20 July 1644 (E 2/25); Godwin, 229–30; Siege Diary, *passim*.

22 HALS 79959X, 46r.

23 Canterbury Cathedral Archives, DCc–CantLet/116, 134, 143; CCA DCc–PET/208, 209; William Prynne, *Canterburies Doome* (1646), 79.

24 There are three exceptions (with apologies for any inadvertent omissions): Charles Carlton (*Going to the Wars*, 241–2), Fiona McCall, *Baal's Priests: The Loyalist Clergy and the English Revolution* (Farnham, 2013), 119–20, 184–5, and especially George Turner, 'Humphrey Peake and Siege Warfare', *Midlands Historical Review* 2 (2018), 1–23, which is the only detailed study of Peake's work.

25 *Englands Loyalty . . . being a true and reall relation of many most remarkable passages which have been lately divulged by one D. Peake Vicar of Tenterden in Kent* (1641) (E 177/19).

26 *CJ*, II, 841, 852; John Walker, *An Attempt Towards Recovering an Account of the Numbers and Sufferings of the Clergy of the Church of England* (1714), II, 8; A. G. Matthews, *Walker Revised, being a revision of John Walker's Sufferings of the Clergy during the Grand Rebellion, 1642–60* (Oxford, 1948), 223.

27 TNA PROB 11/324/435 (Will of Sir Robert Peake, Goldsmith, 26 July 1667); PROB 11/328/120 (Will of Gregory Peake, Gentleman of Middle Temple, 12 Oct 1668). For Sir Robert Peake's sword, escutcheon and watch, see the bottom of the second folio of TNA C 10/110/93. Humfrey Peake's first lectureship was at St Bartholomew's by the Exchange in London (*England's Loyalty*, 3). He also lectured at St Martin-in-the-Fields (*The Further Correspondence of William Laud*, ed. Kenneth Fincham (2018), 71) and may have been 'Mr Pecke the lecturer' of St Sepulchre mentioned in the will of Thomas Johnson's next-door neighbour on Snow Hill (TNA PROB 10/673). Gregory Peake was christened at St Botolph, Aldgate, on 6 December 1618 (LMA P69/BOT2/A/019/MS09234/008 and P69/BOT2/A/001/MS09220). He was a student of the Middle Temple when the war broke out and took up arms for the king. He compounded for his delinquency (citing Kent woodland very close to his father's living in Tenterden) on 1 November 1645. He took the National Covenant on 31 October, which was just two weeks after the storming of Basing House (TNA SP 23/175, 209, 212). He was pardoned by the House of Lords in May 1647 (*HJ*, IX, 213–14). Robert Peake describes his 'friend' and executor Gregory Peake as a grocer and clerk of Innholders Hall, which does not sound like the gentleman of the Middle Temple, but Gregory's will and several leases and lawsuits confirm that it is definitely the same man. See, for e.g. Bedfordshire Archives FN611, FN 618; TNA C 6/190/37; Gwynedd Archives XD2/4701–2.

28 Humfrey Peake, *Meditations upon a Seige* (1646), 106, 29, 28, 108, 37, 31.

29 Ibid., 28, 10–12.

30 Ibid., 14.

31 Ibid., 19–20.

32 Ibid., 103–4.

33   Ibid., 18.
34   Ibid., 28, 107, 78–81.

13 A Special Operation

1   Siege Diary, 13; *The Weekly Account*, 4–11 Sept. 1644 (E 8/29), 425–6; *Mercurius Aulicus*, 1–7 Sept. 1644 (E 10/20), 1147. For Lady Waller, see John Adair, *Roundhead General: A Military Biography of Sir William Waller* (1969), 38, 186–8; Jerome de Groot, 'Mothers, Lovers and Others: Royalist Women', in James Daybell (ed.), *Women and Politics in Early Modern England, 1450–1700* (Aldershot, 2004), esp. 195–6.
2   Clarendon, III, 410. For 'Essex-catching', see Thomas Carte (ed.), *A Collection of Original Letters and Papers, concerning the affairs of England, from the year 1641 to 1660. Found amongst the Duke of Ormonde's papers*, 2 vols. (1739), I, 59: Daniel Oneile to Arthur Trevor, 26 July 1644.
3   Clarendon, III, 222.
4   TNA PROB 10/642/142: Nuncupative will of Hannah Smith alias Bowell, made 'between Midsummer and St Jamestide', 1644.
5   The following account draws on Clarendon, III, 408–15; Siege Diary, 14–15; *Mercurius Aulicus*, 8–14 Sept. 1644 (E 12/18), 1160–4; Edward Walsingham, *Alter Britanniæ Heros, or The Life of the most honourable knight, Sir Henry Gage* (Oxford, 1645) (E 303/6), 11–17; and Henry Gage's 'True Relation' to Lord Digby, Oxford, 16 Sept. 1644, printed in Edward Walker, *Historical Discourses upon Several Occasions* (1705) 90–5.
6   Siege Diary, 14; *Mercurius Aulicus*, 8–14 Sept. 1644 (E 12/18), 1161. For the site of the fight, see Alan Turton, 'A House called Loyalty – The Archaeology of a Civil War Siege', in *Home and Away: The British Experience of War 1618–1721*, ed. Serena Jones (Warwick, 2018), 138.
7   Walsingham, *Alter Britanniæ Heros*, 17. See too Barbara Donagan, *War in England, 1642–1649* (Oxford, 2008), 254–6.

14 The Hand of God

1   Eric Gruber von Arni, *Justice to the Maimed Soldier: Nursing, Medical Care and Welfare for Sick and Wounded Soldiers and their Families during the English Civil Wars and Interregnum, 1642–1660* (Aldershot, 2001), citing TNA E 179/187/468A, 804.
2   Richard Wiseman, *A Treatise of Wounds* (1672), 6, 11.
3   Ibid., 134–5.

4   Ibid., To the Reader; *Herball*, 474. See too To the Reader and An Adver-
     tisement to the Readers (post-index). For Johnson's lectures, discovered
     by Dmitri Levitin, see his article ' "Made Up from Many Experimentall
     Notions": The Society of Apothecaries, Medical Humanism, and the
     Rhetoric of Experience in 1630s London', *Journal of the History of Medi-
     cine and Allied Sciences* 70/4 (2015), 549–87. Levitin also warns against
     falling for the rhetoric of mechanic vs academic, so baldly stated by the
     likes of Wiseman.

5   *The Workes of that famous Chirurgion Ambrose Parey*, translated out of
     Latin and compared with the French by Th. Johnson (1634), 1143. For
     Waller's court-martial papers, see John Adair, *Cheriton* (Kineton, 1973),
     203–4.

6   Keith Thomas, *Religion and the Decline of Magic* (Folio Soc. edn, 2012), 9;
     Stephen M. Rutherford, 'A New Kind of Surgery for a New Kind of War:
     gunshot wounds and their treatment in the British Civil Wars', in *Battle-
     scarred: Mortality, medical care and military welfare in the British Civil Wars*,
     ed. David J. Appleby and Andrew Hopper (Manchester, 2018), 57–77; Eric
     Gruber von Arni and Andrew Hopper, 'Welfare for the Wounded', *His-
     tory Today* 66/7 (July 2016), 48–9; Civil War Petitions Website: West
     Yorkshire History Centre QS 1/8/3/6/3, The petition of Edward Bag-
     shaw of Conisbrough, West Riding, 3 August 1668.

7   Richard Jones, 'Gerard's *Herball* and the treatment of war-wounds and
     contagion during the English Civil War', in *Battle-scarred*, 113–33. With
     thanks to Dr Jones for allowing me to reproduce an image from p. 276 of
     the book.

8   TNA PROB 11/309/596; Society of Apothecaries, Court Minute Book
     1617–51, 475v. John Thomas was in trouble with the College of Physicians
     before the war for attending a private anatomy dissection and for admin-
     istering physic. He reportedly 'slighted the council's warrant, saying it
     was not worth three skips of a louse' (Margaret Pelling and Frances
     White, 'Thomas, John', in *Physicians and Irregular Medical Practitioners in
     London 1550–1640 Database* (2004), *British History Online*). For the connec-
     tion between Thomas and Faithorne (and Peake again), see The
     Goldsmiths' Company Archives, Court Book Z, 105v–106r. 'Mr Thomas
     the apothecary' also appears in Winchester's business agent's account
     book (HRO 11M49/230, 41). For Stephen Fawcett, see TNA SP 23/196,
     71, 77, 79; Richard Smyth, *A Catalogue of all Such Persons Deceased whom I
     knew in their Life Time*, ed. Henry Ellis (1849), 57–8.

9   *Mercurius Aulicus*, 8–14 Sept. 1644 (E 12/18), 1162; Siege Diary, 14.

10   'I am of opinion,' Johnson said in a lecture in 1634, 'that many medicines,
     if used in substance, only beaten to powder and so taken in a convenient
     vehicle, and due proportion, they would work more, and more certain

effects, than the most curious preparations of them, for I think there is none but will confess that God knew better when he created things for medicine what diseases and calamities man should be afflicted withal than any man could ever attain unto; again it is rare to find such cures done speedily in desperate cases by compound medicines as have been wrought by simples' (Folger Shakespeare Library, MS E.a.5, f. 98r). For Johnson's lectures, recently discovered by Dmitri Levitin, see note 4 above.

11 Folger MS E.a.5, 42r, 138v, 32r, 148r, 39r, 144v, 249r, 2v.

12 HRO 76M99/1; *Herball* (1633), 65; *Mercurii Botanici* (1641), 2; D. E. Allen, 'Goodyer, John (c.1592–1664)', *ODNB*.

13 Siege Diary, 15–16; *Mercurius Aulicus*, 15–21 Sept. 1644 (E 13/9), 1172–3.

14 This is, of course, an imagined sequence, but the quotations, in order, come from Johnson, *Mercurii Botanici* (1641), 35; *Herball*, 6; Siege Diary, 14.

15 Siege Diary, 16; Thomas Fuller, *The History of the Worthies of England* (1662), Yorkshire, 204.

16 Richard Symonds, *Diary of the Marches of the Royal Army* (1859), 67; *A True Relation of the Sad Passages, between the two armies in the West* (1644) (E 10/27), 10; Mark Stoyle, 'The Road to Farndon Field: Explaining the Massacre of the Royalist Women at Naseby', *English Historical Review* 123/503 (2008), 917–18.

17 *CSPD, 1644–45*, 60; Siege Diary, 17–18; HMC *Portland MSS*, I (1891), 188–9; *The Letter Books of Sir Samuel Luke*, ed. H. G. Tibbutt, Bedfordshire Historical RS 42 (1963), 45, 362–3.

18 Fuller, *Worthies*, Bark-shire, 112; HALS 79959X, 102v.

19 *CSPD, 1644–5*, 151; Ian J. Gentles, 'Montagu, Edward, second earl of Manchester (1602–1671)', *ODNB*.

20 *The Letter Books of Sir Samuel Luke*, 676; *The Parliament Scout*, 14–21 Nov. 1644 (E 18/6), 593.

21 Siege Diary, 19–20.

22 BL Add MS 18981, f. 323 (Sir Henry Gage to Prince Rupert, 22 Nov. 1644; this letter clears up previous confusion over the dates); Siege Diary, 20–1; Symonds, *Diary*, 154; *The Letter Books of Sir Samuel Luke*, 399–400; Godwin, 279–81; Gentles, 'Montagu, Edward'; William Lilly, *The Starry Messenger; Or, An Interpretation of that strange Apparition of three Suns seene in London, 19. Novemb. 1644. being the Birth Day of King Charles* (1645).

23 *Oliver Cromwell's Letters and Speeches: with elucidations. By Thomas Carlyle*, 3 vols. (1846), I, 207 (5 July 1644).

24 Ian Gentles, 'The Civil Wars in England', in *The Civil Wars: A Military History of England, Scotland, and Ireland 1638–1660*, ed. John Kenyon and Jane Ohlmeyer (Oxford, 1998), 140.

PART FOUR

1   *Oliver Cromwell's Letters and Speeches: with elucidations. By Thomas Carlyle*, 3 vols. (1846), II, 283 (25 Dec. 1650).

15 *Figures Set upon Horory Questions*

1   William Lilly, *History of His Life and Times* (1715, repr. 1823), esp. 25–32, 49–53, 59–61, 76; William Lilly, *Anglicus, Peace, or no Peace* (1645), A3v.

2   William Lilly, *A Prophecy of the White King: And Dreadfull Dead-man Explaned* (1644); William Lilly, *The Starry Messenger* (1645), 20–1.

3   Diane Purkiss, *The English Civil War: A People's History* (2006), 379–88.

4   Bod Ashmole MS 184, 108r.

5   Keith Thomas, *Religion and the Decline of Magic* (Folio Soc., 2012), 296–310; Nadine Akkerman, *Invisible Agents: Women and Espionage in Seventeenth-Century Britain* (Oxford, 2018), 54–5.

6   Bod Ashmole MS 184, 86v, 45v, 3r, 1v.

7   Ibid., 3v, 50v, 95v, 122r, 106v.

8   Ibid., 147r, 151r, 151v, 153v, 156r.

16 *Exodus*

1   Siege Diary, 4.

2   BL Add MS 18981, 323r.

3   *The Royalist Ordnance Papers, 1642–1646*, ed. Ian Roy, 2 parts (Oxfordshire RS, 1964, 1975), I, 217–18; II, 476 n129.

4   HALS 79959X, 72r. See too *The Life of Marmaduke Rawdon of York*, ed. Robert Davies, Camden Society, OS 85 (1863), 6.

5   *Mercurius Britanicus*, 23–30 Dec. 1644 (E 22/19), 498. See too ibid., 20–7 Jan. 1645 (E26/6), 529; 17–24 Feb. 1645 (E 270/15), 568; 10–17 Feb. 1645 (E269/25), 554; *The Weekly Account*, 21–7 August 1644 (E 7/13), 261.

6   *The Parliament Scout*, 1–8 August 1644 (E 4/29), 476.

7   *The Weekly Account*, 4–11 Sept. 1644 (E 8/29), 427; HALS, 79959X, 49r.

8   The Cuffauds descended from Cardinal Pole and had Plantagenet blood. An illuminated pedigree is preserved at The Vyne in Hampshire (National Trust). It was reportedly discovered blocking up a broken window in a cottage in Basingstoke in the nineteenth century (*The History of Holy Ghost Chapel*, Basingstoke, 1819, 74n).

9   *The History of Holy Ghost Chapel*, 28, 74–5, 81–4; G. W. Haws, *The Haws Family and their Seafaring Kin* (Dunfermline, 1932), 145–6; TNA SP 23/142, 450–70.
10 Bod MS Don. G.9, 25v–26r.
11 *CRR*, I, 35, 52, n.198.
12 *Mercurius Britanicus*, 23–30 Dec. 1644 (E 22/19), 498.
13 HRO 40M93/1.
14 HALS 79959X, 46v–47r.
15 Godwin, 170.
16 Surrey History Centre, LM/COR/5/52; TNA SP 19/118, 61.
17 Godwin, 295.
18 *Mercurius Veridicus*, 10–16 May 1645 (E 284/15), 34.
19 Richard Symonds, *Diary of the Marches of the Royal Army* (1859), 162; *The Letter Books of Sir Samuel Luke*, ed. H. G. Tibbutt, Bedfordshire Historical RS 42 (1963), 255. For the charger, see HALS 79959X, 57v.
20 HALS 79959X, 47v, 49r.
21 Ibid., 107v–110r.

17 *The Face of God*

1   Hugh Peter, *Gods Doings, and Mans Duty* (1646) (E 330/11), A4v.
2   John Adair, *Roundhead General: A Military Biography of Sir William Waller* (1969), 168, 176.
3   BL Add MS 46188, 158r; Ian Gentles, *The New Model Army in England, Ireland and Scotland, 1645–1653* (Oxford, 1992), 20.
4   Gentles, *New Model Army*, 28–40, 44 (Venn quotation at 33).
5   Peter, *Gods Doings, and Mans Duty*, 9; Gentles, *New Model Army*, 84.
6   *Mr. Peters Report from Bristol* ([12 Sept.] 1645) (E 301/4), 3; Gentles, *New Model Army*, 64 (and 461 n40), 91, 94–5.
7   Hugh Peter sermon, Christ Church, 7 April 1643: an uncatalogued acquisition now at the Harry Ransom Center, the University of Texas at Austin. For details of this manuscript sermon, see ch. 5 n9 above.
8   Raymond Phineas Stearns, *The Strenuous Puritan: Hugh Peter, 1598–1660* (Urbana, Illinois, 1954), 35; *Mercurius Aulicus*, 30 June–6 July 1644 (E 2/30), 1066; Alexandra Walsham, 'Phanaticus: Hugh Peter, Antipuritanism and the Afterlife of the English Revolution', *Parergon* 32/3 (2015), 71, 74.
9   Joshua Sprigg, *Anglia Rediviva* (1647), 70; John Rushworth, *A Full and Exact Relation of the Storming and Taking of Dartmouth* (1646) (E 317/14), 5.
10 Gentles, *New Model Army*, 45–7, 91–110, 131.
11 C. H. Firth and R. S. Rait (eds.), *Acts and Ordinances of the Interregnum* (1911), I, 554–5. For Hugh Peter at Stonehenge, see Stearns, *Strenuous Puritan*, 250–1.

12   Will Coster, 'Massacre and Codes of Conduct in the English Civil War',
      in *The Massacre in History*, ed. Mark Levene and Penny Roberts (Oxford,
      1999), 96; Stephen Bull, *'The Furie of the Ordnance': Artillery in the English
      Civil Wars* (Woodbridge, 2008), 110–13.

13   *Perfect Occurrences*, 13–20 June 1645 (E 262/10).

14   William Lilly, *Anglicus, Peace, or no Peace* (1645), 67.

15   Stearns, *Strenuous Puritan*, 249.

16   Glenn Foard, *Naseby: The Decisive Campaign* (Whitstable, 1995), *passim* but
      esp. 197–209 for the numbers; Gentles, *New Model Army*, 55–60. For a reassess-
      ment of Goring's actions, see Malcolm Wanklyn and Frank Jones, *A Military
      History of the English Civil War, 1642–1646* (Harlow, 2005), 240–4; for Skippon's
      shooting, which seems to have happened in the first charge, see Ismini Pells,
      '"Stout Skippon hath a wound": the medical treatment of Parliament's
      infantry commander following the battle of Naseby', in *Battle-scarred:
      Mortality, medical care and military welfare in the British Civil Wars*, ed. David
      J. Appleby and Andrew Hopper (Manchester, 2018), 79–80, 84.

17   Michael Braddick, *God's Fury, England's Fire: A New History of the English
      Civil Wars* (2008), 380–3.

18   Gentles, *New Model Army*, 93.

19   *Perfect Occurrences*, 13–20 June 1645 (E 262/10); *A Perfect Diurnall*, 9–16 June
      1645 (E 262/8), 774. See Mark Stoyle, 'The Road to Farndon Field:
      Explaining the Massacre of the Royalist Women at Naseby', *English His-
      torical Review* 123/503 (2008), 895–923. Unless otherwise stated, the
      quotations for the passage below are drawn from this persuasive article.
      See too Stoyle's further point that the presence of a few cross-dressed
      women amongst the king's camp followers might have added further
      fuel to the fire: Mark Stoyle, '"Give mee a Souldier's Coat": Female
      Cross-Dressing during the English Civil War', *History* 103/354 (2018), 22.

20   HMC *Portland MSS*, I (1891), 189.

21   *Parliaments Post*, 3–10 June 1645 (E 287/5), 6. Stoyle ('The Road to Farn-
      don Field', 920–1) suggests that these words, written just four days before
      the battle, may have been 'the final spur for the tragedy'.

22   *A More Exact and Perfect Relation of the Great Victory* (1645) (E 288/28), 4–5;
      The Exchange Intelligencer, 11–18 June 1645 (E 288/32); Stoyle, 'The Road to
      Farndon Field', 909. Mark Stoyle ('Echoes of a Massacre: The Petition of
      Bridget Rumney' (2019), in Civil War Petitions Online) has traced one
      victim: Elizabeth Burgess, a 'herb-woman' at Charles I's court. Her two
      grandsons were also killed that day, though whether on the battlefield or
      by her side on Farndon Field is not known. Her daughter Bridget peti-
      tioned the state for employment fifteen years later. A gentleman usher at
      the Oxford court vouched for her. He had a colleague called Robert Bur-
      gess, who was a 'Knight Harbinger' responsible for providing shelter for

the king on campaign (Jerome De Groot, 'Space, Patronage, Procedure: The Court at Oxford, 1642–46', *EHR* 117/474 (2002), 1226). It seems possible that Robert Burgess was Elizabeth's husband.

23 Gentles, *New Model Army*, 67–9.

24 Peter, *Gods Doings, and Mans Duty*, 21.

25 Thomas Carte, *An History of the Life of James Duke of Ormonde*, 3 vols. (1735–6), III, 422–3.

18 More Sulphur for Basing

1 *The Weekly Account*, 13–20 Aug. 1645 (E 297/7). For Basing as 'a limb of Babylon', see William Beech, *More Sulphure for Basing* (1645) (E 304/3), 28.

2 *The Kingdomes Weekly Intelligencer*, 12–19 August 1645 (E 297/2), 908; *Mercurius Aulicus*, 31 August–7 Sept. 1645 (E 302/14), 1727; TNA SP 16/510, 186r: Sir Robert Honeywood to Sir Henry Vane, 9 Sept. 1645; *The Weekly Account*, 14–21 May 1644 (E 284/25).

3 *Perfect Passages*, 20–6 August 1645 (E 262/51), 351; *A Diary, or, An Exact Journall*, 21–8 August 1645 (E 264/2), 6.

4 *A Diary, or, An Exact Journall*, 18–25 Sept. 1645 (E 303/7), 6; *The Kingdomes Weekly Intelligencer*, 16–23 Sept. 1645 (E 302/23), 945; *The Weekly Account*, 24 Sept.–3 Oct. 1645 (E 303/27); *Mercurius Veridicus*, 20–7 Sept. 1645 (E 303/16), 162.

5 *Mercurius Civicus*, 18–25 Sept. 1645 (E 303/8), 1078; Godwin, 324.

6 HALS 79959X, 49r. Langley does not appear in any of the lists after the storm, nor in the Compounding Papers. He returns, however, in 1660, petitioning for a position in Landgaurd Fort in Suffolk (TNA SP 29/25 98). He claims to have served at both Basing and Faringdon and to have been wounded and imprisoned 'many times'. He had a wife and five children to maintain.

7 *The City-Scout*, 30 Sept.–6 Oct. 1645 (E 304/5), 4; *The Moderate Intelligencer*, 8–15 May 1645 (E 284/6), 82.

8 BL Add MS 29443, 5v. This manuscript refers to the royalists being routed at 'Adderton More'. This cannot be Adwalton Moor as that battle was a resounding victory for the royalists. I think the memoirist, who was prone to errors of detail, must mean Marston Moor. For Colonel Rowland Eyre's regiments and movements at Marston Moor, see Martyn Bennett, 'The Royalist War Effort in the North Midlands 1642–1646' (PhD thesis, Loughborough, 1986), 129–30, 226–8, 328–9.

9 Richard Rowland, *Thomas Heywood's Theatre, 1599–1639* (Farnham, 2010), 250–1; John H. Astington, *Actors and Acting in Shakespeare's Time: The Art of Stage Playing* (Cambridge, 2010), 182–3, 192–3, 212, 217, 238. For Cicely

and William's marriage at St James, Clerkenwell, on 30 July 1622, see LMA P76/JS1/004. Cicely's sister Jane, née Sands, was married to Christopher Beeston. For more on the Sands/Beeston connection and the fascinating history of the Cockpit Theatre, see Christopher M. Matusiak, 'The Beestons and the Art of Theatrical Management in Seventeenth-Century London' (PhD thesis, University of Toronto, 2009), esp. ch. 1.

10   William Prynne, *Histrio-mastix* (1633), 390 and index: '*Women-Actors, notorious whores*'; C. H. Firth and R. S. Rait (eds.), *Acts and Ordinances of the Interregnum* (1911), I, 26–7; Hugh Peter, *The Full and Last Relation, of all things concerning Basing-House* (1645) (E 305/8), 2.

11   *The City-Scout*, 30 Sept.–6 Oct. 1645 (E 304/5), 4, 7; *Mercurius Civicus*, 25 Sept.–1 Oct. 1645 (E 303/30), 1086; *The Moderate Intelligencer*, 18–25 Sept. 1645 (E 303/3). See too Martin van Creveld, *Supplying War: Logistics from Wallenstein to Patton*, (Cambridge, 1980), 41. With thanks to David Flintham for the reference.

12   Godwin, 321.

13   Siege Diary, 7, 11; Timothy Raylor, 'Providence and Technology in the English Civil War: Edmond Felton and his Engine', *Renaissance Studies*, 7/4 (1993), 398–413.

14   M. J. Braddick and M. Greengrass (eds.), 'The Letters of Sir Cheney Culpeper (1641–1657)', *Camden Miscellany* XXXIII, CS 5th ser., 7 (1996), 181 and Introduction. See too Greengrass's entry on Culpeper in *ODNB*.

15   'The Letters of Sir Cheney Culpeper', 179; M. Greengrass, M. Leslie and M. Hannon, *The Hartlib Papers* (2013), published by the Digital Humanities Institute, University of Sheffield (online at http://www.dhi.ac.uk/hartlib), Ephemerides 1643, MS 30/4/92A.

16   'The Letters of Sir Cheney Culpeper', 179–80; *The Hartlib Papers*, 13/12A–14A.

17   Berthold von Deimling, quoted in Bretislav Friedrich, Dieter Hoffmann, Jürgen Renn, Florian Schmaltz and Martin Wolf (eds.), *One Hundred Years of Chemical Warfare: Research, Deployment, Consequences* (Cham, 2017), 26.

18   *The True Informer*, 20–7 Sept. 1645 (E 303/15), 182.

19   *Perfect Occurrences*, 19–26 Sept. 1645 (E 264/19); *The Scottish Dove*, 19–26 Sept. 1645 (E303/10), 800.

20   *Mercurius Veridicus*, 20–7 Sept. 1645 (E 303/16), 155, 161–2.

21   *Mercurius Britanicus*, 22–9 Sept. 1645 (E303/19), 883.

22   *The Parliaments Post*, 23–30 Sept. 1645 (E 303/23), 4.

23   *A Diary, or, An Exact Journal*, 26 Sept.–1 Oct. 1645 (E 303/29), 8.

24   *Mercurius Veridicus*, 27 Sept.–4 Oct. 1645 (E 304/1), 169.

25   William Davenent, *Salmacida Spolia*, in David Lindley (ed.), *Court*

Masques: Jacobean and Caroline Entertainments, 1605–1640 (Oxford, 1995), 200–13, 269; Michael Leapman, *Inigo: The Troubled Life of Inigo Jones, Architect of the English Renaissance* (2003), 326–31.

26   *Inigo Jones on Palladio, being the notes by Inigo Jones in the copy of I Quattro Libri Dell Architettura Di Andrea Palladio, 1601, in the Library of Worcester College, Oxford*, ed. Bruce Allsopp, 2 vols. (Newcastle upon Tyne, 1970), I, 69–74. Vol. II is a facsimile of Jones's copy.

27   *Mercurius Civicus*, 9–16 Oct. 1645 (E 305/5), 1202. The tomb of Mary Wolryche, née Griffith, St Andrew's Church, Quatt, Shropshire. The inscription claims that Mary was 41 in 1678, but the parish register of her father's church, St Mary Magdalen, Old Fish Street, records her christening there on 30 April 1635. See ch. 19 n31 and Epilogue n39 below.

28   David Lloyd, *Memoires of the Lives, Actions, Sufferings & Deaths . . . in our late Intestine Wars* (1668), 521.

29   Matthew Griffith, *Bethel: or, A Forme for Families* (1633), quotations at: title page, 322, 430.

30   Matthew Griffith, *A Patheticall Perswasion to Pray for Publick Peace* (2 Oct. 1642) (E 122/17), 28–30; *A Collection of Speciall Passages and Certaine Informations*, 17 Oct.–1 Nov. 1642 (E 242/2).

31   PA HL/PO/JO/10/1/146, f. 233: Isaac Pennington, Lord Mayor, to the Speaker of the House of Commons, March 1643; *CJ*, II, 987; *LJ*, V, 635; A. G. Matthews, *Walker Revised* (Oxford, 1948), 49; *A General Bill of Mortality, of the Clergie of London* (1646) (E 669.f.10/103), MS note at bottom: 'Decemb: 21, 1646. Supposed to be made by Dr Griffith of Maudlins Old Fishstreet.'

32   Fiona McCall, 'Children of Baal: Clergy Families and Their Memories of Sequestration during the English Civil War', *Huntington Library Quarterly* 76/4 (2013), 628, 630; Michelle Wolfe, ' "There Very Children Were Soe Full of Hatred": Royalist Clerical Families and the Politics of Everyday Conflict in Civil War and Interregnum England', in *Retribution, Repentance, and Reconciliation*, ed. Kate Cooper and Jeremy Gregory (Woodbridge, 2004), 199–200. See too I. M. Green, 'The Persecution of "Scandalous" and "Malignant" Parish Clergy during the English Civil War', *English Historical Review* 94/372 (1979), and for a discussion of the reliability of these accounts, see Fiona McCall, *Baal's Priests: The Loyalist Clergy and the English Revolution* (Farnham, 2013), 41–63.

33   McCall, 'Children of Baal', 627–8.

34   *Wednesday's Mercury*, 25–8 July 1643 (E 62/8), 21; *The Spie*, 30 Jan.–5 Feb. 1644 (E 31/12), 11.

35   Beech, *More Sulphure for Basing* (26 Sept. 1645) (E 304/3), esp. 4–5, 9–10, 14–15, 20–4, 29.

19 Babylon is Fallen

1   *The Parliaments Post*, 30 Sept.–7 Oct. 1645 (E 304/6), 4; *The Kingdomes Weekly Intelligencer*, 7–14 Oct. 1645 (E 304/24), 969.

2   *The Moderate Intelligencer*, 9–16 Oct. 1645 (E 305/3), 161–2.

3   *Mercurius Veridicus*, 4–11 Oct. 1645 (E 304/20), 175; *The Weekly Account*, 8–15 Oct. 1645 (E 304/27); *The Scottish Dove*, 10–17 Oct. 1645 (E 305/6), 820.

4   *The City-Scout*, 7–14 Oct. 1645 E 304/25, 7; *The Weekly Account*, 8–15 Oct. 1645 (E 304/27); Godwin, 347.

5   *The Letter Books of Sir Samuel Luke*, ed. H. G. Tibbutt, Bedfordshire Historical RS 42 (1963), 324; Joshua Sprigg, *Anglia Rediviva* (1647), endnote 130; Ian Gentles, *The New Model Army in England, Ireland and Scotland, 1645–1653* (Oxford, 1992), 96, 100–1.

6   David Farr, *Major-General Thomas Harrison: Millenarianism, Fifth Monarchism and the English Revolution 1616–1660* (Farnham, 2014), esp. 60–2, 73, 76, 81–5, 103–6. For Harrison being in command of Fleetwood's (as well as a list of the other regiments), see *Mercurius Civicus*, 9–16 Oct. 1645 (E 305/5), 1201.

7   Hugh Peter, *Mr. Peters Report from Bristol* ([12 Sept.]1645) (E 301/4), 3; Gentles, *New Model Army*, 93–4.

8   *A Looking-Glasse for the Popish Garrisons* ([24 Oct.] 1645) (E 307/2), 2; *The City-Scout*, 7–14 Oct. 1645 (E 304/25), 7; *The Scottish Dove*, 10–17 Oct. 1645 (E 305/6), 820–1; TNA SP 16/511, 22v: Sir Robert Honeywood to Sir Henry Vane, 13 Oct. 1645. For Sheffield's standard: Gentles, *New Model Army*, 96–7.

9   *Memoirs of Sir John Reresby*, ed. Andrew Browning, 2nd edn ed. Mary K. Geiter and W. A. Speck (1991), 23; John Adair, *Roundhead General: A Military Biography of Sir William Waller* (1969), 179–80; John Morrill, 'Cromwell, Oliver (1599–1658)', *ODNB*.

10   *The Scottish Dove*, 3–10 Oct. 1645 (E 304/18), 816.

11   *The Moderate Intelligencer*, 9–16 Oct. 1645 (E 305/3), 162.

12   *The Kingdomes Weekly Post*, 15 Oct. 1645 (E 304/28), 2; *The Scottish Dove*, 10–17 Oct. 1645 (E 305/6), 820.

13   *The City-Scout*, 7–14 Oct. 1645 (E 304/25), 7–8; *The Scottish Dove*, 10–17 Oct. 1645 (E 305/6), 820; *Perfect Occurrences*, 10–17 Oct. 1645 (E 266/3).

14   *The Memoirs of Edmund Ludlow*, ed. C. H. Firth, 2 vols. (Oxford, 1984), I, 124; G. E. Aylmer, 'Hammond, Robert (1620/21–1654)', *ODNB*; Miranda Malins, '"Dear Robin": The Correspondence of Oliver Cromwell and Robert Hammond', *Cromwelliana* 3/1 (2012), 62–3.

15   *The Weekly Account*, 8–15 Oct. 1645 (E 304/27); *The Kingdomes Weekly Intelligencer*, 7–14 Oct. 1645 (E 304/24), 973.

16 *The Moderate Intelligencer*, 9–16 Oct. 1645 (E 305/3), 162; *The Scottish Dove*, 10–17 Oct. 1645 (E 305/6), 820.

17 *The Kingdomes Weekly Intelligencer*, 7–14 Oct. 1645 (E 304/24), 973.

18 Humfrey Peake, *Meditations upon a Seige* (1646), 130–1.

19 Hugh Peter, *The Full and Last Relation, of all things concerning Basing-House* (1645) (E 305/8), 2.

20 Peter, *Full and Last Relation*, 5. Also Balthazar Gerbier, *The None-such Charles His Character* (1651), 178–9.

21 *A Diary, Or, An Exact Journall*, 9–16 Oct. 1645 (E 305/75), 7. *The Kingdomes Weekly Post*, 15 Oct. 1645 (E 304/28), 8, prints the same post. BL Harl MS 787, 73: Cromwell to Speaker Lenthall, 14 Oct. 1645. This letter was published in various newsbooks, including *A Perfect Diurnall* (E 266/5, 923) and *The True Informer* (E 305/9, 205–6). Cromwell's letter and Hugh Peter's *Full and Last Relation* provide the framework for the account below and are my sources, unless otherwise stated. Nearly all the London newsbooks reported on the storming of Basing House, the most interesting being: *The Kingdomes Weekly Post* (E 304/28); *Mercurius Britanicus* (E 305/12); *Mercurius Civicus* (E 305/5); *The Moderate Intelligencer* (E 305/3); *Perfect Occurrences* (E 266/3); *The Scottish Dove* (E 305/6) and especially *Perfect Passages*, which prints, in its issue of 8–15 Oct. (E 266/2, 407–8), a letter from Cromwell's quarters that is not given elsewhere. (It is not entirely accurate, but interesting on the first rumours.) The next issue of 15–22 Oct. (E 266/6, 415–16) provides the most extensive prisoner list. *Perfect Passages* was an independent-leaning newsbook. See Joad Raymond, *The Invention of the Newspaper: English Newsbooks 1641–1649* (Oxford, 1996), 38–9. No royalist in the house gave his or her story to the press, though two letters written by Tamworth Reresby from Ely Place prison afterwards afford a rare glimpse of the aftermath: West Yorkshire Archive Service, WYL 156/MX/R1/14 and 16.

22 *The Scottish Dove*, 10–17 Oct. 1645 (E 305/6), 820.

23 *Mercurius Civicus*, 9–16 Oct. 1645 (E 305/5), 1202; *Perfect Occurrences*, 10–17 Oct. 1645 (E 266/3); *A Diary, Or, An Exact Journall*, 9–16 Oct. 1645 (E 305/75), 8. For the later claims, see *Mercurius Elencticus*, 26 Dec.–2 Jan. 1648/9 (E 356/31), 551, and James Wright, *Historia Histrionica* (1699), 7–8. In his *ODNB* entry for Thomas Harrison, Ian Gentles states that 'given the New Model Army's usual respect for the laws of war, the story is implausible'. Harrison's biographer David Farr is also sceptical, in *Major-General Thomas Harrison*, 62.

24 *Mercurius Civicus*, 9–16 Oct. 1645 (E 305/5), 1096. For a persuasive case that the defenders fell back over the wooden bridge, rather than the larger stone one connecting the bailey to the Great Gatehouse of the Old House, see Turton, 'A House called Loyalty', 143–4. For the skull, which

was found in 1991, see David Allen and Sue Anderson, *Basing House Hampshire: Excavations 1978–1991*, Hampshire Field Club & Archaeological Society (1999), 99–102.

25   *Perfect Passages*, 8–15 Oct. 1645 (E 266/2), 408.

26   *Mercurius Civicus*, 9–16 Oct. 1645 (E 305/5), 1096.

27   *The Kingdomes Weekly Post*, 15 Oct. 1645 (E 304/28), 8.

28   *The Scottish Dove*, 10–17 Oct. 1645 (E 305/6), 820.

29   *A Looking-Glasse for the Popish Garrisons* ([24 Oct.] 1645), (E 307/2), 2; *The Scottish Dove*, 10–17 Oct. 1645 (E 305/6), 820–1; *The Moderate Intelligencer*, 9–16 Oct. 1645 (E 305/3), 164; *Mercurius Civicus*, 9–16 Oct. 1645 (E 305/5), 1201–2.

30   *The Moderate Intelligencer*, 9–16 Oct. 1645 (E 305/3), 164.

31   Peter, *Full and Last Relation*, 2; John Vicars, *Magnalia Dei Anglicana* (1646), 291. *Perfect Occurrences*, 10–17 Oct. 1645 (E 266/3), describes the slain daughter as a 'gallant gentlewoman', though her name and age are not given. *The Moderate Intelligencer*, 9–16 Oct. 1645 (E 305/3), claims that two of Griffith's daughters tried to pull the soldiers off him and 'adventured very far without hurt'. *The True Informer*, 11–18 Oct. 1645 (E 305/9), 206, claims that two daughters were subsequently taken into custody, whereas *Mercurius Civicus*, 9–16 Oct. 1645 (E 305/5), 1202, claims that there were 'three handsome daughters' afterwards. Vicars (*Magnalia*, 291) also gives three. *Perfect Occurrences*, 10–17 Oct. 1645 (E 266/3), just says that Griffith was 'sore wounded and taken prisoner with his daughters'. According to their mother's tombstone (Anthony Wood, *Athenæ Oxonienses*, III (1817), 713), she had five girls in total, three of whom survived her in 1678. These were Sarah, Elizabeth and Mary. They are also named in their father's will of 1665 (TNA PROB 11/318/690). A fourth girl, Jeane (bapt. 5 Oct. 1630; bur. 22 July 1631), died in infancy. Elizabeth was baptised in her father's church, St Mary Magdalen, Old Fish Street, on 26 April 1629 and Mary on 30 April 1635. Their father was presented to the rectory in 1624, and since the two other girls do not appear later in the register, it can be presumed that Sarah and the unnamed victim at Basing House were both born before 1624. I haven't found a record of their births elsewhere, or for their parents' marriage, though it must have been after Griffith left Christ's College, Cambridge, in 1621.

For the afterlife of this story, see Fiona McCall, *Baal's Priests: The Loyalist Clergy and the English Revolution* (Farnham, 2013), 149. James Heath's claim, in *A Brief Chronicle of the Late Intestine Warr* (1663, p.153), that the 'virgin' was 'shamefully left naked' is not grounded in contemporary evidence, though she may have been 'stripped' of her outer clothes as was customary in a storm.

32   *The Moderate Intelligencer*, 9–16 Oct. 1645 (E 305/3), 164.

33   On 4 October, *The City-Scout* reported that the women in Oxford were having regular nightmares about the New Model Army 'and are so troubled about it that they cannot rest' (E 304/5, 6).

34   Peter, *Full and Last Relation*, 2.

35   *Perfect Passages*, 15–22 Oct. 1645 (E 266/6), 415–16.

36   West Yorkshire Archive Service, WYL 156/MX/R1/14 and 16: Two letters from Tamworth Reresby to his brother Sir John Reresby, n.d. and 26 Nov. [1645].

37   *CJ*, IV, 307; *Perfect Passages*, 8–15 Oct. 1645 (E 266/2), 407–8; *The Weekly Account*, 8–15 Oct. 1645 (E 304/27); *Mercurius Civicus*, 9–16 Oct. 1645 (E 305/5), 1202.

38   Peter, *Full and Last Relation*; *Mercurius Aulicus*, 30 June–6 July 1644 (E 2/30), 1067.

39   *Mercurius Britanicus*, 13–20 Oct. 1645 (E 305/12), 903; *The Moderate Intelligencer*, 9–16 Oct. 1645 (E 305/3), 164. 'Picture-babies' is not, I don't think, a misprint of 'picture Bibles', but a reference to the loose pictures found inside one of Archbishop Laud's illustrated Bibles. *In Canterburies Doome* (1646, p. 66), William Prynne wrote that 'between the leaves of this book, there were 12 several loose pictures in fine vellum, about the bigness of playing cards of the largest size, gloriously and curiously gilded, and set forth with most exquisite colours, some having one, others two or three pictures a piece in them of Christ and the Virgin Mary in several shapes and forms, with glories about their heads, and sometimes crosses on their backs, and the Holy Ghost in form of a dove; pretty babies [dolls] for young children to play with, but most insufferable puppets for an old childish superstitious Archbishop seriously to dote on, if not to reverence, adore, and kindle his private devotions by'. See too George Henderson, 'Bible Illustration in the Age of Laud', *Transactions of the Cambridge Bibliographical Society* 8/2 (1982), 176-7.

40   Peter, *Full and Last Relation*, 2; *Mercurius Aulicus*, 30 June–6 July 1644 (E 2/30), 1066.

41   *Perfect Occurrences*, 10–17 Oct. 1645 (E 266/3); Vicars, *Magnalia*, 291.

42   *The Moderate Intelligencer*, 9–16 Oct. 1645 (E 305/3), 164.

43   Peter, *Full and Last Relation*, p. 3 and frontispiece; Joshua Sprigge, *Anglia Rediviva* (1647), 140.

44   *The Scottish Dove*, 10–17 Oct. 1645 (E 305/6), 821; *Perfect Occurrences* 10–17 Oct. 1645 (E 266/3); *Mercurius Civicus*, 9–16 Oct. 1645 (E 305/5), 1202; *A Diary, Or, An Exact Journall*, 9–16 Oct. 1645 (E 305/75), 8.

45   BL Harl MS 787, 73.

Epilogue

1   *The True Informer*, 11–18 Oct. 1645 (E 305/9), 208; *Mercurius Britanicus*, 13–20 Oct. 1645 (E 305/12), 903; *The Kingdomes Weekly Post*, 15–21 Oct. 1645 (E 305/15), 12.

2   *Mercurius Veridicus*, 11–18 Oct. 1645 (E 305/10), 2. See too *Mercurius Poeticus*, 21–8 Oct. 1645 (E 307/18), 4; *Mercurius Britanicus*, 20–7 Oct. 1645 (E 307/12), 907.

3   *CJ*, IV, 309, 315; *LJ*, VII, 649; *A Perfect Diurnall*, 20–7 Oct. 1645 (E 266/8), 930; BL Harl MS 5910, iv, 135r (for Faithorne).

4   *Mercurius Civicus*, 30 Oct.–6 Nov. 1645 (E 308/15), 1126.

5   *CJ*, IV, 309.

6   TNA SP 19 21/140; 123/186; 6/138. For the golden calf legend (which seems inspired by the Book of Exodus), see Wilf Emberton, *Love Loyalty: The Close and Perilous Siege of Basing House 1643–1645* (Basingstoke, 1972), 101–2. For Lord Bolton's early excavations and the hunt for buried treasure, see David Allen and Sue Anderson, *Basing House Hampshire: Excavations 1978–1991*, Hampshire Field Club & Archaeological Society (1999), ch. 3. Kit Orde-Powlett also kindly shared his memories.

7   *Perfect Passages*, 8–15 Oct. 1645 (E 266/2), 408.

8   TNA SP 23/251, no. 132, f. 272.

9   *The Correspondence of Robert Boyle*, ed. Michael Hunter, Antonio Clericuzio and Lawrence M. Principe (6 vols., 2001), I, 31–3.

10 *The Vindication of Richard Atkyns* (1669), 28; Barbara Donagan, *War in England, 1642–1649* (Oxford, 2008), 171–3; David J. Appleby, 'The Third Army: wandering soldiers and the negotiation of parliamentary authority, 1642–51', in *Battle-scarred: Mortality, medical care and military welfare in the British Civil Wars*, ed. David J. Appleby and Andrew Hopper (Manchester, 2018), 147–50.

11 HALS 79959X, 50v–51r, 56r–68v (Ogilby quotation at 66v). Lady Elizabeth Rawdon's presentation copy of Jones's full funeral sermon is in the Bodleian Library, Oxford: MS Don. G.9, 5r–27v. The scrivener Isaac Rowlett was 'slain in faringdon' (HALS 79959X, 51r; TNA C 7/414/25) and Robert Amery lost his wife there (TNA SP 29/25, 40r).

12 Miranda Malins, '"Dear Robin": The Correspondence of Oliver Cromwell and Robert Hammond', *Cromwelliana* 3/1 (2012), 69–71.

13 David Farr, *Major-General Thomas Harrison: Millenarianism, Fifth Monarchism and the English Revolution 1616–1660* (Farnham, 2014), 90.

14 Raymond Phineas Stearns, *The Strenuous Puritan: Hugh Peter, 1598–1660* (Urbana, Illinois, 1954), 326–36; Ian Gentles, *The New Model Army in England, Ireland and Scotland, 1645–1653* (Oxford, 1992), 300–4.

15   C. V. Wedgwood, *A King Condemned: The Trial and Execution of Charles I* (new edn, 2001), 131; *King Charls his speech made upon the scaffold* (1649) (E 540/17), 9–10.

16   Stearns, *Strenuous Puritan*, ch. 14.

17   Anon, *The Life of that Reverend Divine, and Learned Historian, Dr. Thomas Fuller* (1661), 39–40.

18   BL Add MS 29443, 5v and Add MS 29440, 22r (published in *Memoirs of Sir John Reresby*, ed. Geiter and Speck, 1991, xxxix–xl, 52); TNA SP 23/113, 226; West Yorkshire Archives, MX/R51/43. Several other letters in the Leeds branch of the West Yorkshire Archives (MX/R12/168, MX/R14/8, MX/R14/94, MX/R28/19, MX/R45/23), as well as some Chancery cases in TNA (e.g. C 6/61/40), confirm Tamworth Reresby's indebtedness (and charm). He was 'retired in disgrace' with the Duchess of Buckingham in 1674 (Bod Rawlinson MS D. 204, 17r) and seems to have been involved in a plot against William III in 1689 (*CSPD, 1689–90*, 191–2).

19   TNA SP 29/25, 40–1.

20   Edward Vallance, *Revolutionary England and the National Covenant: State Oaths, Protestantism and the Political Nation, 1553–1682* (Woodbridge, 2005), 125; Michael Leapman, *Inigo: The Troubled Life of Inigo Jones, Architect of the English Renaissance* (2003), 338–9; TNA SP 23/190, 166 (Rosewell); SP 23/177, 777–87 (Jones).

21   Anthony Fletcher, *Gender, Sex and Subordination in England 1500–1800* (1995), 124.

22   *LJ*, VII, 688; VIII, 92–3, 100, X, 549. *CJ*, IV, 407, 425–6, 677, 725–6; V, 3, 294, 422, 521–2, 617; VI, 165. Ronald Hutton, 'Paulet, John, fifth marquess of Winchester (1598?–1675)', *ODNB*. The account book of Winchester's business agent shows that he was in Englefield in 1651: HRO 11M49/230, 9.

23   *A Collection of the State Papers of John Thurloe*, ed. Thomas Birch, 7 vols. (1742), III, 377; IV, 444. Honora's half-brother by marriage, the Marquess of Hertford, was also implicated in the rising (III, 330); *The Triall of the Honourable Colonel John Penruddock of Compton in Wiltshire, and his speech* (1655) (E 845/7), 13.

24   *CSPD, 1655–6*, 105; HRO 11M49/230, 44M69/F5/4/3; Joan Thirsk, 'The Sales of Royalist Land during the Interregnum', *Economic History Review*, n.s., 5/2 (1952), ch. 1.

25   *The Gallery of Heroick Women. Written in French by Peter Le Moyne of the Society of Jesus. Translated into English by the Marquesse of Winchester* (1652), Frontispiece, The Translators Address and p.159. For the text's spirit of cavalier resistance and its influence on Margaret Cavendish, see Hero Chalmers, *Royalist Women Writers 1650–1689* (Oxford, 2004), 40–2.

26   Bod MS Carte 214, 136: Honora, Marchioness of Winchester to Ormond, 10 May 1660.

27   Paul Lay, *Providence Lost: The Rise & Fall of Cromwell's Protectorate* (2020), 129.

28   Bod MS Carte 214, 136.

29   Englefield Church monuments. The parish registers are in Berkshire Record Office, D/P 52/1/1.

30   *LJ*, XI, 472; HRO 44M69/F5/4/3 (2 bundles); Paul Seaward, *The Cavalier Parliament and the Reconstruction of the Old Regime, 1661–1667* (Cambridge, 1988), 205–7. Dryden's poem to the marquess is in Englefield Church.

31   Allen and Anderson, *Basing House Hampshire: Excavations*, 8–11.

32   Gilbert Burnet, *Bishop Burnet's History of his Own Time* (1838), 657; *Memoirs of Sir John Reresby*, ed. Andrew Browning, 2nd edn ed. Mary K. Geiter and W. A. Speck (1991), 466–7; Allen and Anderson, *Basing House Hampshire: Excavations*, 8–11; Alan Turton, 'A House called Loyalty – The Archaeology of a Civil War Siege', in *Home and Away: The British Experience of War 1618–1721*, ed. Serena Jones (Warwick, 2018), 149; David Allen, Briony A. Lalor and Ginny Pringle, 'Excavations at Basing Grange, Basing House, Hampshire, 1999–2006', *Hampshire Studies 2020: Proceedings of the Hampshire Field Club and Archaeological Society* 75/2 (2020).

33   12 Charles II c. 11, clause xxiv.

34   Pepys, *Diary*, 13 Oct. 1660; Farr, *Major-General Thomas Harrison*, chs. 2–3; Ian J. Gentles, 'Harrison, Thomas (bapt. 1616, d. 1660)', *ODNB*.

35   Stearns, *Strenuous Puritan*, 418–19.

36   *CJ*, VIII, 173.

37   David Lloyd, *Memoires of the Lives, Actions, Sufferings & Deaths . . . in our late Intestine Wars* (1668), 521; Anthony Wood, *Athenæ Oxonienses*, III (1817), 711–13; A. G. Matthews, *Walker Revised* (Oxford, 1948) 49.

38   Matthew Griffith, *The Samaritan Revived . . . with a sermon preacht by the same author* (1660), quotation in the Dedicatory Epistle to George Monck. See too Griffith, *The King's Life-Guard* (1665).

39   The tomb of Mary Wolryche née Griffith, St Andrew's Church, Quatt, Shropshire. Mary's marriage to John Wolryche of Dudmaston was investigated by the Court of Arches. See Lambeth Palace Library Film 71, 69v; Film 120, 11; Film 139, 607v–608r; Film 149, 170r–174r. For her first marriage, to George Elphicke, a friend of Wolryche and lawyer of Gray's Inn, see: TNA C 6/215/111; TNA PROB 11/326/91; *The Conway Letters*, ed. Marjorie Hope Nicolson (rev. Sarah Hutton, Oxford, 1992), 144–6, 161, 166. Mary's older sister, Elizabeth, married Lewis (or Ludovic) Napier of Hensington, Woodstock. He composed a Latin elegy to his father-in-law (Payne Fisher, *Elogia Sepulchralia*, 1675, 99), and was also

close to his sister-in-law's husband, 'my dear brother John Wolryche of Dudmaston' (TNA PROB 11/349/200). The third surviving Griffith sister was Sarah Conway in 1665 (Sarah Edwards in 1677).

40 HALS 79959X, 47v, 50v, 51v, 59r; *The Life of Marmaduke Rawdon of York*, ed. Robert Davies, Camden Society, OS 85 (1863), 189–90; TNA SP 16/305, 74 (for John Provest).

41 HALS 79959X, 113v–114r.

42 Kenneth Morgan, *Slavery and the British Empire: From Africa to America* (Oxford, 2007), 12; *Voyages: The Trans-Atlantic Slave Trade Database.*

43 HALS 79959X, 72v, 111r–112r; Clothworkers Apprenticeships (via ROLLCO): James Holdip, 8/8/1609; Matthew Parker, *The Sugar Barons* (2011), 13; Eric Otremba, 'Enlightened Institutions: Science, Plantations, and Slavery in the English Atlantic, 1626–1700' (PhD dissertation, University of Minnesota, 1982), 137–8, 273–80.

44 HALS 79959X, 111v–112r.

45 *Voyages: The Trans-Atlantic Slave Trade Database* (https://slavevoyages. org), 21876; Larry Gragg, *Englishmen Transplanted: The English Colonization of Barbados, 1627–1660* (Oxford, 2003), 119.

46 TNA PROB 11/319/561; Robert Ashton, 'Crisp, Sir Nicholas, first baronet (c.1599–1666)', *ODNB.*

47 *Proceedings and Debates of the British Parliaments respecting North America,* vol. 1, ed. L. F. Stock (Washington DC, 1924–41), 248–63.

48 Aphra Behn, *The Luckey Chance* (1687), 32; John Tradescant, *Musæum Tradescantianum* (1656), To the Ingenious Reader, 4, 7, 47.

49 *Herball*, An Advertisement to the Readers. See too *Mercurii Botanici* (1641), 2.

50 Thomas Fuller, *The History of the Worthies of England* (1662), Yorkshire, 204.

51 TNA SP 23/190, 163–77; HALS 79959X, 50v–51r; Bod MS Rawlinson D 451, 33v–26r.

52 TNA LC3/25, 101, 204; Harold J. Cook, *The Decline of the Old Medical Regime in Stuart London* (1986), 246–53; C. R. B. Barrett, *The History of the Society of Apothecaries* (1905), 72, 76–7; Cecil Wall, H. Charles Cameron, E. Ashworth Underwood, *A History of the Worshipful Society of Apothecaries of London*, Vol. I: 1617–1815 (1963), 116–18. Rosewell is buried in Sunbury Church, Surrey. In her will, his wife Philippa mentions a portrait of him (TNA PROB 11/481/281).

53 BL Harl. MS 5910, iv, 135r–136v: Life of William Faithorne by John Bagford. This is the chief biographical source for Faithorne and was written soon after his death in 1691. Bagford (d. 1716) knew Faithorne and some of his friends and was a careful researcher. His Life is, on the whole,

authoritative, but his much-repeated claim that Wenceslaus Hollar was at Basing House with Faithorne is not corroborated by any other source. Bagford also claimed that Hollar worked at Faithorne's shop after his return from Antwerp, and this seems plausible. Bagford never claimed that Hollar 'lived' with Faithorne. This claim derives from a mistranscription by George Vertue ('Vertue's Note Book A.b.', *The Volume of the Walpole Society* 18 (1929-30), 140) and has led to a lot of needless head-scratching. For Bagford's reliability, see Theodor Harmsen, 'Bagford, John (1650/51–1716)', *ODNB* ; M. McC. Gatch, 'John Bagford, Bookseller and Antiquary', *British Library Journal* 12/2 (1986), 150–71.

54   TNA LC3/25, 113. For the marriage: LMA P69/MIC2/A/003/MS04063/001: St Michael Cornhill, 9 May 1654; St Dunstan-in-the-West, Publications and Marriages, 20 April 1654. Judith's brother was John Graunt, the statistician and author of *Natural and Political Observations mentioned in a following Index, and made upon the Bills of Mortality* (1662). For Faithorne's baptism at St Mary Whitechapel on 29 Sept. 1621: LMA P93/MRY1/001.

55   Valentine Greatrakes, *A Brief Account of Mr Valentine Greatraks* (1666), 47–8, 61–2, 90; Peter Elmer, *The Miraculous Conformist: Valentine Greatrakes, the Body Politic and the Politics of Healing in Restoration Britain* (Oxford, 2013), 188–9.

56   Pepys, *Diary*, 21 May 1662, 7 Nov. 1666, 1 Dec. 1666.

57   Thomas Flatman, 'To my ingenious Friend Mr. Faithorne on his Book', in William Faithorne, *The Art of Graveing and Etching* (1662). See too R. T. Godfrey, 'William Faithorne, Portrait Engraver: 1616–1691', *History Today* 25/3 (1975).

58   Samuel Collins, *Systeme of Anatomy* (1685), The Preface to the Tables. For Faithorne not always making his deadlines, see: *The Correspondence of Robert Boyle*, ed. Michael Hunter, Antonio Clericuzio and Lawrence M. Principe, 6 vols. (2001), II, 304, 316–17, 412 ('Mr Faithorne has now at last promised me with all the asservations imaginable, that he will not fail to finish your picture by the middle of the next week at furthest'), 439–41 (Faithorne 'having so very often and often disappointed by expectation'), 442, 513. He needed a kick up the backside from John Aubrey too: Bod Aubrey MS 12, 158r ('Give yourself the trouble in my absence,' writes John Henley to Aubrey on 29 June 1669, 'of stimulating Mr Faithorne a little at your leisure who I fear may otherwise be too negligent').

59   Meghan C. Doherty, 'Creating Standards of Accuracy: Faithorne's The Art of Graveing and the Royal Society', in *Science in Print: Essays on the History of Science and the Print*, ed. Rima D. Apple, Gregory J. Downey and Stephen L. Vaughn (Madison, WI, 2012), 15–36; Meghan C. Doherty,

'Discovering the "True Form": Hook's Micrographia and the Visual Vocabulary of Engraved Portraits', *Notes & Records of the Royal Society* 66 (2012), 211–34. See too Jacob Kainen's introduction to the De Capo edition of *The Art of Graveing and Etching* (New York, 1970).

60   Neil Jeffares, 'Faithorne, William', *Dictionary of Pastellists before 1800* (2006, online edition: http://www.pastellists.com/Articles/Faithorne. pdf, update 5 July 2020); Bod Ashmole MS 1136, 30v; BL Harl MS 5910, iv, 135v. Bagford adds that 'the misfortunes of his eldest son much broke his spirits'. This possibly refers to William Faithorne junior's dismissal for 'great neglect' as the drawing master of Christ's Hospital school. See LMA MS 12811/6: Christ's Hospital Committee Minute Book, 1687–1698, 565, 670, 675, 699.

61   Faithorne, *Art of Graveing and Etching*, 'To the Right Worshipful Sir Robert Peake Knight'.

62   A point made by Blair Worden in *The English Civil Wars 1640–1660* (2009), 72–3: 'If we could imagine the same conflict being fought a little later in the century, perhaps in the 1660s, amid the growing biographical awareness of the age of Samuel Pepys, we might expect to find accounts of the war that took us further into the feelings of the participants. The same decade, the era also of the start of the Royal Society and of emerging statistical enquiry, might have left us a stronger base of evidence for reckoning the sizes of armies and the numbers of casualties.'

63   Quoted in Fiona McCall, *Baal's Priests: The Loyalist Clergy and the English Revolution* (Farnham, 2013), 54.

64   TNA SP 23/203, 605–20; SP 23/230, 238r; TNA C 10/110/93; *CSPD Ireland, 1633–1647*, 424, 567 (TNA SP 63/261/76 and 63/262/112); Berkshire Record Office D/EBY/E9: A deed of settlement made by John Marquess of Winton, 1661.

65   *CRR*, II, 1176; Anon, *A Panegyrick on the late honourable Sir Robert Peake, Knight, Vice-President and Leader of the Honourable Artillery Company* (1667).

66   BL Harl MS 1099, 39v: the order of the funeral of Sir Robert Peake, 1 Aug. 1667; G. Goold Walker, *The Honourable Artillery Company 1537–1987* (1986), 89.

67   TNA PROB 11/324/435. NB Peake's 'good friends Dr James Hyde of Oxford and his wife Margaret Hyde' (née Saintloe). Peake's 'valentine' Mary Saintloe was the niece of Lancelot Andrewes, Bishop of Winchester. There is some interesting crossover between Peake's will and Hyde's (TNA PROB 11/366/459). Hyde also mentions a loan of £150 to Jane Whorwood. For the examination of John Saintloe after Penruddock's Rising, see *State Papers of John Thurloe*, III, 314–15, 330, and for Hyde's spying, see ibid., IV, 101, and Nadine Akkerman, *Invisible Agents: Women*

and *Espionage in Seventeenth-Century Britain* (Oxford, 2018), 103–6. See too TNA C 10/110/93.

68   BL Add MS 5063, 29.

69   Pepys, *Diary*, 2–7 Sept. 1666; *The Diary of John Evelyn*, ed. E. S. de Beer, 6 vols. (Oxford, 2000), III, 450–63.

70   LMA P69/SEP/B/001/MS03149/002, 101–4.

List of Illustrations

Main Text

Plate Section 1

Plate Section 2

'The Siege of Bazinge House': anon engraving (c. 1644) © The Turton Collection

Sir William Waller by Cornelius Johnson (1643) © National Portrait Gallery, London

Artillery damage to the barn. © Jessie Childs

The postures of the musket: Henry Hexham, *The Principles of the Art Militarie* (1637). Presentation copy given to Charles, Prince of Wales (later Charles II). © Sotheby's

The English Irish Soldier (1642) © British Library Board. All Rights Reserved / Bridgeman Images

Certificate of Protection for John Goodyer of Petersfield (1643) © Hampshire Record Office, 76M99/1

William Faithorne: self-portrait, engraved by John Fillian. © National Portrait Gallery, London

Sir Robert Peake: etching by S & E Harding © The Turton Collection

Hands by William Faithorne: *The Art of Graveing and Etching* (1662)

Inigo Jones by William Dobson (c. 1642) National Maritime Museum, Greenwich, London (BHC2809)

Basing House archaeology: Photos by David Allen. © Hampshire Cultural Trust

Basing House daybed: Private Collection. © Tom Orde-Powlett

Henry Gage by Weesop (1640s) © National Portrait Gallery, London

Charles I in Oxford by William Dobson. Photo © Philip Mould Ltd, London / Bridgeman Images

Mary Griffith in effigy in St Andrew's Church, Quatt, Shropshire. © Jessie Childs

The heavy guns: Henry Hexham, *The Principles of the Art Militarie* (1637)

Oliver Cromwell by Sir Peter Lely (c. 1653). Birmingham Museums and Art Gallery / Bridgeman Images

Decapitated skull: © Hampshire Cultural Trust

Basing House Defended by the Cavaliers, Waterglass painting by Charles West Cope. © Parliamentary Art Collection, WOA 2897

The Plundering of Basing House (exhibited 1836) by Charles Landseer. Bequeathed by Jacob Bell 1859. Photo © Tate

Acknowledgements

First thanks to Alan Turton who was the curator of Basing House from 1987 to 2011. He lived on site, guarded the ruins, sifted its soil and respected its ghosts. I have a happy memory of him and his wife Nicola taking me round in the summer of 2018 when the heatwave brought the old markings out of the ground. They answered every query, commented on an early draft and allowed me to plunder their collection of engravings. Alan also drew the map of Basing House at the beginning of this book. I'm tremendously grateful for their kindness and support.

Immense thanks, too, to Kit Orde-Powlett, descendant of the 5th Marquess of Winchester, for whom Basing House is heritage as well as history. Until the 1970s, his home was a house in the bone-riddled garden. His tales of treasure hunting, spectral photobombing and of his grandfather, Lord Bolton's early excavations (overseen by George Moss, whose ancestor was a drummer boy in the siege) were a privilege to hear. He also very generously allowed me to reproduce his glorious portrait of the 5th marquess. Thanks, too, to Jane Orde-Powlett for sharing her own wonderful memories and for the magnificent marmalade. Their daughter Tora made it all happen, by wondrous serendipity, and also put me in touch with her cousin Tom Orde-Powlett, who revealed not only a portrait of Honora, Marchioness of Winchester, but also – with the magic words 'probably no use for the book, but interesting for us at least' – a daybed that survived the storm. Photos of both are in the plates section and I am so grateful to Tom for sharing them with such enthusiasm and generosity.

Julian Humphrys of the Battlefields Trust went out of his way to show me round Cheriton battlefield in Hampshire, one of the great turning points of the civil war, and Stuart Orme, Curator of the Cromwell Museum in Huntingdon, let me (and, even more bravely, my daughters) handle Cromwell's sword. Vickie Dunlop kindly arranged for St Andrew's Church, Quatt, to be open when I was on my quest for Mary Woolrych (née Griffith) and Brandon Taylor kindly let me rifle through his private archives on the Rawdon family.

A great many other people have helped along the way, including John Adamson, David Allen, Stephen Ede-Borrett, David Flintham, Angus Haldane, Andy Hopper, Richard Jones, Peter Leadbetter, Dmitri Levitin, Simon Marsh, Matthew Parker, Andrew Robertshaw, Mark Stoyle and Gillian Tindall.

Thanks to the librarians, archivists and staff of the Bedfordshire Archives Service, Beinecke Rare Book and Manuscript Library, Berkshire Record Office, the Bodleian Library, the British Library, Caernarfon Record Office, Essex Record Office, Guildhall Library, Hampshire Record Office, Hertfordshire Archives, the Institute of Historical Research, Lambeth Palace Library, London Metropolitan Archives, the National Archives, the National Library of Scotland, Parliamentary Archives, Shropshire Archives, Staffordshire Record Office, Surrey History Centre, the Leeds branch of the West Yorkshire Archive Service, Wiltshire and Swindon Archives and York Minster Library.

The pandemic threw up unique challenges and I'd like to say a special thank you to the staff of the London Library for posting books during the various lockdowns and for being even more elastic than usual in their returns policy; to Janet Payne, Archivist at Apothecaries' Hall, who was brilliantly helpful, as was Hannah Dunmow at the Clothworkers' Company, Eleni Bide at the Goldsmiths' Company and Cressida Williams at Canterbury Cathedral Archives.

At a late stage of my research, the rare-book dealer Dean Cooke sent me his latest catalogue which included a previously unrecorded manuscript sermon given by Hugh Peter, a Puritan preacher who is a key figure in this book. Thanks to Dean and the buyer of the manuscript, Aaron T. Pratt, Pforzheimer Curator of Early Books and Manuscripts at the Harry Ransom Center, University of Texas, for kindly allowing me to see and cite from the text while it was in transit.

Thanks to Georgina Capel, first responder, best of agents and one of life's uppers. She is always there, always positive and always fun, which really matters when you take as long as I do on my books.

Stuart Williams, the brilliant skipper of the good ship Bodley Head has, once again, been a total joy to work with, as have all the crew. Jörg

Hensgen edited every line with intelligence, gentleness and care. Lauren Howard guided the book through every process with deft hands and a cool head. Thanks, too, to Anna Green for the front cover, Bill Donohoe for the maps of London and Hampshire, Jane Selley for the copy-edit, Jane Howard for the proofread, Alex Bell for the index, and Matt Broughton, Beccy Jones, Darren Bennet, Jasmine Marsh and Jessie Spivey.

My dear friend Charlotte Mulford cycled back and forth along the Thames Path with fresh sheaves of the first draft in her basket in order to provide a clever layperson's view of the book. I am so grateful for it.

Love and thanks to friends and family – too numerous to list – for every bit of interest, encouragement and tolerance over the years, especially, as ever, to my sister Anna Richards and my mother Jane Childs, who also drew the Loddon lily ('Summer Snowflake': *Leucojum Aestivum)* which happily grows in her garden – and now mine – and marks the caesura of the book. My darling girls Bella and Lara only required small bribes to traipse over battlefields in driving rain. There will be sun! Above all, thank you, Fletch, for enduring the daily bulletins of agony and ecstasy, for pretending to believe me when I say I'll have so much more time once the book is done, and for making it all such fun.

Jessie Childs
Hammersmith, March 2022

Index